ROYAL REPRESENTATIONS

WOMEN IN CULTURE AND SOCIETY
A series edited by Catharine R. Stimpson

Royal Representations

QUEEN VICTORIA AND
BRITISH CULTURE,
1837–1876

Margaret Homans

THE UNIVERSITY OF CHICAGO PRESS
CHICAGO AND LONDON

MARGARET HOMANS is chair of the Women's Studies Program and professor of English at Yale University, where she has taught since 1978. Among her books are: *Bearing the Word: Language and Female Experience in Nineteenth-Century Women's Writing* (also published by the University of Chicago Press, 1986), and *Women Writers and Poetic Identity: Dorothy Wordsworth, Emily Brontë, and Emily Dickinson* (1980). Her honors and prizes include fellowships from the Whiting Foundation, the Morse Foundation, and the ACLS. She is the recipient of the Theron Rockwell Field Prize and the Keats-Shelley Association Prize.

The University of Chicago Press, Chicago 60637
The University of Chicago Press, Ltd., London
© 1998 by The University of Chicago
All rights reserved. Published 1998
Printed in the United States of America
07 06 05 04 03 02 01 00 99 98   1 2 3 4 5

ISBN: 0-226-35113-0 (cloth)
ISBN: 0-226-35114-9 (paper)

Library of Congress Cataloging-in-Publication Data

Homans, Margaret, 1952–
    Royal representations : Queen Victoria and British culture, 1837–1876 / Margaret Homans
      p. cm.
    Includes bibliographical references and index.
    ISBN 0-226-35113-0 (cloth). — ISBN 0-226-35114-9 (pbk.)
    1. Great Britain—Civilization—19th century. 2. Monarchy—Great Britain—History—19th century. 3. Great Britain—History—Victoria, 1837–1901. 4. Queens—Great Britain—Biography. 5. Queens in literature. 6. Queens in art.
    [1. Victoria, Queen of Great Britain, 1819–1901.]   I. Title.
DA533.H74   1998
941.081—dc21   98-19836
                                                        CIP

∞ The paper used in this publication meets the minimum requirements of the American National Standard for Information Sciences—Permanence of Paper for Printed Library Materials, ANSI Z39.48-1992.

To Marian

Contents

Figures / ix

Foreword, by Catharine R. Stimpson / xiii

Acknowledgments / xvii

Introduction: The Queen's Agency / xix

1
QUEEN VICTORIA'S SOVEREIGN OBEDIENCE / 1

"The Queen Has No Equal": The Problem of a Female Monarchy / 1
Privacy on Display: The Queen as Wife and Mother / 17
The Queenly Courtship of Elizabeth Barrett / 33
Photographic Realism's Abject Queens / 43

2
QUEEN VICTORIA'S WIDOWHOOD AND THE MAKING OF VICTORIAN QUEENS / 58

The Invisible Queen / 58
Domestic Queens: *Miss Marjoribanks* / 67
Making Queens: "Of Queens' Gardens" and the *Alice* Books / 85

3
THE WIDOW AS AUTHOR AND THE ARTS AND POWERS OF CONCEALMENT / 100

Bagehot's *The English Constitution* / 101

The Queen's Books: *The Early Years of His Royal Highness the Prince Consort* / 115
The Queen's Books: *Leaves from the Journal of Our Life in the Highlands* / 131
The Reform Bill and the Queen's Footnotes / 146

4

QUEEN VICTORIA'S MEMORIAL ARTS / 157

Albert Memorials / 157
Tennyson's *Idylls of the King* as an Albert Memorial / 179
Cameron's Photographic *Idylls:* Allegorical Realism and Memorial Art / 202

Epilogue: Empire of Grief / 229

Notes / 245

Index / 277

FIGURES

1. Queen Victoria and Her Servant Abdul Karim. Photograph by Hill and Saunders, 1893. Courtesy of the National Portrait Gallery, London. xxiv
2. Eugene Louis Lami, *Opening of the Great Exhibition 1 May 1851*. Oil painting. With the permission of the Royal Collection, © 1998 Her Majesty Queen Elizabeth II. xxvi
3. "Petticoats for Ever." Broadsheet, c. 1837. *9*
4. "The Coronation." Broadsheet, c. 1837. *10*
5. "The Royal Rose of England." Optical transformation, 1838. *12*
6. "Trying It On." Woodcut, c. 1840. *19*
7. "Albert will you marry me?" Lithograph, 1839. *20*
8. Sir Edwin Landseer, *Queen Victoria and Prince Albert at the Bal Costumé of 12 May 1842*. Oil painting. With the permission of the Royal Collection, © 1998 Her Majesty Queen Elizabeth II. *23*
9. W. J. Linton, "God Save the Queen." Illustration from *A Book of English Song*, 1842. Wood engraving from a picture by H. Warren. *24*
10. "To the Queen's Private Apartments: The Queen and Prince Albert at Home." Lithograph, 1843. *25*
11. "The Royal Family in the Nursery." Hand-colored lithograph, 1845. Courtesy of the Yale Center for British Art, Paul Mellon Collection. *27*
12. Sir Edward Landseer, *Windsor Castle in Modern Times: Queen Victoria, Prince Albert, and Victoria, Princess Royal*. Oil painting, 1841–45. With the permission of the Royal Collection, © 1998 Her Majesty Queen Elizabeth II. *29*
13. Franz Xaver Winterhalter, *The Royal Family in 1846*. Oil painting. With the permission of the Royal Collection, © 1998 Her Majesty Queen Elizabeth II. *31*
14. Queen Victoria's sketch of Winterhalter's *The Royal Family in 1846*. With

the permission of the Royal Collection, © 1998 Her Majesty Queen Elizabeth II. *31*

15. Queen Victoria and Prince Albert, Osborne, 26 July 1859. Photograph by Miss Day. With the permission of the Royal Archives, © 1998 Her Majesty Queen Elizabeth II. *47*

16. Queen Victoria and Prince Albert, 26 July 1859. Photograph by Miss Day. With the permission of the Royal Archives, © 1998 Her Majesty Queen Elizabeth II. *49*

17. Prince Albert on the Terrace at Osborne. Etching after a photograph by Miss Day, 1859. With the permission of the Royal Archives, © 1998 Her Majesty Queen Elizabeth II. *49*

18. Robert Thorburn, *The Prince Consort during His Last Illness, Holding a Draft Memorandum on the "Trent" Question, December 1861*. Painting. With the permission of the Royal Archives, © 1998 Her Majesty Queen Elizabeth II. *49*

19. Queen Victoria, 15 May 1860. Photograph by J. J. E. Mayall. With the permission of the Royal Archives, © 1998 Her Majesty Queen Elizabeth II. *50*

20. Queen Victoria and Prince Albert, 15 May 1860. Photograph by J. J. E. Mayall. With the permission of the Royal Archives, © 1998 Her Majesty Queen Elizabeth II. *52*

21. Queen Victoria and Prince Albert, 15 May 1860. Photograph by J. J. E. Mayall. With the permission of the Royal Archives, © 1998 Her Majesty Queen Elizabeth II. *52*

22. Queen Victoria and Prince Albert, 15 May 1860. Photograph by J. J. E. Mayall. With the permission of the Royal Archives, © 1998 Her Majesty Queen Elizabeth II. *52*

23. Queen Victoria and Prince Albert, 15 May 1860. Photograph by J. J. E. Mayall. With the permission of the Royal Archives, © 1998 Her Majesty Queen Elizabeth II. *54*

24. Queen Victoria and Prince Albert, 15 May 1860. Photograph by J. J. E. Mayall. With the permission of the Royal Archives, © 1998 Her Majesty Queen Elizabeth II. *54*

25. Queen Victoria and Prince Albert, 1 March 1861. Photograph by J. J. E. Mayall. With the permission of the Royal Archives, © 1998 Her Majesty Queen Elizabeth II. *56*

26. Queen Victoria and Prince Albert, 1 March 1861. Photograph by J. J. E. Mayall. With the permission of the Royal Archives, © 1998 Her Majesty Queen Elizabeth II. *56*

27. Queen Victoria and Prince Albert, 1 March 1861. Photograph by J. J. E. Mayall. With the permission of the Royal Archives, © 1998 Her Majesty Queen Elizabeth II. *56*

FIGURES / xi

28. William Powell Frith, *Marriage of The Prince of Wales and Princess Alexandra of Denmark, 10 March 1863*. Oil painting. With the permission of the Royal Collection, © 1998 Her Majesty Queen Elizabeth II.   *61*

29. "Where Is Britannia?" Engraving in *Tomahawk*, June 1867.   *65*

30. "Queen Hermione." Engraving in *Punch*, September 1865.   *66*

31. John Tenniel, two illustrations from chapter 9, "Queen Alice," Lewis Carroll's *Through the Looking Glass*, 1872.   *97*

32. Edward Henry Corbould, *Memorial Portrait of Prince Albert in Armor*. Oil painting, 1864. With the permission of the Royal Collection, © 1998 Her Majesty Queen Elizabeth II.   *167*

33. Henri de Triqueti, cenotaph of Prince Albert, Albert Memorial Chapel, Windsor, completed 1873. Detail. With the permission of the Royal Collection, © 1998 Her Majesty Queen Elizabeth II.   *169*

34. George Gilbert Scott, National Albert Memorial, Kensington Gardens, London, 1862–72. Detail.   *171*

35. Queen Victoria and her second daughter, Princess Alice, with a bust of Prince Albert, 1862. Photograph by Prince Alfred. With the permission of the Royal Archives, © 1998 Her Majesty Queen Elizabeth II.   *173*

36. Queen Victoria, Prince Albert, and Victoria, Princess Royal, on her wedding day, 25 January 1858. Photograph by Williams. With the permission of the Royal Archives, © 1998 Her Majesty Queen Elizabeth II.   *173*

37. Queen Victoria, Victoria, Crown Princess of Prussia, Princess Alice, and Prince Alfred with a bust of Prince Albert, March 1862. Photograph by Bambridge. With the permission of the Royal Archives, © 1998 Her Majesty Queen Elizabeth II.   *175*

38. Julia Margaret Cameron, Maud. Photograph in *Illustrations to Tennyson's Idylls of the King and Other Poems*, 1875.   *207*

39. Julia Margaret Cameron, King Arthur in *Guinevere*. Photograph in *Illustrations to Tennyson's Idylls of the King and Other Poems*, 1875.   *215*

40. Julia Margaret Cameron, King Arthur in *The Passing of Arthur*. Photograph in *Illustrations to Tennyson's Idylls of the King and Other Poems*, 1875.   *215*

41. Julia Margaret Cameron, Elaine in *Lancelot and Elaine*. Photograph in *Illustrations to Tennyson's Idylls of the King and Other Poems*, 1875.   *217*

42. Julia Margaret Cameron, Elaine in *Lancelot and Elaine*. Photograph in *Illustrations to Tennyson's Idylls of the King and Other Poems*, 1875.   *217*

43. Julia Margaret Cameron, Elaine in *Lancelot and Elaine*. Photograph in *Illustrations to Tennyson's Idylls of the King and Other Poems*, 1875.   *220*

44. Julia Margaret Cameron, Elaine in *Lancelot and Elaine.* Photograph in *Illustrations to Tennyson's Idylls of the King and Other Poems,* 1875.   *220*

45. Julia Margaret Cameron, King Arthur in *The Passing of Arthur.* Photograph in *Illustrations to Tennyson's Idylls of the King and Other Poems,* 1875.   *222*

46. Henri de Triqueti, sketch for the cenotaph of Prince Albert, Albert Memorial Chapel, Windsor. With the permission of the Royal Archives, © 1998 Her Majesty Queen Elizabeth II.   *225*

47. Henri de Triqueti, cenotaph of Prince Albert, Albert Memorial Chapel, Windsor, completed 1873. Detail. With the permission of the Royal Collection, © 1998 Her Majesty Queen Elizabeth II.   *226*

Foreword

In 1837 a young woman, Victoria, became queen of Great Britain and Ireland. Because she was the daughter of the fourth son of an earlier king, her ascension had seemed unlikely at her birth in 1819. Once enthroned, she endured throughout the century, ruling until her death in 1901, a time that came to be called the Victorian period.

Margaret Homans, a brilliant and subtle critic, has published two previous books about women writers, *Women Writers and Poetic Identity* (1980) and *Bearing the Word* (1986). *Royal Representations: Queen Victoria and British Culture* is another major book. Homans audaciously, meticulously, and originally explores Victoria as a woman writer. Prolific and conscientious, Victoria wrote journals and diaries from the age of thirteen and continued to produce them as well as thousands of letters throughout her reign. Because she was a royal, she also authorized many texts—such as her parliamentary addresses—that others scripted, not always to her private acclaim. Homans treats these materials as part of her great subject, the ways in which Victoria, operating within the constraints of history and discourse, composed nothing less than the modern British monarchy.

Homans focuses on Victoria's reign between 1837 and 1876 when she became Empress of India as well as queen, a blazing global sign of Great Britain's imperial reach and strength. During these decades, the monarchy as an institution and Victoria as a monarch confronted forces and situations that had to be properly managed if they were not to prove damaging, even fatal. Some of them, social and political in nature, would have daunted a monarch of either gender. Because established hierarchies were dissolving and reform movements growing, royal power was being diluted. Victoria's gender provoked another difficult issue that dragged behind her. She was a queen, a unique role that unites the contradictory realities of public power and womanhood, which historically denotes a lack of public power.

With the clarity, care, and depth that characterize her work, Homans lays bare the strategies Victoria developed to survive and prevail as queen. So doing, Homans shows how profound the connections were among Victoria, her era, and other influential cultural figures such as the poet laureate Alfred Lord Tennyson, the poet Elizabeth Barrett Browning, and the photographer Julia Margaret Cameron. Victoria seemed to grasp that the monarch's role was increasingly symbolic. Her people wanted to exert more control over the affairs of state. Thus, she had to act symbolically, which often meant appearing to be passive and inactive. Constructing effective patterns of royal representation and self-representation, she helped to design and then embodied a paradox—she would hold sway by playing out her willingness to give power away. She assured and reassured her subjects that she would defer to their protocols of what royal behavior ought to be. The royal court would respect the court of public opinion. In her later years, Homans concludes, Victoria was "both captive and despot of her own regime."

Victoria, the royal family, and her supporters deployed a variety of means to make a public spectacle of the mingling of rule and renunciation of rule: official and artlessly unofficial appearances, art itself (paintings and sculpture), the new medium of photography (she and her family pioneered the photo opportunity), and the publication of her judiciously edited writing. Her people were an audience, viewers, and readers.

Among Victoria's greatest triumphs was her treatment of domestic power. For she aligned, with limpid sincerity and passion, the institutions of the monarchy and the middle-class family. Her family role was that of perfect wife to her beloved husband, Prince Albert, a figure of substance in his own right. As queen she might be a sovereign, but as wife she was happily subjugated. As queen she might be a singular figure, but as wife she was an exemplary everywoman to and for her subjects. Homans cites a Christina Rossetti quatrain that illustrates Victoria's balance of throne room and marital bed:

> If I were Queen
> What would I do?
> I'd make you King
> And I'd wait on you.

In 1861 Albert died. Pitched into deep mourning and melancholia, Victoria retreated from public view. Homans is fascinating on the responses of the government, shapers of public opinion, writers, and public to the problem of the queen's disappearance. Appearances were one of her most important techniques of maintaining royal position and authority, and yet she had become visibly invisible. One reaction was to create multiple queens in literature and art. The writers John Ruskin and Lewis Carroll famously participated in this wave of invention. The presence of different queens offered up fantasy substitutes for Victoria. Moreover, by diffusing the power of the monarchy, it abetted in the slaking of democratic thirsts.

When Victoria reemerged onto the public stage, she most often did so in order to memorialize Albert. Her first such major public appearance was in Aberdeen, Scotland, in October 1863, to unveil a seated figure of Albert in military dress. Homans meticulously traces how the mourning Victoria altered her earlier self-representations. Ostensibly and ostentatiously, the bereft widow bowed to the memory of her husband. (Doing so, she seemed to set a counterexample to the contemporaneous efforts on behalf of female suffrage, although overall she shrewdly mixed her signals about this controversial issue.) Victoria, however, is actually far more vital and vivid than Albert. She calls attention to herself as the builder of the monuments that ultimately allegorize and obscure him. Ironically, many images of the dead Albert draw on Victorian representations that associate death with femininity. Long live the queen in her widow's weeds—as the once dominant husband fades into the figure of a powerless woman.

Homans argues accurately that human agency takes historically specific forms. Although Victoria's descendent Queen Elizabeth II has profited from her ancestor's achievements, the conditions of the twentieth century inexorably shape her management of her reign. Nevertheless, Homans's exemplary exploration of history will matter to anyone who wants to understand the relations between powerful figures who are also major celebrities, as Victoria most certainly was, and the rest of us. The representations and self-representations of such figures mediate between their flesh and bloodlines and voracious, demanding, yearning publics. Homans has much to tell us about what these representations are, what they mean, how they work, and how arresting they can be for queens, consorts, courts, and us commoners together.

Catharine R. Stimpson
New York University

Acknowledgments

I am grateful to Yale University's Griswold Fund for help with travel expenses and reproduction permissions. I would like to acknowledge the gracious permission of Her Majesty Elizabeth II to make use of materials in the Royal Archives and the Royal Collection; I am especially grateful to Lady Sheila de Bellaigue, Frances Dimond, and their staffs for assistance at the Archives. My thanks go also to the Yale Center for British Art for help with research and for permission to reproduce material in the Paul Mellon collection, and to the National Portrait Gallery for permission to reprint one of their images. Parts of the Introduction and Chapter 1 appeared in *Victorian Studies* 37 (1993), in *Feminist Measures: Soundings in Poetry and Theory*, ed. Lynn Keller and Christanne Miller (Ann Arbor: University of Michigan Press, 1994), and in *Victorian Literature and the Victorian Visual Imagination*, ed. Carol T. Christ and John O. Jordan (Berkeley: University of California Press, 1995), and are reprinted with permission.

Collaborating on numerous Queen Victoria projects with Adrienne Munich has been a pleasure and an education, and I thank her for her collegiality and for sharing her knowledge of Victoriana. The following people have given generously of their time and expertise in helping me with various aspects of this book, and I thank them here: Linda Anderson, Nancy Armstrong, Jessica Branch, Lauren Chattman, Jay Clayton, Sheila Emerson, Jennifer Green-Lewis, Leigh Coral Harris, Patricia Klindienst, Nancy Marshall, Helena Michie, Robert Patton; Linda Peterson, Margaret Powell, Cathy Shuman, Margery Sokoloff, and Alexander Welsh. I am grateful also to students who have worked with me on Victoria and Victorian culture over the past decade and more, from my first seminar on "Gender and Power in Victorian Literature" at Yale in 1986 to the dissertation group that met in the early 1990s to the group at Breadloaf in the summer of 1997. Katy Homans and Patterson Sims have a better collection of Julia Margaret Cameron books than any library I visited, and I thank them for the long-term loans. Audiences at the City University of New York, Copenhagen University, the English Institute, the Dickens Project, Harvard's CLCS Victorian seminar, Louisiana State University, the Modern Language Association Convention, the Narrative Society, Rice University, the Semiotics Society, the University of New Hampshire, the University of Washington, and Yale University asked me to think harder about my work and made many useful suggestions, and I am grateful to them. I thank Catharine Stimpson for her continued support, and I thank Alan Thomas, Randolph Petilos, Lila Weinberg, and the anonymous readers for the University of Chicago Press for making the publication of this book possible.

My husband Bill has provided all the wise and loving encouragement an author could wish for. My daughter Marian has helped me understand why it is important to think about queens, and this book is dedicated to her, with love.

MARGARET HOMANS
Guilford, Connecticut

INTRODUCTION: THE QUEEN'S AGENCY

> If I were a Queen
> What would I do?
>
> Christina Rossetti, *Sing Song*, 1872

Rossetti's little half-quatrain implies large questions about Britain's Victorian monarch. Can anyone be a Queen, at least in imaginative supposition? And why does being a Queen immediately present "doing" as a problem? For to be a Queen, even in the conditional, is apparently to wonder about action. The conditional and its question seem to open up a horizon of infinite possibilities of action: "What would I do if I could do whatever I liked?" At the same time, they suggest immobilization, the freezing of action: "What on earth would I do if so extraordinary a fate were to befall me?" Moreover, to be a Queen, even in supposition, seems to require that one identify oneself as an "I." But the real Queen—Queen Victoria—never says "I": she says "we" or "she." Those who address her can never say "you"—she is "Your Majesty." Conspicuously not self-identical, she is instead a property ("majesty") belonging to someone—"Her"—who cannot therefore be identified with that majesty. Does that then mean that, after all, no "I" can be Queen, least of all Queen Victoria herself? To what forms of doing, and of being, can the woman who bears the title of Queen lay claim?

This book starts from the double proposition that for Queen Victoria being is a form of doing, but that being Queen never involves a stable identification between the office and the person. Seeming, appearing, or being represented are instances of the Queen's agency, regardless of whether self-representation can be said to have been chosen or actively undertaken. Like her grandfather George III—who comported himself as a family man, disappeared and returned, and challenged definitions of proper regal behavior—Victoria was a monarch whose public and private lives were subject to peculiarly intense scrutiny. Alan Bennett's fictional George III, recovering his sanity and hearing himself told that he "seems more [him]self," recognizes that being King requires only that he "remember how to seem." Because the sign of his recovery is the return of an involuntary speech tic, however, to be himself means to be again in the grip of a compulsion—only now a more acceptable one.[1] At times, this book will argue, Victoria remembered exquisitely well "how to seem," even if it is not always clear whether that remembering and seeming are voluntary; at others, her apparent failure to do so constituted a different way of seeming from what was expected—a different royal representation that was, nonetheless, part of the script for Britain's nineteenth-century monarch.

Victoria's monarchy presents a particularly interesting case for the study of royal agency and royal identity—what the monarch does, what constitutes an action, and who does it when it is done—because to the paradoxes of a constitutional monarch's power at any time are added the complications introduced by Victoria's gender in an era characterized by its heightened and pervasive gender consciousness. Moreover, the terms through which Victorian culture defines and contests woman's "sphere" uncannily echo the distinctive discourse of constitutional monarchy: passivity, moral power, duty, and being and appearing in lieu of originating or executing politically engaged action.[2] Monarchs, as eminently visible beings who are both strikingly powerful and strikingly constructed, are interesting because they may tell us something about the conditions of our own agency, as Aristotle suggests in claiming that the subject of tragedy "must be one who is highly renowned and prosperous—a personage like Oedipus."[3] Because contemporary debates about gender are still framed in Victorian terms (conflicting imperatives about what women should and should not do), a woman monarch makes the power and the constructedness all the more vivid.

Queen Victoria's great achievement—what she "did"—was to smooth the transition to a wholly symbolic monarchy that would have taken place with or without her in the nineteenth century. I would not attempt to challenge the consensus view that by the end of her reign Victoria held less state power than any British monarch before her and passed on to her heirs a monarchy wholly different from that which she inherited. Nonetheless, I would contest the sexist assumptions that have prevented historians from giving her sufficient credit for her understanding of her role and for her efforts to perform it well.[4] Under certain circumstances, passivity is the most appropriate form of action, although it may be difficult to recognize as such.

The nineteenth century was an era of rapidly diversifying technologies for the dissemination of the self, and she performed the action of creating the nineteenth-century monarchy largely through representations. She could manipulate her image, to the extent that her culture made it possible for her to do so; yet many of her representations were made by others. Her resemblance to a bourgeois wife, mother, and later widow was a fiction created both by impressive tricks of deliberate representation and by a certain inevitability in Victorian culture. The degree to which her deliberate choices were involved in constructing this imposture (or what "choice" could mean in such a situation) and the degree to which it was constructed for her by social forces operating independently of her can never be fully established. Nonetheless, while Victoria may have been subject to an ideology over which no individual had control, her subjects also credited her with having an active hand in shaping the ideology that bears her name. She appears to have shared with her subjects a collective fantasy about her powers that is to be identified neither with any specific state or royal authority on the one hand, nor, on the other, with the kind of cultural power that inhabits all subjects. To be fantasized to have the power of influencing ideological shifts is already to be in a position to exert it, and for Victoria exerting this power took the form of yielding to the requirement that she manipulate (as well as be manipulated by) the spectacle of royalty.

Simon Schama remarks generally about the post-1688 British monarchy that "no firm distinction existed between the image and the political reality."[5] Sarah Ellis's writing on the newly crowned Victoria suggests that for Victoria's contemporaries she was both a producer of the royal image and subject to the Victorian construction of all women. Ellis sees Victoria at once as the epitome of the "influence" that serves as excuse for women's containment within the domestic sphere, not differentiating between Victoria's powers and those of her female subjects, and as unique authorizing agent of that containment. The women of England must "prove to their youthful sovereign, that whatever plan she may think it right to sanction for the moral advancement of her subjects . . . will be . . . faithfully supported in every British home by the female influence prevailing there."[6] Victoria is the fantasized authorizer, if not quite author, of Victorian ideology, if it is up to her to "sanction . . . whatever plan"; at the same time, she is the exemplary construct of Victorian ideology, obliged to be interested in the "moral advancement of her subjects" (unlike recent occupants of the throne) because, Ellis claims, those subjects presume her to be so. Ellis's "may" in effect leaves Victoria little room for choice.

Ostensibly directed to exhorting the women of England and so calling them into being as a moral "influence," Ellis's rhetoric simultaneously shows how that "influence" calls Victoria into being. Victoria's subjects subjected her to the myth of her power over them, a paradox we reproduce whenever we use the term "Victorian" to describe Victoria herself.[7] Moreover, some of Victoria's most important functions can hardly be described as acts at all, much less voluntary ones. For example, serving as a resource for the metaphor of middle-class women as "queens" (a metaphor especially pervasive in the 1860s), Victoria was no more a free agent in authorizing or defining queenly powers than her subjects were in assuming them. Nonetheless, the metaphor was and is widely thought to describe, even to create, Victorian women's expanding powers, even though Victoria's powers were themselves constructed in imitation of those same middle-class women.

Twentieth-century clichés about the Queen and about queenly Victorian women tend to emphasize precisely this difficulty of extricating autonomy from construction or power from constraint. Victoria is often recalled in popular twentieth-century representations as the Queen in whose name Britain expanded and maintained its empire, the passive authorizer of world historical aggression. A recent study of imperialism alludes to "Victoria's imperative, articulated through the ideology and practices of her subjects, to civilize barbaric societies."[8] What kind of action is an action undertaken in someone's name, and who is responsible for it? In Caryl Churchill's 1979 play *Cloud 9*, a satire on the continuities between Victorian and modern-day morals and social practices, the Queen is invoked in deliberately clichéd language to authorize patriarchal excesses in the family and in the world.[9] At the opening of the play, somewhere in Africa under a "flagpole with Union Jack," Clive the patriarch recites:

> This is my family. Though far from home
> We serve the Queen wherever we may roam
> I am a father to the natives here,
> And father to my family so dear.
> (*Cloud 9*, 3)

"Serve the Queen" here and in the imperial texts Churchill mocks means undertaking imperial wars of conquest (such as England's "Little Wars" in Africa in the 1880s and 1890s) as well as lording it over the patriarchal family. When British soldiers kill the parents of the native servant Joshua, another character tells Clive, "I think you owe him an apology on behalf of the Queen" (*Cloud 9*, 54). In what sense has the Queen commanded this murderous service? In this scenario she is again rendered passive in her construction by others as an active agent of imperialism. She is obliged to underwrite whatever atrocities her ministers and agents may commit in her name. The satire's joke is that the more she is made responsible for, the less can plausibly be attributed to the actions of Victoria the historical subject. The character in the play called "Victoria" is Clive's young daughter, and she is played by a "dummy," a cloth doll that is unceremoniously tossed from hand to hand during some of the play's action. Clive's wife Betty, "deputizing, as it were, for Victoria in her colonial possessions" (*Rule Britannia,* 120), is forced to represent the static "loving heart without a blot" (*Cloud 9,* 19) for whose comically uncooperative sake Clive and Harry conquer and explore.

> HARRY: Betty, you are a star in my sky. Without you I would have no sense of direction. I need you, and I need you where you are, I need you to be Clive's wife. I need to go up rivers and know you are sitting here thinking of me.
>
> BETTY: I want more than that. Is that wicked of me? (*Cloud 9,* 31)

Betty's queenly "sitting" in the play is not her desire, but the men attribute agency to it anyway. Victoria sat; nonetheless the empire was hers.

The Victorian scene in Woolf's *Between the Acts* similarly evokes, as latter-day cliché, the ironic mismatch between the historical subject Victoria and the powers of Her Majesty as she is called into existence to authorize her empire. The constable played by Budge the publican directs the traffic at Hyde Park corner and in so doing directs "the traffic of 'Er Majesty's Empire":

> THE SHAH OF PERSIA: Sultan of Morocco; or it may be 'Er Majesty in person; or Cook's tourists; black men; white men; sailors, soldiers; crossing the ocean; to proclaim her Empire; all of 'em Obey the Rule of my truncheon.[10]

The "white man's burden," the constable continues, includes policing private life:

> It's a Christian country, our Empire; under the White Queen Victoria. Over thought and religion; drink; dress; manners; marriage too, I wield my truncheon. . . . The ruler of an Empire must keep his eye on the cot. (*Between the Acts,* 162–63)

In the inclusion of "'Er Majesty in person" among those whom he directs, and in the gradual modulation from "her Empire" to "his," the constable—anonymous and depersonalized though he is—makes the Queen his excuse for wielding powers that are as much powers over her as powers she controls. The Queen is subject to the policing power of Victorian ideology as much as are the sailors and soldiers she nominally commands.

An often-reproduced image of Victoria from 1893 (figure 1) provides a gloss both for Churchill's "sitting" queens and for Woolf's constable, directing the traffic of 'Er Majesty's Empire and directing 'Er Majesty too. In this image Victoria sits, at work on her "boxes," perhaps adding to parliamentary bills the signature required to make them the law of the land. They will not become law without her signature, yet she is compelled to sign. She is out-of-doors on the grounds of Windsor Castle: perhaps it is a lovely day, and surely she is of an age to have earned a holiday, but she must attend to her work. Powerful by law yet physically immobilized, she sits inside a tent that echoes the shape of the boxes on which she works. In command of the nation's laws, she is also physically contained by them. Her favorite attendant Abdul Karim, holding a cane, stands guard at the boundary of the space she occupies. Of course, he is there to help her, but he appears also to be policing her, standing sternly over her bowed head as if to keep her at her task. That he is from one of the remoter reaches of her empire, a place she never visited, suggests a further inversion of container and contained. Because he represents the imperial subjugation of India, the picture suggests that that subjugation itself now polices her.[11] Victoria's actions are performatives—the placing of

FIGURE 1   Queen Victoria and Her Servant Abdul Karim. Photograph by Hill and Saunders, 1893.

her signature on a piece of paper to represent her royal assent to law—and they invariably take place within the vast and ornate containers she helped to make. Although any performative may be constrained by context and rules, Victoria exerts her power to call attention to this constraint by putting it on display. An apparent contrast to this picture may be found in Lami's painting of Victoria and her family opening the Great Exhibition in 1851 (figure 2). Full of color in contrast to the photograph's pallette of black and white, the space it represents vast and intricately decorated in contrast to the severe and narrow space of the photograph, this painting too nonetheless represents Victoria in a container, a giant transparent house containing the artifacts of empire and placing the Queen's domestic relations on display. Both the photograph of the Queen working and the painting of her inside the Crystal Palace locate her in spaces that are ambiguously both exterior and interior (a glasshouse, a tent), for the Queen is always performing her containment, her subjection to the law she commands, for the public gaze.

Sitting, allowing a photograph to be made of this action, simply existing—these loom large among the Queen's actions, acts that render power inextricable from constraint, not only in latter-day cliché but in her reign itself. The Queen, however, did more than this. "[T]his country [is] governed by our Sovereign Lady the Queen," remarks one of the defenders of female suffrage in Parliament (London *Times,* 21 May 1867), invoking the benignity and intelligence of the Queen's rule to justify a political change she herself opposed. I turn now to some exemplary moments during the part of her reign this book will explore, moments when the kind of thing she did as monarch and head of state makes visible the difficulty of defining the Queen's agency. This book's focus will be on selected moments from the start of Victoria's reign up to 1876, when her transformation into Empress changes the context of her reign so decisively as to require a different approach from the one I undertake here. Political interventions may be prototypical monarchic actions, but because she was a nineteenth-century monarch, and especially because she was Queen, what she did not do often constitutes a more significant form of agency than what she did, or than what looks at first glance more like an action.[12] It was Victoria's fortune, writes Elizabeth Longford, "to stamp a great age with the royal cypher."[13] The first of these exemplary moments highlights the problem of her "doing," while the second highlights the problem of her identity. (Or, to paraphrase Rossetti, "What would she do, if the Queen were an I?")

During the spring of 1868, Parliament hotly debated the Irish question. The Catholic Irish bitterly opposed the legal establishment of the Anglican Church. The *Daily Telegraph,* the largest circulation daily paper in London,

FIGURE 2   Eugene Louis Lami, *Opening of the Great Exhibition 1 May 1851*. Oil painting.

usually supported reforms that would improve life for the Irish without giving them political autonomy. On 30 April 1868 it ran an editorial on parliamentary discussion of the Irish Church that is really an editorial about the powers of the Queen as constitutional monarch. The question is whether the Queen can cede to Parliament her right to appoint members of the Irish clergy, as Gladstone apparently intends to request. The editorial worries that the House of Commons would be asking the Queen to "break the law" if it asked her to give up "those prerogatives and duties which are imposed upon the Crown . . . by Acts of Parliament, which Her Majesty, as constitutional Sovereign, is bound to obey." Lord Russell has explained, however, that the Queen is not going to be asked to break the law; it is simply that her permission must be sought before the introduction of any bill touching on her prerogatives, and Gladstone wants to introduce a bill to limit the expansion of the Irish (i.e., established, Anglican) Church. The Queen would only be permitting debate on the matter, not giving her assent before the fact to some as yet undetermined outcome. It would be in keeping with the Queen's role in politics—in the language of the editorial, "consistent with complete passiveness and neutrality"—for her to assent to the debate without prejudging its outcome.[14]

By the curious twists of British constitutional logic, the Queen is obliged to retain her prerogatives just as she is obliged to perform her duties: she cannot yield a power she is bound to exert. Her acting to exert that power, moreover, includes the maintenance of her "passiveness" or political neutrality. Is the Queen the most powerful, or the most subjugated, being in the land? Of no one else could it be said that it would take an act of both Houses of Parliament to allow her to give up any of her powers. Bound to her powers, the Queen is rendered inactive in relation to them, while she is obligated to exert her power over Irish Church appointments "with compete passiveness." She is like Jean Ingelow's Mopsa, the fairy who is fated to become Queen of a people who require "a queen of foreign birth [to] come to them against her will."[15] Victoria's power resides in her resistance to using her power. Yet her power is not nothing: her powers are given to her by Parliament; yet they are her powers, not those of Parliament.

The paradoxical agency attributed to the Queen in the *Daily Telegraph* editorial is only one of many such formulations throughout Victoria's reign of what she could and could not, should and should not do. And it is by no means clear how, if at all, "Her Majesty" in this text corresponds to Victoria, the person who lived. *That* Victoria, from what can be known of her, interested herself relatively little in such issues and certainly did not select these ecclesiastical appointments herself. Although her gender would not seem to matter in the editorial's formulation, it is a subtext of all such discussions. Reading the *Daily Telegraph* editorial, it is worth knowing that, although such a debate could have been held at any time during her reign, concerns about her powers and the nature of her agency had become particularly acute at this time, when her widowhood—her overdetermined performance of her gender in relation to the accident of her husband's death—had for over six years brought about her withdrawal from most of her public obligations if not from her behind-the-scenes duties as monarch. The Queen can choose to withdraw from public life. But can she also cease to reign? What more would be required for her to cease to reign, given that she had ceased appearing to reign for so many years? These questions emerge at a moment when calls for her abdication are balanced by fears that she will threaten to abdicate. As the London *Times* had put the matter in 1864, "It is impossible for a recluse to occupy the British Throne without a gradual weakening of that authority which the Sovereign has been accustomed to exert" (16 December 1864). The *Daily Telegraph* editorial of 30 April 1868 implicitly worries such questions, finally asserting not only that she cannot give up her powers but also that Gladstone is not going to ask her to. Pondering—and finding a neat answer to—the question of whether others may ask her to give up her powers seems to be the *Daily Telegraph*'s way of not asking whether she herself might choose, or is choosing, to give them up. The point of the editorial is that no matter how passive she may be—and, indeed, she is to be as passive as possible—she cannot cease to reign; if the "authority which the Sovereign has been accustomed to exert" requires simply passive acceptance of the obligation to be passive, then she can hardly avoid reigning. Nonetheless, it must be counted as one of the decisive actions of her reign that she chose not to abdicate, choosing instead to redefine monarchic power, or to accept such redefinitions as the *Daily Telegraph* offers here.

To read the Queen's speeches opening and dissolving Parliament every winter and summer is to encounter the paradox of her agency in a way that brings to the fore the shifting relation between the public institution of "Her Majesty" and the historical subject Victoria. Usually performed in person up to 1861 (and occasionally thereafter), these speeches were nonetheless written for the Queen by her ministers, for they present the policies that her government has been pursuing and intends to pursue. Given her obligation to be politically neutral and to be guided by her ministers, it would have been shocking had she departed from her set speech. Nonetheless the convention of the Queen's Speech is that all governmental initiatives, including wars and treaties with other nations, are undertaken by the Queen in her own person—the same person who stands up to read the speech—with the advice of

Parliament. Take, for example, her speech opening Parliament on 5 February 1839, which begins:

> My Lords and Gentlemen,
>
> I rejoice to meet you again in Parliament. I am particularly desirous of recurring to your advice and assistance at a period when many matters of great importance demand your serious and deliberate attention.
>
> I continue to receive from foreign Powers gratifying assurances of their desire to maintain with me the most friendly relations.
>
> I have concluded with the Emperor of Austria a Treaty of Commerce, which I trust will extend and improve the intercourse between my subjects and those of the Emperor.
>
> I have also concluded a treaty of the same kind with the Sultan.[16]

Who is saying "I" here? Although Victoria eventually took a strong hand in foreign policy, advising her ministers and insisting that they clear their plans and communications with her in advance,[17] the nineteen-year-old girl giving this speech has no more personally concluded these treaties than she has written the speech in which she claims to have done so. Nonetheless Her Majesty is grammatically and constitutionally accountable for these actions. Hearers and readers of such a speech routinely accept contradictory accounts of the Queen's agency. On the one hand, by virtue of her position, no matter who concludes a treaty, it is she who has done it. On the other, the ostentatious artificiality of these claims calls attention to the legal requirement that she do nothing without her ministers having done it for her. The embodied woman, Victoria, who stands up to speak may have still less to do with these governmental actions; nonetheless it is a matter of state importance that she be there in the flesh to represent those actions as belonging to the speech's "I," Her Majesty the Queen.

The medieval and early modern British legal "fiction of the King's Two Bodies" enabled both the identification and, later, the disarticulation of the monarch's God-given office and his or her natural body.[18] The questions raised by the Queen's performance of her speech cannot be answered just by invoking the idea of the king's two bodies, however, because the Queen is partitioned into at least two sets of two bodies here. There is not only the dualism of the nineteen-year-old girl and the abstract monarchic "I"; there is also the difference between the I who pretends to take dictation from Parliament, the I who pretends to speak for "Her" self, and the I who, while pretending not to take dictation, does pretend to do so. Moreover, that Victoria was monarch only because of a "failure of issue male" means that, whatever else she may represent, she always represents lack.[19]

The difficulty of identifying an action taken by the Queen and knowing who performs it is related to the question of who is speaking when the Queen speaks, a question that becomes further complicated after Albert's death, when Parliament is opened and dissolved "by Commission." At first the Lords Commissioners (including the Lord Chancellor and the Lord Chamberlain) refer to the Queen in the third person, acknowledging her absence, as, for example, when they say, "We are commanded by Her Majesty to release you from further attendance in Parliament" (*Queen's Speeches,* 179). This formulation is in keeping with the convention that it is the Queen who causes Parliament to meet and dissolve, but it is curiously convoluted nonetheless, as—in regard to the dates of Parliament's sitting—it is not she who commands them but rather they who command her. As the years of her widowed absence roll on, however, her ministers take to speaking for her in the first person. In 1867 the second session of Parliament is opened in November by commission, but the speaker ventriloquizes her: "I regret that I have found it necessary to call for your attendance . . . " (*Queen's Speeches,* 230). Victoria has neither written the speech, nor delivered it, nor even turned up to witness its reading; nonetheless Her Majesty's "I" summons the members of her Parliament. Who is the agent for whom? Is the government speaking for Victoria, or is Victoria speaking for her government? When she is not there, who is it that is saying "I"?[20]

Royal performatives would seem to present a clear instance of the verbal cause of a real-world effect. Performatives are generally among a monarch's most formulaic utterances, so the authority they convey may not come solely from the monarch's own person, but Victoria's retirement in widowhood further complicates the question of who is speaking when such a performative is spoken, especially (but not only) when someone else speaks for the Queen. On 29 March 1871, when Victoria made one of her rare public appearances after the death of her husband, to inaugurate the Royal Albert Hall, she whispered something to the Prince of Wales, who walked to the front of the stage and announced: "Her Majesty the Queen declares this Hall now open."[21] The mystery of her whisper is like the mystery of her agency itself. It cannot be said with certainty that either Bertie or the Queen has opened the hall, but opened it was nevertheless. Just so, the building of the Royal Albert Hall might seem to have depended on the historical accident of the Prince's death, yet a venue for the display of England's cultural ambitions would surely have been built on some other pretext. Moreover, it would be difficult to say what is accomplished by the Queen's recessive performance of her performative: she did something—opened a hall, or asked her son to open it—but the opening of the hall may be the least of her action's accomplishments. What that action did might best be described as the public display of Victoria's retiring ways. But what in turn did that display do?

As these examples suggest, the Queen's doings were both overdetermined and indispensable to the life of her nation. Parliament would have opened, and Her Majesty's Empire would likely have expanded, without any one person rather than another occupying the role of monarch; yet the Queen's role in these doings, and her seeming to have some authority over them, was absolutely necessary. She may have been obligated—by her nation's constitution, by the historical relentlessness of empire, by Victorian domestic ideology—to wield the authority and to do the things she did, but in the performance of these obligations, which were also her prerogatives, lies her distinctive form of monarchic agency. The personal styles she adopted, the books she wrote, the works of art she commissioned, the laws she signed, the governments she called into and out of being: all the acts for which she was responsible had enormous consequences, although it is conspicuously difficult to say in what her responsibility consisted or which "she" was or was not responsible. At the same time, whatever she is represented as doing in these episodes (signing documents, retaining her power over the Irish Church, dissolving Parliament, opening the Albert Hall, even justifying imperial violence), that action accomplishes something else in the context of its public display, something that could be approximated as the assertion that she seems to have autonomous power over herself and over her subjects, a seeming that helps the audiences of these acts see themselves as autonomous too.

When they consider what she did, Victoria's biographers and historians have tended to worry such questions as whether she or Albert reigned up to 1861, what impact they and later she had on foreign policy, and to what extent she really reigned during her widowhood. Such questions provide a frame for the more minute study of representational agency this book will pursue. Frank Hardie's 1935 study, unique in the seriousness with which it treats her "political influence," was written, he states, to show that in 1832 "the Crown, ceasing to be powerful, becomes influential," even while he also claims that "[h]er long experience and accurate memory made her political interventions increasingly decisive as the years passed."[22] Similarly, Giles St. Aubyn's recent life differs from most biographies in attributing to Victoria a greater degree of power and autonomy, as when he sums up the contradictory impact of her career: "There is hardly a page of the political history of Queen Victoria's reign which does not bear her impress. . . . nevertheless, the Crown's reputation suffered from the delusion that it had virtually ceased to function."[23] By contrast, Elizabeth Longford's authoritative biography (the first to be based on a thorough study of the Royal Archives) finds that Victoria's power lay not in her annoying and marginally constitutional interventions in foreign policy, or in her insistence on retaining the royal prerogative, but in her seeming to be just like her subjects: "[I]n some inexplicable way the General Will—that most elusive of political concepts—was expressed in her person" (*Queen Victoria*, 567). In opposing ways—Longford through a mystified notion of the representativeness of "her person," Hardie and St. Aubyn by attributing to her a more traditionally masculine kind of political efficacy—these writers attempt to name the kind of agency Victoria had.

Seeking to address the limitations of traditional forms of history and biography, recent studies of British Queens by feminist scholars working in the vein of New Historicism suggest that women sovereigns of any historical period invite consideration through a vocabulary of constructedness and autonomous power. Susan Frye, setting out to write about Elizabeth I's "self-creation," finds Elizabeth participating in a "competition for representation" (the subtitle of her book) on which previous scholars have tended to take sides, emphasizing by turns that Elizabeth controlled or was controlled by her role and images, and that Elizabeth or her handlers or her rivals created these roles and images.[24] Following Louis Montrose, Frye understands Elizabeth's self-creation in the context of discourses that set the terms: although Elizabeth may have chosen to remain a virgin, she could not choose what virginity meant. For Montrose, Elizabeth "had the capacity to *work* the available terms to serve her culturally conditioned needs and interests. By the same token, however, her subjects might rework those terms to serve their turns."[25] Aiming to render more subtly the oscillation she has observed between arguments for constraint and arguments for power, Frye writes that "the extent of [Elizabeth's] power was determined by her willingness to engage and restructure the discourses current in her culture that naturalized gender identity. It is this performance or construction of herself that I term her *agency*" (*Elizabeth I*, 7). Despite her wish to get beyond the alternation of constraint and freedom, Frye's terms and syntax, like those of Montrose, still assume a subject that can get outside of discourse and do things with it, in ways that must be either free or constrained. Frye's definition of agency implies decision and volition, and Montrose too makes allowances for Elizabeth as an independent agent. Although of the "range of strategies" Elizabethans generated to handle the "ideological dissonance" of having a Queen regnant "some . . . were Elizabeth's own" ("Elizabethan Subject," 309), "the historical subject, Elizabeth Tudor, was no more than a privileged agent in the production of the royal image" (317). Finally, Frye notes, Montrose decides in favor of construction, just as she herself finally comes down on the side of "self-creation."[26] These writers cannot avoid taking sides, however carefully, once they have defined their topic in such binary terms.

Where Frye sees competition between Elizabeth and her image-makers, Dorothy Thompson, like Longford, sees convergence between Victoria and her subjects. In adopting the behavior of the middle class, she "encourage[d] trends which were already developing."[27] Although this phrasing echoes the tendency of Renaissance scholars to see the Queen and other makers of the Queen's image as subjects operating independently of each other, it also introduces an emphasis on collaboration. Adrienne Munich's *Queen Victoria's Secrets* is similarly organized around a dialogue between Victoria's image-creating actions and the actions others (ranging from working-class purchasers of cheap jubilee souvenirs to producers of pornography and of high culture) took to create her, although Munich finesses the problem confronted by Montrose and Frye by concentrating more on reading the images produced than on assigning responsibility for producing them. Munich argues that Victoria and her subjects were engaged in an ongoing project of mutual construction about which she writes in antitheses that are sometimes balanced, sometimes weighted to one side or the other. At times conceding to her a primary agency, especially in discussions of costume—"Queen Victoria... reinterpreted her era's cultural codes to fit her self-identity.... she set the stage for performances not of her own contrivance"—Munich, like Montrose, tends to emphasize the Queen's creation by "the imaginative life of her subjects."[28] In line with Munich's view, Nancy Armstrong's Foucauldian approach would, if applied to Victoria, find her to be a woman with no more than any other woman's share of power, a conduit for the sort of power Foucault attributes to all—great, but not the same as the power of autonomous choice.[29] Thus, Victoria appeared as a domestic woman neither because she happened really to be one, nor, by contrast, because she deliberately set about pretending to be one, but rather because this was the role given her by the culture that produced her. She could thus be seen to have performed her gestures of self-representation in concert with other representations of her in the media, gestures that were legible and efficacious because they coincided with representations already in place.

Elizabeth Langland, by contrast, tends to emphasize the Queen's autonomous actions, even when discussing the same kinds of phenomena that Munich explores. Writing about the "discursive instability" of the "domestic ideal" that Victoria so paradoxically exemplified, Langland uses Judith Butler (as does Frye) in an effort to complicate the binarism in which analyses of Queens' agency tend to stall. She quotes: "Construction is not opposed to agency; it is the necessary scene of agency, the very terms in which agency is articulated and becomes culturally intelligible."[30] Despite this disclaimer, however, Langland uses active verbs to emphasize what Victoria did, despite her antifeminism, to authorize advances in women's "power": "That she should . . . take her place as head of the most powerful country in the world bespeaks her own signal role in the construction of a new feminine ideal that endorsed active public management behind a facade of private retirement. . . . Having represented herself in middle-class terms . . . , Victoria facilitated the corollary operation by which middle-class women were represented in regal terms" (*Nobody's Angels*, 63, 66). That Langland believes that the metaphor of "queen" empowers good middle-class women requires that she construct for the Queen a particularly active agency.[31]

Whichever way the antithesis is turned, and however subtle post-Foucauldian abstractions may render it, such discussions seem compelled, when they turn to specific events, to recycle an oppositional vocabulary of free self-creation and constraint. Feminist scholars are particularly likely to turn to such a vocabulary because of the gender of the monarchs they are studying. For in the contexts of liberal and postliberal feminisms, discussions of female monarchs still serve as arenas for testing concerns about women's self-determination. Just as in the 1960s and 1970s it was important to point out the cultural victimization of women—their objectification at the hands of male producers of culture, for example—so in the 1980s and 1990s it became necessary instead to celebrate women's powers, wherever they could be located and however they were compromised. For feminist Victorianists, this meant a rise in the stock of scholars who could demonstrate the public work that private women were doing, as, for example, when Nancy Armstrong contended that the prototypical modern individual was a woman. The interminable oscillation of discussions about social construction throughout this period suggest that there is no truth about agency that will finally be discovered, only a series of historically conditioned descriptions of historically specific situations. The figure of Victoria localizes, exaggerates, and renders compelling and colorful these debates, both as they existed for the Victorians and as they exist for us. Abstractions will have little purchase on the shifting problem of the Queen's agency.

My own examination of Queen Victoria's representations does not avoid articulating Victoria's monarchy through questions of autonomy and social construction, but—to return to Rossetti's verse with which we began—I credit being, seeming, and appearing as forms of monarchic "doing," even as I also acknowledge that Victoria's representational powers could exceed only by degrees those of her subjects. When I turn to things Victoria could be said to have done, I choose moments when lines of responsibility are unclear, as when her widowed reclusiveness makes her seem entirely inactive, or when she gives her consent or approval to a representation generated by someone else. Nor do I take it for granted that when she does something, for example, approving the design of a monument, we know what "she" we are talking about.[32] To be represented, to be passive in relation to her government's policies as well as to cultural artifacts, are among her actions as Queen. Nonetheless, even or especially when Victoria's actions seem most obviously to be original or to have been chosen outside the confines of ideology, even when her actions are at odds with the public's expressed wishes—as when she withdrew from public appearances for a decade, or when she takes a risky, even shocking step such as publishing her intimate memoirs—she is still acting as a creature of her culture. My aim is not to produce one generalization that will cover all cases, but rather to explore the variability of her agency and of its representations across her career and across the varying media and forums in which she so publicly lived.

The chapters that follow will explore in detail some moments in her career that call attention to the peculiarities of Victoria's agency: moments when she did things that both followed and broke the laws she stood for and (in the equivocal way we have observed) had a hand in making, moments when her actions appear both overdetermined and original. If seeming is a kind of doing, then whatever her agency was it chiefly took the form of representation: self-representations such as books or performances, but also authorized and even unauthorized representations by others. Thus, to explore what the Queen did, this book offers readings both of Victoria's works and of works by others, works that were popular then and that have now come to define Victorianness. All include figures of the Queen, although my attention will be as much on the representational mechanisms for producing such figures—the peculiar relation between the Queen and allegory, for example—as on the nature of the figures themselves. Her decision to marry early in her reign and the selection of imagery with which to represent her marriage, her withdrawal from public life after she became a widow and her dramatic performance of her absence, and the production of books and the authorizing of memorial artworks to replace both herself and the Prince Consort—these acts of the first half of her long reign are both original and overdetermined, depending on how they are viewed. In Chapter 1 I argue that Victoria's powers depend upon her active assumption of her powerlessness. Chapters 2, 3, and 4 examine some of the cultural work done by Victoria's doing nothing when, as a widow, she served her nation by withdrawing her presence, even over public protest, to see it replaced with increasingly mediated self-representations that helped make the political and social realignments of the late 1860s and 1870s seem natural and appropriate.

This book emphasizes the part played by Victoria-as-author in the joint cultural production of Victoria. It does so by paying close attention to the texts she produced and authorized and to the acts and agencies by which they were produced and were seen to be produced. But it cannot simply consider Victoria as an author like other authors, even supposing that it were any longer a simple matter to speak of authorship. Just as it is often her ministers, her laureates, and her commissioned artists who perform her self-representations, her self-representations are not hers alone but also the nation's. In focusing on Queen Victoria as an author I am in part performing one of the humbler tasks of feminist literary history, that of honoring, and in many cases of recovering from oblivion, the woman author's subjectivity, signature, and agency. The critique of Western humanism that takes "the death of the author" as its starting point presupposes men's, but not women's, long and comfortable history of publicly acknowledged authorship and subjectivity; as Nancy Miller puts it, "Only those who have it can play with not having it."[33] Although Victoria is hardly an obscure figure, her writing has never received the serious reading that it merits and that I hope to give here.[34] I will not, however, be making a case for inserting Victoria's writing into the canon, for, in emphasizing her creation as an author by her readers, I will be treating her authorship as a historical construct around which some features of Victorian ideology coalesce. Her works will be by turns objects of study in their own right and just a few among the myriad cultural constructions of Victoria's figure. Despite their promise to right the canon's wrongs, author-centered modes of criticism may obscure the ideological constructedness of what appears as freedom or originality. Instead of "freedom fighters," women writers may be merely "role-players in a social dynamic that permitted, perhaps even caused, their rebellion,"[35] precisely the case with Victoria, if we substitute "power" for rebellion here. I will consider Victoria's status as cynosure, the centrality accorded to her cultural productions, not as her just desserts as an author but as part of her construction as holder of powers—powers in relation to which she may be quite passive.

"If I were a Queen / What would I do?" In Rossetti's nursery rhyme, the answer comes in the second half of the quatrain:

> I'd make you a King
> And I'd wait on you.

Creating the terms of her own servitude is what Victoria did in the first years of her reign, to which the next chapter will turn. Through consideration of a series of portraits of Victoria and Albert and of the analogously exceptional case of Elizabeth Barrett, we will explore the compromised nature of Victorian queenly power. Just as Victoria's agency (like, to a lesser degree, that of other exceptional women) is poised between her power over and her subjection to Victorian ideology, so her unusual political and personal powers, like Barrett's, are balanced by her tendency to give away those powers: a tendency created by the ideological scripts "that permitted, even caused" their appearance of having power. Victoria and Barrett can construct their own versions of female authority only by means of the ideology of female submission.[36] Just as I portray Victoria both as a central figure and as a figure whose centrality happens to be her assigned cultural work, I would also argue that it is possible and important to see it both ways about women's power. Victoria and Barrett both exert active agency in posing as inferiors and act out an ideological script prepared beyond their control. Their shared exceptionalness, even as it attests to their submission to ideological strictures, makes them at least seem to exert power beyond that permitted to women. This seeming was a form of doing, and in seeming to exert power, they did.

1

QUEEN VICTORIA'S SOVEREIGN OBEDIENCE

> [Acknowledging] one important truth [will make a successful marriage]—it is the superiority of your husband as a man. It is quite possible that you may have more talent, with higher attainments... but this has nothing whatever to do with your position as a woman, which is, and must be, inferior to his as a man.
>
> Sarah Ellis, *The Wives of England*, 1843

> Since the Queen did herself for a husband "propose,"
> The ladies will all do the same, I suppose;
> Their days of subserviency now will be past,
> For all will "speak first" as they always did last!
> Since the Queen has no equal, "obey" none she need,
> So of course at the altar from such vow she's freed;
> And the women will all follow suit, so they say—
> "Love, honour," they'll promise, but never—"obey."
>
> London street ballad, 1841

"The Queen Has No Equal": The Problem of a Female Monarchy

What made it possible, at a time when women were meant to "obey," for a woman to occupy the throne of England for sixty-three years and to leave the monarchy's domestic and international prestige, if not its political authority, enhanced? Despite notable exceptions, women were never meant to be Britain's monarchs. The throne was patrilineal. Dorothy Thompson indicates how peculiar it is "that in a century in which male dominion and the separation of spheres into sharply defined male and female areas became entrenched in the ideology of all classes, a female in the highest office in the nation seems to have been almost universally accepted."[1] Adrienne Munich points out, moreover, that the idea of "maternal monarchy seems absurd," an outrageous mingling of separate spheres that created a "gap in representability" to be filled only by one paradox after another.[2] And yet it is also arguable, on the model of Nancy Armstrong's contention "that the modern individual was first and foremost a woman" (*Desire and Domestic Fiction*, 8), that, quite apart from the historical accident of Queen Victoria's reigning from 1837 to 1901, the modern British monarch was first and foremost a woman—to be specific, a wife, and a middle-class one. Paradoxical representations of Victoria, as monarch on the one hand and as wife on the other, became an effective strategy both for handling the public relations problem of female rule and, perhaps more important, for completing Britain's transition to parliamentary democracy and symbolic monarchy.

The characteristics required of the monarch of a nineteenth-century parliamentary democracy were those also required of middle-class wives, and if a married woman had not occupied the throne for most of that century, the monarchy would have needed some other way of associating itself with wifeliness. Just like a middle-class wife, the monarch was obliged (since the seventeenth century, but increasingly so) not to intervene in politics. Like a middle-class wife spending her husband's income, she had to spend the wealth of her nation in a manner that displayed both its economic prowess and her dependency; she had to be the chief consumer in a nation of consumers.[3] And she had to serve as a public, highly visible symbol of national identity and of her nation's values, just as a middle-class wife might be expected to display her husband's status. She had to be available for idealization and, by the same token, to be manifestly willing to relinquish active participation in political affairs, so that others could perform remarkable deeds in her name, as when, for example, in 1876 Disraeli presented the crown of empire to his Faery Queen.

Or to look at the matter from another angle: numerous representational problems posed by the fact of a female monarchy could be resolved by defining the Queen as a wife. "By the 1830s and 1840s," write Leonore Davidoff and Catherine Hall, "the belief in the natural differences and complementary roles of men and women . . . had become the common sense of the English middle class."[4] The ideas of "separate spheres" and of "woman's place," they summarize, had come to dominate discussions of sexual difference: the increasing separation of work and home in industrialism, and the rise of middle-class families sufficiently wealthy to mark their status with nonworking wives, meant that sex difference became reified, hypostasized, and consequently hierarchized. For Sarah Ellis women were "relative creatures" whose "proper sphere" was strictly domestic (*Women of England*, 178, 20), and wives were obliged to recognize "the superiority of your husband as a man" and "your position as a woman, which is, and must be, inferior to his as a man."[5] Elaborated and justified throughout the Victorian period, this view reappears in Ruskin's 1864 lecture "Of Queens' Gardens," which argues that "they are in nothing alike" and that "true wifely subjection" is woman's nature and, paradoxically, the aim of her training; and in Darwin's view in 1871 that, thanks to natural selection, "man has ultimately become superior to woman" and that "the present inequality in mental power between the sexes would not be effaced by a . . . course of early training."[6]

Moving from generalities about Victorian sexual ideology to the specific case of Queen Victoria may seem misdirected, given her uniqueness among Victorian women. But owing to the confluence of this ideology with the revival of chivalric gender codes, a woman's construction as special or superior was not seen to contradict her subjection as a wife. Britain, finding itself under female rule, capitalized on the will to limit women's power by making that the excuse for limiting (although, and this is important, not eliminating) the monarchy's powers and entitlements at the same time. By presenting herself as a wife, Queen Victoria offered the perfect solution to Britain's fears of female rule and of excessive monarchic power. At the same time, as if in compensation, the monarchy acquired what is granted to Victorian middle-class wives in exchange for their loss of economic and social autonomy: that ambiguous resource early Victorian ideologues call "influence." Eighteenth-century evangelical writers such as Hannah More had celebrated domesticity while they also, according to Davidoff and Hall, "explored the contradictions between claims for women's [moral] superiority and their social subordination" (*Family Fortunes,* 149). In the popular early Victorian writings of Sarah Ellis, these "contradictions" resolved themselves into the notion of women's "influence," which was both the "secret of women's power" and the excuse for preventing them from "seek[ing] other kinds of legitimation" (*Family Fortunes,* 183). In Victoria the powers of the monarch were limited to symbolic ones, and the monarchy flourished as a result.

Historians generally agree that the Victorian monarchy succeeded—that is, survived into the twentieth century at a time when most other European monarchies disappeared, despite Victoria's wavering popularity from the death of Prince Albert to the first Jubilee—thanks to its public representation as middle-class, domestic, and patriotic, in contrast to the profligate and foreign royalty of the previous generation (see Thompson, *Queen Victoria,* 87). This chapter will explore some specific ways in which Victoria's gender and marital status enabled such representations during the early part of her reign, representations that simultaneously created the appearance of limiting both female and monarchic power and expanded the monarchy's symbolic power and ideological influence. Previous monarchs had represented themselves domestically: Linda Colley shows that George III had revived the monarchy by renovating the royal image as a mixture of regality, domesticity, and (as he grew older) mortal vulnerability, and by identifying himself with a nonpartisan and nostalgic British national identity.[7] Both splendid and ordinary, "glorious and *gemutlich* both," George III set a pattern by which the monarchy was expected to be visible and to participate in a "myth of royal ordinariness" (*Britons,* 232, 233, 235). Simon Schama traces back to seventeenth-century origins the royal penchant for intimate domestic family portraiture ("Domestication of Majesty"). Victoria's reign marked a revival of these strategies with altogether novel meanings and effects. The monarchy's success arose from its transformation into a popular spectacle during the nineteenth century; it was during that time that the association between royal spectacle and middle-class practices and values came to seem the permanent hallmark of the royal family.[8] This spectacle depended for its effectiveness on Victoria's gender. A woman is perhaps more readily transformed into spectacle at any historical period. What the Victorians were treated to during the 1840s and 1850s was, specifically and paradoxically, the spectacle of royal domestic privacy, a privacy that centered on the ever-plumper figure of their Queen as wife and mother.

Victoria's marriage to Prince Albert both enabled and complicated her impersonation of the woman her nation needed her to be. Victoria resembles England's other paradigm of queenly greatness, Elizabeth I, in finding a solution to the anomaly of female rule in being understood as the nation's wife. Louis Montrose cites, among other Elizabethan "strategies" for handling the "ideological dissonance" of having a woman rule, Elizabeth's claim to be "bounde unto an Husband, which is the Kingdom of England" ("Elizabethan Subject," 309). Similarly, Elizabeth publicly displayed her bosom to represent herself as her nation's "bountiful mother," a representation that Montrose argues drew its force from the institution of her virginity.[9] But whereas Elizabeth needed to remain unmarried in her "body natural" in order to remain autonomous as Queen, and so used the spiritual marriage of her "body politic" to her kingdom to justify her not marrying in her "body natural," for Victoria the situation is reversed and, perhaps, more complex. Elizabeth served as the kind of ruler for whom the paradigm could then only be masculine—prince or king. Two centuries and a half later, the monarchy required a symbolic ruler, for which the paradigm might well be a woman. But while the marital status of Victoria's body natural is not opposed to that of her body politic, neither is it identical to it, athough her marriage to Prince

Albert makes possible her appearance as her nation's wife. Similarly, whereas Elizabeth strategically opposed her "weak and feeble" woman's body to her "heart and stomach of a king" ("Elizabethan Subject," 315), confirming her subjects' prejudices about women while asserting the power of her office, Victoria never poses as anything but what she appears to be. Almost from the start, she presents herself as a matronly woman who rules as a woman, not as a prince. Drawing like Montrose on the tradition of "the king's two bodies," Munich locates among the paradoxes of Victoria's maternal rule the fact that "the Queen's maternal body belonged to the private sphere while her sovereign body belonged to the public sphere" ("Victoria, Empire, and Excess," 265), but these spheres often appear to coincide in her person. What being a woman means for this Queen rests on the highly ambiguous relationship—neither the same nor different—between her public and her private identities, between the life of her body politic and that of her body natural.

Just as Victoria both functioned publicly as the nation's wife and was herself, in private, a wife, she both publicly impersonated a domestic woman and really was one. She did indeed appear to be an ordinary, happily married woman. She represents palatial Balmoral Castle and Osborne House, the settings for some of her and Albert's most impressive performances of domesticated monarchy, as homes and herself as an ordinary woman who adored her husband and took an uncommon interest in raising her children. For state occasions she preferred wearing a bonnet to wearing a crown, and she preferred her wedding lace and veil to the robes of state.[10] For her Jubilee procession in 1887 she horrified her advisors by refusing to wear anything more glamorous than her black widow's dress. But the rituals for which she chose such costumes were no less costly for her down-market tastes, and a Queen in a bonnet cuts a very different figure from a commoner so dressed; in Victoria's case, the crown is visible by its absence.[11] Queen Victoria's resemblance to a middle-class wife made her seem ordinary, but its meaning and effectiveness depended on the contrast with her extraordinariness. Her ordinariness was at once genuine and deliberate, that of a unique individual empowered to be exemplary.

Serious-minded middle-class domesticity was becoming the behavioral norm for England, and in behaving publicly like members of the middle class, Victoria and Albert helped their nation to become powerful and prosperous by helping it see itself as a middle-class nation. Sarah Ellis, in the course of defining "the women of England" by the characteristics of women of "the middle class," repeats with approval Napoleon's famous epithet, "a 'nation of shop-keepers,'" and she extols "the number, the influence and the respectability of that portion of the inhabitants who are . . . connected with our trade and merchandise" (*Women of England,* 18–19). The royal couple could not engage in commerce, so their familial behavior instead had to serve as example, as we shall see. Nonetheless, two of Victoria's most important ceremonials of the 1840s and 1850s conferred the royal seal of approval on commerce and manufacturing: the opening of the Royal Exchange in 1844, and the opening of the Great Exhibition in 1851. These ceremonials contributed to the appearance of royal allegiance to middle-class business interests. To the Great Exhibition opening Victoria, though "magnificently dressed," brought her children. Newspaper accounts emphasize the building and its contents, said to be a "crystal store" displaying the world's merchandise, over the ceremony itself (on the day and the day after the London *Times* devotes many more inches of type to detailing and mapping the contents of the exhibition than to the Queen's appearance). The *Times* also uses her family position to subordinate the Queen to her surroundings: under "a glittering arch far more lofty and spacious than the vaults of even our noblest cathedrals . . . was enthroned a youthful matron, the QUEEN of this land, surrounded by her family" (London *Times,* 2 May 1851). Her domestic appearance at the ceremony conduces to the foregrounding of the goods on display.

Her appearance at the Royal Exchange opening on 28 October 1844 rendered her a more spectacularly royal cynosure. She and Albert arrived in a long procession, "her magnificent Royal State carriage drawn by eight beautiful cream-coloured horses." She wore white satin (a dress of Spitalfields manufacture, to show her personal support for English manufactures) and a silver and diamond tiara. The fullsome report in the London *Times* the next day emphasizes both the enthusiasm and the fine appearance of the crowd that had thickly lined the procession route (from Buckingham Palace into the city to the Exchange) since early morning. Not only was "Her Majesty . . . greeted with the greatest enthusiasm—the cheering and waving of hats and handkerchiefs being continued down the whole of the densely crowded line"; but also the spectators were "well-dressed," and in the windows of city houses could be seen "an unusual display of the finery in female attire for which our City ladies have long been celebrated." The Queen provides the occasion, but the news is the prosperity of her spectator-subjects. At the opening ceremony itself the Queen's speech states that "the extension of commerce" is an "object near to my heart," and that she will "rejoice if I am thus enabled, by the blessing of Divine Providence, to promote the prosperity and happiness of all classes of my subjects."

After reading the newspaper reports, Victoria wrote to her Uncle Leopold that "they say *no* Sovereign was *more loved* than I am (I am bold enough to say), and *that,* from our *happy domestic home*—which gives such a good example."[12] At first glance it is difficult to see what the previous day's display of monarchic privilege and splendor could have to do with her and Albert's efforts to seem ordinary or "domestic." But if those efforts are not an end in themselves, but rather aimed at promoting the ascendency of the middle class, then an associative logic emerges: her subjects love her because she promotes and symbolizes commerce and middle-class prosperity; Victoria's life represents the kind of domesticity that can be the fruit of that prosperity; therefore they love her "happy domestic home." Her language echoes the *Times*'s editorial about the great day. Read in full, the editorial is a clear celebration not of Victoria's home life but of Britain's commercial empire, but her letter seamlessly translates public into private terms. The Exchange is

> the real source and center of the greatest and most beneficial earthly dominion.... The Queen of merchants does but close intuitively and inevitably with her high calling, when she holds her court in the Merchants' Hall.... If all other climes toil for us, it is because we toil for them.... Such is... the reign of kindness... in which our Sovereign yesterday placed her throne, the most favored, most loved, and most beneficent of earthly potentates. (London *Times,* 29 October 1844)

Although the *Times* does say she is the "most loved," in context that is because she reflects the benignity of her nation's commercial empire, not because of her own qualities. The Queen's seeming middle-class and domestic, then, like her visit to the Exchange, is her way of positioning herself so as to catch the reflected glory of her "nation of shop-keepers." Nonetheless, the language of benignity and kindness applied to Britain's empire implicitly gains a borrowed persuasiveness from her public image as domestic Queen.

In order for Victoria's monarchy to become and remain popular, the potential disadvantage of a woman on the throne—specifically, the fears of female rule that a Queen regnant would inspire—had to turn into an advantage for the monarchy's middle-class imposture. Victoria's early marriage made this possible: in the report discussed above, the *Times* frequently notes that Her Majesty was "leaning on the arm of Prince Albert." (Indeed, she had given birth to their fourth child just two months before.) Despite her diamonds, her subjects could read her marriage as no different from any other, as a form of privatization through which women were defined as the complements and subordinates of men. Her marriage subdued anxieties about female rule. At the same time it made her a model for the middle class because gender hierarchy was becoming a hallmark specifically of the middle-class family. When Sarah Ellis writes that a wife must recognize "the superiority of [her] husband as a man," she is both addressing and constructing the category of middle-class wives. Ellis's interest, like Victoria's, was explicitly in shaping the emerging middle class, and gender hierarchy within Victoria and Albert's "happy domestic home" would have helped to establish the middle-class nature of that home. Nevertheless, the very success of her marriage in accomplishing these ideological aims also brought with it the attendant risk of making her appear less than a monarch. Her subjects wished to limit their sovereign's political powers, but not to eliminate the monarchy altogether or to find themselves, through their Queen's weakness, autocratically ruled by someone else in her place.

Popular representations of Victoria at the time of her coronation in 1838 betray enormous and sometimes self-contradictory anxieties about female rule. Apprehensions about female rule and the urgency to see Victoria controlled by a husband are complexly dramatized in a pair of broadsheets from this time.[13] In one, titled "Petticoats for Ever" and headed by the image of an enormously fat, menacing-looking woman (figure 3), two characters, Kitty and Joan, hold a conversation about the "wonders" the new Queen will do "all in favour of the women." There will be a Parliament of women (with names like "Mother Mouthalmighty") and an act passed providing "that all women, married or single, are to have a roving commission, to go where they like, do as they like, and work when they like . . . and [that they] shall have . . . a gallon of cream of the valley each to drink health to the Queen." The fear is specifically of female bodily excess as well as of political unrule, and tyranny is linked causally to female rule, so that the comic exaggeration that deflates the threat of female rule also defuses the fear of monarchic tyranny.[14]

Another, and opposite, popular strategy for relieving anxieties about Victoria's accession was in effect to deny that a female monarch would rule at all. A second broadsheet, "The Coronation" (figure 4), represents contrastingly and favorably the sentimental possibilities of the figure of the Queen as a simple woman. Celebrating her sincerely on her coronation day, this doggerel inserts Victoria firmly into the female sphere as dutiful daughter ("Tho' Victoria does the sceptre sway, / Her parent may she still obey") and into her female role as genetic link between generations of men: "E'er she resigns all earthly things, / Be mother to a line of Kings." The broadsheet closes with the image of a coronation, but it is, oddly, of a king, not a queen. The queen appears to be merely a consort sitting uncrowned next to him as he receives the crown, as if to suggest the role England would prefer for Victoria, whose portrait at the top of the page represents her as young, sweet, and unthreatening. But even this soothing image may betray an attendant fear: if the Queen acts only as a consort, as the closing image seems to hope, then an actual consort

FIGURE 3   "Petticoats for Ever." Broadsheet, c. 1837.

may improperly act as king. Desirable though it might be to limit her sovereignty, that might mean only exchanging one authority for a greater one. Taken together, the two broadsheets suggest that female rule is inescapably disadvantageous. On the one hand, being a queen may grant improper power to a woman; on the other, a proper woman may be too weak to be monarch even of a parliamentary democracy.

FIGURE 4 "The Coronation." Broadsheet, c. 1837.

A proper woman may also, paradoxically, be too strong. Sometimes representations of her reassuring innocence and delicacy had the equivocal effect of representing her as unnervingly powerful. At the time of her coronation, Victoria was frequently imaged as a rose:

> Of all the flowers in full bloom,
> Adorn'd with beauty and perfume,
> The fairest is the rose of June,
> Victoria Queen of England.
> (Thompson, *Queen Victoria*, 95)

Despite its saccharine tone and presentation of Victoria's unthreatening virtues, this verse is the refrain of a Chartist ballad whose stanzas enlist Victoria in the causes of rescuing the poor and reforming Parliament: hardly the acts of a sweet girl whose queenly activities would be limited to dutiful daughterhood and lawful procreation. Similarly, a double image from 1838 (figure 5)—one of "Spooner's Transformations," an optical trick that dissolves one image into another when backlit—pictures Queen Victoria as a sweet, scarcely opened rosebud that is also monstrously large, the flower occupying the same space as Victoria's entire body.[15] This "royal rose" draws on sentimental portraits of Victoria at ages six and sixteen holding a rose and anticipates a popular 1842 Winterhalter portrait of her again holding a rose. But it also anticipates much later images in which the massive, voluminously clad Queen appears as Her Majesty the baby, simultaneously aged and baby-faced, taking up all the space and certain to get her way.[16] Spooner's double image appears intended to repeat the strategy for defusing anxiety about female rule represented by "The Coronation" by making Victoria demure. It also, however, conjoins the anxieties represented by both "Petticoats for Ever" and "The Coronation," in representing Victoria as dangerous through the weakness that pattern-book femininity as well as bodily excess entail.

During the years before her marriage, Victoria both found and made ways to assert that her monarchy would allay fears of female rule, but the experience of those years also, to her surprise, made marriage emerge as ultimately the best solution to the problem of female rule. Although prior to her decision to marry other ways of handling the problem had seemed open to her, they depended unpromisingly upon her self-identification as a young and vulnerable woman in need of chivalrous protection. She would later bitterly repent that she had kept Albert waiting.

Queen Elizabeth I provided a chiefly negative paradigm for unmarried and active female rule.[17] Victoria "disliked [her] for her immodesty" (Longford, *Queen Victoria*, 31). The memory of Elizabeth's successful practice of

FIGURE 5   "The Royal Rose of England." Optical transformation, 1838.

adapting female conventions to royal ones survived as anachronism. For example, in the first year of her reign Victoria writes in her diary that "the curious old form of pricking the Sheriffs was gone through; and I had to prick them all, with a huge pin."[18] The names of the High Sheriffs nominated for each county are presented for the monarch's approval on a roll of vellum. "The monarch pierces the appropriate names with the spike of a brass bodkin... a custom believed to date from the time of Queen Elizabeth I who was presented with the Sheriff's Roll for her approval one day when she was sewing in the garden and, having no pen with which to make the usual dots against the chosen names, pricked them with her needle."[19] Elizabeth not only adapted female convention to royal exigency but managed to make sewing immodestly phallic. In Victoria's hands, however, this custom has different meanings. Her diary record of the event focuses on how much she missed the chivalrous protection of her prime minister, Lord Melbourne, who was generally at her side during such performances. Thus she adopts a mode of behavior in self-conscious contrast to Elizabeth's immodest style.[20]

A more immediate paradigm of queenship—just as undesirable as that of Elizabeth but in a different way—was that of Caroline, the Consort of George IV. Although she was accused of adultery, the English people were extravagantly on her side during the divorce proceedings George IV instituted against her in 1820. The dispute became "domestic melodrama," and the

King's failure to win his case was read as vindicating her honor and virtue (*Family Fortunes*, 151). Her supporters appealed to chivalry: "[T]he tenderness and respect with which women were treated in England, it was argued, were the mark of England's advanced state of civilization.... [M]en [could] prove their manhood" by supporting this "poor wronged female" (*Family Fortunes*, 151). As a consequence, when Victoria inherited the monarchy, despite the vast difference between being Queen regnant and Queen Consort, she inherited most immediately this queenly identification with a vulnerable femininity that provides a welcome rationale for chivalric acts.

The highly public text of Victoria's private life in the early part of her reign, both before and after her marriage, demonstrates an intertwining of power and subjection, a mixture shaped by the chivalric ideology that characterizes Victoria's inheritance from Caroline and her reversal of Elizabeth. Enthroned, an object of worship for a nation, she appears to embody the chivalric fantasy of the idealized woman's power over kneeling men. But it is a fantasy that renders her vulnerable even as it glorifies her. At age eighteen Victoria is portrayed, and portrays herself, as intending her role as monarch to supercede constraints on her modesty as a woman. In the much-circulated anecdote about the dramatic predawn announcement of her accession, the Archbishop of Canterbury and the late King's Chamberlain are delayed by Victoria's Household, guarding her sleep; when she is finally summoned, "to prove that she did not keep them waiting, in a few minutes she came into the room in a loose white night-gown and shawl, her nightcap thrown off, and her hair falling upon her shoulders, her feet in slippers, tears in her eyes, but perfectly collected and dignified."[21] In her endeavor to acknowledge that matters of state take precedence over personal modesty, Victoria paradoxically gives rise to potent images of her girlish and unregal vulnerability, the vulnerability that betrays chivalry's illusory idealization of woman's power. Mary Gow and, later, H. T. Wells painted the scene with Victoria standing in flowing white contrasted to the men in black who kneel to pay her homage. The same iconography is repeated in newspaper descriptions of her first dissolution of Parliament, when she appeared in white satin that stood out from the darkness of the room, and in Sir David Wilkie's painting of her first Privy Council, in which Victoria sits on a raised dais, glowing in white, surrounded by black-clad ministers.[22] Later on the day of her accession she saw Melbourne in her room "and of course quite alone as I shall always do all my Ministers" (*Letters and Journals*, 23). Yet her awareness that she is violating codes of proper behavior only emphasizes her deference to those codes, just as the idealization of her virginal figure in white also calls attention to the inappropriateness of her placement in these men-filled rooms. Because she depends on chivalry's vocabulary of idealization to supply her with an imagery of female monarchic power, when she attempts to establish that power she can do so only by giving it away.

Another example: in the spring of 1839, when the Whig Prime Minister Lord Melbourne resigned because his majority in the House of Commons fell to five, to be replaced by the Tories under Sir Robert Peel, a crisis occurred over the question of the Queen's Household. The members of the royal Household, with titles such as "Ladies of the Bedchamber," had long ago been personal attendants, but they were by now understood to be political appointments and ordinarily changed with a change of administration. Peel wanted Victoria "to demonstrate . . . confidence in [his] government" by replacing her Whig friends with the wives of important Tories (*Letters*, 1:159, 8 May 1839).[23] Victoria, however, vehemently protested this protocol. As a new monarch still in her teens, she desired to bolster her own authority and viewed Peel's challenge as "an attempt to see whether she could be led and managed like a child" (*Letters*, 1:163, 9 May 1839). Defying Peel would seem a simple demonstration of her sovereignty, but the way in which she defies him ambiguously constricts, not increases the extent of her power. Victoria is able to confirm her authority as Queen—her right, in this case, to retain her chosen Ladies of the Bedchamber—only by asserting that the Ladies are not political appointments but only friends, and thus that she herself is not involved in politics, at least when at home. Whereas Peel argues that for her there can be no line between the personal and matters of state, Victoria insists upon a private, female sphere distinct from public politics.

Her defense turns on her mocking insistence that women's political views do not matter: "The Ladies his only support!! What an admission of weakness! . . . Was Sir Robert so weak that *even* the Ladies must be of his opinion?" (*Girlhood*, 2:170, 172, 9 May 1839); "I should like to know if they mean to give the Ladies seats in Parliament?" (*Letters*, 1:163, 9 May 1839). In her journal she describes the showdown as if it were a dramatic victory for her own firmness, yet her victory paradoxically empties that firmness of political content.

> Soon after this Sir Robert said, "Now, about the Ladies," upon which I said I could *not* give up *any* of my Ladies, and never imagined such a thing; he asked if I meant to retain them all; all, I said; the Mistress of the Robes and the Ladies of the Bedchamber? he asked. I replied all; for he said they were the Wives of the Opponents of the Government . . . I said that [they] would not interfere, I never talked Politics with them. . . . (*Girlhood*, 2:171, 9 May 1839)

Victoria argues that never before have the Ladies been treated as political appointments. Her analogy is a self-defeating one, however, because previous Ladies of the Bedchamber had attended female consorts; Victoria is in effect standing firm by demoting her status from Queen to Queen Consort. Peel objected that "I was a Queen Regnant, and that made the difference; not here, I said,—and I maintained my right" (*Girlhood*, 2:171, 9 May 1839). Her reply "maintain[s her] right" only by shrinking the profile of her authority.[24]

While the Bedchamber crisis was going on, Victoria was involved in another controversy, one that Dorothy Thompson claims was less politically significant, yet it contributed to her decision to marry, which had enormous consequences for the nature of her reign and power. This controversy and its resolution had a structure cognate to the Bedchamber crisis: the young Queen was able to assert her authority only by giving up some aspect of it. One of her mother's Ladies in Waiting, Lady Flora Hastings, had apparently become pregnant and was the subject of much vicious gossip in the court, gossip promoted by Victoria, perhaps in part because Lady Flora was associated with Tories, perhaps also because Victoria was not on good terms with her mother, for whom Flora became the scapegoat. Indeed, her mother's relationship with her comptroller, Sir John Conroy, was somewhat too intimate, and Victoria's special nastiness toward Lady Flora may have displaced her resentment of her mother's active sexuality. Victoria blamed the supposed pregancy on Conroy, whom she terms "the Monster and Demon Incarnate" (*Letters and Journals*, 42, 2 February 1839).[25]

Lady Flora was not pregnant but dying of liver cancer, which had swollen her body in a simulacrum of pregnancy. But Victoria wished to be rid of her mother, who insisted on living at court as a chaperone, as if it were Victoria, and not the duchess herself, who ran the risk of sexual impropriety. Victoria resented her mother's authority as well as her sexual independence. Melbourne pointed out to Victoria that, if her mother would not leave until Victoria married, "Well, then, there's *that* way of settling it" (*Letters and Journals*, 42, 17 April 1839). The newspapers began prematurely to forecast her marriage throughout 1839 (see *Gossip*, 81, 112). Ashton's retrospective account emphasizes the popular desire to see her marry, and he links the Bedchamber crisis to the Lady Flora scandal and implicitly invokes fears of a "Parliament of Women," when he claims that both episodes "showed it was about time that the Queen was freed from her female *entourage*, and had the protective advice of a husband" (*Gossip*, 89). When the Queen eventually chose Albert, the *Times* (after criticizing her choice of a foreigner) exhorted Albert to save Victoria from the "unhappy bias" that was "hourly undermining the deep foundations of her Throne" (quoted in *Gossip*, 120). The political partisanship that Victoria saw as the sign of her power—a power that she was in any case willing to disclaim when she insisted her Ladies were not political advisers—was taken instead to indicate her need to be subordinated to a husband.

During this period, Victoria disliked the idea of marriage as an unwanted dilution of her position and power as monarch:

> For myself, I said, at present *my* feeling was quite against ever marrying. . . . I observed that marrying a subject was making yourself so much their equal. . . . I said I dreaded the thought of marrying; that I was so accustomed to have my own way, that I thought it was 10 to 1 that I shouldn't agree with any body. (*Girlhood*, 2:153–54, 18 April 1839)

As she saw the matter at this point, to marry for the sake of freedom from her mother's unwanted control would only substitute for it another form of subordination, probably a greater one, and gain one power only by losing another. Moreover, responding to Melbourne's suggestion, Victoria terms marriage "a schocking [sic] alternative." She understood that marriage meant sex as well as not having one's own way. She uses this same term—"schocking"—two months later when she quotes Melbourne discussing Lady Flora's alleged pregnancy (*Letters and Journals*, 42, 43). This echo links the prospect of marriage with sexual impropriety and suggests that Victoria aligned trading her mother's domination for that of a husband with trading the scandal of a mother's sexuality for the public deployment of her own. Just as, in the resolution of the Bedchamber crisis, she "maintain[ed her] right" by claiming lack of involvement in politics, she could suppress her mother's authority and sexual autonomy only at the expense of giving up her own. That she decided to marry anyway indicates her realization that she would sooner or later have to give up her personal autonomy in order to maintain her position. Like Lucilla Marjoribanks, the Queen of Carlingford in Margaret Oliphant's comic novel of 1866, "she had come to an age when most people have husbands, and when an independent position in the world becomes necessary to self-respect. To be sure, Lucilla was independent; but then—there is a difference, as everybody knows."[26] Paradoxically, marriage held out to women the twin prospects of legal disappearance into another's identity and of the only "independence" they could achieve, and Victoria discovered she was not exempt from this social law. Marriage was the only proper way to remove her dominating mother from her household, and marriage would also stabilize her image as Queen of a middle-class nation. She would enhance her particular form of rule, her power as symbol, only by taking the risk of giving away her power over herself.

Privacy on Display: The Queen as Wife and Mother

Replying to her fear that she would cease to have her own way in marriage, Melbourne says, "'Oh! but you would have it still' (my own way)" (*Girlhood*, 2:154, 18 April 1839). The history of Victoria and Albert's marriage is an ambiguous text of sexual and political powers held and given up on both sides, a text that makes use of the confusing, reversible vocabulary of chivalrous worship. Although Victoria adored Albert and at one point sought for him the title of "King Consort" and a position equal to hers, she insisted on her prerogatives as Queen from the start. Before they were married she overruled his desire to choose his own (politically neutral) Household and instead placed close to him Whig candidates of her own choosing. In a letter widely publicized after his death, printed in the Queen's book about him and often quoted in reviews of the book, Albert wrote that his guiding principle was "to sink his own individual existence in that of his wife—to aim at no power by himself, or for himself."[27] And it was she who proposed, not he: or rather, as she puts it in her journal, "[told] Albert of my decision" (*Girlhood*, 2:267, 14 October 1839). As *The Early Years of the Prince Consort* explains it, "[T]he Queen's position . . . must necessarily appear a painful one to those who, deriving their ideas on this subject from the practice of private life, are wont to look upon it as the privilege and happiness of a woman to have her hand sought in marriage, instead of having to offer it herself" (*Early Years*, 225). Reversing the ordinary pattern of engagement gift giving too, she gave Albert a ring, while he gave her a lock of hair. A broadsheet from the time of their marriage depicts Albert as a "sausage maker" so poor that his abjection feminizes even his sexual potency:

> She says now we are wed,
> I must not dare to tease her,
> But strive both day and night,
> All e'er I can to please her.
> I told her I would do
> For her all I was able,
> And when she had a son,
> I would sit and rock the cradle.
> (*English Popular Literature*, 343)

Many popular representations of Albert from the first years of their marriage echo this depiction of him, feminized by his identification with the royal nursery. Victoria proposed to a man she repeatedly describes, using Victorian conventions for describing a beloved woman, as "my dearest Angel," a beauty, with a cheek like a rose, not only at the beginning of the marriage but also, for example, in a letter of 28 January 1845, five years into her marriage (*Letters*, 2:33). Nonetheless, as the years of their marriage went by, all her biographers agree that she came to rely on him more and more, to literalize her language of worshipful devotion as a real dependency.[28]

Victoria's marriage, while it was largely constructed to allay the fear of female rule and transform it into a source of middle-class imagery, did not prevent the twin anxieties—that Victoria would exceed her domestic role, and that she would fail to do so—from continuing to surface, as the doggerel quoted as the second epigraph to this chapter suggests. Victoria did in fact promise to obey Albert, contrary to the verse's assertion,[29] and its erroneous emphasis on her refusal to obey may stem not only from fear that she would unleash female unrule but also, contrariwise, from a wish that she would, indeed, refuse to obey her husband. It would not do for Victoria to appear merely as a private woman and as Albert's subordinate: fears of Albert's foreign loyalties were just as potent as fears of a woman's rule (see Thompson, *Queen Victoria*, 36–41). Another cartoon from the time of the marriage, titled "Trying it on" (figure 6), emphasizes the equal and opposite risks of her status as wife. This cartoon, in which Albert poses admiringly before a mirror wearing the crown of England, expresses the anxiety that the suspect foreigner will be able to take over the monarchy. As Albert puts it in the cartoon's text, "[V]at is yours is mine, now ve *are* married"; because he is her husband, he may use the monarchy more authoritatively than a Queen would. Albert's threat may be in part defused by the presence of the mirror, which feminizes him by representing his vanity, and by the presence of sports equipment that suggests it is all just play, but Victoria looks on horrified and helpless.

Victoria's marriage did on the whole consolidate the image of her as an ordinary and unthreatening woman, but representations of the royal couple had to balance Victoria's reassuring domestication with her equally and oppositely reassuring sovereignty. Another cartoon (figure 7), of Victoria's proposal to Albert, represents that balance by providing two opposing contexts for Victoria's words ("Albert, will you marry me?"). On the one hand, her speaking figure is deferentially curved around his erect if slightly goofy-looking form; on the other, a state portrait hung on the wall at the upper left of the lithograph shows Victoria standing tall and autonomous with the crown on her head. Representing the Queen twice in one image is an extreme way of balancing her different symbolic positions; other images will accomplish the same thing by presenting an ironic distance or equivocation between Victoria's royal and domestic poses.

Perhaps in response both to popular anxieties and to Victoria's own wor-

Trying it on.

Albert.—Ay, I tink I look vere well in it. It just fits me—ha, ha. I now look ike a King; Victoria, mine tear, vat you tink?

Vic.—Oh! Albert, you must'nt touch that! Pray place it where you found it directly—it's not included in our marriage articles for you to wear that. It belongs o' me only!

Albert.—Well, mine lub, I no dispute it; but you know also, mine tuck, dat vat is your's is mine, now ve *are* married; and so I tink I shall take to vear it as o'ten as I like!

Vic.—Well, now, that CROWNS all!!

FIGURE 6 "Trying It On." Woodcut, c. 1840.

ries, representations of Victoria and Albert once they were married—commissioned portraits and cartoons and other popular images alike—helped to disseminate a complex picture of royalty's superordinary domesticity, to publicize the monarchy as middle-class and its female identity as unthreateningly subjugated and yet somehow still reassuringly sovereign. That there was such a congruence between commercial and commissioned works

FIGURE 7   "Albert will you marry me?" Lithograph, 1839.

affirms the presence of a sort of reciprocal shaping between the Queen and her subjects. While the popular press enacts its power to shape her, as England's middle-class Queen, she too, through what Ira Nadel calls "the emergence of... the ideological portrait,"[30] shapes and promulgates herself as a middle-class Queen and therefore shapes her subjects in her own image. I focus on commissioned family portraits in concurrence with Simon Schama's claim that they did not so much illustrate the real state of royal family life as deliberately create a new and politically motivated image of it.[31] These portraits also support my argument that Victoria chose to hold her power in the only way open to her, by giving her power away.

Images of Victoria's marriage play on two contradictory conventions of hierarchy, one a convention of Victorian portraiture, the other a convention of state. First, height conveys power, so that portraits with both husband and wife seated or standing will represent the husband as the more authoritative, as if by nature. Prince Charles had to stand on a step in order to tower appropriately over Lady Diana in their nuptial portrait. Typically in Victorian marital portraits the husband stands while the wife sits, or occasionally, in a convention that reads in essentially the same way, he sits center stage while she leans deferentially against the back of his chair. Both poses emphasize their difference and, secondarily, suggest her bodily weakness and his strength. This convention runs counter to the second, however, that the monarch may sit while others stand, while no one may sit in her presence unless invited.

Victoria's sitting or her standing, in other words, can represent, simultaneously and ambiguously, her power as sovereign and her subordination as wife. Complicating the question is the Victorian revival of chivalric conventions, which Victoria's court wholeheartedly embraced. As we have seen, images of Victoria before her marriage (receiving the news of her accession, holding her first privy council) are strongly saturated with the chivalric conventions that would inform representations of her entire reign. Victoria loved Thorburn's 1844 miniature of Albert in armor and commissioned a statue of the two of them in Anglo-Saxon dress (a memorial to Albert in 1861), suggesting her identification with the days of chivalry.[32] In the iconography of chivalry, the woman's elevation may represent not her real authority (as it might in the first pictorial convention outlined above) but "a tactical inversion of the real relations of power... a strategy for reconciling women to the facts of gender relations [in marriage], that they are called goddesses by the men because they are going to have to treat the men as gods."[33] To place a woman on a pedestal does not necessarily grant her any effective advantage, as (to offer just one example) the fates of George Eliot's majestic heroines always make clear. As the narrator of *The Mill on the Floss* describes the ambiguity of chivalric posing (jocularly addressing his presumptively male reader), "[T]he seat you like best [is] a little above or a little below the one on which your goddess sits—(it is the same thing to the metaphysical mind, and that is the reason why women are at once worshipped and looked down upon)."[34] In *Daniel Deronda* the "queenly" Gwendolen Harleth receives the "devotion" and "easy homage" of her chivalrous suitor Grandcourt, taking her pleasure "as she played at reigning," only to find after marriage that their positions are really reversed: "Any romantic illusions she had had in marrying this man had turned on her power of using him as she liked. He was using her as he liked."[35] Where Victoria's image is elevated, therefore, it is hard to say whether that elevation connotes royal authority or symbolic femininity (fantasmatically powerful, actually vulnerable); indeed, by conflating these two possibilities, such images suggest that a precarious feminine idealization is the only form Victoria's monarchic power can take.

Moreover, confusingly, because Albert himself was often represented as feminized by his role as Consort, his elevation may mean conventional male supremacy or it may mean that he is the woman on the pedestal, just as his deference may be chivalry's cover for male rule or the real deference of a subject. Some of these ambiguities are visible in the monumental 1842 Landseer portrait of Victoria and Albert costumed as Queen Philippa and Edward III (figure 8), as they were for a fancy dress ball that year. Albert is both deferentially lower—his foot a step below hers, his knee bent, his hand chivalrously supporting hers, and his figure turning toward her—and taller by almost a head, his face too much larger than hers than could be accounted for by perspective, since their feet are nearly side by side.[36] Simon Schama and Adrienne Munich both see the portrait "reversing [the] relationship of consort and queen" ("Domestication of Majesty," 161): "Clad in their costumes, the prince no longer seems to be subservient to Victoria. . . . Albert holds his lady's hand, honoring yet ruling her" (*Secrets*, 31). But because one always sees Queen Victoria and her Consort Albert at the same time that one sees King Edward and his Consort, that reversal may itself be open to reversal. Similarly, Thorburn's portrait of Albert in armor, while it celebrates his manliness, nonetheless also objectifies him for Victoria's gaze (she had long wanted such a portrait) and, oddly for this genre, truncates him at the waist, making him a legless warrior.

While some cartoons of Victoria and Albert around the time of their marriage represent them at a standoff—she powerful through sovereignty, he powerful through masculinity—other images in the popular press represent them as any bland, wealthy young couple, sentimentally adorned with the trappings of a fashionable wedding.[37] Popular portraits of the royal pair thereafter frequently represent them embedded in their family, surrounded by increasing numbers of rosy-cheeked children. In the frontispiece to a songbook (figure 9), Victoria is seated, her attention engrossed by the baby she holds in her lap, to connote her identification with the private female sphere. Albert's arms enclose Victoria as well as the children, and his gaze directly returns that of the viewer, to suggest that he takes in public as well as private realms, like any Victorian husband and man of business. Although the words "God Save the Queen" appear prominently, no one wears a crown. A rural scene below the portrait adds connotations of ordinary domestic pleasantness, but it also elevates the royal family to the heavens, to make them objects of veneration in the manner of renaissance ascensions of the virgin. This is the apotheosis of the royal family as middle-class folks, with the Queen imaged as governing paradoxically by removing herself absolutely from the sphere of government.

This representation occupies one extreme of the range of contemporary images, with Victoria as domesticated as possible and Albert firmly en-

FIGURE 8   Sir Edwin Landseer, *Queen Victoria and Prince Albert at the Bal Costumé of 12 May 1842.* (They are dressed as Queen Philippa and Edward III.) Oil painting.

FIGURE 9 W. J. Linton, *God Save the Queen*. Wood engraving from a picture by H. Warren.

sconced in the role of protective and superior Victorian husband. An 1843 colored lithograph published by G. A. H. Dean and Co. (figure 10), while also domestic, at first suggests a contrast. Victoria's figure is the higher of the two, centered in front of an elaborate mirror frame that partially separates her from the rest of the image, while the far from patriarchal Albert on all fours indulgently plays "horsey" with his children. Victoria exchanges no intimate eye or bodily contact with her children, in contrast to her absorption in her children in "God Save the Queen." Perhaps, however, Albert's subordination in this scene—being tugged along by his cravat, decked with flowers, and used as a prop for baby's delight—is all play, thus connoting the reverse of subordination, a reading supported by the light tone of the drawing and by the pose of Victoria's bending, yielding, and smiling figure. Nonetheless, the picture makes even more explicit than "God Save the Queen" the way Victoria could be seen as using her domestic position to reign. The more sentimentally she appears as a pliant wifely figure, the more her subjects grant her the power to model their lives.

Moreover, framed at top and bottom by the words, "To the Queen's Private Apartments: The Queen and Prince Albert at Home," the picture exemplifies Victoria's apparent desire to have her subjects witness her private life, to perform it as a spectacle and model. Presenting itself as an image of privacy on display, the lithograph incorporates the words of its title in an elaborately drawn frame suggesting not so much a painting as a stage set. In one version this surround is fully visible, while in other versions a pair of paper doors have been attached to the sides of this frame, doors that one must open in order to see the lithograph inside.[38] The image of the royal family becomes a sort of peep show, inviting (indeed luring) the public gaze even while constructing

FIGURE 10 "To the Queen's Private Apartments: The Queen and Prince Albert at Home." Lithograph, 1843.

that gaze as invasive. The more privatized her family life appears, the more desirable it seems to be to observe it, and thus the more effective it can become as an ideological influence. There are numerous other peek-a-boo lithographs of the royal family from this period: images of a railway car, of a horse-drawn carriage, and of a boat—a "Royal Aquatic Excursion"—in which members of Victoria's family are concealed and revealed behind a paper flap.[39] Another boating image that does not sport a concealing flap, "The Royal Anglers on Virginia Water," crowds Albert, Victoria, Vicky, Bertie, and the baby Alice into a tiny dinghy, with fishing lines dangling at jaunty angles and an atmosphere of almost working-class pleasure. The boating image with the flap, by contrast, is of a large gondola propelled by five pairs of solemn oarsmen, topped by a stately cabin and decorated by an oversized royal flag. The contrast between grand and formal exterior and cosy and smile-wreathed interior (once the flap has been opened to reveal it) gives this lithograph an impact lacking in the more straightforward image of the family seen all at once in the fishing boat. Images that draw attention to their own status as revelations of a carefully protected private life create an ironic gap between the monarchy and its domestic representations; they also make those representations all the more alluring.

Two other popular lithographs from the early 1840s hint at problems that might emerge from the contradictions—elsewhere represented as attractive—between Victoria's status as Queen and her position in her family. A peek-a-boo image published by Dean and Co. in 1844, "The Antiquarian's Museum," shows, on the outside, a smiling old man about to peek around an interior door. This paper door opens to reveal the old man's shocked face looking at a scene of misrule: three of the royal children are cheerfully playing with the royal robes, crown, sceptre, and other valuables, which they appear to have taken from a large trunk, in a setting resembling an antique store (a suit of armor and some stuffed birds are in the background). Is the Queen, having put the trappings of her royal position into storage, neglecting both her job as Queen and her role as family disciplinarian? If the royal gear can be so toyed with, is the monarchy merely a show, and a haphazardly performed one at that? Another lithograph from the 1845 Dean and Co. series, "The Royal Family in the Nursery" (figure 11), generically recalls "To the Queen's Private Apartments," with its uniformly smiling faces and cartoonish, colorful figures, although now there are five children, a nurse, and a dog as well as Victoria and Albert. Like the 1843 image, it domesticates both Albert and Victoria. But the 1845 image divides into private and public halves, suggesting incompatibility between the two worlds Victoria might be expected to occupy at once.

FIGURE 11   "The Royal Family in the Nursery." Hand-colored lithograph, 1845.

In "The Royal Family in the Nursery," Albert's tall, dark figure as presiding paterfamilias marks the center line. To the left, Victoria sits in an ordinary chair, the nurse behind her, the youngest child in her lap and the two next youngest at her knee with the spaniel. On the right, there is an empty chair that reads as a throne (larger than the other chairs, decorated with a coronet), on which Albert leans his hand and in front of which Bertie stands, waving a Union Jack and pointing to a model ship; Vicky, the eldest, also appears here, with a basket of flowers. Although the entire scene takes place in the nursery, Victoria is identified with the babies on the left while the older children, who have by now assumed gender-appropriate clothing, attempt on the right the adult projects belonging to their genders. The empty throne—which features also in "To the Queen's Private Apartments," at the left side behind the child pulling at Albert's cravat—suggests, as does "The Antiquarian's Museum," a vacancy in the monarchy that can be occupied neither by Victoria (busy with the babies) nor by Bertie nor by Albert, even though his standing posture suggests he might like to try. It is his appearance in the center, after all, that creates the divide in the image—his appearance in the life of the Queen that has plunged her into this Lilliputian domestic life, even while his own feminization and domestication prevents him from playing the role of King. The private world revealed here is appealing, and everyone in it (even the nurse, who has nothing to do) looks happy, but the revelation hints critically at an excess of domestic distraction. These images suggest the fulfillment of the worry represented by such earlier images of the Queen's girlishness as "The Coronation": the worry that the Queen, when she marries, will not reign. The empty thrones in these images (figures 10 and 11) eerily anticipate a mean-spirited cartoon from the period of Victoria's widowhood, a cartoon that pictures an empty throne over the caption "Where Is Britannia?" (figure 29). Albert was to take her away from her throne all her life.

Portraits commissioned by Victoria herself present a similar range of ambiguities as to Victoria and Albert's relationship and relative status and call attention, too, to their revelations of concealed privacy. In Landseer's portrait "Windsor Castle in Modern Times" (figure 12), which Victoria called "very cheerful and pleasing," Victoria stands while Albert is seated, in body-revealing clothes, surrounded by the paraphernalia of hunting. Dogs gaze up at him adoringly, and the toddler Vicky, their first child, toys with one of several dead birds as she stands at the far end of this animal group, mirroring her mother's position at the opposite margin of the picture. The dog between Albert's legs especially suggests his phallic dominance of the scene. The signs of female domesticity are here displaced by the signs of masculine prowess, and Victoria's pose mirrors not only that of her tiny daughter but also that of the dogs: she seems to wait attendance upon Albert as they do.[40] The signifier of her unfeminine authority that might be created by her standing above him seems reversed by these manifold indications that she is any loving Victorian wife, deferring to his centrality, not towering above him— the elevated symbol of domesticity for whom he performs his chivalric, manly deeds, but not the family decision maker. Moreover, remembering the rule that none may sit in the Queen's presence suggests all the more strongly that here she wishes to be seen as wife, not Queen. Paradoxically, their positioning must reverse the usual husband-wife pose in order for him to be read as husband and her as wife.

Nonetheless, the open door framing the picture at the far right serves as a reminder that this model Victorian domestic privacy is being deliberately exposed, and that Victoria's deference in the picture may have other meanings in the context of its display. Indeed, it could also be argued that the composition rises triangularly toward her, and that all eyes really are on her, not on Albert. While the domestic femininity of her form is emphasized by her elaborate lacy dress, his body, while on display as a masculine body, could be said to be feminized too, in that bodily display is itself feminizing. The Byronic tights he wears represent the costume of an earlier age and of outmoded aristocratic pleasures. Real men—prime ministers and businessmen, for example—by now (after 1820) wear pants and make costumes like Albert's here look romantic and effete.[41] It is unusual for a hunter to be shown indoors, and if in one reading it might seem that he has taken over the domestic space with his hunting gear, it could also be said that his masculinity has been captured and tamed by Victoria's coercive domesticity. Turning the paradigm of chivalry the other way, we could say that Victoria is not diminished here by her symbolic elevation. For a constitutional Queen, symbolic power—a woman's power—is the only possible form of royal authority. Perhaps what is really on display here is not, or not only, Victoria's domestic deference toward Albert but, or but also, her sovereignty over a feminized Albert and over an adoring nation.

This ambiguity would seem to receive a somewhat different emphasis in perhaps the most famous portrait of the family, painted in 1846 by Winterhalter (figure 13), who along with Landseer was the chief portraitist to the

FIGURE 12   Sir Edwin Landseer, *Windsor Castle in Modern Times: Queen Victoria, Prince Albert, and Victoria, Princess Royal.* Oil painting, 1841–45.

royal family.[42] Here both Albert and Victoria are seated, this time in regal attire, on throne-like chairs in a formal, stagy setting. Despite the presence of five active children, the parents' expressions are more businesslike than cordial. The painting mingles the genres of the informal family *conversazione* with that of the formal state portrait, and the setting heightens the ambiguity (as to privacy and publicity) we have seen also in the Landseer painting and in the domestic lithographs. While the children in the right foreground seem to tumble about in a domestic space not unlike that in the Landseer portrait, albeit in their best clothes, the left background framing Victoria and Albert is an idealized and undomestic combination of "fine turquoise-blue skies" (specifically requested by Albert) and formal drapery.[43] Are Victoria and Albert public or private, indoors or out, on stage or not? Privacy is being publicized here, and public life privatized. This ambiguity is echoed by the painting's locations: it hung in the dining room at Osborne, Victoria and Albert's most home-like home, but it was also engraved by Samuel Cousins and therefore enjoyed wide public circulation.

These formal ambiguities reinforce those present in the posing of the figures. Although Albert is seated closer to the picture plane and obstructs part of Victoria's figure with his elegantly clad leg, Victoria wears a crown while he does not, and their relative heights have been misrepresented so as to make Victoria almost as tall (against her chair and also in the picture plane) as Albert, despite the shrinking of perspective. Furthermore, in exact contrast to "God Save the Queen" (figure 9), it is now she who gazes unflinchingly out at the spectator, while her husband's gaze is absorbed by his child. There is a baby in the scene, but she (Princess Helena) is at the greatest possible distance from her mother. Of course, the look shared at some distance between father and eldest son differs greatly from the mutual gaze of mother and infant in "God Save the Queen"; it suggests patrilineage and the passage of power from father to son rather than Kristeva's semiotic chora. Yet Victoria's steely gaze looking out between them reminds the viewer that it is her line, not Albert's, that is continued in their son, and that patrilineage in this case is subordinate to other principles of hierarchy. When Victoria and Albert married, there was much public discussion as to whether Albert would even have formal precedence over his own future sons; his rank was finally determined by Victoria's fiat. Victoria's arm around her son thus conveys both domestic maternity and royal lineage, just as the setting conveys both state formality and domestic intimacy.

Although this picture represents her in just about as authoritative and regal a pose as she was willing to occupy in family portraits of this period, and although Victoria was known to have "loved" this picture (*Queen Victoria's*

FIGURE 13   Franz Xaver Winterhalter, *The Royal Family in 1846*. Oil painting.

FIGURE 14   Queen Victoria's sketch of Winterhalter's *The Royal Family in 1846*.

Sketchbook, 112), in the sketch she made of it (figure 14) she revises her own figure in significant ways. She has made her head bow further and more yieldingly toward her son, and has perhaps changed the direction of her gaze from out at the viewer to down toward her son. She has removed or elided the crown on her head and has put a sceptre-like object in the Prince of Wales's hand, as if to emphasize her role as uncrowned "mother to a line of Kings." Appreciating Winterhalter's relatively regal and public vision of her, she nonetheless domesticates it further. Or perhaps she liked the picture because she saw it in the way that she sketches it, with emphasis on its domestication of her regality.

At least one review found that the painting domesticated her too thoroughly. The reviewer for the *Atheneum* wrote in 1847 that the figures of the Queen and Prince were "sensual and fleshly versions" and that the Queen's arms and hands were "expressed in contours that speak more of hard work in the kitchen than of the occupations of a palace."[44] The composition also implies oddly deflationary parallels between the Queen and baby Helena, despite the distance between their figures. Albert's hands gesture toward each one's hand, and these two alone look out at the viewer, as if to suggest that Victoria's regal pose is not so very far removed, after all, from that of Helena's tumbled and horizontal sprawl. This connection recalls Victoria's assimilation, in "The Royal Rose of England" (figure 5), to a vast pink rosebud. Representing the monarchy domestically risks exposing its potential resemblance to a baby's irrational if charming tyranny, even though that domesticity is invoked in the first place to replace the image of monarch as autocrat with the image of monarch as harmless middle-class citizen.

Equivocally domestic images such as these, generated to allay fears that Victoria would be either too powerful or not powerful enough, suggest that there is no such thing as an unthreatening—or even an internally consistent—image of a Queen regnant. If it is surprising that the Queen's own commissioned images betray this faultline, it is worth recalling that the popular images considered earlier are often more frank in their depiction of the Queen's contradictory roles. In 1852 a letter attests that she thinks of herself as handling ideological contradiction by holding apart in their separate spheres yet conjoining the roles of good woman and concerned ruler. Contrasting Albert's fitness for rule to her dislike of it she writes, "We women are not *made* for governing—and if we are good women we must *dislike* these masculine occupations; but there are times which force one to take *interest* in them . . . and *I* do, of course, *intensely*" (*Letters*, 2:362, 3 February 1852). Her popularity during her married years suggests successful enough management of this conflict, even if it remained visible as a conflict. By 1844, in the letter quoted above claiming that "*no* Sovereign was *more loved* than I am . . . and *that,* from our *happy domestic home,*" Victoria can insist that she is a dutiful Victorian wife and that that, paradoxically, is the source of her authority as Queen. She holds her sovereignty by the popularity she accrues by behaving like an ordinary wife, ruling in the only way she can, by giving over her authority. One reflection of how convincing this strategy was—or how ready her subjects were to credit it—appears in Caroline Norton's 1855 pamphlet, *A Letter to the Queen,* which calls for support for improved divorce laws. Norton openly acknowledges, "I know that the throne is powerless to redress [my wrongs]."[45] Instead, Norton sees the Queen as a woman like herself who relies on the chivalric protection of a patriarch, and who would understand Norton's wish to have the Law serve as her guardian from the outlawry of her husband (see Hadley, *Melodramatic Tactics,* 161–66). If historians have been able to agree that during his life Albert managed the monarchy, it may be a triumph of Victoria's art of ruling that she understood and supplied the image her subjects wanted, an image all too easily taken at face value. To succeed by making her subjects think she was not interested in success was a shrewd if ultimately self-effacing strategy, even if it was not so much deliberately undertaken as it was evidence of Victorian ideology's effectiveness in shaping all women.

The Queenly Courtship of Elizabeth Barrett

During these early years of Victoria's reign, another exceptional woman courted and married a man her financial and social inferior. One of the most celebrated poets of her day, highly educated, wellborn and well-to-do, Elizabeth Barrett shared with Victoria an ideologically contradictory position as well as an elevation that subjected her.[46] The language of her poems about Victoria and about other queenly women, like the language of her courtship correspondence with Robert Browning (the poor and obscure poet she was to marry in 1846), suggests how fully the rhetoric of the Queen's life story had saturated Victorian culture. Or to look at it in another way, the resemblances between the (pictorial and verbal) rhetoric of the Queen's story and Barrett's poems and letters suggests how typical that rhetoric was of early Victorian elite women's strategies for balancing personal autonomy with feminine and domestic subordination. Barrett's poems about queenly women helped to create the conditions of legibility for Victoria's early life choices; Victoria in turn provided a model, if an equivocal one, for how a woman might be shaped by, yet also make use of, the seductions of chivalric and "separate spheres" ideology. Barrett's work from the late 1830s and the 1840s supplies a close-up picture of the ideology to which Victoria was herself subjected and to which she helped to subject others.

Barrett's volume of 1838 contains two poems on Queen Victoria, "The Young Queen" and "Victoria's Tears."[47] The poems sentimentalize the figure of the eighteen-year-old monarch by describing Victoria implausibly weeping for the death of her "wicked uncle" William IV (Thompson, *Queen Victoria*, 15) and by exaggerating Victoria's love for and dependence upon her mother, the Duchess of Kent.[48] Poems on the Queen published in Barrett's volume of 1844, however, focus, as do Victoria's writings and the images we have discussed, on the ambiguous relation between her status as wife and her status as Queen. Barrett's poem "Crowned and Wedded," printed five days after the royal wedding, insists on the separation between Queen and wife and celebrates, for the day, Victoria the woman:

> Let none say, God preserve the queen! but rather, Bless the bride!
> None blow the trump, none bend the knee, none violate the dream
> Wherein no monarch but a wife she to herself may seem.
> Or if ye say, Preserve the queen! oh, breathe it inward low—
> She is a *woman*, and *beloved*! and 'tis enough but so.
> (Lines 46–50)

Although the poem ends by leveling Victoria's personal happiness with that of her subjects—"The blessings happy PEASANTS have, be thine, O crowned queen!"—it nonetheless betrays anxiety about the conflict between wifely subordination and the monarchy's prerogatives. Like the street ballad on Victoria's marriage ("'obey' none she need"), it has Victoria vowing to love but conspicuously not to obey, and it makes a rhetorical compromise by re-crowning her even while her crown is off: "And hold her uncrowned womanhood to be the royal thing" (line 58). Even as it reconstructs Victoria as an ordinary wife, it cannot uncrown her altogether.

It is not this poem, however, but a more celebrated one in the same volume that most vividly reflects Barrett's identification (whether as an inadvertent reflection of the same ideology or as a deliberate strategy) with the sexual politics Victoria made visible, the poem for which Victoria's public image serves as the important intertext. The most popular of the poems in the 1844 volume was "Lady Geraldine's Courtship," a dramatic monologue in the form of a letter written by a lowly but talented poet, Bertram, about his love for Lady Geraldine. Especially important to the Browning-Barrett relationship because it prompted Browning to write to her, the poem appears uncannily to project the real relation between Barrett and Browning. In order to give its reading of the Queen its due, however, we will need first to examine in some detail the courtship correspondence that ensued for its deployment of chivalric and separate spheres gender ideology.

"I love your verses with all my heart, dear Miss Barrett.... and I love you too": thus Robert Browning opens this famous correspondence.[49] What can he possibly mean? They have never met; he cannot mean that he loves a Miss Barrett that he knows separately from her poems; indeed, so to declare himself to such a Miss Barrett would be an astonishing indiscretion. Only a supposed identification between the poet and her poems can legitimate Browning's remark, an identification that, as readers of Browning's poems know, Browning himself fastidiously eschewed.[50] Thus his courtship of Miss Barrett begins simultaneously with extravagant praise and with denigration of her as a writer, a combination that persists not only on his side of the correspondence but on hers as well.[51] Each writer gains an advantage over the other through adopting a pose of abject humility, but this apparently gender-neutral strategy has differing resonances for a man's and for a woman writer's authority in Victorian England.

Browning continues, in all his humble arrogance. Once before he nearly visited her, and he felt "close ... to some world's-wonder in chapel or crypt" (*Letters*, 1:3–4). Responding in kind, she professes herself to be "a devout admirer & student of your works" and claims "the humble, low voice, which is so excellent a thing in women," pointedly inserting humility into Lear's description of Cordelia's voice (as "soft, low, and gentle"). In a lighter vein, she also cautions him that had he entered the so-called crypt, he "might have caught cold" (*Letters*, 1:5, 11 January 1845). Thus she mockingly elbows him out of his worshipful pose by simultaneously declaring herself unworthy of the compliment and pointing out that to compare her to a corpse in a crypt is hardly flattering. But she does so only in order to occupy the pose of worshipper herself.

In this first exchange the writers have begun to discuss the "faults" in Barrett's poems. Browning accuses himself of failure—of failing to find any "faults" and thus of being unable to "do you some little good ... as a loyal fellow-craftsman" (*Letters*, 1:3)—thus managing to praise her and disparage himself in the same phrase. In reply, she "begs" to be informed of her faults. Her "fault," which he claims to admire, is an excess that reveals the poet behind the poem: "for an instructed eye loves to see where the brush has dipped twice in a lustrous colour, has lain insistingly along a favorite outline ... — for these 'too muches' for the everybody's picture are so many helps to the making out the real painter's-picture as he had it in his brain" (*Letters*, 1:7, 13 January 1845). (That the erotic as well as the poetic is on his mind is suggested by the example he proposes: "Titian's Naples Magdalene.") This faulty, praiseworthy revelation of the artist behind the work leads Browning to his best-known formulation of their difference: "You speak out, *you*,—I only make men & women speak," a formulation that confirms Browning's initial and paradoxically derogatory premise that to love her poems is to love her. Her self-revealing insistency, her speaking out from herself, constitutes for Browning her limitation as a poet, able to speak in only one voice, or only to paint the same line again and again. Moreover, the letter ends with Browning's refusal to admit that she has successfully dismantled his "crypt" figure: he waits for the spring "and my Chapel-sight after all!"

Disguising his criticism—really his condescension—as humble praise ("I *only* make men & women speak"), Browning again claims advantage through humility, and Barrett in return does the same. "The fault was clearly with me & not with you" (*Letters*, 1:8, 15 January 1845) she begins, faulting herself for misreading his first mention of faults. She accuses herself of being "headlong" both in her misreading of his letter and in her poetry, equating that term with the insistency Browning described. Indeed, she discusses at great length the fault "which many wd call superfluity" (*Letters*, 1:9), thus aggressively repeating—in her own insistency in the letter—the fault of which he originally accuses her. She also castigates her poems for a "difference between the thing desired & the thing attained, between the idea in the writer's mind & the εἴδωλον cast off in his work." But this confession of weakness actually defends against Browning's criticism, for she claims a gap between mind and poem in place of too much self-revelation. Moreover, she uses Greek to make this point, and she introduces the term "headlong" with reference to "an Italian master" she had "years ago," thus reminding Browning of the elite and unfeminine education that makes her his intellectual peer, even while humbling herself before his disparagements.

Nonetheless, she closes this section of the letter by defining their difference as a gender difference that is also qualitative: "Then you are 'masculine' to the height—and I, as a woman, have studied some of your gestures of language & intonation wistfully, as a thing beyond me far! & the more admirable for being beyond." This arrangement of low femininity relative to masculine height reverses Browning's stance of worshipfulness, locating Barrett herself as a woman in the position of worshipper.

Reading the early letters, Browning's biographer Betty Miller points out that the two poets "stood, or attempted to stand, in the same, wholly reverential attitude."[52] Barrett's recent feminist critics have pointed out, about the correspondence in general, that the two poets "competed in their letters for the lowest place" (Mermin, *Barrett Browning*, 133); "Each insisted on being the lesser artist," writes Angela Leighton, and "the lover, not the beloved."[53] Both seeking to be "secondary," they are said to have achieved a relationship characterized by "collaboration" and "reciprocity" (Mermin, *Barrett Browning*, 124); for Yopie Prins "they solve the problem of power by re-allocating it between themselves and calling it love."[54] Like Victoria vowing to "obey" and Albert promising to "sink his . . . existence in that of his wife," Barrett's and Browning's poses of self-abasement look virtually identical. But the asymmetry of gendered meanings in the Victorian context prevents these poses from producing symmetrical effects in either case. When we look at the literary context, for example, early poems by Browning and Barrett show how differently the pose of admiring, seeking quester constructs male and female identities. In Browning's "Pauline," the "fallen" speaker elevates his beloved Pauline to a celestial height and then elevates Shelley to the same height, using his worship of the celestial and now feminized Shelley subtly to displace Shelley, for example, by calling him "still" a star—still in the sense of "everlastingly" but also stilled, stuck, unchanging.[55] The speaker enthusiastically embraces secondariness as his solution to Shelley's unalterable priority, delighting in

> "the contented lowness
> "With which I gaze on him I keep for ever
> "Above me; I to rise and rival him?
> "Feed his fame rather from my heart's best blood,
> "Wither unseen that he may flourish still."
> (Lines 554–59)

The speaker renders himself active and Shelley passive by making himself the agent of Shelley's elevation ("him I keep"). And to be second is always to have "some better essence" to quest after. Fixing Pauline and Shelley as stilled celestial ideals, the speaker seizes the initiative and makes from his abjection a position of power. Moreover, the equation of Shelley and Pauline suggests how Browning equates poetic secondariness with the sort of erotic self-subordination he performs in the letters to Barrett. Crudely put, he makes Barrett another Pauline, and perhaps also another Shelley.[56]

This equation and embrace of erotic and poetic secondariness reveals the gendered meanings of posing as "the lowest": in this instance it takes its meaning from the speaker's masculinity, as Shelley's rival and Pauline's lover.[57] Barrett's relation to the poetic past, as well as to present erotic possibilities, is not likely to follow such a model; for Barrett, posing as "the lowest" has different meanings, resonances, and, possibly, sources.[58] Conventions about absolute and hierarchical sex difference clearly operate within Victorian literature, and Mermin, Helen Cooper, and others have discussed Barrett's paradoxical relation to a poetic tradition that divides human possibility into silent feminine object and questing male subject. "The Lost Bower" (1844), a poem in which a young girl penetrates through a wood to an enclosed garden-like space, only to find on a return trip that it has vanished, is in Mermin's astute reading (*Barrett Browning,* 102) a sad account of the impossibility of a girl's being both (male) quester and (female) destination, so that she might enjoy more active human possibilities than conventional femininity alone permits.[59] In her quest, the girl-speaker's

> little struggling fingers
> Tore asunder gyve and thong
> Of the brambles which entrapped me, and
> the barrier branches strong.

In the letter about being "headlong" Barrett again precariously places herself in that traditionally masculine role: "Headlong I was at first, and headlong I continue—precipitously rushing forward through all manner of nettles & briars instead of keeping the path." Worshipping Browning and impersonating a chivalric troubador may likewise constitute Barrett's attempt to occupy a powerful speaking position in writing, given that Browning uses that pose to such self-empowering effect. Yet while he can firmly position himself as active, subjective quester in relation to Pauline and Shelley, Barrett's girl-speaker, and perhaps the "headlong" Barrett of the letters as well, can occupy the role of questing subject only fleetingly.

In emphasizing gender asymmetry here, I am pursuing, in part, a line of argument Mermin parenthetically advances at the start of her book. Mermin writes that Barrett Browning tends to reuse traditional metaphors in a way that is "disconcertingly literal," and that she does so "most often in amatory protestations of subordination or dependency (flattery when men use them, but painfully close to the social reality of women's lives)" (*Barrett Browning,* 6). To extend Mermin's idea into a reading of the letters, it could be said that for Browning to claim abjection is a flattering conceit. As a Victorian man, even an obscure and lowborn one, his relation to the pose of worshipper is ironic or playful: a superior posing, in effect, as an inferior. For Barrett to claim abjection, however, is doubly ironic. As a woman, even a famous and wellborn one, she is an inferior posing as a superior posing as an inferior, with an irony that returns upon and undoes itself. Pretending subordination, to reiterate Mermin's parenthesis, is "painfully close to the social reality of women's lives."[60]

Barrett's recent critics have tended to avoid these social meanings of seeking "the lowest place," meanings that bear directly on understanding the epistolary and poetic relationship we are tracing here, as if Barrett were exempt in her exceptionalness from such social constraints. Yet as we have seen, uniqueness does not so exempt Victoria. When the two poets met, Barrett was famous already, and richer and of higher social status than Browning, who became a celebrity only later in his life. And yet even in these regards, Barrett may have been as typical as she was exceptional. Davidoff and Hall point out that much of the writing of early Victorian ideologues "explored the contradictions between the claims for women's [moral] superiority and their social subordination," and they note that Ellis's popularity was due in part to "the tension" in her writing "between the notion of women as 'relative creatures' and a celebratory view of their potential power" (*Family Fortunes*, 149, 183). If Browning asserts his superiority to Barrett by asserting her superiority to him, then it is indeed part of, not an exception to, the Victorian ideology of women's subordination that Barrett should be in some ways his superior. The terms in which she achieved her contemporary fame are saturated with "separate spheres" ideology, despite reviewers' admiration for her classical learning: reviewers singled out for praise her most sentimental poems in preference to more original ones and belittled her as "our fair author," a "poetess" (Cooper, *Barrett Browning*, 22–25). Like her Queen, her very unusualness as a Victorian woman, her status as a star, is what brings her into line with ordinary women whom chivalric rhetoric emptily idealizes; her superiority subjects her.

When a genuinely successful mid-nineteenth-century woman acts the part of inferior toward an embodiment of manliness, her rhetorical act as well as its unpredictable consequences create a resemblance between her and her Queen. Barrett's "Lady Geraldine's Courtship" both draws upon and helps to create an equivocal poetics of Victorian queenliness. Not literally a queen, Geraldine nonetheless has wealth and "kingly blood . . . / And the shadow of a monarch's crown is softened in her hair" (stanza II). This image of a shadowy crown connects Geraldine to Barrett's Victoria by recalling the ambiguous presence and absence of a crown on Victoria's head in "Crowned and Wedded" earlier in the same volume. Moreover, Lady Geraldine is so highborn compared to Bertram ("born of English peasants") that she might as well be a queen, and he frequently compares her to one. "Many vassals bow before her as her carriage sweeps their doorways; / She has blessed their little children, as a priest or queen were she" (VI). Bertram adores the "queenly" Geraldine in the manner of Browning's speaker in "Pauline," or in the rhetorical manner of Browning addressing Barrett in the letters: "Oh, she walked so high above me, she appeared to my abasement, / In her lovely silken murmur, like an angel clad in wings!" (V).

One day Bertram overhears an earl's proposal to Geraldine and the disclaimer she makes on refusing him: "Whom I marry shall be noble, / Ay, and wealthy. I shall never blush to think how he was born" (LXVI). Her words are meant figuratively and refer, cryptically, to Bertram's metaphoric rank and wealth as an artist. Bertram, misunderstanding her irony, delivers a tirade about her hypocrisy (the two of them having earlier conversed on the social ills of England), even while declaring his love for her in the familiar rhetoric of high and low ("I would kneel down where I stand . . ." [LXXIX]). Then he faints and has to be carried away by Geraldine's minions. In a conclusion, a third-person narrator describes the sequel. Bertram receives a visit from Lady Geraldine, who significantly stands while he stays seated. He addresses her in echoes of the opening of "Pauline" ("Pauline, mine own, bend o'er me"): "Vision of a lady! stand there silent, stand there steady!" (Conclusion, V). But she too adopts the pose of humble worshipper and asks: "Dost thou, Bertram, truly love me? Is no woman far above me / Found more worthy of thy poet-heart than such a one as *I?*" (Conclusion, VIII). The last stanza has them vying for the pose of the lowest: "on his knee he fell before her, / And she whispered low in triumph . . . " (Conclusion, XI), and what she whispers restates what she said to the earl, elevating Bertram to her own or a higher rank by virtue of his poethood. For both, it is, as in the Browning-Barrett letters, a pose of humbleness that conceals "triumph;" she has won her point, and he has won her.

This poem's recent readers, like those of the letters, have emphasized this apparent symmetry.[61] Symmetrical as the poem's close may appear, however, Barrett echoes the scene of a poet kneeling to a queen a year later in a letter to Browning that helps to expose the asymmetry that underlies Geraldine and Bertram's relationship. Bewigged and wearing a borrowed ceremonial sword for an audience with Queen Victoria, the aged laureate Wordsworth "fell down upon both knees in the superfluity of etiquette, & had to be picked up by two lords in waiting" (*Letters,* 1:84), like Bertram, who is picked up by his queen's servants when he faints at her feet. Despite the bathos of the scene, Barrett continues in a serious vein to praise Wordsworth for honoring the laureateship, an office disparaged by some. She concludes: "And won't the court laurel (such as it is) be all the worthier of *you* for Wordsworth's having worn it first?"[62] His homage to her (Wordsworth's to the Queen) leads to her even greater homage to him (Barrett's to Browning). Barrett writes this letter in the wake of a letter from Browning, now lost, which scholars think contained a proposal, or at least declarations of his admiration that Barrett was within reason to take for a proposal: an instance, one might say, of his embarrassingly excessive kneeling. Except (and this may be the subtext of both

"Lady Geraldine's Courtship" and the letter about Wordsworth) it is Barrett who ends up the more embarrassed: he caddishly makes her look foolish by implying that she imagined the proposal. "Will you not think me very brutal if I tell you I could almost smile at your misapprehension of what I meant to write?" writes Browning, as he goes on to reassert "my real inferiority to you" (*Letters*, 1:74).

For a woman to have imagined a proposal would have been for her to expose desires that Victorian culture's double sexual standard made it an offense to feel, much less to show. Browning's proposal and its sequels expose the asymmetry between the two poets' kneelings: a man whose desire is rebuffed is merely a wounded suitor, but a woman who betrays her desire has compromised herself. The exceptional case of Victoria, when she proposed to Albert, only made this asymmetry in Victorian sexual ideology all the more visible and justified its further enforcement for everyone besides her, as the broadsides discussed earlier indicate. Unlike Victoria only in this regard, but like Barrett, Geraldine cannot propose to the man she loves, and can speak her desire for him only in terms so cryptic that she risks being completely misunderstood. That the poem breaks off after the scene of the misunderstanding, and can be completed only by another narrator in a conclusion with a different numerical sequence, may reinforce the sense of social rupture aroused by a woman's attempting to speak her love. It is true (as Mermin and Stephenson optimistically emphasize) that Geraldine takes the active and risky step of visiting Bertram in his room, yet the words she speaks are highly constrained: she can speak only about his desire for her ("Dost thou, Bertram, truly love me?") and within the fiction of his "vision" of her ("Bertram, if I say I love thee, . . . 't is the vision only speaks"), or repeat her cryptic lines on the nobility of her successful lover, this time making the point easier to grasp ("It shall be as I have sworn. / Very rich he is in virtues, very noble—noble certes; / And I shall not blush in knowing that men call him lowly born"). In her letter a few days after the exchange about his proposal, implicitly linking Browning to Wordsworth and Bertram and herself to the Queen and Lady Geraldine, Barrett admonishes Browning to give up excessive kneeling. Perhaps she does so because his kneeling might really humiliate, not him, but her.

"Lady Geraldine's Courtship" thus enables a close look at the conflicts between a woman's authority—be it poetic, political, or simply emotional—and the position in courtship and marriage that Victoria's unique yet typical case made visible to women of her day. Like Barrett's letters, the poem depends on the maintenance of a precarious double irony: Geraldine's posing as the lower, like Barrett's, carries the risk of being taken literally or unironically by the man who, as her husband, can legally expect her to obey.[63] This point is underscored by the presence of irony as the poem's most conspicuous rhetorical trope, for the meaning of Lady Geraldine's final words depends entirely on the maintenance of ironic doubleness, just as Victoria's pose as subservient wife depends for its effectiveness as a monarchic strategy upon the ironic distance between the pose and the political and economic reality.[64] Bertram can be identified as the object of Geraldine's desire only if nobility and wealth are taken figuratively. Bertram's proclivity to lecture her and his history of deafness to her delicate ironies makes it uncertain whether the irony of Geraldine's position will stay open and continue to give her room to maneuver.

A lowborn poet courting a higher-born lady, Browning may have imagined that Barrett's poem licensed his addresses.[65] In his reading—"you speak out, *you*"—the poem represents Barrett's own sincere and even insistent feeling. But this reading erases the poem's artifice as a dramatic monologue spoken by the male poet and not the highborn lady. Turning Barrett into her own queenly heroine, he overrides her rhetorical acts as a poet, and to make her a queen is thus—as is true of the correspondence generally—to make her at once a superior and a subjected being. Misreading her gives him the masculine advantage, both poetically and erotically.

Whereas throughout the 1840s and 1850s Victoria's public image continued to express conventional middle-class wifely deference, Barrett eventually abandoned whatever queenly identification may have initially seemed useful to her, although, as we shall see, deliberately rejecting it did not mean that she could entirely get free of it. Barrett's *Sonnets from the Portuguese,* written in 1846 just before the wedding, successfully (according to Mermin, Cooper, and Leighton) insert a woman's voice into the conventionally male place of speaker in the amatory sonnet tradition; in evenly distributing the roles of subject and object, they represent a "fine balance of literary power" between Browning and Barrett (Leighton, *Barrett Browning,* 99). I concur with these readings, and I would only suggest further that—either as a cause or as a symptom—the *Sonnets'* effectiveness may be related to Barrett's rejection of any queenly associations for herself. Instead, she places (in his view) "a strange, heavy crown" on Browning's head, a "wreath of Sonnets" that renders the beloved "noble and like a king" (XVI) and endows him with "sovranty" (XXXVII). The speaker is "a poor, tired, wandering singer" (III) with no royalty except what he gives her, no elevated position except that to which he "lift[s]" her.[66] At about the same time, Barrett in a letter to Browning facetiously retells an anecdote about Queen Victoria (the last of her allusions to the Queen in the correspondence): "I heard once of her most gracious Majesty's throwing a tea cup,—whereupon Albertus Magnus, who is no conjurer, could find nothing better to do than to walk out of the room in solemn silence. If I had been he, I should have tied the royal hands, I think" (*Letters*, 2:733, 25 May 1846). Thoroughly debunking the myth of the Queen's domestic virtue at the same time that it represents her power as mere bad temper such as any commoner might display (Barrett connects this anecdote to a scene a friend witnessed in which a woman threw a cup and saucer at her husband in a restaurant), the anecdote dissociates Barrett from identification with Victoria.

Barrett, it would seem, has finally seen through the appeal of Victoria's embrace of secondariness, to rid herself of that seductive yet compromising model of female authority. Before her marriage, Queen Victoria gave away her power in order to have it, perhaps in the process really giving up more than she intended; during her marriage she kept her power by continuously giving it away. Yet Barrett rejects queenly associations in the *Sonnets* only to abase herself all the more entirely. To make someone else a king as Barrett does in the *Sonnets*—as Rossetti's quatrain and Victoria's one-time effort to have Albert made King Consort suggest—may only be to place oneself back again in the position of subservient Queen ("I'd make you a King / And I'd wait on you"). Although Barrett's feminist critics have amply demonstrated that this strategy can be construed as enhancing Barrett's authority as speaker, the *Sonnets* remain for many readers sheer sentimentality, the gauge of her true inferiority, or her irredeemable Victorianness, as a poet. What is power (rhetorical or political) without an audience that acknowledges it as such? Literary history has largely joined Browning in representing Barrett as the Lady in a Victorian erotic drama, not as the speaker of her own. Barrett accurately names canonical realities—of her own as well as of our day—when she defines Browning's superiority as masculine and her inferiority as female. For all his talk of being beneath, they do not discuss *his* "faults"; when she finds fault with herself, it is not frivolous posing as it is for Browning but rather an anticipation of androcentric canon formation. Just as Barrett's ironic assumption of the role of humble student is all too easily taken literally, the Queen was all too successful in convincing others of her lack of ambition. History has remembered Barrett's poetic faults instead of her successes and has emptied the name Victoria of political significance: her name identifies an ideology but evokes no images of well-used authority.

Photographic Realism's Abject Queens

Wisely if ineffectually, Barrett discarded the tempting identification with "queen" that Victorian chivalry held out to women like her like a poisoned apple. Victoria lacked this option and had in any case more uses for chivalry: her "social reality" meant its promises could come true. Nonetheless, the last years of Victoria's marriage coincide with a change in the dominant genre of her pictorial representations, and the last section of this chapter will trace the effects of the photographic realism of late portraits of Victoria and Albert. Ruling in her subjects' minds without taking part in politics of state may be much the most potent kind of rule, as Langland argues about Victoria and Ruskin's queens. But it is more likely to appear to be so when the polish of chivalric discourse is on it, as in the romantic and sentimental cartoons and oils of the 1840s and 1850s, and even in Barrett's romances of low and high. In the harsh light of the marriage photographs, the effectiveness and the appeal of symbolic rule fade.

By 1860 in England, costly and traditional oil portraiture had lost ground to a newer method of representation, for "hand-tinted portrait photographs were being praised as 'truthful beyond the artist's power.'"[67] Along with its relative cheapness and availability, photography's claim to offer greater realism—for it "promised a superior grasp of reality, a realism more real than the thing itself"[68]—made it the middle class's favored method of recording itself. The royal family began to commission photographs too.[69] The daguerreotype was invented in the year of Victoria's accession, and commissioned photographs of the royal family date from as early as 1842, only a year after developments in technology made exposure times brief enough to photograph human subjects and Fox Talbot devised a process for printing on paper. The first is an 1842 portrait of Albert, made by a Mr. Beard (*Gossip*, 185); the first of Victoria is an 1844 or 1845 calotype by Henry Collen of the Queen with her arm around her daughter Vicky, who has her arms around her doll: as paradigmatically domestic a scene as could be imagined. For photography's representation of "reality" had quickly come to mean certain genres of imagery and not others. Helmut and Alison Gernsheim note that "among the many hundreds of photographs of Queen Victoria, few show her as sovereign. She preferred to be portrayed as wife and mother" (*Victoria R.*, 257.) The technology of the middle classes brings with it an intensification of the royal family's middle-class appearance. Just as photography supplanted oil painting, so trousers supplant knee breeches and hose as Albert's habitual portrait costume, while Victoria's dress rarely suggests her rank. In these photographic portraits the Queen never wears a crown,[70] but Albert sometimes wears or holds a top hat, which, reversing the iconography of the Winterhalter family portrait (figure 13), tends to privilege his masculine height over her royal precedence.

Like realism in fiction, photographic realism is a highly artificial genre, as artificial as the high gloss on Victoria's crown in Landseer's costume portrait. For Victoria and Albert to travel to Mayall's studio, to pose themselves amongst his props and try out this expression and that for his camera is just as much to make something up as it is for Winterhalter to paint them in his imaginary spaces. Realism can only refer to other texts, not to some extratextual reality "out there," as, for example, when George Eliot's 1859 narrator, defining the realist method of *Adam Bede,* compares it to a "mirror [that] is doubtless defective," to narration "in the witness-box," to a pencil drawing of "a real unexaggerated lion," and to "Dutch painting."[71] And Victorian realism, writes Jennifer Green-Lewis, "use[s] the idea of photography as a structuring principle or standard of truth to which the language itself aspires."[72] But photography and mid-century realism share a generic commitment to an idea of "the real" that was part of the middle class's strategy for making its values normative for all British society. Green-Lewis argues that "it is through its implicit affirmation of a community of viewers who see in similar ways that photography enters the domain of realism.... [T]here is in realism a homogenization of represented experience which prescribes a way of being, a 'normality.'"[73] Mrs. Henry Wood's 1861 bestselling novel *East Lynne*—not otherwise known for its commitment to realism—casually uses photography as a benchmark both for descriptive realism and for the desirability of middle-class norms when, following a detailed description of Afy Hallijohn's fancy dress, the narrator states: "and if I had but a photographing machine at hand—or whatever may be the scientific name for the thing— you should certainly have been regaled with the sight of her."[74] Afy's purpose in dressing up in "the fashion" (which includes "a mauve silk dress with eighteen flounces, and about eighteen hundred steel buttons") is at once to display and to put into effect her aspiration to join the middle class: once a servant, she is about to marry the shopkeeper Mr. Jiffin. Photographs of Victoria and Albert likewise regale us with the sight of a couple dressed for mobility—though in this case, downward—into the middle class.

These photographs, strikingly different from the oils of just a decade earlier in their apparent refusal of her regality, may constitute the logical extension of earlier representations of Victoria as middle-class Queen; even so, they adjust Victoria and Albert's relationship in ways that recall the oils' ambiguous projection of the Queen as both subject wife and lofty monarch. Unlike the oils, however, the photographs—produced within the documentary portrait genre favored by the royal family—are unwilling, or unable, to flatter the Queen's appearance. Even Winterhalter represents her as much younger and more in conformity with the fashionable type of Victorian beauty than the photographs suggest she was. In making this observation, I am not claiming that the photographs tell the truth whereas the oils lie; rather, the photographs construct a different reality and a different kind of queen. (A genre of photography more fanciful, romantic, or sentimental than the kind practiced by Day, Mayall, Fenton, and the other royal portrait photographers might well have produced yet another kind of royal image.) Although the homeliness of her looks contributes to making her seem ordinary in the photographs, it also has the reverse effect of saving her from the stereotyping to which her paint portraitists, the popular lithographers, and even most cartoonists subjected her. The photographs record her physical uniqueness and thus contribute to constituting her regality—as sole monarch—even as they diminish her grandeur.[75] That Victoria preferred to be represented in all her frumpy particularity is suggested by her practice of "press[ing] photographs on the artists she employed" (*Victoria R.*, 256).

The preservation of various images from a single session with a photographer enacts and accentuates the ambiguity of the Queen's image as wife and as sovereign. Not only are single images often equivocal, but several images taken at the same time may constitute a range of ideological positions as regards the royal marital hierarchy, as if the photographer and her or his subjects were experimenting together as they tried out different poses. Of the many available images I will discuss examples from three groups of photographs made in the three years before Albert's death: records of one session with a Miss Day on 26 July 1859 at Osborne House and of two sittings with John Edwin Mayall in 1860 and 1861, in all of which Victoria and Albert are dressed as an ordinary wealthy middle-class couple. One of Day's photographs was engraved for public circulation, and Mayall's images were published as *cartes de visite:* they are part of the royal family's deliberate promulgation of its domestic image. It is impossible to know the order in which the poses from any given session were taken; in what follows I will try to avoid constructing a narrative that depends upon the sequence in which I describe the photos; my intention is instead to describe the range of possibilities that the photographs explore. There are, however, narratives implicit in the choices Victoria and Albert made as to which images would be published and the popularity of some published images over others.

The royal photograph albums contain altogether ten images from the session with Miss Day, all of them posing royal family members against the creamy walls of Osborne House.[76] Two are of Victoria alone seated on a stone bench built into a wall, three represent Victoria on the same bench with "Baby" (Princess Beatrice), and the remaining five pair Victoria and Albert in various arrangements. In two of these she sits and he stands, in two others they both stand, and their hats and elements of the background are variously

FIGURE 15   Queen Victoria and Prince Albert, Osborne, 26 July 1859. Photograph by Miss Day.

disposed so as to alter the appearance of their relative heights. Figure 15 shows them standing rather casually together, the difference in their heights clearly visible but minimized by her hat, his slouching posture, and by a tree that softens his silhouette. That they are looking in the same direction further equalizes them by suggesting they have some interest in common. A similar pose places Victoria in front of the tree, which adds to her height relative to his; yet another has Victoria again in front of the tree and includes a statue that towers over them both, tending even further to minimize the difference between husband and wife.[77] Does the democratizing potential of photography influence the content of the image? Perhaps, but the image that was engraved for public circulation (figure 16) exaggerates the difference between them that gender makes. Albert leans rather casually against a wall, holding his hat, and looking an exaggerated distance down at the seated Victoria, in a pose that suggests disengagement and even weariness, while she gazes up at him intensely with an expression of agitation and needfulness. Here, she is seated, not with the precedence of a Queen but with the humility and even bodily weakness of a worshipful, yearning wife. In all probability, it was the Queen's choice to have this one engraved and circulated, and that choice constitutes the Queen's decision to represent Albert's authority as "lawful husband"—in the words of an 1840 cartoon—prevailing over hers as "lord and master" (Thompson, *Queen Victoria*, 37).[78]

Miss Day's two images of Victoria alone portray her seated on the same bench, looking to the right and to the left; in the context of the other photos, she looks not self-sufficient but lonely, looking off-camera for the man who has just posed with her or is about to do so. There is no record of Albert having been photographed alone, but an engraving was made (figure 17) that isolates him from figure 16, shows him reading a letter, and replaces the yearning Victoria with a small rose lying unnoticed on the stone bench. This image was later adapted yet again (figure 18) by the painter Thorburn, who places Albert in an interior, clothes him in a dressing gown, and shows him looking at the memorandum on the Trent question, to represent his last great deed as international peacemaker before his death in December 1861. The lonely rose that represents Victoria in the engraving of Albert reading alone is replaced in the Thorburn painting by a framed image of Victoria's face on the wall above him; either way, Victoria is reduced to a sentimental image to foreground Albert's important and manly work. Although Victoria having been photographed alone suggests her centrality as photographic subject, contrasted to Albert appearing only in photos with her, the overall effect of looking at this collection of images is to find that the Queen does not stand iconographically on her own, whereas the Prince can and does. She searches for him with her eyes; he reads important documents.

The American photographer J. E. Mayall photographed Victoria and Albert at Buckingham Palace on 15 May 1860. These images were made to be published as *cartes de visite,* although not all were finally selected for the "Royal Album," fourteen *cartes* of members of the royal Household published in August 1860.[79] Helmut and Alison Gernsheim report that "hundreds of thousands of Mayall's *cartes* were quickly sold," and that the English craze for collecting and trading *cartes*—which led to "three or four hundred million *cartes* [being] sold annually in England" in the early 1860s—began with Mayall's publication (*Victoria R.,* 261). Victoria's interest in promoting the circulation of her image is suggested by her successful obstruction of several proposed taxes on photographs. Like Day's photographs, this session produced images of Victoria alone and some of her with Baby as well as images of Victoria and Albert. The stiff poses simulate the domestic through the use of furniture and books as props. Victoria's figure alone can appear relatively regal and self-sufficient (as in two three-quarters profile images), or—

FIGURE 16   Queen Victoria and Prince Albert, 26 July 1859. Photograph by Miss Day.

FIGURE 17   Prince Albert on the Terrace at Osborne. Etching after a photograph by Miss Day, 1859.

FIGURE 18   Robert Thorburn, *The Prince Consort during His Last Illness, Holding a Draft Memorandum on the "Trent" Question, December 1861*. Painting.

FIGURE 19 Queen Victoria, 15 May 1860. Photograph by J. J. E. Mayall.

as in two images of her seated—it can express the lack of Albert. In figure 19 she ignores the nearby table and books and looks off-camera, her body turned as well as her head, her whole figure expressing the action of looking for someone.[80] On the one hand, Victoria's action violates the decorum of conventional photographic portraits of women: "The pose of a lady should not have that boldness of action which you would give a man, but be modest and retiring" (quoted in Linkman, *Victorians,* 46). On the other hand, Victoria's mimed dependency on Albert substitutes (to excess) for the modesty her figure fails to express.[81]

Victoria and Albert appear together in seven images, in various combinations of seated and standing poses using table, chair, and books. In four he sits and she stands, while in three she sits and he stands, but most convey his masculine authority and her wifely deference, a message especially visible in those most widely circulated, even though the range of poses suggests that

Mayall and his subjects anticipated the public would like to see their Queen in a variety of ideologically contradictory attitudes. When Albert stands and she sits (figure 20), he faces the camera with his arm cocked on his hip, while she looks down at the book in her lap. The pose suggests a middle-aged version of "God Save the Queen" (figure 9), in which he faces the world while her eyes are lowered modestly on a private occupation. Although the image conveys nothing like the emotional intensity of Day's engraved photo (figure 16), it conveys a similar ideology of marital precedence. In another pose of Albert standing and Victoria seated, he looks at a book while she looks up at it (figure 21). His reading while standing recalls Thorburn's painted version of Day's standing figure more than it resembles Victoria seated and reading from the book in her lap: for a man to read while standing suggests he is preoccupied with important business, while her looks convey dependence on his interests. The third pose of Albert standing and Victoria seated (figure 22), by contrast to the other two, resembles figure 20 but implies a much more equitable relationship: he looks down at the book in her lap, which she has turned to show him, even though it seems unlikely he could read it at such a distance.[82]

In the four images from this session of her standing and him seated,[83] the implied narratives again convey a marital relationship that is sometimes profoundly hierarchical, sometimes less so. He sits, a book in his hands, his legs crossed and stretched across the picture plane, taking up space in a way that even her voluminous but contained skirt does not. In figures 23 and 24 he looks up at her as if interrupted while reading, while she stands, eyes downcast, her arm on his shoulder, her figure partly obscured by his. In figure 23, Albert's attitude is markedly confident and Victoria's pose seems apologetic, almost servile. She stands, but her relative height in the picture plane does not convey power or precedence. Her head bowed, she appears to be looking at the floor, as if awaiting his command. In figure 24, however, a slight shift of the pose from that of figure 23 complicates the appearance of Victoria's servility. Victoria now looks at the book Albert holds, while Albert's gaze seems more questioning, as if he were studying her face for her reaction, less assertive than in figure 23. When the Picture Post Library published this photo, it added the caption, "The Prince verifies a reference," the editors projecting onto the picture what it meant to them. On the one hand, his verifying a reference would make him the authority to whom Victoria defers, and that is what her stance conveys here as well as in her seated poses; on the other hand, if he is verifying a reference, his eyes deferential toward her act of reading, we are being reminded for whom he works: Victoria Regina. The caption brings out the ambiguity of these images by seeming at

FIGURES 20 (*above left*), 21 (*above right*), and 22 (*below*)
Queen Victoria and Prince Albert, 15 May 1860. Photograph by J. J. E. Mayall.

once to disguise her servility as her mastery and to disguise her real mastery as feigned servility.[84] While this group of photos suggests that the same marital hierarchy can be read in opposite poses, it also suggests that very nearly the same pose can be made to convey quite different phases of relationship, ranging from her servility to his servility to their mutual disregard.

In a portrait session six months before the Prince's death (1 March 1861), Mayall uses a step and other props—Albert's top hat and Victoria's parasol—to play explicitly with both accentuating and neutralizing the signifying difference in their heights. Once again there is a group (five) taken of Victoria alone, and there are also five of Albert alone, as well as seven or eight images of the couple together.[85] Figure 25, taken with Victoria and Albert standing together on the studio floor, represents their very different heights (he appears about a foot taller) undisguised by hats or other gear. And yet it could be said that Victoria's bulk compensates for her short stature: her ample and conspicuous dress obscures his legs, and her distinctive profile denaturalizes her, making her appear institutional, even hieratic, her silhouette like that on a stamp. Linkman reports that photographers found profiles made the subject appear "'isolated, dignified and contemplative but "a trifle stern"'" and reserved them for "older people or prominent personalities."[86] That we see Albert's flashy striped vest in this image makes him seem Victoria's fashion accessory.[87] In figure 26, by contrast, Victoria stands on a step so that her face is almost on a level with Albert's, although she looks slightly downward.[88] His top hat and her hatlessness and lowered parasol, however, rehierarchize the carefully dehierarchized pose. The ostentatious failure to conceal the machinery by which she is made to appear his height suggests that the very idea is a sort of somber joke. His top hat and the concealment of his flashy vest make him look more businesslike than in figure 25, while her parasol muddles her profile and makes her look relatively frivolous. Having her face on a level with his, then, is no guarantee that the image will convey marital equality, much less sovereignty: to the contrary; just as having her face lower than his in figure 25 does not preclude her appearing the stronger figure.

The third set of closely related poses from this session with Mayall (nos. 2931 and 3336) shows Victoria standing as if alone, while Albert stands with his arm behind her but seeming not to touch her, looking away from her out of the picture plane; they seem to be in no relation whatsoever. Finally, in the fourth pose from this group, figure 27, the image that seems to have been most widely circulated ("Mayall Fecit" is scratched into the negative at the lower right), Albert and Victoria again stand so that their heads are level; again Albert wears his towering hat; but in addition, while she looks steadily

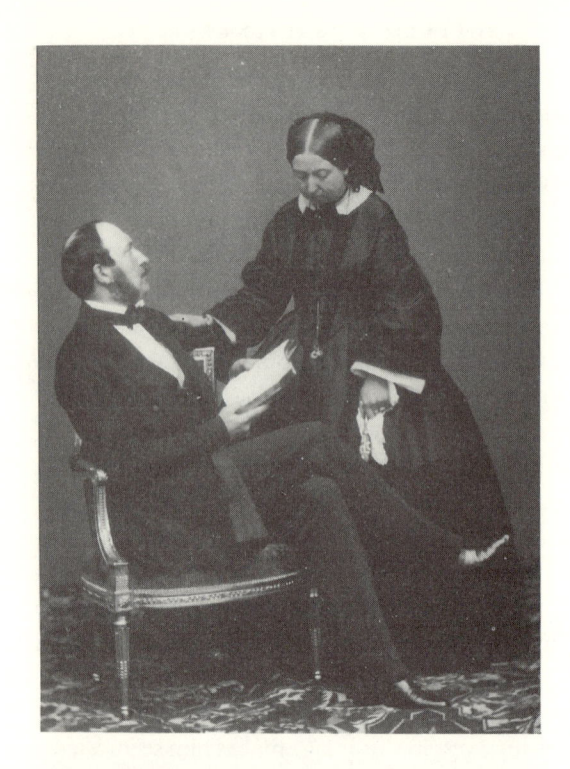

FIGURES 23 (*left*) and 24 (*below*) Queen Victoria and Prince Albert, 15 May 1860. Photograph by J. J. E. Mayall.

at him, he looks away, partly out toward the viewer, his stance jaunty, left knee conspicuously crooked, walking stick at an angle. He seems to be caught in the instant of turning away from her, to set off on a stroll into the public world. Her hat in her hands suggests humility, and with her body pitched slightly forward so that her skirts are all behind her, she lacks the solidity of stance she maintains in figure 25 and even in figure 26.

Seated below, standing over, or standing on a level with him, Victoria in the majority of these images conveys less sovereignty than proper wifely humility, subordination, even abjection toward her husband. To recall the words of *The Mill on the Floss*, to stand or be seated "a little above or a little below . . . your goddess [amounts to] the same thing." The poses in figures 26 and 27 recall the 1842 Landseer costume portrait (figure 8), because he both stands beneath her and towers above her, and to a certain degree these images share that painting's ambiguities as to who is the sovereign. Yet the medium of photography and the costuming (not as sovereigns but as citizens) eliminates the allusion to chivalry that had enabled Landseer's image to represent Albert's deference both as the pretend deference of the knight to his lady on the pedestal and as the genuine deference of a subject. In the photographs, in the dull light of Mayall's studio and without the magical shine and trappings of chivalry, he looks scarcely deferential at all; interested, rather, in the wider world at which he seems to look out, away from his beseeching Queen, his erect and glossy top hat trumping her lowered hat and parasol as the new crown of a middle-class monarchy. Chivalric poses no longer yield chivalric meanings.

And yet in the context of their dissemination these photographs could be read as we read the popular images (figures 7, 9, 10, and 11) and the Landseer painting of Albert as a hunter (figure 12), through the paradox that typifies Victoria's reign, as a display of her female subordination that reinforces her ideological rule—a successful deployment of the ironic distance between her appearance and her status as Queen. In the pictorial medium of the middle classes, Victoria and Albert assume increasingly the guise of the middle classes, their clothes and most important their rigid gender hierarchy; and that declassing and gender subordination paradoxically confirm Victoria's highest ambitions, to lead by her example a middle-class nation. Posing as ordinary was Victoria's mode of sovereignty: to put her ordinariness on royal display for popular admiration. Holding her sovereignty by the popularity she accrues by appearing as an ordinary wife, she rules in the only way she can, by giving over her authority. If what she wanted to and did accomplish was the predominance of a worldview in which the middle-class wife's subordination underwrites middle-class supremacy, she is both agent and prod-

FIGURES 25 (*above left*), 26 (*above right*), and 27 (*below*)
Queen Victoria and Prince Albert, 1 March 1861. Photograph by J. J. E. Mayall.

uct of her own ideological designs. Either way, her portraits remain as a testimony to her and her popular image-makers' skill in manipulating conventions for representing gender difference and class status, and as a record, too, of the ideological complexity of the problem, for art and for the Queen herself, of representing a Queen regnant in an era desiring to see the end of female power.

Printing off thousands of copies of the Queen on *cartes de visite* for ordinary subjects to purchase and collect, Mayall and others presented her as at once unique (her face so particularized) and infinitely duplicable. After 1861, the Queen's reproducibility takes on particular meanings in light of her withdrawal in mourning, as seen in the next chapter. Even at the time of her accession, however, popular literature had expressed fears about her duplicability, the fear that every female subject would become a queen, and an unruly one. Using the metaphor of the playing card to express (in comically exaggerated form) this fear of infinitely extensive female unrule, the 1839 broadside "Petticoats for Ever" (figure 3) anticipates the rage for photographic *cartes* and their reproduction of the Queen's uniquely powerful yet common visage:

> So all you young girls who are out of your teens,
> When it comes to your turn you'll all be made Queens;
> If you marry a spoony then give him hard thumps,
> And we'll let him know he's turn'd up Queen of Trumps.
> (*English Popular Literature*, 340)

A figure at once of total power and of impossibility (there is no such thing, yet every card player wants one), the Queen of Trumps is Victoria multiplied by popular image-making. In this chapter we have explored the construction of the Queen as everywoman; the next chapter will explore what it might mean for every woman to be a queen.

2

QUEEN VICTORIA'S WIDOWHOOD AND THE MAKING OF VICTORIAN QUEENS

The Invisible Queen

During the years of Queen Victoria's marriage, from February 1840 to December 1861, the popularity of the monarchy depended in large part on the apparent authenticity of Victoria's performance as an ordinary middle-class wife, even though the maintenance of her monarchic power depended equally on the ironic distance between these two roles. She represented the monarchy in her own person: she and Albert and their growing brood of children appeared frequently in public, and these appearances tended to rouse patriotic sentiment and loyal affection for the monarchy. Looking back from the vantage point of 1864, the London *Times* writes:

> In the early days of Her Majesty's reign nothing was more gratifying to the public than to learn that there was a Royal Speech at the opening or close of the Session.... Equally beneficial was it to the interests of the Constitution that with the chief enterprises of the day the name of the Queen should be connected. Whether it was an industrial exhibition, or a naval review, or a new public building, it pleased the people and strengthened the Throne when Her Majesty was on the spot as the chief patroness of the work. (*Times*, 15 December 1864)

Her person and her family life were on stage for public display. When she became a widow, however, as Lytton Strachey writes,

> a veil descends. Only occasionally, at fitful and disconnected intervals, does it lift for a moment or two; a few main outlines, a few remarkable details may be discerned; the rest is all conjecture and ambiguity.[1]

Her life became virtually invisible to the public eye and thus virtually unknowable to the irritated biographer. Although the publication of her letters makes it possible now to say more than Strachey could about her life as a widow, Strachey's comment points to the representational problem posed by Victoria's widowhood, during much of which she almost entirely disappeared from public view. What form could monarchic power take if the Queen was not visible?

Although by the nineteenth century state power may have come to approximate Bentham's panopticon, in which power is invisible but all-seeing, monarchic power—much reduced though it may have been relative to the powers of other parts of government—was understood to remain theatrical, as it had been in Elizabethan times. Walter Bagehot's *The English Constitution* lists the monarch among "the theatrical elements" of government and offers royal weddings as an example of the kind of spectacle that appeals to the public eye.[2] The monarch's power would seem to depend upon a unique representational responsibility: the responsibility to be present in the body, if for no other reason than to ground referentially the proliferation of monarchic images on stamps and coins, the value of which the monarch serves to guarantee. Granted that a monarch's body is never coextensive with its representations, the years following December 1861 nonetheless constitute an anomalous period in Britain's royal history, a historical moment in which the monarch's chief representational form is her invisibility. If the kind of power Victoria held before Albert's death was largely that of public relations—the projection of a favorable image of the monarchy through her public appearances and the power of influencing her admiring middle-class subjects to act more like the middle-class image she projected—what happened to her power when she disappeared behind Strachey's veil of widowhood?

One immediate answer, of course, is that she came near the verge of losing it. Although for two years her seclusion was appropriate to Victorian mourning customs,[3] her extended mourning beyond that time put the paradox of her reign to the test. Expected as a wife to mourn deeply, she was also expected, as Queen, to violate mourning practices and appear on display as usual. "The Press was almost unanimous in denouncing her seclusion," reports Giles St. Aubyn (*Queen Victoria*, 344). After three years, her "insistence on a national preoccupation with memorials . . . awakened revulsion in the most understanding of her subjects" (Weintraub, *Victoria*, 324). She was expected either to abdicate (Weintraub, 321; Thompson, *Queen Victoria*, 58, 105; St. Aubyn, *Queen Victoria*, 344) or to resume her public work of opening Parliament, holding balls, levees, and drawing rooms for the elite, and making public appearances. By 1864 cartoons as well as editorials were appearing about her extended mourning, and by 1871, even though her seclusion had lessened somewhat after 1866, there was a small but serious republican movement afoot. Victoria's power did not disappear just because she did, but her invisibility provoked a disconcerting shift in the representational forms associated with her. Whereas before Albert's death she represented the middle-class monarchy in her publicly available person, afterward a growing gap developed between her and the representations of her compelled into existence by her absence. Among these new forms of representation are what I call "performances of absence" or dramatizations of her concealment and the "Queens' Books" (to be discussed in Chapter 3); this chapter will consider a variety of ways in which the Queen's absence came to be represented by others, both as a diminishment and—surprisingly—as an augmentation of her power, through the making of multiple alternative queens.

Victoria was aware that she was a show or spectacle for her people, and her letters and journals during her widowhood attest to her resistance to the pressure to perform. She asserts the importance of her work behind the scenes as monarch and claims ill health and shattered nerves. The royal wedding Bagehot alludes to was that of the Prince of Wales in March 1863, which Victoria describes in her journal at length as "a scene in a play" (*Letters and Journals*, 173). That the public found this spectacle "interesting" is shown by the jump in the *Times*'s circulation from 60-65,000 to 108,000 the next day.[4] Among the first occasions demanding her public appearance after Albert's death, the wedding was nonetheless on a much smaller scale than might have been expected, held in St. George's Chapel at Windsor rather than in London. Although the performers in this case are her son and daughter-in-law, a contemporary painting of the event by Frith (figure 28) suggests that Victoria was as much spectacle as spectator—or at any rate that in a publicly disseminated image of the event it was thought desirable to convey this message. In the painting's upper right-hand corner, Victoria sits in Catherine of Aragon's closet, a gallery overlooking the stage where the ceremony is in progress, "rather as she might watch an opera from her box at Covent Garden" (St. Aubyn, *Queen Victoria*, 399). The painting's lighting highlights her figure—her brightly illuminated face and white widow's veil emerging dramatically from the shadows of her black dress and the darkened balcony—as much as it does the more evenly lit whites and reds of the couple and their train, despite her dislocation from the center of the picture. Her black garb, however, makes a pointed contrast to the whites or light colors she wears in images of ceremonial occasions before Albert's death, images in which her conspicuous bright dress is generally the central focal point, for example, a colored engraving by Vautier showing Victoria visiting the French king in 1855 in which Victoria's fluffy white skirts are visually echoed by the massive white chandeliers that fill the hall, or the many images of the Queen opening

FIGURE 28   William Powell Frith, *Marriage of The Prince of Wales and Princess Alexandra of Denmark, 10 March 1863*. Oil painting.

the Great Exhibition (see, for example, figure 2).[5] In Frith's painting, most spectators' eyes are directed toward the ceremony, but several are pointedly lifted to gaze at Victoria as she gazes downward; Disraeli is known to have "raised his quizzing glass" to her face, only to be stared down by her (Longford, *Queen Victoria*, 316–17).

The arrangement of the figures closely resembles one model of royal theater design: Stephen Orgel shows that the royal box after 1500 was placed directly opposite the stage or—during the regency—that the two royal boxes were those adjacent to the stage.[6] Victoria's placement in a "box" next to the stage where her son performs his vows suggests at once that she is not quite the monarch (regent or incompetent king) and, to the contrary, that she is the regal cynosure—the spectacle that gains authority from the spectacle on stage. Another helpful comparison is presented by the staging of the 1842 costume ball, at which Victoria and Albert sat and watched the dancing from a raised dais but also descended to the floor to dance themselves (Ashton, *Gossip*, 188). At the Prince's wedding, Victoria again performs, but solely as spectator. The painting conveys both Victoria's resistance to and her acceptance of performing her spectacular part in the theater of royalty. Although it was rumored that she would abdicate following Bertie's marriage (see, for example, Weintraub, *Victoria,* 321), the painting reveals something more complex than her absence or a simple desire for it: rather, she actively performs her absence. That reporters were treated well on the occasion, a dozen of them even being allowed in the organ loft of the chapel, underscores the Queen's active pursuit of publicity—even if it is publicity about her withdrawal (*Victorian News,* 145).

Throughout the years of her seclusion, the *Times,* the *Daily Telegraph,* and the other London papers printed a daily notice (under the title "The Court" or "Court Circular") of the doings of the Queen and any of her children who were in residence with her. Very often—with a peculiarly ironic effect on days when momentous news is being reported elsewhere in the paper—the notice reads merely "The Queen rode out on her pony" or "The Queen walked in the grounds yesterday," with mention of a daughter or two accompanying her. The notices are generally posted from Osborne, Balmoral, or Windsor. The brevity and monotony of these notices call attention to how seldom the Queen ventureed away from her homes (and they do not report the hours she spent reviewing and signing government papers); but it is worth noting that the Queen had an official "court newsman" (documented in 1874 but probably throughout this period; *Victorian News,* 146) who sent out these reports. Again, she promulgates the evidence of her absence rather than simply not appearing.

As her mourning extended on and on, public criticism of her inaccessibility grew. On 13 October 1863 she traveled from her retreat in Balmoral to Aberdeen to unveil a memorial statue of Albert, but—in another active dramatization of her felt absence—citizens were asked to "refrain from cheering, employing bands of music, and from decorating their houses and the streets with the usual banners, triumphal arches, and flowers of such occasions."[7] As the newspaper the *Scotsman* put it the next day, the procession moved through "the densely packed streets amid the deepest silence of the asssemblage, everybody seeming to be animated by a desire to abstain from any popular demonstration that might be distasteful to Her Majesty."[8] The ceremony, carried out in pouring rain and consisting of the silent exchange of written "addresses" by the Queen and the provost, was "more 'funereal than festive.'"[9] In March 1864 someone put up a poster outside Buckingham Palace that read, "These commanding premises to be let or sold, in consequence of the late occupant's declining business" (see Longford, *Queen Victoria,* 321). A similar April Fool's joke in the London *Times* led her to authorize the publication (in her name and voice) of a letter insisting that she save her strength for other duties than "mere representation"—that is, appearances in person.

An erroneous idea seems generally to prevail, and has latterly found frequent expression in the newspapers, that the Queen is about to resume the place in society which she occupied before her great affliction; that is, that she is about again to hold levees and drawing-rooms in person, and to appear as before at Court balls, concerts, &c. This idea cannot be too explicitly contradicted.

The Queen heartily appreciates the desire of her subjects to see her, and whatever she *can* do to gratify them in this loyal and affectionate wish she *will* do. . . .

But there are other and higher duties than those of mere representation which are now thrown upon the Queen, alone and unassisted—duties which she cannot neglect without injury to the public service. (*Times,* 6 April 1864)

The letter goes on to claim that her "health and strength . . . have been seriously impaired" by both grief and overwork, and that "mere State ceremonies . . . can be equally well performed by other members of her family." She will "do what she can" to meet her subjects' wishes and "to afford that support and countenance to society, and to give that encouragement to trade, which is desired of her."[10]

"Mere representation" here means misrepresentation: she never uses the term except to distance herself from it and to distinguish it from what she considers the real but invisible work of monarchy, to which she repeatedly refers as "duties," such as reviewing and signing papers and consulting with her ministers. Her use of the term creates its own retrospective history, as if long ago, in her youth as in Elizabethan times, representation exactly coincided with the monarch being represented. Now, "representation" means the ostentatious performance of ceremonies in which the leading role could well be performed by another royal family member, such as the "scene" of the wedding performed by the Prince and Princess of Wales or indeed the balls, drawing rooms, and levees that they (and occasionally Vicky, the Crown Princess) held on her behalf during the 1860s. "Mere representation," the letter stresses, threatens her health: because she is already "overwhelm[ed] with work and anxiety," to require that she also perform publicly "is to ask her to run the risk of entirely disabling herself" for those unspectacular duties on which the nation's safety depends.

After Albert's death, she had a particular dislike for her once-familiar practice of driving in an open carriage so that her subjects could see her. Not until 21 June 1864 did she take such a drive (not a long distance: through the park from Windsor Castle to the Windsor train station). This appearance, "though very painful, pleased people more than anything," she concedes (*Letters and Journals*, 185). (There was also a drive from Buckingham Palace to Paddington Station, and an appearance at a Horticultural Show, during 1863–64.) More sustained "representations," however, still proved too much for her. Although one of the chief performances of her year was opening Parliament by reading the Queen's Speech, the policy statement written by her ministers, she declined this duty in the years 1862 through 1865. Complaining to Lord Russell about the 1865 opening, her term for what she dislikes is again "representation:" "[N]o child can feel more shrinking and nervous than the poor Queen does, when she has to do anything, which approaches to representation" (*Letters and Journals*, 186, 8 December 1864). Called upon to perform such a "representation," the Queen does not feel like herself when seen in public; the monarch divides from and succumbs to the shrinking child. The mourning and working private self is distinguished from the "representations" that so jangle on the nerves of that private self.

Although she agreed to open Parliament in 1866, to support Lord Russell's attempt to pass a Reform Bill, her bitter complaints reflect the same understanding that her "use," to use Bagehot's term, is as a performer. She writes again to Russell:

> That the public should wish to see her she fully understands, and has no wish to prevent . . . but why this wish should be of so unreasonable and unfeeling a nature, as to long to witness the spectacle of a poor, broken-hearted widow, nervous and shrinking, dragged in deep mourning, alone in State as a Show, where she used to go supported by her husband, to be gazed at, without delicacy of feeling, is a thing she cannot understand, and she never could wish her bitterest foe to be exposed to! (*Letters and Journals*, 193, 22 January 1866)

This prospect she compares to an execution, which remained a public spectacle until 1868. Her journal for the day records her costume and the enthusiasm of the crowds along the way. It is the performance inside Commons that distresses her: "all eyes fixed on me, and there I sat alone" (*Letters and Journals*, 193, 6 February 1866). Distressing though this experience may have been, she did not even read the Queen's Speech: the Lord Chancellor read it for her, while she sat crownless, dressed in black, staring rigidly ahead, her royal robes merely draped over the throne behind her (Longford, *Queen Victoria*, 348). Once again, she does not fail to perform; rather, she dramatically performs, in her own person, her reluctance to perform. A vivid contrast is provided by the newspaper description of Victoria's first appearance in Parliament in 1837 (discussed in Chapter 1), a description that emphasizes her

WHERE IS BRITANNIA ?

FIGURE 29 "Where Is Britannia?" Engraving in *Tomahawk*, June 1867.

presence through the expressiveness and vividness of her body and costume: "Her emotion was plainly discernible in the rapid heaving of her bosom, and the brilliancy of her diamond stomacher, which sparkled out . . . " (*Gossip*, 4). A cartoon published in June 1867 in the satiric periodical *Tomahawk* (figure 29) illustrates a scene of Victoria's visible absence very like the one staged in Parliament in 1866: titled "Where is Britannia?" it pictures an empty throne draped in royal robes on which is precariously perched the crown.[11]

One of the cartoons protesting her extended mourning, in *Punch* in September 1864 (figure 30), portrays Victoria as "Queen Hermione," standing in her court robes and crown (which she had not worn since she became a widow) on a raised curtained stage, the curtain being drawn back by Paulina garbed as Britannia, who is saying, "'Tis time! Descend; be stone no more." Iconographically affiliated both to Frith's painting of the 1863 royal wedding—the Queen is sequestered in an enclosed yet theatricalized space—and to the later *Tomahawk* cartoon (both depict royal robes to complain of their disuse), the *Punch* cartoon offers a wishful solution to the problem they identify. Hermione here is a figure who conflates human being with representation; she is both herself and a statue of herself. Whereas the Frith painting

FIGURE 30 "Queen Hermione." Engraving in *Punch*, September 1865. The caption reads: Paulina (Britannia) unveils the statue.— "'Tis time! Descend; be stone no more!" (*Winter's Tale*, act V, scene 3).

(figure 28) and the *Tomahawk* cartoon (figure 29) dramatize Victoria's dramatic absence from her usual forms of monarchic self-representation, the Hermione cartoon expresses a wish that Victoria would return, not merely to life but to performing monarchy in her own person. Although ostensibly the cartoon urges her to stop being a statue (and perhaps to stop devoting herself to making stone monuments to Albert) and be instead a person, the moment chosen for visual representation is the moment when Hermione is in between states, at once monument and living being. Refusing to be her own statue and indeed castigating such calls as unreasonable demands for "mere representation" that could injure and disable her, Victoria provokes through her absence a new range of representational forms, produced both by herself and by others.

This chapter will explore how some literary texts from the first ten years of her widowhood produced multiple queens in the vacuum created by Victoria's absence. Ruskin's "Of Queens' Gardens," given as a lecture in 1864 and published in 1865, and Oliphant's 1866 novel *Miss Marjoribanks* place many and explicitly reproducible queens in the domestic drawing rooms of England. In doing so they both affirm and call into question the authority of the Queen to which their constructions refer. In this regard, the ambiguity of Victoria's power during her widowhood is not far different from the ambiguity discussed in Chapter 1: in the 1860s as in the 1840s and 1850s, domesticity both enlarges and compromises queenly power. What is new is that, in the absence of a central focus for this ideology, it is located diffusely—in a multiplication of queens—throughout the imagined homes of Britain. The final section of this chapter will explore a related representational issue: the way Ruskin's "Of Queens' Gardens" and Lewis Carroll's two *Alice* books, published in 1865 and 1871, reflect on the difficult process of making queens. Chapter 3 will take up another representational strategy employed both by the Queen and by those writing about her: the representation of absence and concealment as presence and power.

Domestic Queens: *Miss Marjoribanks*

Summarizing the laws concerning women in Britain in 1854, Barbara Leigh-Smith Bodichon writes of women's all-too-familiar exclusions: from voting in parliamentary elections, from possessing property if they are married, from engaging in most professions. She writes: "The church and nearly all offices under government are closed to women. The Post-office affords some little employment to them; but there is no important office which they can hold, with the single exception of that of Sovereign."[12] The highly skilled and rewarding job held by the Queen is the anomaly that makes the rule for Bodichon, and her attention is on the Queen's uniqueness. Ten years later, John Ruskin finds queens everywhere. The women of England, according to Ruskin, by which he means the middle-class women, "are called to a true queenly power," and "the territories over which [women] reign [are] 'Queens' Gardens'" ("Of Queens' Gardens," 49.) "Oh—you queens—you queens!" he addresses them in his peroration (79);

> you must be, in many a heart, enthroned: there is no putting by that crown; queens you must always be; queens to your lovers; queens to your husbands and your sons; queens of higher mystery to the world beyond, which bows itself, and will forever bow, before the myrtle crown, and the stainless sceptre, of womanhood. But alas! you are too often idle and careless queens, grasping at majesty in the least things, while you abdicate it in the greatest. ("Of Queens' Gardens," 74)

Ruskin's insistent repetition of the word "queen" in this passage and throughout the essay formally reinforces the proliferation of queens that is his theme and indeed his exhortation, for all middle-class women are to be queens not only in their own households but also in the public thoroughfares of Britain. To survey the British literary scene of this time is to find queens multiplying everywhere. All of George Eliot's heroines are described as queens or queenly. Margaret Oliphant, the so-called Queen of Popular Fiction—herself the Queen's double in living as a widow in Windsor and later writing the Queen's life—makes one of her heroines the "Queen of Carlingford." The Victorian gothic revival brought with it numerous narratives and portraits of queens, fairy queens, princesses, and other female royalty. Multiple queens abound in fantasy literature of the period, such as the *Alice* books, Jean Ingelow's *Mopsa the Fairy*, and Christina Rossetti's *Speaking Likenesses*.[13]

There has recently been considerable critical debate about the political meaning of this proliferation of figurative queens. Building on the assumption that when Ruskin uses the word "queen" he indicates Victoria,[14] such critics as Elizabeth Langland and Sharon Aronofsky Weltman have argued that the reference to Victoria injects into Ruskin's use of the term "queen" to describe middle-class women an unexpected element of power, or as Langland puts it, "a new feminine ideal that endorsed active public management behind a facade of private retirement."[15] Following up on Dorothy Thompson's speculation that "there must have been many ways in which the presence of a woman at the head of the state worked at a deeper level to weaken prejudice" against women taking part in public life (Thompson, *Queen Vic-*

toria, 145; quoted in *Nobody's Angels,* 65), these critics emphasize Ruskin's use of the term "queen" to urge women to get out of the house. For Sharon Weltman, "Ruskin aggrandizes housewives by urging them . . . to don symbolically the mantle of public queenship" ("'Be no more housewives,'" 111). Langland sees Victoria as an enabling figure for middle-class women. In Langland's view, Ruskin acknowledges that "women were already effective social arbiters" (*Nobody's Angels,* 78), and she argues that with reference to Queen Victoria Ruskin helped to produce the "new woman" by naturalizing associations between women and power (79). This line of argument would run counter to an earlier feminist argument, that mounted by Kate Millett (who finds support in J. S. Mill's proleptic critique of Ruskin for granting women power at the cost of their liberty), the argument that emphasizes Ruskin's eerie limitation of women to the role of a helpmate ("Of Queens' Gardens," 50) who may guide but does not determine (59) and whose education should extend "only so far as may enable her to sympathise in her husband's pleasures" (65).[16] Given that it is feminist writer Bodichon who focuses on the Queen's uniqueness to highlight ordinary womens' lack of power and entitlement, Ruskin's figurative and multiplicative use of "queen" might well seem linked to a conservative social agenda. Following Mary Poovey and Nancy Armstrong, we might see that Ruskin naturalizes and thus enforces middle-class behavioral rules for women by relabeling them as queenly and so appearing to take them out of the register of class altogether.[17] In this vein, Cathy Shuman has argued that Ruskin uses an "obsolete class categor[y] to describe women's position" ("'Different for Girls,'" 50) in order to "locate power exclusively in gender relations, allowing them to mystify its presence in economic relations" (54). Coventry Patmore's *Angel in the House* makes copious use of the figure of queen, and Tennyson puts his most explicitly conservative statements about women and gender in his dramatic poem *The Princess.*[18]

But the debate over whether Ruskin would constrict or enlarge the powers of middle-class women by calling them "queens" presupposes that "queen"—whether or not it refers to Victoria—constitutes a fixed reference point outside the text. (Were I to participate in this debate, my account in Chapter 1 of the compromised nature of Victoria's power would lead me to argue that Victoria may just as likely model loss of power in Ruskin's text as model a new form of it.)[19] Instead, we should be asking how Ruskin is making Queen Victoria by using her to describe middle-class women; his presentation of her is determined by, as well as helping to determine, the character of his proliferating middle-class queens. For December 1864 was a time when the British public imagination was engaged with particular acuteness in the project of creating new Victorias to replace the one missing for three years. If, up to 1861, Victoria and her middle-class subjects had been engaged in an ongoing project of mutual construction, by which Victoria modeled her values on those of the middle class, which in turn used her to authorize their own practices, her widowhood shifted this balance and left it up to her subjects to do more of the making—often to their resentment as well as to hers.

Ruskin gave his lecture on 14 December 1864, the third anniversary of Albert's death, to a middle-class audience in Manchester, as part of an effort to raise money for schools for the poor. On December 15 the London *Times* published an attack on the Queen's "indulgence of an unavailing grief" and its ill effects on the nation. "It is impossible," states this article, "for a recluse to occupy the British Throne without a gradual weakening of that authority which the Sovereign has been accustomed to exert." Although "law or usage . . . dispenses with the Royal presence, and allows every public act to be performed by deputy" (as indeed her letter to the *Times* earlier that year claimed was necessary), the article demands that the Queen's "public functions . . . should once more be performed in person." The article grounds this demand on the claims of loyalty: her continued neglect of these functions would "confirm in their views those who suggest that the Throne is only an antiquarian relic and Royalty itself a ceremony." Fortunately for the monarch, "the great mass of the nation" believe her political judgment matters, but her ability to "stand as the representative of the nation" depends on "a proper intercourse with the world" that her seclusion denies her.

Over the next few days, this article provoked a flurry of responses defending the Queen, all carefully preserved in scrapbooks in the Royal Archives. These responses reveal that the *Times* was understood to be complaining largely about Victoria's failure to sponsor social events for London's elite: the *Times* had said that "the society of England requires its chief hostess and natural leader" and had managed to connect her political abilities to the frequency of her appearances at balls ("proper intercourse with the world"). The next day's *Morning Post,* for example, asserted that the loyalty of the people of England transcends her participation in ceremonials; "In seclusion or in society, Queen Victoria will reign in the hearts of her subjects." The *Morning Star* accused the *Times* of disloyalty when it insisted "that Royalty becomes useless when it does not show itself at balls and figure in state ceremonials"; readers of this paper can be presumed to believe in the superior importance of her behind-the-scenes duties and in the tenet, "These duties the Queen never has put aside." The "society" in whose name the *Times* critizes the Queen "means, of course, some few thousand people living in a western corner of the British metropolis. It has nothing to do with the millions who make up the British population. These may be satisfied with their Queen" because she does her duty and, moreover, because "she shows that she has the deep-feeling heart of a woman." Other papers echoed these themes, attacking the *Times,* asserting the superior loyalty of the Queen's non-Society subjects, and expressing the certainty that the Queen is doing her duty and that she deserves every sympathy. The Queen herself was furious at the "vulgar and heartless article in the Times," and, when Palmerston hinted that the *Times* might be right, she objected to being told she was neglecting her duties by not "taking part in the frivolous amusements of the world.... but the Queen knows this is not the feeling of the nation—for she has never received more marks of devotion, loyalty and true sympathy from her subjects than within these three last sad years—and it is only amongst a certain set that her conduct and her health are misunderstood and disregarded."[20] Her journal reveals that in December she was eagerly watching the progress of her two books which, as will be seen in Chapter 3, she hoped would serve as substitutes for public appearances in person.

Criticism of her seclusion thus becomes the occasion for augmented expressions of loyalty to her; complaints of her absence highlight the importance of her invisible work and bring her figure freshly into the public imagination. The image of the sorrowing yet hardworking Queen reproduced in each of these newspaper editorials offers an imaginary solution to the real problem of the Queen's absence. But it is a solution that, like many moments earlier in her reign, gives up even while it gains. The Queen is defended only by being rendered as an ordinary woman, subject to ordinary feelings, linked with what she would call "the lower classes" (everyone beneath aristocratic "Society"), exempted from colorful ceremonials and relegated to hard work in the privacy of her home. Ruskin's speech, delivered on the eve of this controversy to an audience emphatically not part of carping "Society," does not directly address this controversy, but it does arguably offer a related imaginary solution to the problem of the missing Victoria: it multiplies her figure and locates her in ordinary homes across the land. And yet, just as the editorials defending the Queen must first repeat and perpetuate the slanders against her, and then must defend her by rendering her as "a woman," Ruskin's multiplication of queenly women—like the multiple queens in the fantasy literature mentioned above—supplies an equivocal reconstruction of vanished monarchy.

To use "queen" as a figure at all, especially as a figure for a class of women, suggests equivocation not only about Victoria's powers but also about her ontological status. The difference between Bodichon's 1854 emphasis on the Queen's uniqueness and Ruskin's formulation ten years later may be attributable not only to the difference between feminist and conservative social agendas but also to the difference her widowhood made. When Ruskin and others imagine a proliferation of queens in every home in the nation, whether or not it means a bold claim for the housewives of England, it may also or alternatively mean the dispersal of Victoria's royal presence, a forgetting of the monarch's uniqueness to which Barbara Bodichon called attention in 1854 and a leveling of her with any mourner. Ruskin vehemently opposed mechanical reproduction in the arts because it removes the personal presence of the artist or artisan in the work of art; but in the context of Victoria's widowhood, his interpellation of multiple Victorian queens seems both to respond to and to confirm Victoria's absence. And for Victoria's powerful presence to be vitiated through her multiplication would then in turn disable the claim that she is an enabling, empowering model when she is reproduced in the fictions about women that abound in this period.

Although Ruskin uses the term "queen" throughout the essay—"true queenly power" appears on its second page—he does not begin hyperbolically to emphasize it in the manner of the longer quotation with which this section began until the essay is winding to its close. In the essay's third and last section Ruskin asks, "What is her queenly office with respect to the state?" ("Of Queens' Gardens," 71), and it is here that he gets women out of the house into the dark, dangerous streets of Manchester with their feeble florets in need of succor, here that Ruskin apparently (for Weltman and Langland) draws on Victoria's monarchy to support the empowering of women in the public sphere. Here women have

> power to heal, to redeem, to guide, and to guard. Power of the sceptre and shield; the power of the royal hand that heals in touching,—that binds the fiend, and looses the captive; the throne that is founded on the rock of Justice, and descended from only by steps of mercy. Will you not covet such power as this, and seek such throne as this, and be no more housewives, but queens? ("Of Queens' Gardens," 72–73)

If we take "queen" to be grounded in an extratextual reality and to mean something unequivocally powerful, then Ruskin's claims here are certainly strong and novel. But if we understand "queen" in section 3 as a term already defined by the earlier sections of the essay, which describe women's ideally sweet and sympathetic character and outline the education needed to produce that character, then we are compelled to pay close attention to the way those sections preemptively qualify the empowering effect the term appears to have later. In the vacuum of Victoria's absence, Ruskin is free to invent his paradigm queen and her duplicates in any way he chooses.

In Ruskin's catalogue of women from literature—the "testimony" he adduces from Shakepeare, Dante, Homer, and the Greek playwrights to prove that women are better than men—notably absent are the one queen after whom Shakespeare named a play, Cleopatra (no paragon of domestic virtue); his equivocal queen of the fairies, Titania; and the former queen of the Amazons, Hyppolyta. Even more conspicuously absent are those royal figures from Greek drama, Medea and Clytemnestra. In place of these queens, we hear about "the bowing down of Iphegenia, lamb-like and silent" and a catalogue of Shakespearean female perfection, culminating in "perhaps loveliest, Virgilia" (51), best known in Coriolanus's words as "my gracious silence." The conspicuous absence of queens represented as actively wielding power in the texts they inhabit suggests Ruskin's aversion to queenly political power and his need to evacuate from the term queen any referent in historical monarchy. Moreover, for Ruskin to make Iphegenia and Penelope (with her "housewifely calm") into paradigms not only of female virtue but of women's power is to give the lie explicitly to his subsequent claim that no "calamity" would "recur . . . were it but rightly mourned by her" (63), and, in section 3, that "[t]here is not a war in the world, no, nor an injustice, but you women are answerable for it; not in that you have provoked, but in that you have not hindered" (75).[21] For had Iphegenia and Penelope, by their mourning, succeeded in hindering the Trojan War, there would have been no heroic verse about it, or, indeed, about them. If he takes Penelope for a paradigm queen at the start of the essay, he cannot later mean queens to have the power his apologists claim.

Multiple queens in fantasy literature in the period—in Ruskin, but also in the *Alice* books and in Ingelow's and Rossetti's stories of girl-queens—tend to lack monarchic power in proportion to their numbers. The more queens Alice encounters in wonderland and in looking-glass land—or the more hyperbolically multiplied their supposed powers are—the less they have power to disturb Alice, as we shall see. In Ingelow's 1869 *Mopsa the Fairy,* the glamorous fairy queen whom the human hero Jack frees from slavery announces herself to be "the Fairy Queen" (*Mopsa,* 110) but turns out to be subject to her mother and to be only one of many possible queens of one of many alternative fairylands ("hundreds," speculates one character). When the child-fairy Mopsa discovers that she is growing into a rival queen, the first queen, notifying her that "[t]here cannot be two queens in one hive" (*Mopsa,* 153), introduces Mopsa to a deputation from another fairyland that needs a queen. Mopsa, disliking the proposed terms, runs away with Jack, but she ends the story installed as that fairyland's queen anyway, under highly ambiguous conditions. The place is better than expected, but she becomes a mournful somnambulist who must say goodbye to Jack and whose country is controlled not by herself but by three fairies (white, brown, and black), while she herself remains under the care and instruction of an older "dame" until she grows up.[22] Rossetti's *Speaking Likenesses,* moralizing tales for girls published in 1874, opens with the story of an eight-year-old girl whose selfishness as "queen of the feast" at her birthday obliges her to suffer through a nightmarish dream vision. In a room "lined throughout with looking-glasses," a nasty "birthday Queen, reflected over and over again in five hundred mirrors, look[s] frightful," presides over a series of violent, "horrid game[s]," and consumes gargantuan quantities of sweets.[23] Quarreling, shrieking "you're another" at each other, and hurling slabs of colored glass, the queen and her companions teach Flora her lesson: to "bear . . . disappointments" and "be obliging and good-humored" (*Speaking Likenesses,* 49). Queen, in these tales, means a domesticated, rule-bound, diminutive creature whose fantasmatic augmentation only means her ultimate reduction.

Similarly, when "queen" appears as a description of the heroine in Victorian realist novels, what might appear to be a grounding of the heroine in the real (if ambiguous) powers of Victoria can have instead the effect of constructing Victoria as an ordinary citizen. Novel heroines and Victoria—and particularly the mourning Victoria—are involved in a relation of mutual ungrounding, because as a culturally meaningful icon she is created in the uses of her to describe heroines just as much as they are created with reference to her. And in creating Victoria by making her so often and so ordinary, these novels, like Ruskin's essay and the children's tales that echo it, may serve to demystify and even to dismantle the monarchic aura upon which they would seem to rely. When a George Eliot heroine is described as a queen or "queenly" (and every one of her heroines is), the term generally refers to her outward beauty, with ironic emphasis on the discrepancy between appearance and either moral strength or effectiveness in the world.[24] To glance only at Eliot heroines from the 1860s: Maggie Tulliver's childhood aspiration to be a colonizing, domesticating "Queen of the gypsies" (*Mill on the Floss,* 121) is cruelly undercut by her own naivety; later, neither her "queenly head" (310) nor her "jet crown" (393), although these attributes suggest a more natural and therefore more appealing kind of regality, save her from the grief to which her passions and "the world's wife" subject her.[25] Esther's "high crown of shining brown plaits" make her the "fine lady" Felix initially dislikes; of her apparently innate fine tastes and her father's subjection the narrator comments, "There will be queens in spite of Salic or other laws of later date than Adam and Eve; and here, in this small dingy house of the minister in Malt-House Yard, there was a light-footed, sweet-voiced Queen Esther."[26] After she learns she is an heiress, Harold Transome—whose frame of reference is orientalist—calls her an empress (501). Tempted to believe in his chivalric assurances "that she had power over him to make him do what she liked, [she] quite forgot the many impressions which had convinced her that Harold had a padded yoke ready for the neck of every man, woman, and child that depended on him" (538), including his "majestic" (585) mother Mrs. Transome. To want to be a queen is what Esther must learn not to do. Similarly, Romola (who has a "queenly step," and who "'cast[s] around, as it were, an odour of queenliness'")[27] is painted as "the crowned Ariadne" (246, 397) and is married in a "circlet" of gold and pearls. But when she decides to leave Tito, she sobs to notice again that "in a tiny gold loop of the circlet a sugar-plum had lodged—a pink hailstone from the shower of sweets" (389), and the chapter is titled "Ariadne Discrowns Herself." Her crowning, thus ironized, is strictly domestic, whereas her wholly positive associations with the Madonna continue into her larger life tending the sick. To describe her as a queen is a way of indicating her constraints and limitations.

On the positive side, Esther (in the manner of a Ruskinian queen) exerts a benign influence by generating sympathy for Felix at his trial; but when she does so she is compared not to a queen but to one of the devout "making a confession of faith" (573). In a similar episode in the last book of *Middlemarch,* Dorothea (from whom the worshipful Ladislaw "longs for some queenly recognition," and to whom Celia says, "James always said you ought to be a queen")[28] ventures to extend her private credit as a highborn and exemplary woman into the public world; by convincing Middlemarch of her belief in Lydgate's goodness, she hopes to save him from the worst consequences of his entanglement with Bulstrode. But her "impetuous generosity . . . underwent a melancholy check" (790) as her male advisers talk her out of this plan for doing good in public; in the end, she privately persuades only four men and one woman. She can do Lydgate no lasting good, and the most important indirect consequence of her persuasiveness is a benefit to herself (the temporarily chastened Rosamond restores Dorothea's good opinion of Ladislaw). This mixed result expresses Eliot's sense of the limits of this queenly influence. Thus "queen" in Eliot comes to mean a heroine who attempts (not necessarily successfully) to extend the powers of the private sphere into unexpected areas and, more often, a heroine who finds her personal autonomy and authority curtailed. While Eliot's queens nonetheless manage to retain a sheen of timeless, mystified uniqueness, other novels multiply their decidedly Victorian queens in more pedestrian contexts, even while they worry, as do Eliot's novels, the consequences of subjecting their queens to "social reality." One such novel that recreates the missing Victoria in the person of a middle-class girl is Margaret Oliphant's 1866 *Miss Marjoribanks*.

Miss Marjoribanks locates a middle-class queen amongst the citizenry of a small country town and tests, with a delicate satiric touch, the Ruskinian proposition that queens are or should be everywhere.[29] Lucilla Marjoribanks, the "queen in Carlingford" and "sovereign of Grange Lane" (102, 268), makes the members of Carlingford "society" into her admiring "subjects" under the guise of being "a comfort to papa," her widowed but not particularly grief-stricken father, "who became aware . . . that he had abdicated, without knowing it, and that the reins of state had been smilingly withdrawn from his unconscious hands" (*Miss Marjoribanks*, 50). The cook becomes her prime minister. Although Oliphant proposes many models for Lucilla's power in addition to that of queen—Lucilla is also, though less consistently, a genius, a student of political economy, a dictator, an MP or prime minister, a "general," a "soldier of fortune," and a revolutionary—when Oliphant uses the term "queen" to constitute Lucilla, the term resonates with available representations of Victoria and her peculiarly domestic monarchy.

The book is written in mock-heroic style, consistently substituting small domestic acts where the tone would seem to call for large public ones. One of her first acts on beginning her "illustrious and glorious reign at home" (40) is the redecoration of her father's drawing room, a project she initiates with great seriousness in the presence of her father and her visiting cousin Tom:

> Lucilla was found in the act of pacing the room. . . . [She] was tall enough to go through this process without any great drawback in point of grace—the long step giving rather a tragedy-queen effect to her handsome but substantial person and long, sweeping dress. She stopped short, however, when she saw them, and withdrew to the sofa, on which she had established her throne. (*Miss Marjoribanks*, 65)

Her father mockingly suggests she is rehearsing for Lady Macbeth, but she deflates his mockery by claiming equal gravity for what she *is* doing: measuring for the new carpet. Lucilla, making her body public in the manner of Elizabeth I, will decorate to match her person. "'I think,' said Miss Marjoribanks, rising and looking at herself seriously in the glass, 'that I have enough complexion at present to venture upon a pale spring green'" (67). On which the narrator comments: "Lucilla was quite in earnest in thinking that the colour of the drawing-room was an important matter, and that a woman of sense had very good reason for suiting it to her complexion" (68).

Lucilla's monarchy bears a curiously chiastic relation to Victoria's. Lucilla is a private woman behaving like a queen: but queen only of her drawing room, or at most, of the upper-middle-class inhabitants of Grange Lane, Carlingford; while Victoria, especially the mourning Victoria of 1866 (and of 1864–65, the years in which the novel was written), is a queen behaving like a private woman whose sphere often appears to be as small as a drawing room. Lucilla's figurative monarchy and Victoria's actual one are engaged in a relation of mutual construction that amounts to a relation of mutual ungrounding, whereby circular reference to the other prevents each from achieving a firm cultural meaning. The novel asks: Can a domestic woman's activities be as significant and wide-reaching as those of a queen; or, conversely, does Victoria's restricted style of monarchy limit both her own and Lucilla's significance to the drawing room? If the latter is the case, and if Victoria is the monarch on whom Lucilla's monarchy is based, does that then reduce the extensiveness of Lucilla's implied queenly powers; or, if the former is the case (that a domestic woman's activities can be as significant as a queen's), and if Victoria's reign is modeled on domestic monarchies like that of Lucilla, does that then expand the sense of what a domesticated monarch like Victoria could do after all? These are the same questions raised by "Of Queens' Gardens" two years earlier, in which the proliferation of queens in every home in the nation suggests at first a bold claim for the housewives of England, yet simultaneously a dilution and diminution of the authority of Queen Victoria. If Victoria is diminished by her mass production in Ruskin and by her duplication in *Miss Marjoribanks* and countless other novels, that would in turn diminish the boldness of claims for domestic women. As the novel proceeds, the possibility of answering these questions depends largely on how one reads the novel's very delicate satiric tone. Given that readers have varied so widely in their interpretations of this tone, it may be undecidable whether Lucilla and her narrator believe in the world historical importance of her social maneuverings. Irony keeps open the question of what and how extensive any queenly power may be.

In the first part of the novel, what Lucilla accomplishes under the banner of "being a comfort to papa" seems to assert that great actions can be taken in the name of domestic femininity. This positive reading is emphasized by Joseph O'Mealy, who remarks of Lucilla, "She takes the Victorian home, which was supposed to be the realm of the private, and turns it into the public, subverting the Victorian 'ideology of home and family [which] was consistently employed to oppose emergent feminism.'"[30] Dressed in her "white frock [worn] *high*" (100, 110), holding court in the spring green drawing room, Lucilla not only consolidates Grange Lane Society, subduing some of its more anarchic elements (such as Mrs. Woodburn) and bringing old and young together, but she also executes a series of elaborate and brilliant social manipulations, matchmaking and rescuing her friend Mr. Cavendish from disgrace when he is about to be exposed as a class impostor.[31] Proclaiming that she "ought to be Prime Minister," Mr. Cavendish calls Lucilla's activities "social politics" (111). Brilliantly though she has schemed, however, when the monarchic or in this case ministerial metaphor is removed, Lucilla has done nothing beyond the domestic sphere. The chief import of Mr. Cavendish's praise, after all, is that he contemplates proposing to her. And then he does not do so after all.

By contrast, in the second part of the novel (starting at chapter 36, the last third of the novel), which takes place ten years later, Lucilla affects the outcome of a parliamentary election. Here the novel does start to propose genuinely enlarged, public sphere powers for Lucilla as a domestic woman. In this part of the novel the narrator notes that she is now old enough to "have gone into Parliament herself had there been no disqualification of sex" and that "there are instincts that go even beyond dinners, and Lucilla had become conscious that her capabilities were greater than her work" (*Miss Marjoribanks*, 395). Her ambition hardly resembles the charitable acts Ruskin has in mind for his queens, such as stopping wars and saving the poor, but it does take an irreproachably "feminine" form. Campaigning aggressively, Lucilla nonetheless represents herself as a merely inspirational figure, an "influence," not a political agent. In doing so, she follows (or at any rate seems to follow) Oliphant's own recommendation that women find their power in influence, not in clamoring for the vote. Getting the vote for women, Oliphant wrote in an essay for *Blackwood's*, would concede that women were at present lacking in some way: "something less than woman, something almost man."[32] Claiming that her candidate's solidity as a man—his class position and his discreet lifestyle—outweighs the dubiousness of his political views, Lucilla (like a model queen) holds herself above politics both in choosing her man and in working for him. Silencing Mr. Ashburton's fear that what she calls his "opinions" do not match those of the important men of Carlingford, she outlines his successful campaign strategy and its slogan:

> I would not pay the least attention to Tories or Whigs, or anything of the sort. For my part I don't see any difference. All that has to be said about it is simply that you are the right man. Papa might object to one thing and the Colonel might object to another, and then if Sir John, as you say, is of quite another way of thinking—But you are the man for Carlingford all the same, and none of them can say a word against that. (*Miss Marjoribanks*, 346–47)

Extending women's moral responsibilities from the drawing room to the nation, and keeping her hearers from deciding whether her discourse is lightheaded or profound, Lucilla nonetheless keeps her politics of influence safely feminine.

Demonstrating that her politics retains its ties to the drawing room, Lucilla identifies the moral with the aesthetic, as in the next moment she leaps characteristically to the

> "one thing that is really important, and must be fixed upon. . . ."
>
> "What?" said the candidate eagerly—"about Reform? . . ."
>
> Lucilla smiled compassionately, and with the gentlest tolerance, at this wild suggestion. "I was not thinking of Reform. . . . I was thinking of what your colours were to be." (*Miss Marjoribanks*, 348)

Choosing once again in accordance with her complexion (the colors are to be green and violet), literally replicating the drawing room in the coloration of the campaign, Lucilla may well be right, despite Mr. Ashburton's laughter, that visual symbols are just as likely to turn elections as are political views. The reader, like Mr. Ashburton, would be forgiven for "thinking she was joking, or acting, or doing something quite different from the severe sincerity which was her leading principle" (348); Sarah Ellis mentions the colors of political parties among the topics on which women "prattle," thereby betraying "littleness of soul" (*Wives of England*, 84). But this ambiguity makes the running joke of the novel, which makes it impossible to decide whether Lucilla really thinks only about trivia or whether she is cynically manipulating the language of female domestic values—with its curiously impartial emphasis on personal rectitude and on color scheme—to achieve her personal ambitions in the public sphere; whether her "sincerity" means her innocent, lightheaded belief in the importance of her complexion or means instead her shrewd knowledge of how easily voters may be fooled. Mr. Ashburton, seduced by her apparent frivolity, soon comes round to thinking her "very clever" (349). Making it impossible to decide about the moral weight of Lucilla's opinions also keeps open, by implication, such a question as how Victoria's monarchy is being constituted, her focus on the moral and familial and on the decorative and symbolic being represented here as at once appropriate and ludicrous, at once the crucial form of power and its evasion.

Whatever the case, Lucilla's "right man" wins—her ultrafeminine behavior with the ribbons having encouraged his self-identification as the "man"—chiefly because at the eleventh hour his opponent, the problematic Mr. Cavendish, reveals his lack of good breeding and proves that Mr. Ashburton is indeed the better man, that is, the more genteel. Mr. Cavendish exposes the inborn class affiliation Lucilla had earlier aided him to conceal by making the aesthetic mistake of publicly romancing the cheaply clad Barbara Lake ("in that same silk dress which rustled like tin," 450) on the eve of the election. ("A man ain't the man for Carlingford as takes up with that sort," says Lucilla's former butler, 447.) With Mr. Ashburton Carlingford appears to be getting a conservative MP, associated with land and tradition, cautious about Reform, in favor—like Oliphant in her essays for *Blackwood's*—of symbolic rather than numerical representation; but the voters seem not to care about these issues one way or the other. The satire is directed as much at Lucilla's constituents as at herself; for such voters, a queen who chooses the right colors is more welcome and useful than a queen who understands (much less wants) Reform.

At the moment of Mr. Ashburton's election in Carlingford, the actual Queen's colors were not purple and green but black. While voters were making choices about Reform, she concerned herself with aesthetics (not ribbons but books about and statues of Prince Albert). Whether she had chosen the right colors was, as we have seen, like Reform itself the subject of public debate throughout the period when Oliphant was working on the novel. When Lucilla's domestic monarchy and her successful involvement in political campaigning through "influence" and symbolic performance reconstitute the missing Queen by locating her in a house in Carlingford, the "young sovereign" (49) so reconstituted most clearly resembles the young Victoria who, as Langland points out, "began her reign in her late teens" (*Nobody's Angels*, 158). But the novel also represents Victoria's widowhood and registers the difference it made for her powers as a monarch and for the possibilities of royal representation. *Miss Marjoribanks* manages to turn the unmarried queen of Carlingford into a widow about half way through its second part, and in doing so both comments critically upon and helps to define Victoria's royal mourning. Attending to the changing conditions of Victoria's power helps us to historicize the question of whether invoking Victoria would have signified powerlessness or power.[33] When the term "queen" is used in 1864 or even in the 1870s, it means something rather different from what it meant in 1837, in 1850, or in 1890, and to that difference we will now turn.

The ambiguity of Lucilla's political powers are, like Victoria's, exaggerated even further when her mourning removes her from the public sphere. Lucilla's father dies about half-way through the second part of the novel, before the election actually takes place, leaving her not only genuinely grieving for him but also suddenly poor. As a result, she withdraws from the business of campaigning into deep mourning and also into the exclusive company of her aunt, who appears at just this point to serve as the sort of bossy chaperon that Lucilla has successfully avoided so far. That Lucilla's sphere of action is thus drastically reduced to the literally domestic—she does not venture outside her house—emphasizes how far she had moved beyond the drawing room while still adhering to its principles. Her reduced circumstances lead her neighbors to assume she will "abdicate at once" (420). Precisely because (unlike Elizabeth I) Victoria and Lucilla have held themselves to the same standards of behavior to which they hold their female subjects, Victoria and Lucilla are both hard pressed to sustain their authority when mourning customs—indistinguishable from genuine feelings of grief—cause them actually to stay home and not just appear to do so. While queens have "a duty to be looked at," widows have a "right," indeed a duty, "to hide themselves" (Longford, *Queen Victoria*, 317).

Lucilla's privatizing mourning leads her into marriage, however, rather than away from it, in the novel's curious merger of Victoria's gloomy story with the conventions of comic closure. In this way the novel follows the cultural logic of Victoria's widowhood while at the same time delivering Lucilla into the conventions of the marriage plot. The novel's relation to Victoria's reign is here again chiastic: a marriage follows widowhood rather than widowhood following marriage. In mourning, Lucilla acquires psychological depth, a quality she has done very well without so far. The night he dies, her usually undemonstrative father pats her shoulder in a good-night gesture that she compulsively recalls. Even the ordinarily dry narrative voice veers suddenly toward pathos in its narration of the doctor's death. While others are wondering what Lucilla will do with her life now, her first response to his death is emotional and not at all strategic:

> She did not think at all that first long snowy, troubled day, but went about the house, on the bedroom floor, wringing her hands like a creature distracted. "If I had only sat up," she said; and then she would recall the touch of his hand on her shoulder, which she seemed still to be feeling, and cry out. (*Miss Marjoribanks*, 404)

Victoria's threats to fall to pieces, her going to sleep every night with Albert's nightshirt and a cast of his hand, are perhaps alluded to here. When Lucilla learns about the failure of her father's investments, "a sudden sense of utter gloom and cold and bewildering uncertainty came over Lucilla" (410). When she considers his restraint in keeping his worries to himself, "'Poor papa!' she said to herself; and as she was not much given to employing her imagination in this way, and realizing the feeling of others, the effect was all the greater" (411). She sobs again and again to learn that all he said when he himself received the news from his lawyer was "Poor Lucilla!" "Giddy, . . . ashamed of her weakness," shut up in her room "with the blinds down, and the black dresses everywhere about, for so many dreary days" (412), Lucilla has become another sort of heroine altogether from the one we have been treated to so far.

Lucilla has become what Nancy Armstrong's *Desire and Domestic Fiction* identifies as the hallmark of the rising middle class and its authorizing fictions: the psychologically deep heroine whose emotions create and justify the perpetuation of a separate private, domestic sphere. Although the bold and original tactician will soon return, for Lucilla defies expectations by determining to stay on in her father's expensive house, this new emotional Lucilla never entirely goes away.

It is this privatized, emotional Lucilla who is finally receptive to a marriage proposal from her cousin Tom, suddenly returned from India on the news of his uncle's death. Mr. Ashburton, having won the election, now feels obligated to propose and is on the verge of doing so when Lucilla's quiet drawing room is invaded by the sounds of a cab in a hurry and of the doctor's disused bell "peal[ing] through the silence." At these sounds Lucilla's color changes and her heart "leaps" and "jumps." Although Tom is still "a blunderer," India has transformed him into "a man with a beard" (472) who has the audacity to kiss her on first arriving, and Lucilla loses command. Admitting that she does not want Ashburton, but not yet ready to accept Tom, Lucilla finds that her

> powers seemed to fail her.... She broke down just at the moment when she had most need to have all her wits about her.... the fact was that Lucilla relinquished her superior position for the time being, and suffered him to make any assertion he pleased, and was so weak as to cry, for the second time, too—which, of all things in the world, was surely the last thing to have been expected of Miss Marjoribanks at the moment which decided her fate. (*Miss Marjoribanks*, 476)

The bracing return of the mock-heroic tone at the end of this passage goes some way to restoring Lucilla the comic mastermind, just as that version of Lucilla had returned when people piled into her house to celebrate the election and she "forgot that she was not able for it" (461). Married to Tom and living on the ancestral estate, Lucilla will still have a "Career," repairing the "disarray" of the Marchbank village and perhaps helping her husband into Parliament ("there are Members for counties too," 493). (When Lucilla, asserting that she must have "something to do," allows Tom to think that she has been ministering to the poor while really she has served as Carlingford's "chief hostess," Oliphant may allude to the 1864 attempt of the newspapers to minimize Victoria's role at the head of elite society in favor of her more modest "duties.") Nonetheless, the acceptance of Tom's proposal confirms the existence of the new emotional Lucilla created by her mourning.

Like the widowed Victoria, Lucilla retreats from public to private, from strategy to emotionality, a tendency confirmed by the structure of the narrative, which produces as its climax not the vindication of Lucilla's political views but the resolution of her private life. One passage rhetorically equates marriage and mourning by juxtaposing, in quick succession, Lucilla's notion that "I don't mean to be Lucilla Marjoribanks forever" and her sensations upon returning from her first excursion out of the house: "When she put back her thick black veil, the last climax of painful change came upon Miss Marjoribanks. She did not feel as if she were Lucilla; so discouraged and depressed and pale, and tired with her walk as she was" (424–25). Marriage and mourning are here equated as institutions that change the heroine into someone other than herself. Using the marriage plot to exaggerate the privatization Victoria's widowhood produced, the novel in this way indicates what "queen" means in the 1860s: someone whose public powers—whether direct or indirect—are subordinated to the exigencies of her domestic life; and someone who no longer fits her prior, public self-image. Just as Victoria shrinks nervously away from the "representations" she might once have inhabited comfortably, so Lucilla "did not feel as if she were Lucilla" and indeed does not intend to remain Lucilla Marjoribanks. Lucilla is like the Queen, but the absent Queen is also being made in the image of a privatized Lucilla, a Lucilla who has become dislocated from her public image.

There is one important difference between Lucilla and Victoria in their responses to mourning. While Lucilla's subjects expect her to "abdicate"—to rent out her father's costly house and live modestly elsewhere, perhaps with her aunt, on the income—her boldest decision is to stay on in the house and maintain a public profile by holding on to the signifiers of her reign. In this regard Oliphant arranges for Lucilla to behave differently from Victoria, whose abdication (as we have seen) had been rumored and indeed called for when her mourning did not lighten after two or three years.

> As long as she remained in Grange Lane, even though retired and in crape, the constitutional monarch was still present among her subjects; and nobody could usurp her place or show that utter indifference to her regulations which some revolutionaries had dreamed of. Such an idea would have gone direct in the face of the British Constitution, and the sense of the community would have been dead against it. (*Miss Marjoribanks*, 421)

Although in Victoria's case abdication would have led not to a republic but to the probably even less desirable reign of her son, Oliphant's novel conflates the prospect of Lucilla's abdication with republicanism, a possibility that is raised only to be quelled:

> Lucilla's subjects contemplated their emancipation with a certain guilty delight. . . . But when the fact was really known, it would be difficult to de-

scribe the sense of guilt and horror which filled many innocent bosoms. The bound of freedom had been premature—liberty and equality had not come yet, notwithstanding that too early unwise *elan* of republican satisfaction. (420–21)

Republicanism was not yet a serious movement in England when Oliphant was writing *Miss Marjoribanks,* yet the novel proleptically wards it off by constituting its queen's widowed retirement as an aid to her continued occupation of monarchic space rather than as a cause of her departure from it. The Queen herself had in mind something like this strategy when, as we have seen, she wrote to Palmerston in December 1864 that "she has never received more marks of devotion, loyalty and true sympathy from her subjects than within these last three sad years." Her retirement may indeed have enabled or provoked into being the very proliferation of domestic queens we have observed in Ruskin, Oliphant, and elsewhere, queens whose reconstitutions of the missing Queen at once expand and diminish her domain. Thus the novel both borrows from the stock of Victoria's model domestic monarchy, and, having shrewdly diagnosed Victoria's powers as powers of representation, urges her to find ways of republicizing her monarchy (and itself exemplifies some of them) even in the midst of—and indeed by way of—her retirement.

The novel's ending also seconds the urging of the cartoon of Victoria as Hermione, the wish that Victoria would once again coincide with her monumental public representations. The closing lines of the novel reflect on the fact that Lucilla's name will after all not change even though she is to marry, for her husband's name is the same as her own (and both are cognate with the name of their future home, Marchbank). Readers have tended to see in this plot twist an autobiographical gesture, as Oliphant herself married a cousin who gave her for a married name the name of her own mother. Allusion is also being made to Victoria, who married a cousin and whose name remained the same in marriage. But even more striking, that Lucilla "will never be anything but Lucilla Marjoribanks" is instrumental in the mock-heroic monumentalization of the heroine as the novel takes leave of her:

> If there could be any name that would have suited her better, or is surrounded by more touching associations, we leave it to her other friends to find out; for at the moment of taking leave of her, there is something consoling to our own mind in the thought that Lucilla can now suffer no change of name. As she was in the first freshness of her youthful daring, when she rose like the sun upon the chaos of society in Carlingford, so is she now as she goes forth into the County to carry light and progress there. (*Miss Marjoribanks,* 498–99)

As a mourner retreating into her private life, Lucilla became disjunct from her name and public image; now returning to her public, rendered monumental and changeless (also because the novel is over), Lucilla will once again coincide with the mock-heroic image of her projected in every part of the novel except the psychologizing chapters on her mourning and courtship, the "queen" whose lack of interiority makes her all the more powerful an image of successfully projected monarchy. Like the iconic "Queen of Trumps" in the 1839 broadside, she is at once everywoman and fantasmatically powerful beyond the limits of mortal women. Thus the novel ultimately brings its queen back from the privacy of widowhood and emotionality and reimagines her in a world where monarchic "representation" is never "mere representation" but identical to the Queen herself.

Making Queens: "Of Queens' Gardens" and the *Alice* Books

Ruskin's "Of Queens' Gardens" and Lewis Carroll's two *Alice* books, published in 1865 and 1871, reflect on the difficult process of making queens.[34] In these texts, perennial literary anxieties about representation cluster insistently around figures of queens, in texts that *make* queens by turning girls into queens and that multiply queens fantasmatically in ways that both augment and vitiate the powers of the actual monarch. These texts could be said not so much to recreate the missing Queen (as *Miss Marjoribanks* or the supportive articles in the papers of December 1864 could be said to do), although that may be among their ambitions and effects, as to worry the question of how to make her. If they do remake her, they remake her as an absence. There are without doubt other possible sources for Ruskin's and Dodgson's fantasies about manufacturing multiple queens whose powers are simultaneously vast and trivial, their shared pedophilia, for example: Ruskin as well as Carroll was struck by the attractions of Alice Liddell. One would still have to explain, however, why pedophilic expression took this particular form at this time in British history, and why these texts were such popular successes. The Queen's seclusion, if initiated by the random and underdetermined event of her husband's death, became in the decade following December 1864 an overdetermined cultural nexus where all sorts of issues—among them pedophilia with its horror of mature women, the postromantic anxiety about the mind's relation to nature, as well as political fears of female authority in the age of agitation for female suffrage and higher education—could converge and find expression.

The stated aim of "Of Queens' Gardens" is to explain why and how to turn all middle-class British girls into queens. In the course of doing so,

Ruskin insistently and sometimes hysterically repeats the word "queen," and this rhetorical effect combined with his explicit exhortations serves, as I suggested earlier in this chapter, not so much to augment the authority of the ordinary British woman so exhorted or that of the Queen who is thus mined as a resource for metaphor, but instead to construct the Queen in the image of the ordinary woman and to disperse her powerful presence across the landscape. With its multiplication of queens, the essay both echoes and attempts to compensate for Queen Victoria's absence by locating queens everywhere. Here I would like to focus more narrowly on the essay's preoccupation with how queens are made, and on the *Alice* books' comic confirmation of Ruskin's logic.

My suggestion in the first part of this chapter that Ruskin's essay creates the Queen as much as it draws on her takes its start in part from J. Hillis Miller's argument that nineteenth-century realist fiction exemplifies the trope of catachresis, naming figuratively what lacks a literal name (the face of a mountain, the leg of a table).[35] In this case, "queen" appears to refer to a reality outside the text but instead constructs, by so naming it, a certain otherwise unnameable womanly ideal. The queenly women, and the queen or queens used apparently to ground Ruskin's exhortations, are personifications of desirable traits more than they are representations of actual women, least of all Queen Victoria. Miller points out that personification or prosopopoeia is the correct rhetorical term for Ruskin's "pathetic fallacy," or the projection of human qualities onto nature, and that Ruskin avoids using its proper name because he is anxious to deny the unavoidability of prosopopoeia, aspiring instead to allegory, in which the visible world would simply reveal intrinsic meanings. Harold Bloom, after observing that for Ruskin "all great poetry whatsoever is allegorical," calls *Sesame and Lilies* a "giant Pathetic Fallacy" or a failed allegory, apparently because Ruskin exposes the process of projecting onto queens and gardens his own ideas instead of simply telling an intrinsically meaningful story, that is, an allegory with queens and gardens.[36] Thus Ruskin's personification of his female ideal as "queen" is attended by considerable anxiousness.

Moreover, in light of what some Ruskin scholars have argued about the place of "Of Queens' Gardens" in Ruskin's oeuvre, we could say that the essay constitutes pathetic fallacy at two removes: Ruskin not only projects his ideas about womanhood onto queens and gardens but also, prior to that, projects onto womanhood certain needs of his own. Dinah Birch and David Sonstroem have both argued, in different contexts, that Ruskin creates his queenly women not so much out of a wish to indoctrinate Victorian women in a certain ideal of womanhood but rather to meet his own needs, be they psychosocial or sociopolitical.[37] Sheila Emerson traces Ruskin's lifelong identification with queenly girls to his need to represent his own secondariness as a critic.[38] Sharon Aronofsky Weltman has argued about *The Ethics of the Dust* that Ruskin identifies personification, metaphor, and the pathetic fallacy all as feminine, because they all exemplify connectedness and syncretism—his own pet projects of revealing how, as Weltman puts it, "every real thing inheres in every real thing."[39]

Whether we read the pathetic fallacy with Bloom as a sign of "post-Romantic . . . mingled grandeur and ruin" ("Introduction," 13) or with Weltman, Birch, and Emerson as a more neutral or even favorable self-description of Ruskin's own feminized "second rank" among writers, it is politically important to understand that "Of Queens' Gardens" is a work of personification, an example of the pathetic fallacy, and not a work of referential or realist representation. Paul Sawyer articulates why: Ruskin's essay is about the idealized figure of "woman" as it is deployed to justify patriarchal social order, "an order that maintains its control . . . by appeals to the feminine images of domestic harmony" but that is unrelated to powers any actual woman might control or any meanings she might intrinsically bear.[40] Sheila Emerson, too, concluding her discussion of Ruskin's identification with girls, points out "his rejection of the actual lives of those girls" and the importance of distinguishing between such lives and Ruskin's female "garb," a "garb so artful, that no female who puts it on will ever grow up to make art" (*Ruskin*, 228).[41]

Ruskin begins, then, with an idea (about himself, or about art and criticism, or about the powers of sympathy), projects that onto middle-class women, and projects this ideal onto the figure "queen," about whom he tells a story. The claim that this story is true serves as Ruskin's excuse for scolding middle-class women for not behaving as if they were allegories of his meaning, radiant with the intrinsic queenly power to change the world. The essay's frenetic tone and its insistence on its key term or personification "queen" exemplify Ruskin's anxiety to coerce personification to become allegory, to coerce women to bear naturally the meanings he would impose on them. (Or to put it another way, he is trying to literalize his metaphor "queen" so as to make women not be like queens but be queens.) Indeed, as a tract about education, in which Ruskin describes how to turn a girl into a queen, the essay could be understood as a slow-motion narrative about how personification or pathetic fallacy comes about, how meaning gets applied to a natural object. John Stuart Mill proleptically criticizes Ruskin's educational program for laboring to produce that which he simultaneously claims exists naturally (the girl/woman as queen), pointing out that there is no need to pass laws to prevent women from doing what nature disinclines them to do.[42] This paradoxical feature of the essay could also be understood as a narrativizing of Ruskin's wish to turn pathetic fallacy into allegory. Women and girls, it would seem, personify personification: again and again, it is in stories about trying to form women that he reveals his efforts to make natural objects mean. His insistence that women must *be* queens suggests that Ruskin's use of pathetic fallacy makes him anxious about referentiality even as he goes on quite deliberately deploying it. Perhaps these linked anxieties, about regulating the powers of women and about making them mean referentially, are the same. Getting women to be what he wants them to be and getting figures to embody (and not just analogize) the meanings he would like them to embody pose equivalent difficulties.

In her reading of *The Ethics of the Dust,* Sharon Weltman discusses Ruskin's insistence that crystals really are the things he wants them to mean, which takes the form of his insistence that the crystals are alive. The girls repeatedly question this assertion: "It is very delightful to imagine the mountains to be alive; but then,—*are* they alive?" (quoted in "Gender and the Archtectonics," 54). Weltman takes this questioning to be Ruskin's way of emphasizing the importance of personification. But in "Of Queens' Gardens" Ruskin eliminates the questioners, so that there is no one to ask "But then,—*are* they queens?," the very question that makes Ruskin anxious, both as regards women and as regards his desire to produce seamless allegory or referential language. There must be no question that they are queens, and yet, of course, the doubt remains.[43]

That "Of Queens' Gardens" anxiously acknowledges its status as "a giant Pathetic Fallacy," and identifies that anxiety with an anxiety about women, is suggested by Ruskin's choice to close the essay by quoting some of the same lines from Tennyson's *Maud* that he uses as his final defining example of the pathetic fallacy in *Modern Painters.* Here is the passage as it appears in *Modern Painters:*

> There has fallen a splendid tear
> From the passion-flower at the gate.
> .... [Ruskin's omission]
> The red rose cries, "She is near, she is near!"
> And the white rose weeps, "She is late."
> The larkspur listens, "I hear, I hear!"
> And the lily whispers, "I wait."[44]

"Of Queens' Gardens" ends with a clumsy allegory about "torn" and "broken" flowers (poor women, prostitutes) who need queens (middle-class women) to tend them. In the course of his peroration Ruskin quotes from *Maud* the invitation by the mad young man—"Come into the garden, Maud / I am here at the gate alone"—so as, bizarrely, to attribute these words to the "feeble florets" (77), and then he quotes the flowers to which the mad young man has given voice: "The Larkspur listens—I hear, I hear! And the Lily whispers—I wait" (quoted in "Of Queens' Gardens," 78), as if these too were the words of his own feeble florets. Ruskin's queens thus occupy Maud's place as the object of the talking flowers' eager waiting. In context, Tennyson makes the young man responsible for the use of pathetic fallacy and has him envoice the flowers as a way of characterizing his delusion. But by quoting in the way he does, Ruskin eliminates the ironic distance between poet and unhinged fictive speaker and incorporates that speaker's exaggerated, pathological pathetic fallacy into his own personification of the feeble florets and the queens. His anxious forcing of figures to bear his meanings, like his anxious forcing of Tennyson's lines to fit his purposes (amongst his continuous miscitations of literary texts throughout the essay), testifies to the difficulty of establishing seamless referentiality. That it is a scene of waiting for someone who may never come dramatizes the anxiety attendant upon trying to make connections in much the same way that Ruskin's educational scenario does. And that it is a woman who is awaited here suggests again that there is some necessary connection between anxiety about establishing referentiality and the anxious hope that women will do what he wants. But this was an anxiety already exhibited at the start of the essay in his wild claim that classic authors' female figures constitute "testimony" about women as they should really be.

In "Of Queens' Gardens" literary texts are treated as referential "testimony" rather than as fictions or projections, and having given them this status Ruskin then tries to get them to mean things it is scarcely credible they could ever mean (for example, that the Greek dramatists thought women were better than men; "Of Queens' Gardens," 50, 55–56). He quotes Tennyson tendentiously, and he edits one of Wordsworth's Lucy poems to exhibit it as another great poet's ideal of natural femininity, neglecting to include the stanza in which Lucy dies from the effects of her education ("Of Queens' Gardens," 61). But it is not only literary texts that Ruskin treats in this way; words themselves are obliged to mean what Ruskin wants them to mean, and to do so intrinsically, that is to say, etymologically. The bogus etymology is a familiar feature of Ruskin's writing generally, but in "Of Queens' Gardens" his argument depends upon it to an unusual degree, starting on the first page with the word "state." By making it seem that the meaning he is asserting is intrinsic to the words themselves, he appears to ground his argument irrefutably, just as he insists that the crystals are alive and that the women are queens, even though he knows he is the one who has just made them so. Like literary "testimony," his use of etymology is a trick, of course: even if his etymologies were accurate, there is still no final or literal meaning of words—no natural connection between a phoneme and a meaning.[45] But he makes it appear that there is, and furthermore that it is the meaning that best supports his argument.

On their way to becoming queens, Ruskin says, he would like women to

> claim the title of Lady, provided they claim, not merely the title, but the office and duty signified by it. Lady means "bread-giver" or "loaf-giver," and Lord means "maintainer of laws," and both titles have reference, not to the law which is maintained in the house, not to the bread which is given to the household; but to law maintained for the multitude, and to bread broken among the multitude. ("Of Queens' Gardens," 73)

English women, he complains, have appropriated the term "Lady" simply as a class marker, but he wants to restore it to its original and thus ostensibly literal meaning, with its attendant responsibilities. This sounds good, but Ruskin is making it up. According to Skeat and to the OED, a lady is etymologically, from the Anglo-Saxon, a loaf-kneader, while a lord is a loaf-keeper (and a servant is a loaf-eater), with implications far less spiritually elevated than Ruskin's argument permits him to acknowledge. Similarly, he points out that Rex and Regina mean "Right-doers" (74). This may be so, but he fails to point out that the more relevant term "king" derives less splendidly from "kin," and that "queen" derives from the gothic word for "woman"; "cwen" was used interchangeably in Wessex with the word we now know as "lady." His key terms do not bear intrinsically the meanings he desires for them, but that does not stop him from pretending that they do.[46] And significantly it is for the purpose of coercing women to be what he wants them to be that he obliges words to bear intrinsically the meanings he needs them to bear.[47]

Although Carroll's *Alice* books, especially *Through the Looking-Glass*, oppose Ruskin's essay in many ways, they share a preoccupation with the process by which queens are made—Ruskin's insistence betraying his fear that they cannot be made, Carroll's wit exposing the improbability of their manufacture.[48] *Alice's Adventures in Wonderland*, and the earlier manuscript version *Alice's Adventures under Ground* on which it is based, are largely about Alice's efforts to master her growth. Her unpredictable growth and shrinkage make her uncertain who she is through much of the story, unable to explain herself to the caterpillar "because I'm not myself, you see" (*Wonderland*, 35).

Although she does not grow into a queen (and that she does so in *Through the Looking-Glass* makes that story instead the main focus of my attention here), Alice's eventual mastery of her growth brings her the dubious benefit of meeting the Queen of Hearts and her retinue in the croquet ground, a queen whose authority Alice learns to rival and reject. Her maturation teaches her that queens are "nothing but a pack of cards" (*Wonderland,* 97). Although Carroll and Ruskin both remake the missing Queen of England in the form of her own lack or absence, to read *Through the Looking-Glass* after reading Ruskin's essay is to find in it a hilarious parody and trenchant critique of Ruskin's endeavor, through pathetic fallacy, to turn girls into queens. Carroll's writing mocks both Ruskin's flamboyant rhetorical tricks and his views on women, and mocks the one through his mockery of the other.

Humpty Dumpty, the egg-headed philologist of *Through the Looking-Glass,* is, in my view, Carroll's dyspeptic version of Ruskin the bogus etymologist in "Of Queens' Gardens." Here is the familiar passage, beloved by the many commentators on Carroll's linguistic play. Humpty Dumpty is discoursing on the merits of unbirthday presents, and concludes,

> "There's glory for you!"
> "I don't know what you mean by 'glory,'" Alice said.
> Humpty Dumpty smiled contemptuously. "Of course you don't—till I tell you. I meant, 'there's a nice knock-down argument for you!'"
> "But 'glory' doesn't mean 'a nice knock-down argument,'" Alice objected.
> "When *I* use a word," Humpty Dumpty said, in a rather scornful tone, "it means just what I choose it to mean—neither more nor less."
> "The question is," said Alice, "whether you *can* make words mean so many different things."
> "The question is," said Humpty Dumpty, "which is to be master—that's all." (*Looking-Glass,* 163)

Humpty Dumpty does deliberately, even ostentatiously, what Ruskin does on the sly: get words to mean whatever he wants them to. In doing so he reveals that effort (whether mastery or submission) is involved on both sides. A radical nominalist in this exchange, Humpty Dumpty is thus not very far from Ruskin the radical but bogus essentialist. That these two positions are linked, not opposed, is made evident by the next topic of Alice's conversation with the humanoid egg, in which he eagerly explicates the meanings of Lewis Carroll's portmanteau words and other neologisms in "Jabberwocky," relying on a para-etymological strategy that laughs again but in a different way at Ruskin's practice in "Of Queens' Gardens":

"And '*the wabe*' is the grass-plot round a sun-dial, I suppose?" said Alice, surprised at her own ingenuity.

"Of course it is. It's called '*wabe*' you know, because it goes a long way before it, and a long way behind it—"

"And a long way beyond it on each side," Alice added.

"Exactly so." (*Looking-Glass,* 165)

In looking-glass land, anyone with "ingenuity" (such as Ruskin, or Alice) can invent words as well as their meanings, and—better still—once they are made, you can pretend they were always there.

In Ruskin, coercing or paying words to mean what you want is linked, as is the use of pathetic fallacy, to coercing women to *be* queens, not just to be like them. The same pattern appears in *Through the Looking-Glass*—the rhetorical practice and the thematics about girls and women giving shape to each other—but with just the opposite effect. Just as Ruskin's essay contains a narrative of educating girls to be queens, Carroll's story is plotted as the transformation of Alice into a queen on the chessboard of life. But just as Carroll spoofs Ruskin's coercive etymologies, he also mocks Ruskin's coercive educational scheme, since Alice's so-called education consists in her being moved involuntarily across the board and, at the end, being not-quite-certified a queen by two wholly incompetent examiners, the Red and White Queens. Alice's queening makes that of the women in Ruskin look ridiculous, in part because in the looking-glass world it becomes clear that "queen" is a position to be arbitrarily assumed, not, as in Ruskin, an identity or essence. Cathy Shuman points out that in both narratives of girls' education, indirection and backward travel substitute for progress ("Different for Girls," 1, 77–78). (With a similarly self-reversing plot logic, in *Mopsa the Fairy* Mopsa becomes a potential queen when Jack kisses her and his kiss retards her growth, in contrast to her companions who reach their full growth rapidly and fly away; she is only ten when she becomes dependent queen of "the place she thought she had run away from," *Mopsa,* 194.)[49] Ruskin the pedophile aims to retain his women's "majestic childishness" ("Of Queens' Gardens," 62); Carroll the pedophile protests the very idea that little girls must grow up. When Alice remarks to Humpty Dumpty, early in their conversation, "that one can't help growing older," the reply is, "*One* can't, perhaps . . . but *two* can. With proper assistance, you might have left off at seven" (*Looking-Glass,* 162). Carroll's radical pedophilia laughs at the socially uplifting forms in which Ruskin's masks itself.

Carroll dramatizes the link between the coercion of girls and the coercion of words when he has Alice "suddenly" remark, directly after the exchange about growth,

"What a beautiful belt you've got on!"... (They had had quite enough of the subject of age, she thought: and, if they really were to take turns in choosing subjects, it was *her* turn now.) "At least," she corrected herself on second thoughts, "a beautiful cravat, I should have said—no, a belt, I mean—I beg your pardon!" she added in dismay, for Humpty Dumpty looked thoroughly offended. (*Looking-Glass*, 162)

That Alice must grow—and grow into a queen—is dramatized both by her discomfort with the topic and by her attention to good manners; but her entanglement in the question of "which was neck and which was waist" also propels her into the next conversational topic, the relation of words to things discussed above. As for Ruskin, the problem of turning girls into queens is the same as the problem of getting words to mean, although whereas Ruskin anxiously wishes for these projects to succeed, Carroll opposes them by revealing their shared arbitrariness.

Along with bogus etymology, pathetic fallacy is Ruskin's chief rhetorical analogy for the attempted queening of girls, and Carroll mocks Ruskin's use of pathetic fallacy as well as his bogus etymologies, on his way to mocking Ruskinian queening. Near the start of *Through the Looking-Glass* Alice comes upon the garden of talking flowers. They introduce her to the looking-glass world's characteristic rhetorical gesture of punningly taking figures of speech literally, the humorist's version of Ruskin's attempt to make literal the metaphor of queen for women. The tiger-lily explains that in most gardens the flowers do not talk because the beds are so soft and put the flowers to sleep; the daisy and the rose explain that the tree in their midst could protect them by barking and saying "boughwough" (*Looking-Glass*, 122). They mention that there is in the garden another flower like Alice, with Alice's awkward shape but with short red petals and spikes that Alice lacks. Thus announcing the Red Queen, the flowers turn out to come from Tennyson's *Maud*: "'She's coming!' cried the Larkspur. 'I hear her footstep, thump, thump, along the gravel-walk!'" (*Looking-Glass*, 123). In literalizing Tennyson's figures of speech, turning the mad young man's prosopopoeia into embodied characters, Carroll is also literalizing Ruskin's figures of speech, for these are the lines from *Maud* that Ruskin uses, as we saw, both to exemplify the pathetic fallacy in *Modern Painters* and to appeal to women in "Of Queens' Gardens."[50] The looking-glass flowers literalize Ruskin's prosopopoeia in a manner consistent with their tendency toward literalizing puns; their queen makes the same kind of puns, and, thumping heavily into the garden, literalizes and concretizes Tennyson's and Ruskin's etherially figurative queens. In the garden, Alice's promotion to the rank of queen is foreshadowed by her initially mistaking the flowers' description of the queen for a description of "another little girl in the garden . . . like me" (123) and by the rose's surprise that Alice does not have spikes like the queen's (she will soon). Again, Carroll's parody of Ruskin's awkwardly coercive prosopopoeia coincides with the arbitrary making of girls into queens.

As John Hollander suggests, because the *Alice* books are dream visions (a traditional framing device of allegory), they invite allegorical reading; that is, each tells a more or less internally coherent story that seems, to quote J. Hillis Miller's definition of the kind of allegory Ruskin fails to achieve, to "stand for what is immeasurably above [it] in a mode of non-correspondence or unlikeness."[51] Thus Carroll would seem to have succeeded in producing the allegory to which Ruskin in vain aspired. But of course that seeming, teasing allegory is part of the joke. Readers too sober to get it have fallen into Carroll's trap and explicated the *Alice* books as allegories of many things, such as the secret history of the Oxford movement or the intrauterine development of the child.[52] But rather than *being* allegories, the books parody allegory, or the aspiration to allegorize, by taking pathetic fallacy (or prosopopoeia or failed allegory) to its literalizing limit. Every thing is animate—cards, chess pieces, flowers—and every animal is anthropomorphic. Humpty Dumpty is doubly personified, in that human traits have been projected onto an egg and in that he embodies or literalizes a nursery rhyme. Carroll mocks Ruskin's project to lift prosopopoeia to the level of allegory, to get the women to be queens and the "feeble florets" to be the suffering of England, and he does so by collapsing the distance between tenor and vehicle. By making the flowers talk and the chess pieces walk Carroll makes them more human than Ruskin can manage within the discourse of high seriousness, but, of course, at the expense of higher meaning: they have none. Ruskin's queen becomes, instead of a paragon of sympathy, a heavy-footed, governessy type whose opening remarks to Alice are distinctly testy. When Alice then remarks that she has lost her way, the Red Queen replies with a looking-glass pun, "'I don't know what you mean by *your* way, . . . all the ways about here belong to *me*'" (*Looking-Glass*, 124). Like Humpty Dumpty, the Red Queen exposes the reductiveness of Ruskin's proprietary attitude toward words. In looking-glass land, just as words and idioms used figuratively—such as "way" and "bed"—are collapsed into their literal meanings (or dead metaphors are revived), so the queens of Ruskin's dreams are made all too real, in being given dramatic and pictorial life as literalizing pun makers. Were Ruskin's anxious implicit query "but then,—*are* they queens?" to be asked here, the question would have to be answered in the affirmative, but not because allegory has been achieved—instead, because its terms have been collapsed into each other.

That this mockery of Ruskin's ambitious pathetic fallacy is also directed toward his project to turn girls into queens is suggested by what happens in chapter 9 of *Through the Looking-Glass*, when Alice becomes a queen. Alice crosses the brook from the White Knight's square and finds on her head—initially to her dismay (like Mopsa, who becomes queen "against her will," *Mopsa*, 205)—a golden crown. The White and Red Queens materialize to test her readiness. Their nonsensical examination is predictably characterized by puns that take figurative idioms literally and that bring dead metaphors to life. A peculiarly resonant instance of the latter occurs when Alice tries to excuse herself for the apparent arrogance of saying "if I really am a Queen:"

> "I'm sure I didn't mean—" Alice was beginning, but the Red Queen interrupted her impatiently.
> "That's just what I complain of! You *should* have meant! What do you suppose is the use of a child without any meaning?" (*Looking-Glass*, 192–93)

Collapsing the transitive, etiquette sense of "I mean" into the weightier notion of a self's intrinsic meaning, the Red Queen confirms a point of Carroll's spoof of Ruskin: what Alice understands to be an arbitrary matter of semantics the Red Queen mistakes for essential being or, alternatively, for intrinsic or allegorical significance. For Alice and for Carroll, to become a queen is to arrive arbitrarily at a certain position that may be designated by a sign such as the crown and spoken of in the conditional. For the Red Queen, by contrast, to become a queen is essentially to be one, or intrinsically to embody the meaning of queen, in just the way Ruskin hopes for the girls he would educate.[53] To take signifiers too literally, as the Red Queen and Ruskin do, is to enforce a notion of intrinsic meaning, and intrinsic queening, that oppresses the girl who wears the crown.

The anxieties about representation that were mobilized by the Queen's absence in widowhood would then, in Ruskin and Carroll, take opposing forms. Where Ruskin anxiously and self-defeatingly coerces the presence of a preferred kind of queen in a multitude of self-representing figures, Carroll equally hyperbolically displays the gap between sign and meaning, the impossibility of making a queen at all. But these opposed figurings of the Queen are two sides of the same coin, and both texts (like the cartoon of Victoria's empty throne, figure 29) remake the absent Queen as a vividly dramatized absence, the site of an evacuated authority. These links between Carroll and Ruskin emerge at the end of the scene of Alice's queening, when the Red and White Queens fall asleep with their heads on Alice's two shoulders. Alice remarks for the first time on the Ruskinian multiplication of queens in the story, the multiplication that Tenniel's two illustrations make especially vivid by doubling each other (figure 31): "'I don't think it *ever* happened before, that any one had to take care of two Queens asleep at once! No, not in all the History of England—it couldn't, you know, because there never was more than one Queen at a time'" (*Looking-Glass,* 197). It is curious here that Alice, who has up to now accepted the premise from chess that there can be two queens at the same time—red and white—suddenly shifts paradigms to royal history, in which there cannot be two, and certainly not three.[54] The multiplication of queens she notices here, emphasized as it is by the prevalence of arithmetic in the two queens' exam questions, coincides with their derealization: they fall asleep and shortly after they vanish. This point should recall the potentially vitiating effects of multiplying queens in Ruskin, in the fairy tales, and in Oliphant's novel.

Here, for all his mockery of Ruskin in other regards, Carroll's explicit representation of female power aligns exactly with the effects of Ruskin's writing and also that of Oliphant. The more queens there are, the less value they may hold and the less present they become, Carroll confirms; the more queens there are, the more "queen" comes to seem an arbitrary signifier and less an intrinsically (or allegorically) meaningful term. Literalizing Ruskin's queens in a form that lends itself to infinite reproduction (every chess set has two, and there are many chess sets), Carroll with his inconsequential looking-glass queens confirms that Victoria, and the notion of female sovereignty itself, is made less by her multiplication.[55] The very effort to reproduce her, to replace her absence, only calls attention to her absence and confirms that absentness is the form in which she now appears. The same point could be made about *Alice's Adventures in Wonderland,* where the more frequently the Queen of Hearts screams "Off with their heads!" the less credible her authority becomes, to the point where the King of Hearts quietly pardons them all; and where Alice's realization that they are "nothing but a pack of cards!"—as multiple and reproducible as chess pieces, as fantasmatic as the Queen of Trumps—coincides with her waking up and mastering her dream.[56] Fictions of making queens only call attention to the vacuousness of the task.

Through the Looking-Glass, then, may be about the work of constructing the cultural icon Queen Victoria without being about Queen Victoria. It would be a mistake to look for direct representations of her in the *Alice* books' queens, despite the tempting resemblance offered by the peremptory Queen of Hearts or by the plump, dowdy White Queen who can add but not subtract.[57] But the story repels attempts at allegorical decoding, a point made abundantly clear by the perpetrators of *Queen Victoria's Alice in Wonderland,* a clumsy parody of deconstructive and historicist critical methods that pretends to argue that Queen Victoria wrote *Alice* as a crypto autobiog-

FIGURE 31 John Tenniel, two illustrations from chapter 9, "Queen Alice," Lewis Carroll's *Through the Looking Glass*, 1872.

raphy.[58] Victoria cannot be found in these texts any more than she can be found in "Of Queens' Gardens" or in any of the texts that multiply queens in this period. But if they are not simply about Queen Victoria, the *Alice* books do reveal something about the process of making Queen Victoria, the kind of process that occurs when "Of Queens' Gardens," *Miss Marjoribanks,* and Eliot's novels manufacture the image of female monarchy that they simultaneously draw upon.

Both *Alice* books are characterized by tropological reversibility: although I have emphasized that the chess pieces constitute the literalizing of figures—especially of Ruskin's and Tennyson's prosopopoeias—it is also true that they are figures, as chess pieces represent real kings and queens, and also insofar as the Red Queen is an anthropomorphic transformation of Alice's real-world black kitten. (The same would be true of the cards in *Wonderland:* they are both stylized, figurative representations of actual royalty and—because they are, after all, things—literalizations of the idea of royalty.) And in like manner Alice never solves the puzzle of whether she is dreaming the Red King or the Red King is dreaming her. Similarly the looking-glass insects—the rocking-horse-fly, the bread-and-butter-fly—are identical with their ordinary-language names (132). Although these names pun on the names of real insects, it is impossible to say whether the creatures or the words came first, whether they have intrinsic meanings or are personifications, words given form. Humpty Dumpty, Tweedledum and Tweedledee, and the other characters drawn from nursery rhymes are determined by the rhymes' words (mastered by them, as it were: Humpty Dumpty will inexorably fall off the wall), and yet they see themselves as independent agents of which the rhymes are secondary descriptions. This array of reversible representational relations corresponds to my suggestion that *Miss Marjoribanks* and "Of Queens' Gardens" construct Queen Victoria fully as much as Victoria can be said to be a resource for those texts' figurations. Both lead to the same circular logic in which each of two terms depends upon the other for its definition. This is the looking-glass logic of signification, but it is also a theory of cultural production that resonates powerfully in the decade of the Queen's absence.

The varied attention the *Alice* books pay to naming and to possible disjunctions between creatures and their names corresponds not only to the literary effort to constitute the Queen or to represent her absence, but also to the Queen's own worries about representation during her widowhood discussed in the first part of this chapter. "Mere representation" is her name for such public appearances as performing the Queen's Speech or presiding over a drawing room or levee, performances from which she "shrinks" and to which she claims to feel no connection, even if, before Albert's death, she might once have done so. (In *Through the Looking-Glass* what most closely approximates her expressed feeling is the woods where creatures lose their names altogether, and Alice and the fawn can exist in temporary harmony.) These "representations" misrepresent her and can best be visualized through images of her separation from the standard iconography of royalty: Frith's picture of her spectacularly ghostly appearance at the Prince of Wales's wedding, her silent and rigid presence during the reading of the 1866 Queen's Speech, the *Tomahawk* cartoon of empty throne and royal robes. The Queen's failure or refusal to embody or be her representations, or to perform them convincingly, her retreat from and behind them into an invisible world of "duties" and grief, partakes of something like the representational structure of Ruskin's prosopopoeia or failed allegory in "Of Queen's Gardens." Our anxious Ruskinian question, "But,—*are* they queens?" if asked of the Queen's "representations" at this time would have to be answered in the negative, despite her family's, her secretaries', and her ministers' wishes to the contrary. If the desired condition would be that of Lucilla Marjoribanks at the end of her story, luminously at one with her own monumental representation, the Queen's seclusion has made her into a failed allegory, a personification with the seams showing. No longer radiant with the intrinsic meaning of "Queen"—at least not for all spectators—she verges on exposing the arbitrariness with which the meaning of "Queen" is assigned to her, just as Ruskin's and Carroll's texts in their opposite ways expose the arbitrariness of their efforts to make girls into queens. The *Times*—dyspeptically complaining of failed allegory—implies that she ceases to be Queen when she is not performing in public; her defenders—maintaining that Queen is her intrinsic meaning—claim that "in seclusion or in society, Queen Victoria will reign in the hearts of her subjects." Ruskin's text expresses something like the same wish expressed by the 1864 cartoon of Victoria as Hermione, that she would coincide with her own statuesque representation. While the impossibly euphoric ending of Oliphant's novel devises a queen identical to her name and to her monumental queenly image, *Through the Looking-Glass* gleefully, and "Of Queens' Gardens" mournfully, show the difficulty of making that wish real.

3

THE WIDOW AS AUTHOR AND THE ARTS AND POWERS OF CONCEALMENT

During the 1860s the chief issue of Victoria's monarchy was representational: what representational forms her monarchy could assume given her personal seclusion in widowhood. But the same period also witnessed debate and agitation about another kind of representation—electoral reform—culminating in the passage of the Reform Bill of 1867. As Catherine Gallagher has argued, the debate over reform was at heart a debate not only about who should be represented but also about the nature of representation.[1] Electoral reform would have arrived in any event, but that the passage of this particular phase of it occurred when it did meant that it gave meaning to and took meaning from Victoria's reclusiveness. This chapter will consider in the context of the reform debate one representational strategy adopted by Victoria and by others writing about her during this period: the representation of absence as presence and of concealment as power. This chapter will argue that there is an inverse and complementary relation between, on the one hand, Britain's slow movement toward direct or "descriptive" representation of constituencies in Parliament and, on the other, Victoria's sudden change from immediate and personal self-presentation to more indirect and displaced forms of representation. Her subjects come to occupy some of the space of self-representation left vacant by the mourning Queen. Neither the Queen nor her subjects, of course, have access to transparent or accurate self-representation. For commentators on both kinds of representation—that of the Queen and that of the people—"representation" is virtually equivalent to "misrepresentation," despite, or especially in the presence of, insistence on "truth." As the Queen moved from one form of misrepresentation to another, so did the people of Britain move from yet another kind of misrepresentation to another still. Nonetheless, the Queen's retreat from embodied self-representation (which is also a disguise) into doubly displaced literary forms of representation (which, although they involve disguise, seem to readers "truthful," and more so than her previous "representations") complements the movement toward greater popular political representation, unsatisfactory though the results of the 1867 Reform Bill initially were.

Monarchic power was by no means all that stood in the way of British democracy, and yet demands for electoral progress coincided exactly with the accidents of Victoria's life that removed her from public view during the 1860s. In Chapter 1, I argued that the monarch of nineteenth-century Britain had to be a woman, and a married woman; here I will argue that, for the monarchy to complete its transformation into a wholly symbolic function at the head of a representative state, the best possible occupant of the throne was a widow.

Bagehot's *The English Constitution*

Writings and speeches from the 1860s about reform and about the British government testify to uncertainties about the adequacy of existing representational forms, literary and political. Catherine Gallagher, writing about the 1840s and the 1860s, shows that changes in the theory and practice of literary and political representation evolved together through the medium of changing ideas about literary realism. I wish to take her approach as my starting point, reaching different conclusions from hers by attending to a different canon of representational forms. Tracing the afterlife of Coleridge's faith in the state as "representative symbol" of God's will, she shows that Disraeli initially favored a strong monarchy and aristocracy in his "antidescriptive theory of Parliamentary representation," a theory opposed to Chartist demands for numerical or descriptive representation of the people and to James Mill's utilitarian call for a "detailed, proportional rendering of English society" (*Industrial Reformation*, 195, 203, 222). Inheriting this opposition in the reform debates of the 1860s, the difference between the radical reformer John Bright and his liberal opponent Robert Lowe was, Gallagher argues, an opposition between descriptive or numerical representation on the one hand and, on the other, symbolic representation, an opposition that found its equivalent in literary practice of the day. For Arnold, "true culture [is] the representation of the best self formed through an acquaintance with true representations of 'the nature of things'" (249). Although George Eliot had begun her career as a novelist espousing synecdochal realism, she also extended Arnold's idea of pure culture as the representation of representations to the realm of politics, endorsing the Arnoldian solution of replacing parliamentary representation for the masses with pure representations of culture. In this way she and other culture conservatives could privilege symbolic representation in the realm of politics.[2] Although Queen Victoria's literary and political practices, like those of the monarchy's supporters, initially appear to conform to the view Gallagher ascribes to Arnold and Eliot (and stretching back through Disraeli to Coleridge), careful reading of the texts of her widowhood in the 1860s suggest as well a countercurrent of support for other, more populist forms of representation.

Walter Bagehot's 1866 *The English Constitution*, fluently and rapidly written as a series of magazine articles for the *Fortnightly Review*, opens with a curiously expressed anxiety about representation.

> "On all great subjects," says Mr. Mill, "much remains to be said," and of none is this more true than of the English Constitution. The literature which has accumulated upon it is huge. But an observer who looks at the living reality will wonder at the contrast to the paper description.[3]

The next few paragraphs go on to detail some of the misconceptions that have arisen about the Constitution. R. H. S. Crossman explains the allusion to Mill as Bagehot's polite criticism of Mill's failure, in *Representative Government* (1861), to understand the importance of the Cabinet in the real or "efficient" workings of government.[4] While Bagehot claims greater accuracy or descriptive realism for his account, he also claims to have a clearer idea of the representational structure of government itself, for his great discovery is the separation between what he calls "the dignified parts" and the "efficient parts ... of the Constitution" (*English Constitution*, 61). The monarchy and Lords comprise the "dignified" part, which puts on a good show, as contrasted to the "efficient" parts, Commons and above all the Cabinet, which Mill had overlooked as the place where the real work of governing the country is done. Each of these parts has its own dignified and efficient aspects; even the monarchy has its efficient side. The dignified parts of the government are a disguise or outward (mis)representation of the efficient parts, and this representational structure Mill had failed accurately to represent.

At the same time that Bagehot claims greater accuracy for his account of government, he also implies a fear that any such representation will only entail further representations, as indeed Mill's has. And when introducing the 1872 second edition of the book, Bagehot refers self-deprecatingly to "his representations" of the living reality of government as necessarily inaccurate (267). By beginning his book with the difficulty and endlessness of writing about the Constitution, Bagehot implies that having a Constitution is equivalent to attempting to represent it, or to finding the difficulty of representing it. The Constitution lives on only in the discourse about it and, as a representational structure, must itself be represented in order to be effective. This suggestion would seem to displace the issue, obviously urgent in 1866, of another kind of representation: the debate over who shall elect parliamentary representatives for the counties and boroughs of Britain.

Focusing attention on representing the Constitution rather than on representing the people, and on representational structures internal to government rather than on the government's success or failure in representing the nation, might seem to add Bagehot to the list of Arnoldian conservatives such as Eliot who, in Gallagher's view, sought to replace expansion of the vote with representations of representations. Certainly Bagehot was as opposed as Mill was to democracy, both of them fearing "the tyranny of the majority."[5] But Bagehot's account of this representational structure within government may also illuminate what the representation of Britain's peoples meant to him and others debating reform. His anxiety about correctly representing the Constitution, and his argument that the dignified parts constitute the deliberate misrepresentation of the efficient parts, suggest doubts about whether any constituency's desire to be represented can or even should be met. To Gallagher's dialectic between descriptive on the one hand and, on the other, symbolic and eventually "pure" or cultural representation, I would add a related dialectic between descriptive representation and representational disguise. Whereas, in Gallagher's account, Felix Holt "represents a pure, disinterested politics and a pure, disinterested culture that ostensibly represent only one another. . . . independen[tly of] the very things politics and culture had been formerly said to represent: the social and the divine" (*Industrial Reformation*, 245, 248), in Bagehot's writing representations are neither synecdochally descriptive of nor purely independent from what they would seem to represent: instead, they deliberately misrepresent so as to conceal.

Comprehending Bagehot's account of the monarch's role as a disguise requires that we first explore more fully how Bagehot and other participants in the reform debates use the terms "representation," "represent," and "representative." As applied to the selection of members of Parliament, these terms slide back and forth between two ends of a spectrum of meanings. On one end of this spectrum is the relatively descriptive or synecdochal kind of representation that would create democracy; at the other end is the relatively symbolic representation that would create a Parliament composed of the wisest and the best. We might now call this the difference between "speaking as" and "speaking for [but not as]." Bagehot's attitude toward these two kinds of representation shifts back and forth as well. When he writes that the majority of the House of Commons "ought to represent the general average intelligence of that country; its various members ought to represent the various special interests" (*English Constitution*, 76), he seems to indicate and recommend descriptive representation. Elsewhere, however, Bagehot explicitly criticizes descriptive representation, so as to make that earlier favorable comment seem retrospectively to have referred instead to symbolic representation. "A representative public meeting is subject to a defect. . . . It may not be independent. The constituencies may not let it alone" (161). In a democratic system, Bagehot acerbically notes, the towns "would send up persons representing the beliefs or unbeliefs of the lowest classes" (162). Parliament works best, Bagehot concludes, when "the overwhelming majority of the representatives are men essentially moderate, of no marked varieties, free from class prejudices" (163), that is, symbolic representatives who would then of necessity best represent by misrepresenting (or ignoring the low-class concerns of) their constituencies.

By contrast, a few pages later symbolic representation comes in for criticism: in an obvious injustice, "Half the boroughs in England are represented by considerable landowners" (173). Descriptive representation again starts to gain points: "[T]he true reason for admitting the working classes to a share in the representation" is the benefit the public would receive from the expression of the "ideas . . . feelings [and] intellectual life" of the "town artisans" (181). Even so, it is not they themselves but their "advocates" Bagehot wishes to see included. In this wish he was in the majority, as the denial of any salary to MPs until 1912 effectively prevented any working-class person from synecdochally representing his class.[6] In this passage, moreover, "the representation" (a phrase often used in this period) suggests a static entity to which workers may or may not be admitted. Either way, "representation" means misrepresentation of the interests of those groups now seeking the franchise.

Bagehot's equivocation both about the definition of "representation" and about its value is reflected in writings and speeches by others at the time, including ardent reformers. According to historian F. B. Smith, "The Reformers' advocacy of a selective enfranchisement on the grounds of social utility necessarily involved the rejection of any claim that the franchise was a natural right"; the franchise was a trust that would be awarded only to a man "who was likely to use his vote rationally and independently to elect representatives who would uphold the good order and best interests of the State" (*Making*, 26). If the vote was a right, pointed out the radical Sir Francis Crossley, it would have to be given to women (*Making*, 27); that few in Parliament sought to enfranchise women suggests that those involved in the debate preferred some version of symbolic representation to purely descriptive or numerical representation.[7] Even the proreform *Saturday Review* rejected the idea that Parliament should comprise "500 members who shall be a little England in miniature," seeing instead as the aim of reform "to give political power to large, flourishing, modernized constituencies, and to take it away from small, decaying, antique constituencies."[8] The "Resolutions" drafted by Disraeli and Derby in 1867 after the failure of the Liberal party to pass reform in 1866 included formulations that again treated representation as a static entity that could be "given" or "supplied" to classes and places not then enfranchised (quoted in *Making*, 138). Likewise, the liberal Samuel Laing did not want "the representation" to be numerical (*Making*, 215). Resistance to numerical representation is also suggested by repeated calls, not only from Bagehot but also from Mill and other reformers—from right and left—for the country to be protected from majority rule.[9]

Nonetheless, F. B. Smith concludes that the country was gradually shifting its definition of representation. The workers who attended Bright's mass urban meetings between parliamentary sessions believed in their "honest rights" (*Making*, 140–41). The "minority clause," which gave a third MP to twelve constituencies, functioning as something like a Derridean supplement,

> [b]y providing a representative for the upper-class minority in the great towns and counties, . . . implicitly denied the old theory that members represented the total range of interests in their locality. (*Making*, 240)

Although its proponents treated it as a mechanism to restore an older, symbolic notion of representation—"you would obtain in the persons of those who would be the representatives of the minority in these large constituencies a body of men of great intelligence and of great independence"—the editorial in which the *Daily Telegraph* thus quotes Lord Cairns (1 August 1867) sees straight through this ruse and makes it clear that an upper-class minority is no different from any other minority that must accept its disappointment: "Even if Lord Cairns secured a member for one minority . . . there would always be a further minority unrecognised." The editorial thus establishes that Lord Cairns is seeking exactly the opposite kind of representation to what he claims: claiming to enable the choice of the wisest and the best, he merely wants "an exponent of [his] political views." In Smith's view, "the minority clause accelerated the movement towards the representation of numbers rather than localities" (*Making*, 241), because it established a precedent for ensuring representation of all classes. The minority clause was the only amendment proposed by Lords that survived in the final bill as passed by Commons and was considered by many to be a "sop to the Lords" to make the bill "almost palatable" to conservative MPs,[10] and yet its ultimate effect may have been, as Smith suggests, among the most radical of the bill as a whole.

Smith's analysis thus points to the equivocal effects of the Reform Bill as regards representation. Just as its contemporary opponents and advocates wavered between two opposing senses of the word representation, historians have emphasized, on the one hand, that it decisively changed the electorate (which now included renters in addition to owners, for example) and initiated progress toward numerical or descriptive representation, and, on the other hand, that it tended in effect to preserve the older, symbolic notion of representation.[11] That symbolic notion of representation—on its way out, yet enduring for the time—corresponds to Bagehot's use of "representation" to articulate both his worry that he can only misrepresent the Constitution and his theory that monarchy is a "disguise." Although Bagehot's adherence to this older idea of representation prevents him from actively seeking any alternative to it and leads him instead to advocate ever more indirect and displaced forms of representation, I will also suggest that his argument contains and proposes its reverse, and that Victoria too undermines her own endorsement of symbolic or cultural representation.

Bagehot's initial chapter, on the Cabinet as the efficient part of the Constitution, emphasizes that the apparent and traditional division of government into three separate and balanced parts—"Kings, Lords, and Commons"—is not, contrary to popular understanding, the "inner moving essence" (*English Constitution*, 60) of government. Instead, the dignified parts, especially the monarchy, are what "excite and preserve the reverence of the population" (61). Given the ignorance and credulity of most of that population, these are necessarily

> the *theatrical* elements—those which appeal to the senses, which claim to be embodiments of the greatest human ideas, which boast in some cases of far more than human origin. That which is mystic in its claims; that which is occult in its mode of action; that which is brilliant to the eye; that which is seen vividly for a moment, and then is seen no more; that which is hidden and unhidden; ... this ... is the sort of thing ... which yet comes home to the mass of men. (*English Constitution*, 64)

Bagehot insists upon his theatrical metaphor: later he describes royalty as a "pageant" (90), a "procession" (249), or a "theatrical show" (248).

While scholars of the English Renaissance such as Stephen Greenblatt and Stephen Orgel have long argued that its monarchy was essentially theatrical, existing as a spectacular display of power—citing, for example, Elizabeth I's famous dictum, "[w]e princes ... are set on stages, in the sight and view of all the world duly observed"—the theatricality of the Victorian monarchy is of a different kind, in Bagehot's account.[12] Whereas Elizabethans do not distinguish between the appearance and reality of power, for Bagehot monarchic theater is mere theater, separated from governmental power; there is a clear line between the thing itself and its representation. Monarchic pageantry, he argues, serves as a "disguise" (97) for the efficient workings of government, which are all the more effective for going on in secret. The great benefit of monarchy is that it makes for "an intelligible government" (82), one that is more "comprehensible" (85) than an unadorned republic because it focuses attention on "one person doing interesting actions" instead of on "many, who are all doing uninteresting actions" (86), and on "difficult ideas" (85). A family is particularly "interesting" to the common mind, Bagehot says, especially to women, who "care fifty times more for a marriage than for a ministry" (85).[13] The book concludes with a footnote—itself a sort of concealed text—on the likelihood that a "cabman" will not have heard of Downing Street "and will not in the least know where to take you" (266).

This notion of monarchy as disguise resembles Disraeli's 1845 position, according to Gallagher, that the monarchy is the symbolic representative both of the "nation as a whole" and (following Coleridge) of "God's sovereignty" (*Industrial Reformation*, 201–2). But whereas Disraeli treats this symbolic function reverentially, and is undisturbed by the manifest noncorrespondence between the monarch and what she is said to represent (or between aristocratic Tory MPs and the populace they are said to represent), Bagehot's focus on the dramatic difference between the monarch and the government she conceals, his focus on disguise and misrepresentation, suggests equivocation about the representational structure he outlines and ostensibly praises.[14] His tone is often condescending both toward hereditary monarchy, where "dullness" of mind must predominate, and toward the ignorant populace that is its dupe.

Although Victoria hardly shared Bagehot's cynicism about the deliberately misleading quality of her role as show or spectacle, she was aware of the value placed by others on her role as performer.[15] Moreover, that she shared his understanding of the structure of her job, divided between its own dignified and efficient parts, is suggested by her resistance (as discussed in Chapter 2) to the pressure to perform and her belief in the greater importance of her behind-the-scenes work as monarch. The marriage Bagehot alludes to was that of the Prince of Wales in March 1863, discussed above in terms of Victoria's understanding of it as "a scene in a play" (*Letters and Journals*, 173). The "mere representation" to which the Queen objects in the letter she authorized in the London *Times* (6 April 1864) is associated with performance (ceremonies that can be "performed" by any royal family member, like the "scene" of the Prince of Wales's wedding), and she clearly distinguishes it from the work to which she refers as "duties," the "efficient" part of her job. Although she takes those duties much more seriously than does Bagehot and protests against the performances that would weaken her for what she sees as her real work, her account concurs with his demarcation between "dignified" performance and efficient work. In the letter to the *Times* and in her response to being asked to open Parliament in 1865, "representation" or "mere representation" refers to the "dignified" part of her job, yet she invariably uses the term negatively, as when Bagehot calls his inaccuracies "representations." When "representation" means "misrepresentation," confirming a distinction between the monarch's private and public (or efficient and dignified) aspects, Bagehot's theory of statecraft proves true: when (mis)representing herself in her body, she is also serving (according to Bagehot) as a disguise or misrepresentation for something else. Widowhood, with its accentuation of the gap between Queen and representation, makes her the ideal modern monarch of a parliamentary state.[16]

When objecting to her "use" as a performer, Victoria most frequently refers to her ceremonial obligations inside Parliament, but, recording her response to opening Parliament in 1867 (the year reform finally passed), she finds that the performance outside Parliament is just as painful:

> that stupid Reform agitation has excited and irritated people, and there was a good deal of hissing, some groans and calls for Reform, which I—in my present forlorn position—ought not to be exposed to. There were many, nasty faces—and I felt it painfully. At such times the Sovereign should not be there.[17]

Here, her performance or "representation" of herself as herself (which is in turn a misrepresentation of herself and a disguise for or misrepresentation of the working government) conflicts with another kind of representation, the democratic representation for which these "nasty faces" agitate. These two self-representations cannot coincide, for they make identical and mutually exclusive claims to sovereignty. "At such times the Sovereign should not be there": the direct representation of the people (which is only another form of misrepresentation, but one that they demand) will eventually replace Victoria's embodied "representations."

The Queen's opinion about the Reform Bill and about earlier and subsequent parliamentary efforts toward electoral reform was sufficiently equivocal to cause disagreement among her biographers. On the one hand, Giles St.

Aubyn stresses her favorable view, quoting her observation of "a growing feeling for it in the country amongst all the respectable classes" (*Queen Victoria*, 374–75, quoting RA Queen Victoria's Journal, 9 October 1866). This emphasis is possibly supported by a letter in which, prompted by her daughter Vicky's progressivism, she inveighs against the dissolute habits of "the higher classes—expecially the aristocracy"—and then writes: "The lower classes are becoming so well-informed, are so intelligent and earn their bread and riches so deservedly—that they cannot and ought not to be kept back—to be abused by the wretched, ignorant, high-born beings who live only to kill time" (*Your Dear Letter*, 165, 18 December 1867). The controversy in the papers in December 1864 (see Chapter 2) helps suggest why she might have favored "the people"—by which she means the working and middle classes—over elite "Society": it was not "the people" who complained when she canceled fancy state balls and levees (see Longford, *Queen Victoria*, 352).

On the other hand, Longford quotes these same remarks as favoring reform, but she cites also the Queen's annoyance with "this wretched reform" in April 1866 (Longford, *Queen Victoria*, 349), because it was causing a ministerial crisis at a time of impending war between Prussia and Austria. The Queen's letter indicates her priorities: "if anything can be done [Lord Russell] is most anxious to effect it; but there are many troubles at home and I fear a Ministerial crisis is impending on account of this wretched Reform which I fear has been brought too hurriedly and carelessly forward" (*Your Dear Letter*, 24 March 1866, 63). Thus, both aristocrats and reformers are "wretched," the term she also uses to characterize the winter day when her appearance to open Parliament drew "hissing, some groans and calls for Reform:" "a wretched day" (*Your Dear Letter*, 120, 5 February 1867). Longford concludes that while Victoria was sentimentally favorable to reform, her chief wish was for both sides to "buckle to" (Longford, *Queen Victoria*, 352, quoting RA Queen Victoria's Journal, 24 July 1867). Stanley Weintraub too finds her impatient with the issue (*Victoria*, 341). Moreover, in 1880 she wrote that she "*cannot* and will not be the Queen of a *democratic monarchy;* and those who have spoken and agitated, for the sake of party and to injure their opponents, in a very radical sense must look for *another monarch;* and she doubts they will find one."[18]

Her sentimental preference for "the people" thus does not necessarily translate into a desire to enfranchise them. Elaine Hadley argues that her use as a heroine in the "royal melodrama" was to help "manage [or contain] the energies of social change," including the impulse to reform (*Melodramatic Tactics*, 138). It appears that she opposed democracy and that, even with her mildly favorable view of electoral reform, it was not among her favorite causes. If she was eager to see the matter settled, it was so as to stave off further attempts at democracy and so that her Government (whichever it was at the time) could attend to more important business, such as the Prussian-Austrian war, or allocating funds for building more memorials to Albert. Thus, despite her lack of active partisanship for seeing "the people" represented in Parliament, her wish to cease representing herself lends inadvertent authority to their wish to take "the representation" over as their own. If they are going to agitate for reform, "the Sovereign should not be there;" and if they achieve democracy, they "must look for another monarch." Her representations—or those of any alternative monarch—and theirs cannot occupy the same stage. I will argue later in this chapter that although she may have preferred to see her subjects' power as a reflection of her own, her writing expresses a wish to consent to their self-representation.

When Victoria appeared in Parliament in 1866, dramatically performing her reluctance to perform by sitting silent and crownless while the Lord Chancellor read the Queen's Speech, she forced the "efficient" part of government to express or represent itself. While her widowhood might seem helpfully to clarify the gap between monarch and government, or between dignified and efficient parts of government, to widen that gap too far is to put at risk the cover under which government efficiently functions, just as her desire to absent herself from scenes of democratic agitation inadvertently gives room to those agitations. Her dramatic performance of her absence revealed where the real workings of government lay. But Bagehot is arguing against democracy, and wishes the monarchy to keep up its function as "disguise" for the real work of government by skilled and intelligent ministers acting in secrecy. This wish again corresponds, but with a difference, to Disraeli's hope in 1845 that the symbolic function of monarchy might forestall the arrival of descriptive representation sought by reformers. This disguise "enables our real rulers to change without heedless people knowing it" (*English Constitution*, 97). Moreover,

> [t]he excitement of choosing our rulers is prevented by the apparent existence of an unchosen ruler. The poorer and more ignorant classes—those who would most feel excitement, who would most be misled by excitement—really believe that the Queen governs. You could not explain to them the recondite difference between "reigning" and "governing;" the words necessary to express it do not exist in their dialect. (*English Constitution*, 241)

The masses of people take the figure of the Queen literally, for Bagehot, and their naivete is at once rhetorical and historical. They take "reign" as a figure for "govern," because, anachronistically keyed to an older idea of monarchy in which the spectacle of government was the government, they find the dead metaphor of the Queen's power alive and well. Belief in the efficient power of the monarchy is like belief in the truth claims of outworn maxims: "every generation inherits a series of inapt words—of maxims once true, but of which the truth is ceasing or has ceased" (*English Constitution,* 59). (This comment about discerning the "living reality" of the Constitution beyond the "paper description" applies equally to Bagehot's idea of the monarchy.) Explaining that the real head of government is the prime minister elected by Commons, even if officially named by the Queen, Bagehot writes that monarchic government is a set of words that are no longer literally true. "A century ago the Crown had a real choice of Ministers. . . . They were not only in name, as now, but in fact, the Queen's servants" (66). Although the gap that widowhood accentuates between the private Queen and her (mis)representations serves Bagehot's polemic nicely, like gaps between words and their referents, that gap is helpful only so long as both terms are sustained. For the Queen to perform her absence as dramatically as she did in February 1866 threatens to undermine his hopes for a royal disguise that would dampen agitation for democracy. Should the people observe that the Cabinet and not the Queen governs—as her nonperformance in Parliament gave them an opportunity to do—their desire to choose that Cabinet might well increase. Bagehot should wish the monarchic spectacle to remain as showy and distracting as possible.[19]

Bagehot therefore insists that government correctly goes to some lengths to sustain the fiction or "theory" (*English Constitution,* 229) of the monarch's agency, by continuing to attribute to her the power to dissolve Parliament and to summon a new government, and by insisting that she read the Queen's Speech. "In theory," Bagehot concedes, the Queen does have these powers, but they are "yearly ebbing" through disuse (231). (The only agency Bagehot wants to attribute to the Queen is the fictive one granted her by government; what her real agency might be, or what she thinks it is, we would have to learn elsewhere.) In Trollope's *Can You Forgive Her?* (serialized 1864–65) the sycophant Mr. Bott insists on unchivalrously puncturing this fiction:

> "You don't mean to say that the Queen will send for Planty Pall?" said the young member.
> "I mean to say that the Queen will send for anyone that the House of Commons may direct her to call upon," said Mr. Bott, who conceived himself to have gauged the very depths of our glorious Constitution. "How hard it is to make anyone understand that the Queen has really nothing to do with it!"[20]

Bott is advised by Calder Jones, the author's figure for himself in the novel, to "draw it mild," but even so he is punished by being made nearly the most obnoxious character in the novel and by not being returned at the next election. The novel, like Bagehot, acknowledges that the Queen's agency is a fiction even as it insists that all decent Englishmen must be invested in maintaining its credibility. Even Victoria's heartfelt emphasis on the value of her behind-the-scenes work (the "duties" she shoulders in the letter to the *Times*) contributes to maintaining this fiction, by giving the appearance that she herself believes in it.

Given Bagehot's insistence on maintaining the fiction of the Queen's agency, even if as a fiction, and on describing the monarchy as the visible show behind which real government is concealed, it is odd that he also emphasizes, in writing about the monarchy as theatrical spectacle, that its disappearance is as important as its appearance. "English royalty . . . is commonly hidden like a mystery" (*English Constitution*, 90). It is "seen vividly for a moment, and then is seen no more" (64). Bagehot's emphasis suggests that Victoria's widowhood is his paradigm, since almost all that was on view during the years of his book was her invisibility. Describing the monarch's role as "head of our society" (*English Constitution*, 90–96), Bagehot attempts to reconcile Victoria's conspicuous absence from society with her position at the head of it. Far from being a problem that "the Court is not quite as gorgeous as we might wish to see it," it is advantageous, for any greater show would encourage the aristocracy in unseemly displays of "showy wealth—if it gave the sanction of its dignity to the race of expenditure" (96). The monarchy "is of use so long as it keeps others out of the first place, and is guarded and retired in that place." A retired widow (if not also her unemployed son), in the famous opening phrase of the chapter on monarchy, would seem, paradoxically, to be the ideal head of society; and yet, as we have seen, her retirement—when carried too far—risks undoing the very structure of disguise Bagehot celebrates. Why, then, does Bagehot emphasize her hiddenness?

In "hidden monarch" dramas from the reign of James I, Leonard Tennenhouse can discern a celebration of monarchic authority: in plays such as *Measure for Measure* the ruler vanishes only so that the play can celebrate his return and the return of law and order with him. Victoria's hiddenness, for those living through the 1860s, had no such tidy prospect of closure.[21] Indeed, whereas Tennenhouse finds that the Jacobean plays' representation of a gap between ruler and state power (formerly, "the state walk[ed] with him" [*Power on Display*, 155]) seeks its own closure, Bagehot seeks to maintain the separation between monarch and state, between real government and its disguise. Tennenhouse's hidden monarchs are essentially variants on the spectacularly visible monarchs Stephen Orgel writes about, their concealment only leading to their dramatically contrasted reappearance. Bagehot's writing specifically about Victoria's concealment carries no secure sense that the monarch will or even should be reunited with the state that she represents. He values her hiddenness for itself. In this age of internalized regimes of surveillance in which power is constitutively invisible and all-seeing, the hiddenness of Victoria furthers the even more truly hidden power of government.

Bagehot's praise for Victoria is not moderate: "If we look to history, we shall find that it is only during the period of the present reign that in England the duties of a constitutional sovereign have ever been well performed" (*English Constitution*, 117). Victoria's withdrawal, then, as much the maintenance of the distracting fiction of her agency—her absence as much as her presence—fulfills the Constitutional description of the monarch's role, according to Bagehot's equivocal account. For Bagehot she serves as "disguise" even when she is refusing to perform these "representations," for her retirement and the ebbing of her powers make just as interesting a show as her earlier presence and appearance of power had been—a paradox confirmed by the painting of the Prince of Wales's wedding, with its spectacular display of Victoria's nonparticipation, or by her spectacularly vacant presence on the occasion of opening Parliament.

In thus celebrating her exemplary absence, however, Bagehot risks compromising his own antidemocratic stance: democratic and even republican agitation takes its cue from her ceasing to perform the monarchy. Republicanism surfaced as serious movement during her reign only in 1870–71, provoked in part by continued objections to her disappearance (and then defused by the national enthusiasm over the recovery of the Prince of Wales and later of the Queen from life-threatening illnesses, recoveries that occasioned massive public spectacles displaying the healthy royals to their subjects). Historians tend to give the radical John Bright credit for chivalrous behavior when, in response to attacks on the Queen for her disappearance, he celebrated her deep mourning for its promise that she would sympathize with suffering working men; yet he may only have been saying that men like him could do very well without her now. Her absence makes the monarchy appear unthreatening—a pitiable widow for Bright, not worth bothering to overthrow, a social leader who discourages extravagance for Bagehot—even as her absence also showed how unnecessary the monarch was to the continuous operation of government. Her invisibility earns her Bagehot's praise, yet he wants her invisibility to remain on display—a visible absence, not an absence *tout court*.

When Bagehot commends her retirement, what he really has in mind is the way her retirement signifies her real if hidden power, as each side of his argument folds into the other. The Queen is a conspicuous disguise for real government, but then it must be admitted that she is not conspicuous; even so, behind the dramatic front of her retirement, it turns out he claims the Queen still holds her prerogatives. Behind the facade of doing a lot (summoning governments into being and dissolving them), the monarchy actually does very little (it is really Commons who decides), but this little doing turns out to be an appearance too, for behind it "the Crown does more than it seems. . . . the best Liberal politicians say, '*We* shall never know . . . what we owe to the Queen and Prince Albert'" (*English Constitution,* 100).[22] (Indeed, in 1864, although she did not open Parliament, she "dinned into the Prime Minister's ears" her insistence that Britain stay out of the Prussian war, while the bellicose Parliament took the side of the Danes, and thus influenced the composition of the Queen's Speech even if she did not perform it [Longford, *Queen Victoria,* 319–20].) Her "secret prerogatives" (*English Constitution,* 100) are ghostly, both present and absent. Referring to her quite legal but unsuccessful attempt to create some life peers, Bagehot writes that "the Queen has a hundred such powers which waver between reality and desuetude" (99). Because presence and absence disguise each other, her power is fundamentally unrepresentable: "There is no authentic explicit information as to what the Queen can do, any more than of what she does" (99).

Here and elsewhere in the volume, Bagehot conjures a vast shadowy realm of queenly powers that are simultaneously present and absent either because it is legally unclear whether they exist or because their use has ceased to be customary. He dramatizes the ambiguous status of these powers through his rhetorical use of *occupatio*. *Occupatio* is Bagehot's rhetorical model for the equivocal monarchic presence and absence that he both observes and recommends. For the Queen to destroy a ministry with a secure majority in Parliament, although she may in theory do so, would seem to the people "like a volcanic eruption from Primrose Hill" (*English Constitution,* 229). What remains in the mind is not the proper ebbing of her prerogatives (for which Bagehot is ostensibly arguing), but the presence of the volcano. Bagehot includes in his 1872 introduction to the second edition a catalogue of "what the Queen can by law do without consulting Parliament":

> [S]he could disband the army . . . ; she could dismiss all the officers, from the General Commanding-in-Chief downwards; she could dismiss all the sailors too; she could sell off all our ships of war and all our naval stores; she could make a peace by the sacrifice of Cornwall, and begin a war for the conquest of Brittany. She could make every citizen in the United King-

dom, male or female, a peer; she could make every parish in the United Kingdom a 'university'; she could dismiss most of the civil servants; she could pardon all offenders. In a word, the Queen could by prerogative upset all the action of civil government within the Government, could disgrace the nation by a bad war or peace, and could, by disbanding our forces, whether land or sea, leave us defenceless against foreign nations. (*English Constitution*, 287)

Bagehot invokes monarchic powers only to assure readers that the absent Queen will never use them. His assurances, however, fall somewhat short. The only "checks" on the Queen's powers he can cite are threats Parliament might make to her ministers: the threat of impeachment or of change of government. Having cited her powers in order to alleviate fear of them, those powers remain rhetorically vivid. The hyperbolic tone of the passage, arising in part from Bagehot's manic repetition of what was already excessive, recalls the comedy of Wonderland: like the multiplication of queens in the *Alice* books, his multiplication of fantasmatic queenly powers (which could be paraphrased "Off with their heads!") serves to make the Queen present, but by representing her absence in terms of the things she will never do. In place of and parallel to Ruskin's and Carroll's proliferation of queenly figures that suggest both a desire for her presence and a defensive trivializing of it, Bagehot constitutes Victoria herself as at once inordinately powerful and entirely lacking in monarchic power; powerful by way of her absence and yet, as a mere figurehead, powerless.

This is the context—Bagehot's celebration of Victoria as a spectacle of monarchic agency that is overtly fictitious (a misrepresentation of something else), visibly invisible, and powerful as an absence—in which I would like now to turn to the Queen's Books and their reception. Bagehot's use of *occupatio* offers a rhetorical model for understanding the strategy the Queen's own books will deploy when, writing from her widowhood, she offers both enactments and representations of her own concealment, with the effect of both compensating for her missing and regretted presence and confirming her desired absence.

The Queen's Books: *The Early Years of His Royal Highness the Prince Consort*

The death of Albert occasioned not only the abrupt end of Victoria's self-representations in public spaces but also her adoption of various substitute forms of royal representation, notably the publication of books originally produced for private circulation.[23] Even before the decision to publish them, these books seem designed to compensate for her absence: her journals for 1864 and 1865 regularly juxtapose remarks about the composition of both books and expressions of her wish to avoid public appearances. In her journal for 7 December 1864, just before the heated controversy in the newspapers discussed in Chapter 2, the Queen notes that both the private edition of her Highland journal and "the beloved Life" (still for private use at that time) were "getting on" (RA Queen Victoria's Journal). Both Elizabeth Longford and Giles St. Aubyn, Victoria's most reliable biographers, state that she hoped the books would substitute for her public presence. Longford writes: "There is more than a hint that she believed the *Leaves* would in future look after her popularity, rendering a drastic alteration in her way of life superfluous" (Longford, *Queen Victoria*, 375; and see St. Aubyn, *Queen Victoria*, 365). In certain ways the books accomplished this aim. Reviewers' use of the phrase "The Queen's Book" to describe each in turn suggests that readers were hungry for some alternative to the increasingly empty convention of the Queen's Speech, as well as for a supplement to her meager public appearances, and the near-universal praise for both books and the immense popularity of the *Leaves* suggest that readers were to some degree satisfied. But formally and thematically these books also represent and emphasize the Queen's continued disappearance, a feature also highlighted by the reviews. Literary self-representation of any kind would of course substitute words for the Queen's body. With *The Early Years of His Royal Highness the Prince Consort* (1867), concealment is a conspicuous formal feature of the narrative and the signature. In *Leaves from the Journal of Our Life in the Highlands* (1868)—whose authorship is not disputed—concealment is a central theme. Even so, reviews emphasize that these indirect forms of representation provide more satisfactory "truth" and "presence" than the Queen's embodied "representations" had lately done.

At the same time, the coincidence of the publication of these books with the passage of the Reform Bill in the summer of 1867 and its delayed extension to Scotland and Ireland in 1868 invites speculation about the relation between the Queen's literary self-representations and "the Representation of the People" (as the bill was formally titled), or electoral representation. Compiled for private circulation during the years of most intense criticism of the Queen's reclusiveness, their public appearance at a slightly later date places both the Queen's motivations in publishing them and their public reception in the context not only of her withdrawal but also of urgent and extended public discussion of the franchise. The "Queen's Books" may have both opposed democracy—by attempting in an Arnoldian way to replace it with literary representation—and encouraged it, by ceding the public space of self-misrepresentation to others. "The representation of Scotland," states the *Daily Telegraph* a month after the publication of *Leaves* (Victoria's book about Scotland), "ought to be increased" (17 February 1868): this statement could be taken as a symptom that *Leaves* has failed in whatever Arnoldian aims it may have had; it could also be taken to show that the Queen's literary representations of Scotland lend support to Scots reform. By publicly representing herself, but as an ambiguously concealed presence, the Queen may have tacitly endorsed the nation's clamor for access to more direct political power. Historians and biographers have loosely correlated her absence with the agitation for reform (Longford hints at this in *Queen Victoria*, 351, although her absence more clearly correlates with republicanism); and her enthusiasm for "the people" could appear to be a common thread in *Leaves* and, as we have seen, in one aspect of her view of reform. But these loose correlations deserve to be examined in more detail and with more care for the texts involved. These historical speculations, I will argue, are likely right, but for reasons less obvious than these apparently straightforward correlations can suggest. The remaining sections of this chapter will examine the literary evidence for a view that reverses what Gallagher's argument would have lead us to expect.

The Early Years of His Royal Highness the Prince Consort, completed for private circulation in 1866 and published in July 1867, is the second of three volumes the Queen was to publish in the aftermath of her husband's death, the first being *Speeches and Addresses of the Prince Consort*, edited by Arthur Helps (1862), and the third being *Leaves from the Journal of Our Life in the Highlands*, privately printed in 1865 but not revised and given to the public until January 1868. (In 1884 she published *More Leaves from the Journal of a Life in the Highlands*, selected from the years after Albert's death.)[24] While the authorship of the other books is not disputed, not only contemporary reviewers but even Victoria's recent biographers differ about the authorship of *Early Years*, the title page of which continues: "compiled, under the direction of Her Majesty the Queen, by Lieut.-General the Hon. C. Grey." Giles St. Aubyn's biography states categorically that it was "written by General Grey," confirming his earlier assertion that "General Grey's *Early Years* made use of her letters and diaries, and was written under her direction."[25] Stanley Weintraub explores the matter more fully if perhaps more speculatively. Amongst other forms of commemoration already in process, "there had to be a biography.... What, then, but to write it herself?" (*Victoria*, 336). According to Weintraub, "Victoria brought her manuscript to General Sir Charles Grey, her principal secretary, and asked him to see it through to publication." Grey "found it so candid and guileless that he worried about letting it loose";[26] he urged printing it only for private circulation to family and close friends, on the model of *Leaves.* Weintraub points out that Grey's preface implies that he transformed the raw material of the Queen's journals and memoranda and the Prince's letters into a book, yet Weintraub also believes that Grey's request to have Professor Adam Sedgwick review the contents for historical accuracy "adds weight to the likelihood that [Grey's] substantive role was small." In a letter included in Grey's preface to the published volume, Sedgwick writes of "'Victoria lay[ing] open the innermost recesses of her heart.' . . . Such a work was clearly not General Grey's" (Weintraub, *Victoria,* 337, quoting *Early Years,* Preface, xi). (Elizabeth Longford is silent on the question of authorship.)

As Victoria's secretary, Grey often served as Victoria's pseudonym: she habitually used him, as she used her doctors, to transmit as if they were his own opinions her excuses for not seeing her ministers.[27] As we have seen, Grey (according to the Queen herself) wrote the 6 April 1864 letter to the *Times,* using the Queen's voice effectively enough to convince readers of her authorship (see Chapter 2). Although this habit would lend support to Weintraub's view, during the days of Albert the pseudonymity often went the other way. Albert would draft memoranda for Victoria to "adopt" as her own and deliver as if representing her own opinion (for example, *Early Years,* 304, on the Trent affair). Her ministers wrote the Queen's Speech with which she—or someone else, reading in her name—opened Parliament. Perhaps, rather than Victoria hiding her true authorship behind the name of Grey (Weintraub's view), Grey flatters Victoria by deferentially referring to her "guidance" of a project he himself undertook (St. Aubyn's view). There may be two authors, or, as in the Finale of *Middlemarch,* there may be no author at all. Fred Vincy has written a book on agriculture, and Mary Garth has written a book of stories taken from Plutarch, but Middlemarch decides otherwise. "[M]ost persons there were inclined to believe that the merit of Fred's authorship was due to his wife," while as for Mary's book, "everyone in the town was willing to give the credit of this work to Fred," thanks to his university training. "There was no need to praise anybody for writing a book, since it was always done by somebody else" (*Middlemarch,* 89–91).

An examination of the text of *Early Years* suggests that the case could be made for either position and many in between. The title page of the first published London edition prints the word "Queen" in type only slightly larger than that used for "Grey," but the New York edition (by Harper's) prints "Queen" in type so large that she is indexed as author. Grey refers to himself as "editor of this volume" (Preface, *Early Years,* xii) who has merely "arranged and connected" the materials supplied him (Letter to the Queen, *Early Years,* xv), grateful for having "been allowed to assist in your Majesty's work of love"; and yet these phrases appear in his "Letter to the Queen on Completing the Volume for Private Circulation," and he refers also to his "execution of the work." The Queen's journals and letters lend weight to the argument that Grey took some responsibility for the writing and not merely for "arranging." On 31 January 1863 Victoria writes to Vicky that she is "trying to collect and put together the beginning of that private life,"[28] which suggests not merely assembling materials but also writing them into a narrative; but in May of the same year she writes that she is getting "everything I can together . . . for the private life. General Grey is working at that" (*Dearest Mama*, 220). In the same letter she mentions a book of her own that she differentiates from Grey's project. On 2 February 1864 she writes in her journal: "Saw General Grey and talked of the admirable beginning he has made of the precious Life, which I have just been looking over"; the next day she saw Mr. Helps "about the precious Life and gave him all the papers which we have at present put together" (RA Queen Victoria's Journal, 2 and 3 February 1864). Nonetheless on 3 April 1864 she writes, "Dictated some things to Lenchen, for the precious Life." Similar remarks indicating her at least partial authorship appear in entries for April 11 and 22. The book in one way or another constitutes the Queen's representation of herself, but at several removes from her former practice of making physical appearances.

Whether she did or did not write what she appeared to be pretending Grey wrote for her, resolving the question of who wrote it is less interesting than exploring the reception of the book—especially the public's insistence on attributing it to her—and the uses made of it and of its puzzling authorship. Reviewers differed on the question of Victoria's authorship. Like St. Aubyn the reviewer for the London *Times* takes the title page at face value and states that "it was originally compiled by General Grey, under Her Majesty's direction," although "enriched by numerous memoranda from Her Majesty's own hand" (27 July 1867). The review in *Fraser's Magazine* (by Charles Anthony Froude) likewise states that "[i]t was written under the Queen's eye by General Grey," and with no hint of uncertainty introduces a quotation with the words "General Grey says,"[29] a practice generally followed also by the *Daily Telegraph*. Whereas *Fraser's* narrow view of the Queen's authorship matches its skepticism about the book's hagiographic aims (questioning, for example, whether Prince Albert was "heroic" just for recovering quickly from seasickness [271], as *Early Years* insists), the more simply laudatory review in the newer *London Quarterly Review* states as a "fact that it is substantially the Queen's work," and attributes to this "fact" its "immense circulation" and its high visibility in the newspapers.[30] "For this is truly 'the Queen's Book,'" this review continues; "General Grey has no doubt done his work of editing exceedingly well; but one hand may be traced all through" (201). Margaret Oliphant, writing in *Blackwood's*, emphasizes the Queen's agency, referring to "the volume which her Majesty has just given to the world," and even constructing a theory as to why only the Queen could be the author: just as only a Queen could propose marriage, so only a Queen can be so frank about "the touching and sympathetic story of her own heart and love."[31]

Some reviewers equivocate. Even the *Times*, despite its clear statement that the Queen was not the author, sees the Queen taking "her subjects unreservedly into her confidence. She opens her heart to them in the volume." The *Daily Telegraph* similarly opens with "the simple confidence which the Queen here makes to her people," even though the body of the review distinguishes between Grey's narrative and quotations from the Queen's diary and her notes. The notice in the *Saturday Review* shifts in its first paragraph from calling it "General Grey's record" with "interpolations by a more tender hand" to ascribing it to "the devoted wife who records his virtues."[32] Charles Kingsley, reviewing *Leaves* for *Fraser's*, opens with a puzzlingly equivocal mention of the authorship of *Early Years:* he refers to "its authors," but he also writes, "By telling her own story, simply, earnestly, confidently, her Majesty has appealed . . . ," thus contradicting Froude's view of *Early Years* in the same magazine.[33] The review in the older *London Quarterly Review* asserts that whereas previous acts of apparently royal authorship (except Elizabeth I's) have turned out to be "cheats," "such galling criticisms . . . could not touch the high motives or sacred feelings which have led to the newest example of such a production." Waving aside the evidence of the title page, the reviewer calls it "essentially a royal work."[34]

This review, deepening the complexity of the question of authorship, goes on to explain how Grey's imposture actually enhances the sense of Victoria's authorial presence:

> [I]n many places the mask of authorship is not ungracefully assumed by the gallant General. But every reader of the volume will feel that its real interest is derived from the writing of another; whose presence is never more perceived than when it seems most to be withholden. (*London Quarterly Review 123* [October 1867]: 148)

Hinting, with this allusion to the general's gallantry, at the properly feminine privacy and modesty that would make openly claimed authorship a burden to the Queen, this reader finds Victoria's presence to be best represented by her absence, or by the "withhold[ing]" of her presence. As for Bagehot, her absence in widowhood serves just as well as a monarchic "disguise" as did her more colorful presence. The review then reinforces this paradox by going on to emphasize two opposing features of the writing in *Early Years:* on the one hand, the writing is "simple," "natural," unselfconscious, and "genuine"; on the other, it represents or indeed performs the Queen's silence, her "speechless grief":

> [N]o desire of display, no longing to be enrolled in the catalog of authors, have led to the writing of this volume. It is a genuine and unmistakable offering of love. . . . It is the Sovereign casting herself in her speechless grief upon the sympathy of her people. (*London Quarterly Review* 123 [October 1867]: 148)

A document of many words, it nonetheless conveys "speechless grief"; as the reviewer goes on in this vein, the "mere fact" of the book's existence makes "an appeal the truth and eloquence of which can scarcely be exceeded by any articulate utterance." This note is introduced in the volume itself in a quotation from Dr. Macleod's memorial sermon: the "eloquent preacher" asks his audience "to acknowledge the demand [for sympathy] which 'now arises in mute eloquence from the throne'" (*Early Years*, xxxi). The Ciceronian echo here has the odd effect not so much of advertising the Queen's eloquence as of enforcing her silence.

Quite possibly, the reviewer for the older *London Quarterly Review* does not literally believe in Victoria's authorship, as the mention of fraudulent royal books may suggest to the careful reader. But evidently this reviewer feels compelled to maintain the fiction that it is the Queen's Book. He may not even mean his readers literally to believe in her authorship, either: later in the review he lets slip, "The Queen has allowed it to be recorded that . . . " and then follows a quotation from the book (123 [October 1867]: 159). For in his view, Victoria's authorship is proven by her silence, her "mute eloquence." The more she seems not to have written the book, the more evident it is that she did and that it expresses her. Her authorship takes the form of silence, just as according to Bagehot her agency is expressed through her invisibility and her loss of power.

This review, like the others that attribute authorship to Victoria and like the many reviews of *Leaves*, focuses much of its commentary on Victoria's "artless" language and in so doing suggests one reason why reviewers may have felt justified in finding her the author. The preface excuses the Queen's "giv[ing] her consent to the present publication" on the grounds that "the free and unreserved expression . . . of her own feelings . . . if made public (however unusual such publicity may be), will command the entire sympathy" of her people and also enhance appreciation of the Prince's character

(*Early Years,* x). Sedgwick, in the letter quoted at the end of this preface, asks "why should not our honored and beloved Queen lay open the innermost recesses of her heart" (xi). Although the *Daily Telegraph* eventually clarifies its view that Grey is the author, for purposes of speculating on the book's popular reception it emphasizes Victoria's direct communication with her people: "This pathetic book—glowing with household fondnesses, and plain to boldness in its resolute wish to let nothing go of the Dead that can be saved—will speak to the millions the things they understand best" (27 July 1867). The *Times* remarks on the Queen's sacrifice of her privacy and praises her willingness to "lay open [her] private thought and feelings." The *London Quarterly Review* writer defends against the "vulgar" who would "question the propriety of such a revelation of the Sovereign's inner life" (123 [October 1867]: 158) and praises letting "the veil be somewhat lifted."[35] Even Margaret Oliphant, who was privately bored by the prospect of "try[ing] to make something of the Royal lucubrations," testifies (if negatively) to the effect of candor produced by the book: in a note sent with her *Blackwood's* review she writes that "the book proves that at least her Majesty is an innocent-minded woman—it is wonderfully youthful and unsophisticated."[36] All the reviews emphasize that *Early Years* was initially written only for private circulation and detail the Queen's reasons for letting it be published. The newer *London Quarterly Review* praises the volume's "simplicity and entire frankness" and claims that "this undisguised disclosure of the innermost privacy, and even the personal thoughts and feelings of our royal lady, is due to the fact that the widowed mother wrote for her children, and for them only" (29 [October 1867]: 200). The private, the inner self, finds unmediated expression in the published text.

Whether or not the book constitutes an exact representation of Albert seems of less interest to these reviewers than that it seems to constitute an exact revelation of the writer-Queen's self.[37] The model of linguistic transparency here is nostalgically close to the Renaissance concept that the monarch is coextensive with her theatrical display—as if the Queen's Book were another sort of performance art.[38] This emphasis betrays a widespread need among readers from a range of classes for Victoria to be present among them, as if a literary equivalent for personal appearances could be found. Indeed, if "representation" suggests deliberate and artful performance, then a literary work that can be praised for its truthfulness, or whose verity can be asserted in the papers, may really be preferable. Even Froude's review in *Fraser's,* skeptical of both Albert's saintliness and Victoria's authorship, testifies to this longing. Froude notes the "harshness which is almost insolence" with which the Queen has been "taken to task" for her "retirement." "Without her presence" the court loses both its "brilliancy" and its moral tone, "as if her presence would have been a check upon licentiousness" (Froude, "The Late Prince Consort," 269). The emphasis on the term "presence" recurs when the book is introduced:

> In the midst of all this, her Majesty has suddenly appeared among us in a form not utterly unlooked for; not personally among the favoured thousand who might have been admitted into her presence, but in a book compiled under her own directions. ("The Late Prince Consort," 270)

The review continues in this vein, emphasizing the exposure of private spaces:

> The present is, we believe, the first instance in history in which a living sovereign has discarded the conventionalities of her position, and has presented herself. (270)

The awkward and unnecessary echo of "presence" and "has presented herself" in "the present [instance]" (simply to designate the book) suggests an unconscious textual overinsistence on the book's status as an equivalent or simulacrum of queenly presence. That Froude does not admit to believing in the Queen's authorship testifies all the more strongly to the compulsion to find in her book not just words or representations but "presence"; and this delivery of her presence does not require her authorship—indeed, it seems to exclude her authorship. *Fraser's* joins the newer *London Quarterly Review* in criticizing the *Times*'s "coarse" attacks on the Queen's retirement, here on the grounds that the book has made up for her absence:

> And who can now regret Her Majesty's almost conventual retirement? Never did grief more worthily relieve itself. Never did widowed love build up a more beautiful and touching memorial than is contained in this admirable book. (*London Quarterly Review* 29 [October 1867]: 200)

If the memorial somehow makes up for her retirement (the claim also made in Kingsley's review of *Leaves* in *Fraser's*, 154), then literary representation has adequately—or such is the earnest hope—substituted for presence.

In *The Early Years* itself, to turn to the materials on which these reviewers constructed their theories of authorship, one can find evidence for all positions. To begin with what might be counted as evidence for her authorship, the perspective is often the Queen's. The volume contains information about her childhood that bears only tangentially on the Prince's story, and the plot is frankly teleological, modeled as it is on the courtship plot, and intertwining the Queen's story with the Prince's long before they meet.[39] "Prince Albert's letters to his father at this time," the narrative coolly comments, "are chiefly interesting from their allusion to England and the young Queen" (*Early Years*, 144). Moreover, the narrator makes remarks so sentimental it is difficult to imagine anyone but the Queen writing them. On quoting from the Queen's journal of 14 October 1839 recording Melbourne's satisfaction that, with the decision to marry, she would never have to "stand alone," the narrator comments, "Can we wonder that the Queen, recalling these circumstances, should exclaim, 'Alas! Alas! the poor Queen now stands in that painful position!'" (*Early Years*, 224). About prayers for their happiness offered to the Queen and the Prince on their wedding day, the narrative comments that "we can estimate but too well how completely those prayers were granted, writing as we do when all that happiness has passed away" (*Early Years*, 313; see also 322). Either the Queen is speaking or Grey is impudently successful in impersonating her campy voice. That the Queen would in any case write of herself in the third person singular or the first person plural helps to highlight the question of whether she or Grey is writing, while neatly obscuring the answer. Oliphant's article on the Commonwealth autobiography of Lucy Hutchinson confirms that Victorian readers accepted the existence of a tradition of women's autobiography in which the woman writing tells her husband's story and writes of herself in the third person. Although "there is never an I in the book from beginning to end," Oliphant emphasizes nonetheless the episodes in which Lucy takes action; it is still the story of her life even if this "autobiography is given under another name."[40] Seen in the light of this tradition, *Early Years* can be understood as the Queen's autobiography.

Nonetheless, the text contains formal evidence for the view that the Queen contributed to it but did not wholly write it (the position the Queen's journal, cited above, best supports). Many of the most vivid expressions of the Queen's perspective are demarcated as paraphrases of or quotations from "The Queen's journal written at the time," from "Note[s] by the Queen," or from an evidently extensive "Memorandum by the Queen" that is deployed among other memoranda by old friends and relations of Albert's who were asked to write their reminiscences (his tutor Herr Florschutz, for example, or his cousin Count Mensdorff). Very likely, the Queen's "authorship" extends only as far as the penning of this memorandum, which Grey then used liberally in his writing of the book. This view of the relation of the Queen's memorandum to Grey's apparent authorship of the rest may be most explicitly exemplified in a passage on Albert's fitness for his new position:

"How this early promise of distinction was fulfilled," the Queen says in the memorandum from which this account is taken, "how immeasurably all the most sanguine expectations were surpassed ... we all know!" (*Early Years*, 214–15; see also 255)

The narrator here distinguishes between the memorandum and the book based upon it. But reviewers could take considerable liberties in interpreting this textual relationship. The reviewer for the newer *London Quarterly Review* who asserts the Queen's authorship quotes an emotion-filled passage from the Memorandum (which appears in the text clearly set off by quotation marks) without noting its source, as if to imply that it is continuous with the narrative as a whole: "Nor can the Queen think without indignation against herself of her wish to keep the Prince waiting for probably three or four years" (*London Quarterly Review* 29 [October 1867]: 215). In framing their quotations of the same passage, both *Blackwood's* and the *Saturday Review* similarly imply that the words are not set off as a quotation in the book. The reviewer for *Fraser's* who sees Grey as the author, by contrast, quotes the same passage with a clear attribution at the end: "(Memorandum by the Queen, p. 220)." Reviewers with different understandings of her authorship can thus give widely different impressions of the Queen's role in shaping the narrative point of view of the whole.[41]

The Queen's comments are often clearly differentiated from the rest of the narrative, and it is likely that Grey wrote the book using her writing only in the places indicated. But acknowledging that the Queen's point of view is sometimes localized in these quotations does not necessarily prove that she did not write some of the rest, or all of the rest, of *Early Years*. She could be quoting herself, distancing her most personal remarks, in order to imply that Grey is writing the rest; for were these passages not demarcated by quotation marks, readers would more likely take the whole for her composition. The reviews that call her author of the entire work are implicitly subscribing to this scenario. In this reading, she has devised a strategy to gratify two opposite imperatives: to be seen as self-confessing author and emotive woman, making her presence available to her subjects in words; and to be seen as shy of public appearance, an author whose deepest feelings are best represented by their modest, appropriately feminine concealment behind the fiction of her loyal secretary's authorship—and indeed whose absence is also, paradoxically, required by the very public that seeks her reconstituted presence.[42] These imperatives are equivalent to the conflicted imperatives to be the Queen (who must make herself present in public) and to be a woman, wife, and mother (who must behave as an example of domestic privacy to other women). And yet this strategy would require of the Queen an artfulness that those who appear to believe in her artless authorship—her self-revelation as woman not as Queen—are at pains to deny. In other words, if she wrote the whole book, exposing herself in candor, then she has also concealed something: her authorship. If she did not write the book, she has not lied, but neither has she fully revealed herself, for she is hiding behind Grey. This contradiction suggests that belief in the Queen's authorship is being embraced openly as a fiction, as a fantasy reconciling belief in her transparent self-display with acceptance of the deviousness necessary to literary work. Whatever the case about the real signature of *Early Years,* it is clear that the public's investment in the book's constituting the Queen's presence compelled reviewers to go to considerable lengths to sustain it.

The relation between the Queen and Grey in these accounts of the authorship of *Early Years* is like the relation between the Queen and the Cabinet in Bagehot. The Queen may be a distracting misrepresentation of real government, serving to entertain those who believe that "reign" means "govern" and to lure the public eye away from secret power; nonetheless, Victoria is nearly invisible herself, and retains considerable if shadowy monarchic powers that lend her absence a mysterious agency that exceeds her role as mere disguise. In just the same way, the public reception of *Early Years* at once fantasmatically constructs her authorship to cover up what may be Grey's "efficient" role (to borrow Bagehot's term for the Cabinet) in producing the book, and seeks to deny her authorship as implying immodesty, praising her "silence" and finding her presence where "it seems most to be withholden." Depending on point of view, "the Queen's Book" can seem like the Queen's Speech, a ghost-written document read by someone else while she stares into space; or it can seem like the fiction that the institution of the Queen's Speech is meant to maintain, the fiction of her rule that Bagehot suggests could still come true. At times the relation between Victoria and Grey reverses that between Queen and Cabinet, if Grey (like a monarch) is the disguise for the real, secret author (like the Cabinet), who can then be uncovered behind his pretense of authorship. But that would be like Bagehot's uncovering of the Queen's prerogatives behind the screen of constitutional government. In both Bagehot's account of the Constitution and in the reviews of *Early Years,* the Queen's presence is desired, yet it seems most effectively delivered by her absence, an absence filled with mysterious powers and simulating "presence." Whether the Queen is a disguise for real government or real government is a thin blind for the Queen's powers, whether Grey is a disguise for the Queen's authorship or the Queen's authorship is a disguise for Grey's, both sets of representations find the Queen's presence in her absence, her agency in her powerlessness; both, too, make a virtue of her absence by reconciling the Queen's public duties with her retiring feelings and by providing the public with a reason to accept, praise, and encourage her absence.

When the book came out and reviews began appearing in late July 1867, the Reform Bill had just been passed by Commons, after months of debate and revision, and was making its way through the House of Lords, which could add amendments to the bill that would nonetheless be subject to the acceptance or rejection of Commons. None of the reviews discussed here explicitly connects these two events, but the *Daily Telegraph*'s reviewing, perhaps because of the political heatedness of the moment, suggests an eagerness to find political meanings in the Queen's Book. There are not one but three separate reviews, published on July 27, 29, and 31. While the first is the relatively conventional review mentioned above, which emphasizes and sentimentalizes the Queen's authorship, the second review sets out explicitly to identify the work's "political interest" and focuses on "the relations of the Court to the State," pursuing in detail the book's account of Albert's position and entitlements. The third review simply excerpts material on King Leopold of the Belgians, for "it has historical value independently of the fact that the writer was the uncle of Prince Albert." Thus the *Daily Telegraph*—which will later express disappointment that *Leaves* omits politics—seeks ways to emphasize that *Early Years* is a political work. Although I have found no evidence that the publication date was chosen for its proximity to the end of the Parliament that was sure to pass reform, both the Queen's journal and the publications we have discussed, in reporting the two events side by side, suggest, however indirectly and equivocally, that the book's publication was a political act, implicated in the representational politics of reform.

The Queen's journal juxtaposes her delight about the reviews with her comments on the difficult and sluggish journey of the Reform Bill, its mixed progress toward and retreat from adequate electoral reform. On July 27 she writes: "The precious Life of my beloved Albert has just been published, and has been received in the most satisfactory spirit. The *Times, Morning Herald,* and especially the *Daily Telegraph* are most gratifying. . . . General Grey spoke of the debate on the Reform Bill in the House of Lords. The Bill makes slow progress" (RA Queen Victoria's Journal, 27 July 1867). Entries for July 28 and 30 comment on similarly good reviews. She sees praise of the book as "unbounded admiration for my beloved one," and she believes in the transparency of her prose: "I feel as if my fondest, most earnest wish, that his perfect character should be thoroughly known and understood . . . was about to be realised." On August 3 she records a conversation with the Duke of Marlborough about reconciling differences between Commons and Lords. Commons will restore its version of the lodgers clause, enfranchising lodgers who paid an annual rent of 10£, despite the Lords' wish to raise the minimum to 15£. Apparently confused, at the beginning of the entry she writes that the

Duke "said he feared the House of Commons would not adopt the alterations," but at the end of the same sentence, "twenty of the alterations would probably be adopted." In the event, with one exception, Commons rejected the Lords' amendments "one after another almost as fast as it could vote."[43] Against the Queen's hopes, Commons' entitlement to reject these amendments made the processing of the bill through Lords no more than an annoying impediment to reform.

In these entries, the book's transparency as a representational form, representing Albert's goodness and her intentions with absolute immediacy, contrasts strikingly with the compromises and imperfections of the Reform Bill both in representing the intentions of its many authors and in representing the Queen's subjects. Maurice Cowling cites the lodgers franchise as an example of the mixed results of the bill: "Though many Radical objectives were achieved, they were matched by conservative clauses, motions and amendments, the success of which guaranteed Conservative acquiescence in the bill as a whole. Though the lodger franchise was low, it had a twelve-month residential qualification and stipulations about furniture added to it, which seemed likely to neutralize its effect" (*1867: Disraeli, Gladstone,* 225–26). Indeed, F. B. Smith reports that when the bill became law, "the ancillary lodger franchise was almost inoperative, because the registration of lodgers presented almost insuperable difficulties" (*Making,* 236–37). Even though they were disappointed in their hope for the Lords' amendments, the Duke's and the Queen's "fear" about the lodgers clause proved needless. In her comments about the certain passage of the bill, the Queen expresses measured enthusiasm for "the good sense of the country" (RA Queen Victoria's Journal, 10 August 1867; the bill passed five days later). Nonetheless, from the Queen's point of view it is clear which form of representation—the clarity and simplicity of literary self-representation or the muddle of reform—is preferable. To look at the Queen's explicit response is to see at work the Arnoldian view of representation.

The Queen reconciles herself to reform in her journal by referring to the popular belief that whereas shopkeepers and the wealthier artisans (the class the Whigs would have enfranchised) would vote Whig, with Disraeli's deeper extension of the franchise "the class who would get more power . . . were infinitely more loyal than those just above them" (RA Queen Victoria's Journal, 10 August 1867). An article in the August *Blackwood's* shares this notion with the Queen, praising the Conservatives for designing their Reform Bill to reach "the people of England [who] look up with respect to the aristocracy and the crown."[44] The *Saturday Review,* by contrast, repeatedly attacks this idea, arguing that the reason to enfranchise the lower classes is that their views cannot be predicted and therefore should be heard, and mocking the notion that "the Residuum" are "a loyal class—a class too ignorant to have any political opinions, but who just know the name of the QUEEN."[45] But the *Saturday Review*'s perfectly typical account of *Early Years* later in the same issue conveys the same mindless loyalty, and the same belief in the fiction of the Queen's powers, that the political article mocks. In this light, the many reviews that sustain the fiction of the Queen's authorship and that seek to affirm her presence even as a powerful absence could be seen as implicitly supporting the view—expressed in adjacent articles—that reform will ultimately have conservative effects. In this reading, the Queen's Book would have accomplished its Arnoldian aim of furthering a conservative loyalism.

Disraeli's final speech about the bill, the end of which *Blackwood's* quotes as the close of its own conservative-leaning account, evokes an abstract personification of England to project his confidence in the "safe" effects of the bill. This personification is predictably female:

> I think England is safe in the race of men who inhabit her; that she is safe in something much more precious than her accumulated capital—her accumulated experience. (Cheers.) She is safe in her national character, in her fame, in the traditions of a thousand years, and in the glorious future which I believe awaits her. (The right hon. gentleman sat down amidst loud cheering.) ("The Bill as It Is," 256)

This shadowy Britannia evokes the equally shadowy Queen, whose partially illusory presence as concealed author of the Queen's Book is so powerfully evoked in *Blackwood's* and other contemporary reviews of *Early Years*. Reassurances about the effects of reform require that the Queen remain present as a fiction or abstraction, as a constitutional or "dignified" figurehead, as the absence that the fiction of her authorship makes her. Even the ferociously proreform *Daily Telegraph*—the paper, of all those cited here, read by the lowest class of readers—celebrates the bill in prose that echoes the values that the paper had celebrated in *Early Years* and would later celebrate in its review of *Leaves:* the values of patriarchal domesticity. England will establish

> side by side with all the venerable traditions of the land the principle of household suffrage as the basis for Government. Our island-word "home" ... has new significance now that it has become the chief word of the kingdom's political life, as it was before of its social and civil genius. Henceforth whoever has his "home" in England, a hearthstone where his family gathers, a key that the owner can turn against the cares and troubles of the day ... that man is a citizen in the fullest sense. (*Daily Telegraph*, 10 August 1867)

Going on to celebrate the enfranchisement of "the classes of industry" that figured largely in its readership, the *Daily Telegraph* nonetheless understands this franchise in the terms established by the kind of sentimental representation of which *Early Years* ("glowing with household fondnesses") had presented so recent an example. Once again—in a publication ideologically opposite to *Blackwood's*—a literary representation aids the presentation of reform as a reassuringly "safe" development.

Nonetheless, despite the decisiveness with which Commons rejected the Lords' amendments and adhered to its own text of the bill, debate and confusion accompanied it to the end. In the ideological self-contradictoriness of the bill as passed may be found a reflection of the self-contradictory literary effects of the Queen's Book: both to make her present and to confirm her absence. Apart from the lodgers clause, the two amendments most heavily debated were the minority clause, discussed above with regard to its ambiguous assumptions about "representation," and an amendment to institute voting papers, a mechanism by which people could have their votes delivered to the polls and avoid the unpleasantness of election day mobs. (This amendment was rejected but had support in Commons.) Voting papers represented, on the one hand, the privilege of the rich and, on the other, a potential mechanism (a precursor of the secret ballot) for protecting tenants and workers from pressure from their superiors. Like *Early Years,* voting papers permit a written representation to substitute for physical presence, but also as in the case of the Queen's Books, it was unclear at the time whether voting papers would favor the old order or the new. Both types of written representation substitute for the public performance of public duties (and the Queen's Book perhaps unduly protects her both from the "many, nasty faces" who agitate for reform and from the elite who demand her presence at State ceremonies) and encourage those previously disenfranchised to take possession of their new entitlements. The minority clause, similarly, meant either a return to older, symbolic notions of electoral representation—like the Arnoldian idea that the Queen's book would enhance her presence—or, by contrast, a foot in the door for the principle of numerical or descriptive representation, which would correspond to the reception of Queen's book that celebrates her absence. The equivocal meaning of Victoria's absence mirrors the uncertainty about what these measures might mean for reform.

On July 20 the *Daily Telegraph* juxtaposed on the last three columns of page 5 three items of interest to us: an announcement of Earl Grey's proposed amendment—"impossible for the government to accept"—criticizing the Reform Bill; an even briefer notice in fine print excerpted from the *Lancet* on "The Health of Her Majesty"; and an extensive account of "Mr. Bright on the Reform Bill." The paraphrase of Bright's speech to his constituents at Birmingham emphasizes the hypocrisy of the Tories in passing reform, a point underscored by the notice about Grey's unhelpful amendment. The item about the Queen reads as follows:

> We have good grounds for stating that the absence of the Queen from public evening festivities is really due to the fact that agitation, over-worry, or much talking in the evening is followed by restless nights, most distressing sick headache, and sense of great exhaustion.

Bright's speech, made in the evening at "a crowded meeting," suggests a different social world from that of the "much talking in the evening" that disables the Queen: the *Lancet* refers to elite entertainments. Yet in its graphic juxtaposition of these two items, the newspaper implies that the Queen's reclusiveness has indeed made way symbolically for the prevalence of "talking in the evening" of the sort Bright and the *Daily Telegraph* favor. Bright's speech ultimately had more purchase than Grey's amendment, although the Queen would have liked neither. Nonetheless, the Queen's Book, to be reviewed a week later, supplies the Queen with an excuse to give up "talking in the evening," as if she were graciously stepping aside to let Bright and his constituents occupy what we have called the public space of self-misrepresentation. But the reception of the second of the Queen's Books will tell a more complete story of the relation between the Queen's representational forms and those of "the people."

The Queen's Books: *Leaves from the Journal of Our Life in the Highlands*

When *Leaves from the Journal of Our Life in the Highlands* was published in January 1868, having been in private circulation since 1865, it became a bestseller—selling out all 20,000 copies within two weeks, with second and cheap editions rapidly produced thereafter—and was greeted by many loyal and laudatory reviews. When Arthur Helps writes the story of the book's publication in the preface, he calls attention to the Queen's exemplary modesty, her disclaimer of literary "skill" and her "extreme reluctan[ce] to publish anything written by herself" (*Leaves*, viii). This claim positions *Leaves* as the emphatic opposite of the Queen's Speech, written for performance and publication but not by her. At the same time, her intense privacy is said to forge an immediate personal connection with her reader-subjects. The reason to publish, as for *Early Years*, is that "it would be very gratifying to her subjects, who had always shown a sincere and ready sympathy with the personal joys and sorrows of their Sovereign" (*Leaves,* viii–ix), Bagehot's "one person doing interesting actions" (*English Constitution,* 86).

The preface thus echoes the terms in which *Early Years* was received, and reviewers celebrated in it many of the same traits that were noted in the earlier work: its "perfect naturalness . . . its simplicity, its truthfulness,"[46] its "simplicity and naturalness" (London *Times,* 10 January 1868), meaning both transparency of representation and "homeliness" of subject matter.[47] "[W]ritten without a thought of the critics . . . it does not mind being called 'simple'" (*Daily Telegraph,* 10 January 1868). Margaret Oliphant characterizes it as "the simple record . . . of simple enjoyment";[48] the *Edinburgh Review* emphasizes both the "genuine simplicity" of the Queen's "simple avocations" at Balmoral and the "inimitable artlessness" of her style in describing that life.[49] Once again the Queen "opens to us her heart" (*Times*), to let her subjects "know what thoughts went and came in [her] candid soul" ("The Queen of the Highlands," 243), and "appeals . . . directly to the common heart" (*Times*). Because the story of this marriage is "closed," "the veil" that normally conceals "the happy fireside" is lifted here (*Daily Telegraph*). The Queen is seen "to lay aside for a moment that Majesty which constitutes the grandeur and solitude of the throne" (*Edinburgh Review,* 127 [January 1868]: 281); "she lays aside her robes of state and enters into friendly conversation with her subjects on the mere footing of a warmhearted, cultivated gentlewoman" (*Times*); "the queen is lost in the woman" (*London Quarterly Review* 30 [April 1868]: 84).

Suggesting a literary representation exactly opposite but equivalent to the public "representation" she now reluctantly undertakes as Bagehot's "disguise," these characterizations show that readers are still eager for signs of the Queen's presence. The *Daily Telegraph* makes explicitly the point that the book should compensate for the Queen's absence, both in its review and in the lead editorial with which it announced the book's publication as an important news item:

> [I]f any of her subjects have regretted that when she has gone amongst them in public they could not come near enough to see her face, to hear her voice, to know what she does and how she does it, they may be consoled in reading this book; for, through its pages, they are drawn nearer to the every-day life of a living QUEEN than any persons not courtiers ever came before. . . . Those who have been impatient with the wish to see Her Majesty more in public will at least comprehend how real was the home in the ruins of which she has had to mourn the stroke of Death. (*Daily Telegraph,* 10 January 1868)

Reviewers, responding not only to the intrinsic qualities of the text but also to their readers' desires, claim the book delivers their Queen to them unmediated even by her rank. The Queen herself understood its reception in these terms: she is "overcome" by the flood of favorable reviews and letters saying "how much more I would endear myself to the people, than ever before!" (RA Queen Victoria's Journal, 14 January 1868).

Also like *Early Years, Leaves* is celebrated for offering an "example" to the public as well as for supplying the missing presence of the Queen. (All reviews of *Early Years* praised Victoria and Albert's exemplary behavior, and *Fraser's* specifically excused Victoria's absence on the grounds that her "unappeasable grief" set a better example than her "presence" would do.) The *Daily Telegraph* editorial emphasizes this theme, praising Albert and the Queen "not solely for what they did and said during their united reign, but for what they were essentially.... the Queen and he set a high example" (*Daily Telegraph*, 10 January 1868). The chief reason for publication that Victoria had offered to her daughter Vicky was that "it would, from its simplicity and the kindly feelings expressed to those below us, do so much good" (*Your Dear Letter*, 166, 21 December 1867) and set a good example. On 14 January 1868 she rejoices in reviews and letters that tell her "what good the book would do" (RA Queen Victoria's Journal). By being understood to set a good example as well as to make her present, the book doubly recuperates her absence. Her invisibility and privacy are part of her typicality, her appealing participation in common humanity. Within the world of the 1840s and 1850s covered by *Leaves* the invisibility is not that of her widowhood but rather of her private married life, but because the book appeared during her widowhood, reviewers can tacitly excuse (or even praise) her mournful retirement by praising her domestic privacy in marriage. Like Bagehot, reviewers sought ways to recuperate her widowhood for a positive monarchic image. The life at Balmoral is admirable for its difference from the "tinsel" and "artifice" (*Edinburgh Review* 127 [January 1868]: 283) of court life and for its similarity to ordinary private homes:

> There are, no doubt, many such houses in Scotland and in England too. Such abodes are best known to those who have had the good fortune to frequent them. But it would not be easy in any of them to draw a more pleasing and accurate picture of life and character than the Queen has given us from Balmoral. (*Edinburgh Review* 127 [January 1868]: 283).

The *Daily Telegraph* exclaims, "Thank GOD there are many thousand English homes like this.... her home was but one of many like it, and ... she had no Royal monopoly of that pure light of household love which shines by so many English hearths" (*Daily Telegraph,* 10 January 1868). Oliphant similarly writes "that in family hoards all over the country at this present moment similar records [of the pleasures of a Highland vacation] abound" ("The Queen of the Highlands," 243). The Queen's Book both follows and sets an example for how to live comfortably in a country house, or indeed by any hearth; reading her book will teach you to live well too.

The book's power to set an example depends upon maintaining the fiction of its transparently revealed privacy, its "absence of self-consciousness" (*London Quarterly Review* 30 [April 1868]: 93). This review continues:

> Without any intention to do so, she has drawn for us, both in the outpourings of her own heart, and in the description of her ways of life, the ideal of "a perfect woman, nobly planned." (93)

"Nobly planned" suggests (probably unintentionally) that the portrayal is not so unselfconscious as this reviewer claims, but the review concludes by reiterating this emphasis on the dependence of her moral exemplariness upon the transparency or unselfconsciousness of her self-representation:

> We lay down the book with a feeling of the deepest thankfulness that so pure and refreshing a work has been given—given out of a broken heart—by our beloved and gracious Queen to her subjects. It will convey moral health wherever it goes; it will intensify the domestic affections of every family which it may enter; it has already deepened beyond expression the attachment of her people to Queen Victoria. (98)

The book improves the behavior of Victoria's subjects both by setting so fine an example of private behavior and by delivering that example so transparently: by letting subjects feel that they "have looked into another interior" ("The Queen of the Highlands," 243). This transparency is not just a means to an end (the end of discerning the Queen's example); it is also an end in itself. The Queen's "truth," which conveys the Queen's presence, is a virtue, the virtue of realism. The *Daily Telegraph* review characterizes the virtuousness of the book's truth in a different way: the Queen "has been willing—or, we might add, has been able—to put the leaves of her own private daily notebook into the hands of her people" because "she has nothing to conceal" (*Daily Telegraph,* 10 January 1868).

The authenticity of the Queen's authorship and voice is not in doubt here.[50] Because her privacy never obstructs her candor, the recovery of her vanished presence seems to come even more easily through her authorship than in the case of *Early Years*. But the book's thematics raise concerns about what that recovered presence really might amount to, or be worth. In *Leaves,*

Victoria does not pretend not to be the author; she pretends not to be the Queen. This pretense takes two forms: the elimination—by Victoria and Mr. Helps, acting as editor—of all overt references to matters of state (which, however, return in figurative and domestic form); and a series of episodes, excerpted by nearly all the reviewers, in which Victoria and Albert appear in disguise. These episodes include Victoria's visits to poor old women in the neighborhood of Balmoral and several overnight expeditions the royal couple made with small parties from Balmoral, tours in which they dressed and traveled as private citizens. Disguise allows the Queen to perform herself as a private person. These episodes suggest that, rather than having a private life that can be "looked into" by her lucky readers, the Queen is making and performing privacy of a kind more artificial than reviewers acknowledge. Purportedly compensating for her absence at court with the delivery of her presence as a private person, these episodes instead reveal the absence behind her private self as well. They confirm Bagehot's theory that her essence is disguise.

Both the *Times* and Margaret Oliphant are quick to associate the pleasures of readers' voyeurism with the pleasure the Queen takes, as her book reveals, in traveling in disguise. Readers enjoy looking at what they think is her real privacy, even as she takes pleasure in assuming the disguise of an artificial privacy. Nowhere is this contradiction acknowledged openly, however, just as the reviews of *Early Years* fail to acknowledge that the Queen's supposed candor depends upon artful disguise. The *Times* review opens, as described above, with emphasis on the simplicity and directness with which the Queen portrays both her heart and her activities. But that there is "no show about it whatever, except the simple show of fine natural feeling," suggests that the Queen's privacy is not after all so transparently represented as the review would wish readers to understand. Moreover (still in the first paragraph), the review identifies her disguises with her candor:

> [O]f all the days . . . those were the most enjoyed, and the pleasure of them were the most eagerly sought to be renewed, on which the Queen and her party could go forth in disguise roaming among the hills and about the villages unrecognized, received as private persons. . . . And since Her Majesty is pleased to come to us in this way without ceremony, we venture to meet her, as she would wish, without compliments. (*Times*, 10 January 1868)

The reviewer implies that the Queen's self-presentation in her publication is like her disguise in the Highlands: if it is a revelation of her true inner and private life, it is one that has to be performed with special costumes and assumed names. A letter from the Queen to Theodore Martin acknowledges that the book's candor was a product of her art: "[I]t was the simplicity of the style and the absence of all appearance of writing for effect which had given her book such immense and undeserved success"; the Queen has inserted the words "appearance of."[51]

Oliphant too cites the incognito tours early in her review, to denote what differentiates Victoria's writing from private journals, just as the *Times* reviewer emphasizes that for the Queen privacy is an unusual performance, not a continuous state of being. For the Queen there can be no ordinary private life; or if there is such a thing, to reveal it is to make it theatrical. In focusing on the incognito tours, then, the reviews hint that the Queen cannot be made fully present for readers, even when she is performing her privacy publicly, even when they are happily claiming, as does the *Times,* that her disguise reveals her "without ceremony." Bagehot argued that the Queen serves as "disguise" for government whether she is withdrawn or on view; she both *is* a disguise and is *in* disguise whether she wears robes of State or her drabbest morning dress and bonnet. The Queen might contest the unavoidability of disguise, taking the view that she can give up public ceremonial "representations" with their immediacy and yet falseness, and replace them with displaced self-representations that are somehow more "true" (writing her life as an ordinary woman and traveling incognito). Yet the reviews suggest with Bagehot that she can only substitute one disguise for another.

In the scenes from Victoria's early career discussed earlier in this book, we found Victoria's pose as a middle-class domestic woman to be an equivocal one that both convinces and displays itself as a pose. The retrospective structure of *Leaves* complicates the matter: while the characters represented in the text of *Leaves*—the Queen and her dear dependents during the 1840s and 1850s—are occupied in just such posing, the Queen who is understood to be made available in and by the book is the widowed Queen of the 1860s, involved in a different kind of royal theater, in which the issue is not so much what kind of pose as whether she will be present on stage at all. Thematics of public and private domesticity that were most prominent before Albert's death now serve as vehicles for the concerns of the 1860s about Victoria's presence and absence. If the incognito tours were, in their original context, exercises in domestic posing, now, at the time of publication, they become attempts to assert that displaced representations—literary descriptions of inhabiting a disguise—can substitute adequately for her presence, make tolerable her absence, and answer her subjects' desire for her to appear before them once again. In the reading that follows, I will attempt to show how the 1840s' and 1850s' open pose of apolitical domesticity serves the needs of 1868 as well.

Because Helps states the principles of editing he and Victoria agreed on rather than silently removing references to matters of state, the volume proclaims its own artificiality in contriving to isolate the private (or what resembles the private in Victoria's life) away from the public aspects of the Queen's daily life. The volume represents Victoria not just as an ordinary woman but as a monarch trying to impersonate ordinariness; she displays for public consumption the effort to create a public persona and the acts of exclusion that creation demands. As Arthur Ponsonby pointed out about *Leaves*, "It would not require much research . . . to pick out a date recording some colourless, unimportant incident and to find in her correspondence on the same day some letter to the Prime Minister or the Private Secretary expressing in the most vehement language her desire to interfere in high matters of national importance" (quoted by Weintraub, *Victoria*, 383). Helps's wording in the preface is curious: he writes that "[a]ll references to political questions, or to the affairs of Government, have, for obvious reasons, been studiously omitted." The *Daily Telegraph*, anticipating that "some persons may be disappointed at the entire absence of political affairs from this volume," expresses bafflement that "the particular reason [for Helps's decision] is not distinctly stated" and suggests the reason may be a desire not to anticipate Martin's forthcoming, full-length *Life of the Prince Consort*. Helps's awkward "obvious" calls attention to his labor in its attempt to finesse the complexity of possible reasons: state security may be implied here, but what seems uppermost in the editor's mind is his desire arbitrarily to present Victoria's writings as "the natural expression of a mind rejoicing in the beauties of nature, and throwing itself . . . into a life removed, for the moment, from the pressure of public cares." The *Daily Telegraph* knows this is an imposture, noting that "she maintains her prerogatives" and that it is sure "of the conscientious care and the judgement uniformly shown by the Queen in the exercise of her public duties." In the statements by Ponsonby and Helps the Queen's involvement in "political questions" is not denied, rather it is deemed inappropriate to the volume at hand. Adrienne Munich sees Victoria working while on vacation as one of her "secrets" (*Secrets*, 41).

Nonetheless, Victoria and Helps let public subtexts emerge in many apparently private scenes. For Charles Kingsley (whose review in *Fraser's* is admittedly anomalous in various ways) the point of the book is the attention it calls to Scotland. Alone among the reviewers he does not extensively quote from *Leaves* and instead uses the review as an occasion to attack the legal causes of poverty in Scotland and to argue for its reforestation. Looking for evidence that it is a political work, Kingsley fends off the implication that *Leaves* presents the Queen's life as one of "idleness" (*Fraser's* 77 [February

1868]: 160): when the Queen mentions once that, on her yacht, she spent hours reading despatches and conducting business, "one account, set down by accident [or more accurately, included in the volume by apparent accident], of a morning so spent, will be a guarantee that hundreds of other mornings have been spent as well" (160). The book "at least hints to us that her duties have been performed." Kingsley's tone is sufficiently skeptical in the rest of the review to suggest that when he says he does not "regret the elimination" of political references, he means the reverse of what he says.

The book "hints" at the Queen's performance of monarchic duties in descriptions of her and Albert's leisure activities as well. Her youthful tourist excursions outside England and her decision to buy Balmoral are simultaneously ordinary acts of holiday making and royal progresses that assert her imperial possession of territories and peoples. The book came out at a time of heated debates about the "Irish Question" in the wake of the "Fenian Outrages" (as the papers termed a fatal explosion at Clerkenwell Prison in December 1867). When Parliament met a month after the book's publication, it quickly passed a bill suspending Habeas Corpus in Ireland and opened debate on Reform Bills for Scotland and Ireland. The stir that surrounded these events would have highlighted the book's imperial theme for readers. Two reviews make explicit the imperial motives behind Victoria's tourism. The *London Quarterly Review* account extensively compares Victoria's travels to the royal progresses of Elizabeth I, who, it claims, "wished to see things with her own eyes [and] enjoyed not a little the incense so freely burned before her in the great provincial houses where she halted" (*London Quarterly Review* 124 [January 1868]: 30). Although the review emphasizes the difference between Elizabeth's "unsettled" life and Victoria's stable marriage, and the difference between the "mystery" surrounding Elizabeth's personal life and Victoria's "minuteness of description" (31), the review by implication extends to Victoria Elizabeth's territorial motives. Later the same review describes "the purchase of Balmoral as what it is so desirable that the Queen of Great Britain should possess—a really Highland home" (35). Similarly, the *Edinburgh Review* notes the significance of Victoria's innovation in visiting Scotland: no Hanover sovereign (apparently the Prince Regent's visit does not count) "had ever set foot in Scotland; . . . Queen Victoria was the first sovereign, since the accession of James VI to the English throne, who made Scotland a home" (*Edinburgh Review* 127 [January 1868]: 284). Among the first passages this review quotes is one that records Victoria's politely imperial visit to Perth and to Scone, to see "the mound on which the ancient Scotch kings were always crowned" and to sign "a curious old book . . . in which the last signatures are those of James I (of England) and of Charles I"

(285). The *Daily Telegraph* does not emphasize imperial politics in its review, but in various articles in 1867 and 1868 it urges the royal family to visit or to purchase homes in Ireland as gestures of confidence, and in a later article it alludes to a passage in *Leaves*—"which few persons have missed reading wholly or in part"—in its reporting of the visit of the Prince and Princess of Wales to Ireland on 14 April 1868.

At Balmoral, Albert is almost continually hunting, in passages that revive the dead metaphor of hunting as martial conquest. Victoria writes, for example, that once when they spotted some deer, a "'council of war' was held in a whisper" (*Leaves*, 108, 18 September 1848).[52] Albert kills "a magnificent stag, 'a royal'" (110). This monarchic slaughter of local royalty looks back to England's imperial violence to Scotland, or, more immediately, to Ireland, and ahead to the imperial violence of Victoria's own armies around the globe (for example, the "Abyssinian Expedition" is being reported heavily in the papers in the winter of 1868). Her phrasing represents the private pleasure of hunting at Balmoral as a practice filled with public significance. The killing of a royal stag also recalls the killing of the tame stag in Book VII of the *Aeneid*, the stag whose death at the hand of Ascanius sparks the war that will end with Aeneas's imperial conquest of Italy. Nonetheless, the Highlanders attribute Albert's success to Her Majesty's "lucky foot," as if her most valuable power were this accidental, private, and, indeed, imaginary one. The attention to her "luck" and the reduction of conquered peoples to casually slaughtered animals trivialize the subject of imperialism even as they make it safe for inclusion in the book. Moreover, just as Ponsonby claims, the day's entry in the original journal ends with the Queen's noting that in Ireland "the people are burning and attacking houses, and forcing people to join them" (RA Queen Victoria's Journal, 18 September 1848); the day before, the Queen had met with Lord Russell "about Ireland, and the certainly very bad news from there. Risings in Waterford and Wexford, and in all directions" (RA Queen Victoria's Journal, 17 September 1848). The unpublished entry for September 19 begins and ends with consultations about the Irish situation, with Albert deer stalking and the Queen visiting cottages in between. (Ireland in the time of the book's publication was in just as much turmoil as it was in 1848.) Reading what has been omitted from the original helps bring into focus the political subtexts of Victoria's rural pleasures, but those pleasures signify politics allegorically in any case.

In an entry made a few years later Victoria recounts two events that signify vividly in much the same way. One day, they build a stone cairn "to commemorate our taking possession of this dear place" (*Leaves*, 139, 11 October 1852). The family's acquisition of Balmoral is the explicit referent, but England's imperial conquest of Scotland is implied in this memorializing too.[53] But the building of any cairn for such memorial purposes is already an act of cultural imperialism. Cairns were originally built in the Highlands when men, going off to fight, each left a stone in a pile; those returning removed a stone, so that the stones that remained became a memorial to the war dead. (The best cairn would then be a vanished one, and the large heaps of stones the royal family makes therefore suggest heaps of vanquished Scots.) Victoria's family thus doubly appropriates Scotland in appropriating this custom for their own purposes. That this cairn matters politically as well as domestically is suggested also by an editorial change: either Victoria or Helps has changed "I placed a stone first" (as it appears in Beatrice's transcript) to the monumentalizing "I then placed the first stone" (140). Later the same day, Albert shoots yet another stag, and the household builds another cairn to "mark the spot" (142), while Victoria sketches the corpse (the sketch appears in the published volume).[54] The repeated act of cairn building links the owning of property to the violence of killing the stag, and it links the private (Balmoral as home, hunting as mere sport) to the public (Scotland as conquered territory, hunting as martial exercise). Moreover, Victoria's sketching, as a memorializing activity parallel to cairn building, firmly implicates her female domestic arts in public conquest as well. Her journal writing itself, then, by extension becomes another sort of cairn, a record of domestic life that carries world-historical significance. Victoria claims that her part in this masculine, public activity is only as observer and recorder, yet monarchy's domestic front turns out to be replete with the signifiers of royal power.

Imperial politics enters explicitly in the entry for 10 September 1855 when the vacationing household receives the news of the fall of Sevastopol, and thus of the successful termination of the Crimean war. (Several reviews note this passage, together with a passage on the death of the Duke of Wellington, as the only public events to violate the privacy of Balmoral, or rather the fiction of its privacy created by author and editor.) The household and village turn out to light a celebratory bonfire on top of the cairn, the very cairn that ostensibly celebrates only their possession of the house, but that here doubles as—and is revealed to have been all along—a sign of empire as well. The purchase of the property turns out to signify the subjection of Scotland, which turns out to signify Britain's global power. Victoria presents this scene in exclusively private, domestic terms, however, for she begins her account by saying "the new house seems to be lucky, indeed; for, from the first moment of our arrival, we have had good news" (*Leaves,* 152). By mentioning the war at all, Victoria acknowledges her journal's royal identity, but by attributing Britain's success in imperial war to the happiness of her domestic home and to the banality of her personal "good luck," as in the passage on her "lucky foot," Victoria is also concealing that royal identity.

"Luck" is what Bagehot's "secret prerogative . . . waver[ing] between reality and desuetude" translates into in the relentlessly lighthearted idiom of *Leaves:* a name for the monarchic agency that functions by means of its obscurity. Victoria can take credit for the Crimean victory only through magical metaphors, and yet her correspondence (as Ponsonby predicted) reveals an intense involvement in the war, both hidden and public, and some measurable impact on its effect on Britain. Informed in detail about the troops and battlefields, she conveyed her advice on the conduct of the war to her ministers. Albert's behind-the-scenes letters from "a valiant campaign of his own against bureaucratic obstruction" fill fifty bound volumes in the Royal Archives (St. Aubyn, *Queen Victoria,* 295). Praising Victoria's handling of the ministerial crisis occasioned in the winter of 1855 by the war, Longford writes: she "showed that she could take an active, even central part in providing the country with a government"; "the Queen's part in extricating the country from the political crisis in the middle of the war, together with her own and her husband's labours in so many other fields, gave a temporary fillip to the power of the Monarchy" (Longford, *Queen Victoria,* 245, 255).[55] Publicly visible encouraging "her beloved troops," protesting their unnecessary sufferings, awarding medals, visiting hospitals, giving away artificial limbs, and pensioning the disabled, the Queen also served her country more lastingly but less visibly by exercising her right to send for a new ministry. These powers, however, can appear in her book only as "luck," and she is able to exercise them because her subjects know them as nothing more than that.

The strategy of both revealing and concealing her royal identity—posing as private and exposing that imposture—is repeated in the journal extracts that the reviews most emphasize. As the reviews note, Victoria's greatest pleasure in Scotland derives from impersonating one of her own subjects or being treated like an ordinary lady even when she is recognized as Queen. Long quotations from the incognito tours generally form the climax of the reviews, but the reviews also invariably include summaries of and passages from an earlier episode in which Victoria visits poor women in her neighborhood. While this episode tends to be described under other headings—class relations, the noble character of the Scots, her interest in her servants—it too involves a certain degree of imposture or disguise.[56]

On 26 September 1857 Victoria takes a walk with two of her daughters and Lady Churchill, for the purpose of buying and distributing some goods to the poor. Impersonating one of her own subjects, dressed just like any charitable lady with time and money on her hands, Victoria nonetheless takes along a local friend, Mrs. P. Farquharson, to "show me where the poor people lived, and tell them who I was."[57] Victoria gives an old woman "a warm petticoat" and is gratified by a display of the desired emotion: "[T]he tears rolled down her old cheeks, and she shook my hands, and prayed God to bless me: it was very touching" (*Leaves*, 161). Victoria represents herself as especially pleased when the old women speak to her without regard for precedence or protocol. "Old widow Symons . . . was most friendly, shaking hands with us all, asking which was I" (162), and blessing Victoria and Vicky. "Old Mrs. Grant" expresses herself frankly on the subject of Vicky's upcoming marriage ("I'm very sorry, and I think she is sorry hersel'"), and then half-apologizes: "'I always say just what I think, not what is fut' (fit)" (163; Beatrice's transcript omits Mrs. Grant's remark). Saying just what she thinks, not what is fit, is also the way Arthur Helps characterizes Victoria's own prose in his preface ("the writer describes what she thinks and feels, rather than what she might be expected to think and feel," x–xi), and the reviewers say so too, to imply that—thanks to the careful orchestration of spontaneity—Victoria is indeed not so different from her subjects. And yet in recording Scots dialect ("fut"), to repudiate it immediately with the King's English ("fit"), Victoria suggests that she assumes the disguise of the locale only for the purpose of taking it off ostentatiously.

Widow Symons's need to be told which is the Queen and the Queen's need for her friend to do advance publicity for her visit point to an ambiguity in the episode that reappears in the incognito tours, in which disguise is even more deliberately assumed and sustained. Victoria likes her subjects to treat her without excessive deference. Mrs. Grant's insubordination only elicits Victoria's pleased comment, "Dear old lady; she is such a pleasant person." And yet she also wants them to know who she is. She wants both to succeed in impersonation and to have the impersonation recognized for what it is, to be both absent as Queen and present as Queen. (Beatrice's omissions would effectively disable this reading, if hers were the only version we had.) As an event of the 1850s the episode exemplifies Victoria's public and regal performance of private and ordinary life; edited and published in 1868, it dramatizes the power of concealment to serve as public performance that both delivers and desirably withholds Victoria's presence.

The political background this time is the "Cawnpore massacre" of August 1857. In the days preceding her "Visits to the Old Women," the Queen is reacting in the unpublished sections of her journal to telegrams and delayed newspaper accounts reporting the recent spread of the "mutiny." In this context the usual tales of dead stags become especially eerie: on September 18, after reading that the courtyard at Cawnpore was two inches deep in

English blood, Victoria and Albert hold a ball in a room decorated with dead stags' heads. If Strachey is right that "the power of a dependent still remains, by a psychological sleight of hand, one's own power,"[58] then her pleasure in the deliberately contained insubordination of the old women suggests Victoria's effort to confirm British rule—now seriously threatened in India—in an unthreatening context.

Soon after this episode come the incognito tours, expeditions ranging so far from Balmoral that overnight stays in country hotels were necessary, and these follow the same pattern of concealment and recognition. The first is a "delightful, successful excursion!" of September 1860 during which Albert and Victoria pass themselves off as Lord and Lady Churchill, demoting their companions, General Grey and Lady Churchill, to Dr. Grey and Miss Spencer (*Leaves,* 194). What they see and do while traveling in disguise can hardly account for Victoria's delight.[59] After a night of bad sleep in a tiny room (the price of traveling unknown), they pass the entire day in rain or drizzle, and in addition to some lovely scenery they drive through "the most tumble-down, poor-looking place I ever saw . . . the dirtiest, poorest village in the whole of the Highlands" (199–200).[60] What makes this a "delightful, successful excursion!" is the semi-transparent disguise itself and the comedy it generates. That they half expected or half desired to be found out is suggested by their neglecting to remove from one of their carriages the royal insignia of Balmoral. During the course of the excursion Victoria seems disappointed by the success of the imposture, as when "the few people about stared vacantly at the two simple vehicles" (195). The fun comes from accidents that threaten to expose them: "Brown once forgot this, and called me 'Your Majesty' as I was getting into the carriage; and Grant on the box once called Albert 'Your Royal Highness'; which set us off laughing, but no one observed it" (194). Again, the next day, the innkeeper tells Grant, "'Dr. Grey wants you,' which nearly upset the gravity of all the others: then they told Jane [Victoria's maid], 'Your lady gives no trouble'" (197).[61]

Finally the secret gets out, and townspeople wave flags and handkerchiefs as the carriages pass. After some further description of the places they visit, Victoria ends the account on this note, with an explanation of how the secret got out (someone recognized Albert) and her pleasure at the reaction she imagines:

> When they heard who it was, they were ready to drop with astonishment and fright. I fear I have but poorly recounted this very amusing and never to be forgotten expedition, which will always be remembered with delight. (*Leaves,* 203)

It matters greatly to Victoria, as in the episode with the old women, not only not to be recognized but also to be recognized, and to be recognized as having concealed herself. Victoria mentions the following detail from the narrative of their discovery:

> "The lady must be terribly rich," [a] woman observed, as I had so many gold rings on my fingers!—I told Lady Churchill she had on many more than I had. (202–3)

Characteristically, Victoria assumes that she herself, and not Lady Churchill, is the rich lady this woman notices, despite her lesser number of rings: it matters to Victoria that she be perceived as the first in any group, despite, or because of, her efforts to hide her status; the disguise must not succeed too well.

The reviews pick out for special note the incognito details of the subsequent three tours (in 1861), even though in these cases the disguise is not so much emphasized in Victoria's text as in the first tour. In September 1861 a traveler staying in the country-town hotel with them has to be turned away (with a fabrication about a wedding party) from the dining room the royal party occupies (*Leaves,* 211–12), but here the proprietors are in on the secret, and it appears the royals did not use assumed names. In October a few people assemble at the inn of Dalwhinnie, "and I thought they knew us; but it seems they did not, and it was only when we arrived that one of the maids recognized me" (225–26). This evening provides "no fun," whether because of the lackluster reception or because of the wet weather and the poor meal. The next day she is cheered by the appearance of volunteers playing fife and drum and by the sight of "the fat old landlady [who] had put on a black satin dress, with white ribbons and orange flowers!" (227). The reviews similarly focus attention on the one incognito episode in the accounts of "Earlier Visits to Scotland" that precede the selections from the Balmoral journal, a sentimentally sketched return to Taymouth, one of the first places Victoria and Albert visited in Scotland in 1842. This incognito episode appears in an 1866 footnote to the original visit (*Leaves,* 22; it reappears in *More Leaves,* 34). The footnote by itself is the first long quotation by both the *London Quarterly Review* (30 [April 1868]: 85–86) and by Oliphant, and it is also quoted by the *Times,* the *Edinburgh Review* (127 [January 1868]: 286), and the *Daily Telegraph,* which notes that it "illustrates the quiet habit of the Royal Writer to go unknown among her people." This unexpected privileging of a footnote emphasizes the reviews' attentiveness to themes of concealment: what is hidden, in this text, is what is worth looking for.

Another incognito feature of the journal highlighted by the reviews is Albert's deer stalking. Of the many hunting episodes in *Leaves,* the reviewers single out for attention those in which concealment is especially emphasized. One review, in accounting for the Highlands' great appeal for Victoria and Albert, links the two kinds of hiding explicitly:

> [T]here can be little doubt that the entire seclusion of Balmoral, the distance from railways, and the perfect contrast to the conventional and stately splendour of court life, had very much to do in influencing the selection; not to speak of the Prince's intense love of sport, especially the difficult, but exciting, sport of "deer-stalking," for which the neighborhood affords such splendid opportunities. (*London Quarterly Review* 30 [April 1868]: 88)

The reviewer then quotes a letter by Albert that Victoria inserted in her account of their first visit to Scotland. As with the reviews' copious quoting of the footnote about Taymouth, it is peculiar that so much attention should be focused on passages that are not properly part of the Queen's journal.

> "Without doubt deer-stalking is one of the most fatiguing, but it is also one of the most interesting of pursuits. There is not a tree, or a bush behind which you can hide yourself . . . [elipsis in original]. One has, therefore, to be constantly on the alert in order to circumvent them; and to keep under the hill out of their wind, crawling on hands and knees, and dressed entirely in grey." (*Leaves*, 35)[62]

In the newer *London Quarterly Review*, this episode is directly followed by a deer-stalking episode from the Balmoral journal in which, having concealed himself with Victoria and a servant, Albert shoots a roe. The sport is interrupted by the sudden appearance of a witch-like old woman on crutches; when the beaters "were told to take up the roe, they first saw the old woman, and started, and stared with horror—which was very amusing to see" (*Leaves*, 114–15).[63] When Victoria and Albert hide, their target changes from a deer into a witch, linking this episode to the "Visits to the Old Women" in which Victoria, like a deer stalker, once again takes pleasure in both concealing and revealing herself. (Giving the lie to Victoria's pose of sympathetic identification with poor old Scotswomen, this episode also recalls Victoria's "amus[ement]" and "delight" over the "astonishment and fright" felt by the citizens who recognize the royal party belatedly on the first expedition.) Albert's attention to the importance of dressing entirely in grey resonates adventitiously with the importance later of General Grey in facilitating their incognito tour, the General Grey who enables Victoria's imposture as the concealed and revealed author of *Early Years*. Deer stalking (and the verbal coincidence is not needed to make this connection) is another form of the royal disguise through which Victoria gives narrative life both to the performance of privacy that the Queens' Books together constitute and to the performance of her own vanishing, performances designed both to replace and to emphasize the absence to which they refer.

Leaves functions like the authentic Scots cairns it so unnoticingly displaces: its presence, like a cairn, marks an absence, while its simultaneous status as monumental absence—its signification of Victoria's absence from public life—marks her living presence. The compulsively energetic royal family can never build enough cairns, just as the task of memorializing or representing life can never be complete. Victoria's ostensible purpose is to memorialize Albert by publishing *Leaves,* to make every word and every heap of stones refer to him and recuperate his loss. She even built a cairn at Balmoral to commemorate the spot where he killed his last stag. But, for a public considerably more interested in her than in Albert, the volume transforms the memorializing of him into the self-memorializing of her, in the double sense that it aggrandizes her presence and enables (or even effects) her disappearance. "While she tried to raise a monument to the Prince Consort, [she] added a stalwart buttress to her own throne," writes Kingsley in *Fraser's*. Chapter 4 will consider in more detail the nonliterary monuments Victoria raised to Albert's memory and their tendency, like the books, to represent her more than him; but this chapter will close with a closer look at the ways in which *Leaves* was perceived to represent Victoria's subjects.

The Reform Bill and the Queen's Footnotes

This chapter began by proposing that the Queen's staged absences, together with her books, coincided both with the retarding of electoral reform (in that they assert her presence and constitute symbolic representations or representations of culture that would replace direct democratic representation) and with its arrival, in that they assert her absence and cede the space of public representation to others. This equivocal effect matches the double view of the Reform Bill that Bagehot's equivocal account of "representation" exemplifies. There is, however, a feature of *Leaves* that suggests, in balance, that the Queen's book was seen as more encouraging than discouraging to reform, just as, above, I suggested we take seriously the substitution of Bright's "much talking in the evening" for the Queen's just after the publication of *Early Years.* The close of this chapter will turn again to Kingsley's anomalous review of *Leaves* in *Fraser's* to offer further support for this equivocal claim and, too, for the view that *Leaves* had a predominantly democratizing effect. This review curiously connects the "Queen's Book" to her status as constitutional monarch, a monarch who rules by what Kingsley calls the "suffrage" of her subjects.

In Europe, Kingsley writes, "the king has always been more or less the elected ideal of his people. His authority has been, in the long run, a moral authority, dependent on the public opinion of free men" (155). Christopher Pye supports the notion that England has a long tradition of viewing the monarch as "sovereign representative": he shows that for Hobbes the seventeenth-century king is *made* by his subjects to provide a visually coherent form for the commonwealth, and that he then "forms their wills," but only in the image in which they create him ("The Sovereign, the Theater," 89). Whereas in France the kings attempted to imitate "a sort of Eastern sultanship" and had to be removed, according to Kingsley, in England the Hanoverian monarchs have retained their position "by public opinion and really universal suffrage" (156). This "suffrage" becomes a distinctly literary category when Kingsley applies it to the book at hand. By revealing how much her life resembles the lives of her subjects, the Queen reinforces her claim to their "suffrage." To "peruse these pages" is to

> find that the British people are at least following the example of their Queen, and that she is, in this as in other things, the representative of her subjects. (157)

She rules because she represents them, and she represents them because she is like them, although she is like them because they follow her example, after the fashion of Hobbes's mutually creating subjects and monarch. Lord Salisbury, St. Aubyn points out, claimed that "once he had ascertained what the Queen thought, he 'knew pretty certainly what view her subjects would take, and especially the middle class of her subjects'" (St. Aubyn, *Queen Victoria*, 367).[64]

This notion of her representativeness makes explicit what Oliphant implies when she writes in *Blackwood's* that Victoria's journals resemble "similar records" in "family hoards" all over Britain, or what the *Edinburgh Review* suggests in saying that the "Queen's Book" describes a country-house life that is not far off from typical ("it would not be easy for any of them to draw a more pleasing and accurate picture . . . than the Queen has given us from Balmoral"). Being like her subjects means, in Kingsley's review, that they could have written her book for her. Those who think they know nothing of queens and kings

> could form a much more faithful picture—at least of the English court—by appealing to their own better feelings. . . . the average Briton should be

able to sketch for himself what royalty ought to do in the retirement of a country house. On reading these pages, he will find his sketch forestalled by the Queen's. (155)

Kingsley curiously figures the Queen's ability to represent her people as their ability to have written, or represented, her, where to write her is to consult their own feelings. They follow her example, but that is because she is modeled on them. Like the situation of authorial concealment and revelation in *Early Years,* whereby Grey and Victoria each seem to have authored and not to have authored the work, *Leaves* too seems to be written now by the Queen, now by the common life of the upper middle class. And this shared and submerged authorship constitutes the condition under which Queen Victoria can come to "represent" her subjects. Pye shows that while Hobbes thought he was exalting the sovereign's power by making him a "sovereign representative," he can also be read as paving the way for 1642, by reducing the king to an artificial—and therefore dispensable—body. Victoria, unlike the unfortunate sovereign of 1642, retains her sovereignty by vanishing into the world created by her subjects, "her home," in the words of the *Daily Telegraph,* "but one of many like it."

This way of representing her subjects would seem to differ greatly from Bagehot's notion that the Queen's representational function is to misrepresent the government. And yet it is also curiously akin to the queenly powers Bagehot names under the trope of *occupatio,* the lack of power that conceals the presence of the Queen's never-exercised powers to transform or destroy the nation. Like the idea that the end of the Crimean war can be attributed to her "luck," Bagehot's list of her unused powers and Kingsley's notion that she is a representative at once minimize and vastly expand claims made for her power. She becomes trivial and Everywoman at the same time. The Queen vanishes, and in her vanishing lies her power.

Kingsley's sense that she represents her subjects by being indistinguishable from them and written by them seems to combine the two senses of "represent" used in the reform debate. It sounds like symbolic representation; and yet the Queen is understood not so much to speak for her subjects, as a symbolically representative aristocratic MP would be understood to do, as to be like them, as descriptive representation would require. This focus on her representation of her people may be why Kingsley—the only reviewer to claim that *Leaves* is an openly political book—singles out for his only extensive quotation the visits to the poor old women (and why all the others quote this episode, too), with commentary emphasizing Victoria's wish to see the classes "blend" through their "community of interests" (157, quoting Helps's preface, *Leaves,* xii); and why not only Kingsley but all the other reviews discussed here mention Victoria's extensive footnotes detailing the life histories of her servants.

In her close supervision of the book's production, Victoria took pains to ensure that the published book, and especially these footnotes, would be easily accessible. Reviewing *Early Years,* the *Daily Telegraph* had said that "her Majesty makes friends of her readers." She wrote to Arthur Helps that she wanted *Leaves* to be "much read, especially by the *people,* her *real* friends," so she wanted the price low enough "so that *everyone can* buy it." (By "the *people,*" she means everyone below the elite few thousands who might complain of the loss of royal balls and levees; she does not distinguish between middle and working classes.) She wanted them especially to be able to read the footnotes: "[T]he Queen thinks it a pity that the *notes* are in such small print—containing as they do so much matter. *Will* they be *enough* read?"[65] Victoria had written to Vicky that "the kindly feelings expressed to those below us" would "do so much good" (*Your Dear Letter,* 166, 21 December 1867), and after the book appeared, she understood its popularity to confirm these motives. On 12 January 1868 a Mr. Van de Weger tells her it is "so much liked" because of "the simple narrative of our happy home life, the love dearest Albert and I bore to one another, and the kindly feeling and friendly footing, in which we lived with our people" (RA Queen Victoria's Journal, 12 January 1868). She had expressed to Vicky her view of the social purpose of *Leaves* only three days after writing to her that "the lower classes . . . ought not to be kept back" (*Your Dear Letter,* 165, 18 December 1867). *Leaves* is Victoria's own private Reform Bill, in which she reconciles high and low by exhibiting the virtues of the low for the benefit of the high and by exhibiting her own model behavior toward "our people."

As in Catherine Gallagher's reading of Disraeli and, too, of Eliot, the loyal Kingsley suggests that literary representations may serve as an alternative to political representation, and the Queen's way of merging symbolic and descriptive representation would further strengthen her claim to obviate any form of popular representation. Oliphant's idea that the Queen's Book resembles "similar records" would thus be of a piece with their shared opposition to women's suffrage; the Queen represents well enough.[66] In Kingsley's review, the Queen's rule and her story represent women in particular:

> By telling her own story, simply, earnestly, confidently, Her Majesty has appealed to women's suffrage, of a most subtle and potent kind.

If votes for women would, according to Sir Francis Crossley, prove (as he did not want it proven) that voting is a right not a trust, then the "women's suffrage" Kingsley claims for *Leaves* reinforces his other claims for the Queen's capacity to "represent" and to counteract the case for numerical democracy. If the Queen is making an Arnoldian claim to represent her nation literally, in keeping with her lukewarm enthusiasm for any expansion of the electorate, then the Queen's Books would indeed seem intended to obstruct her subjects' search for their own forms of representation, whether symbolic or descriptive.

At the same time, however, those footnotes urge the opposite argument as well. Even though any written representation may constitute symbolic representation, the footnotes, on the evidence of the response they provoked, do more than simply co-opt (by replacing it) "the representation of the people." Subordinate to the story of the Queen's doings, outside the text proper, semi-concealed by their small print, they draw attention to themselves by their obscurity, as does the footnote about Victoria's incognito return to Taymouth discussed above. As with Victoria's performances of her absence, they spring to view because they seem hidden. To cite one of the most notorious examples:

> Saturday, September 16, 1848. At half-past nine o'clock Albert and I set off in a postchaise, and drove to the bridge in the wood of Balloch Buie, about five miles from Balmoral, where our ponies and people were. Here we mounted, and were attended by a keeper of Mr. Farquharson's as guide, Macdonald*—who, with his shooting-jacket, and in his kilt, looked a picture—Grant† on a pony, with our luncheon in two baskets, and Batterbury* on another pony. (*Leaves*, 103–4)

From this passage depend three footnotes, on each of the attendants, including the following on Grant:

> †Head-keeper. He had been nearly twenty years with Sir Robert Gordon, nine as keeper; he was born in Braemar, in the year 1810. He is an excellent man, most trustworthy, of singular shrewdness and discretion, and most devotedly attached to the Prince and myself. He has a fine intelligent countenance. The Prince was very fond of him. He has six sons,—the second, Alick, is wardrobe-man to our son Leopold: all are good, well-disposed lads, and getting on well in their different occupations. His mother, a fine, hale, old woman of eighty years, "stops" in a small cottage which the Prince built for her in our village. He, himself, lives in a pretty Lodge called Croft, a mile from Balmoral, which the Prince built for him. (*Leaves*, 103–4)

Even though the Queen describes Macdonald, Grant, and Batterbury as "ours" and moralizes freely about them, the footnotes also acknowledge that those who figure marginally in her text have a life of their own outside the text. Widow Symons is not just insubordinate to the Queen; she also gets a footnote stating when she died (in January 1865; *Leaves,* 162), as if her life counted for something beyond the anecdote she usefully supplies. The footnote is the only mechanism available to the Queen (who is otherwise so proprietary) for gesturing beyond her text.

Moreover, the footnotes not only attracted the favorable attention of all the reviewers I have mentioned, they also aroused the anger of Vicky and other royal family members and intimates, who seem on this evidence to have found in them a radical potential contained neither by their formal diminutiveness nor by their generally patronizing tone. Vicky and Lady Augusta Stanley disliked the display of socially leveling intimacy with servants (St. Aubyn, *Queen Victoria,* 365). As Longford recounts it, Lady Augusta stutters fixatedly over the very term "footnote," as if the word itself embodied the social relations she deplores: she "resented the footnotes retailing the life histories of footmen as if they had been gentlemen: it gave the dangerous impression 'that all are on the same footing'" (Longford, *Queen Victoria,* 375). Footnotes should not put footmen on a footing with "our dear One." The longest footnote, the one most often cited in reviews, recounts the life and connections of John Brown (*Leaves,* 128–29), whose intimacy with the Queen was a particular source of discomfort for her children.[67]

Arthur Helps's preface also betrays anxiety about the footnotes. He devotes two out of his eight pages to his commentary on them, and he writes of them—and this remark is quoted by most of the reviews that mention the footnotes—that they

> illustrate, in a striking manner, the Patriarchal feeling (if one may apply such a word as "patriarchal" to a lady) which is so strong in the present occupant of the Throne. (*Leaves,* xii)

Helps wants to show that the notes reinforce the Queen's hierarchical relation to those she patronizes, yet his embarrassed use of "Patriarchal" suggests a defensive overinsistence on hierarchy. He is so anxious to assert social hierarchy that he tampers with the ordinarily sacrosanct hierarchy of gender. He moreover compulsively returns to the topic ("the Editor cannot refrain" from doing so) when, in closing, he includes himself among those who "render . . . services and attentions" (xiv) to the Queen and are grateful for her gratitude, as if his preface itself were an additional footnote, his small opportunity to be heard.

Reading for the footnotes may also be an aid to rereading those moments in the text proper when one suspects other voices may be breaking through the Queen's bland prose. Such moments might include the Highlanders' dwelling on the Queen's "lucky foot." She takes this to betoken their friendliness, but it suggests also the trivialization of her nation's rule over theirs, an interpretation possibly supported by Beatrice's fastidious omission of this phrase in her transcription of the original journal (see notes 52 and 61); she seems to have liked her mother's familiarity with the servants as little as her older siblings. The *Daily Telegraph*—the publication that, of all those I have cited, had the widest circulation, was read by workers, and supported reform the most unequivocally—curiously chooses the "lucky foot" passage to illustrate its claim that "never is the name of an attendant mentioned without some generous tribute or gracious recollection of service." This is not a passage notable for its generosity or graciousness toward servants, even though elsewhere this review like all the others quotes some of the footnotes about servants and emphasizes the visits to old women. The "lucky foot" passage is thus made to bear alone the burden of the newspaper's claim that Victoria is good to her servants. Perhaps her benign interpretation of their insubordination is what counts as "generosity." The *Daily Telegraph* also uses the footnote form to make a little class-leveling joke: just before quoting the Queen's footnotes on "our people," it supplies its own footnotes to explain the identities of "the Baby," "Bertie," and "Vicky," putting the royal children graphically on a footing with the servants. The Queen herself, employing the near-cognate term that bothered Lady Augusta Stanley, uses the phrase "friendly footing" to describe her book's account of class relations. "Pleasant" insubordination such as that of the old women—"I always say just what I think, not what is fut"—may not entirely fit Strachey's notion that "the power of a dependent still remains . . . one's own power"; but it is to the Queen's credit that she never wavers in her tolerance for "what is [not] fut."

In a letter to her daughter Alice, the Queen recommends her book both as a "*Memorial*" to herself after she is dead and for the "*tributes* in it to our *good people* which I should be glad the world knew."[68] In a single formulation, she imagines her own nonexistence and the continued life and value of her servants. There is of course no intent here to enfranchise them; if anything, the reverse. But such a formulation lends textual support to the counterargument I have been proposing, that the Queen's recourse to highly displaced forms of self-representation conceded to her subjects the public space of self-misrepresentation. If she represents her people by vanishing into them and becoming indistinguishable from them, as Kingsley claims, then her monarchic agency is, as in Bagehot, being expressed through her lack of agency and her appearance as disappearance. She is at once spectacle, the showy disguise of real government, and an invisible disguise, standing as she does at the double remove of literary self-representation that (in the case of *Early Years*) constitutes her authorship as her silence or (in the case of *Leaves*) makes concealment its central theme. Literary self-representation ultimately concedes the open secret that Bagehot himself is at no pains to keep—that the monarch cannot ever be present. And it concedes that "The Representation of the People," however flawed, is worth trying. But it took a widowed Queen and her representational choices to show that that is so.

The Queen did not disappear forever; her Jubilees of 1887 and 1897 placed her body as well as her much-duplicated image before the public in massive and successful celebrations. But she had already resumed a limited degree of public performance in the late 1860s and early 1870s. In the early and mid-1860s she made some rare appearances to unveil statues of Albert; these will be discussed in the next chapter. Shortly after the publication of *Leaves*, the Queen began to appear more frequently, in apparent contradiction of her belief that the book's success would eliminate the need for her to do so. The appearances, however, continued to call attention to her absence. On 6 March 1868 she held a Court at Buckingham Palace; she wore the Koh-i-noor diamond along with her black silk and her miniature portrait of Albert. A few weeks later she inspected her troops at Aldershot. The reporter for the *Times* curiously emphasizes the difficulty of catching sight of the Queen and her troops, and the lack of interest there is in seeing her. Most of the camp is "deserted," and the off-duty soldiers waiting for the Queen's arrival lounge about "with apparently as much sense of expectation as some few groups of ordinary persons, who . . . stood beneath the leafless trees, as if for shelter from the hot sun" (*Times*, 16 April 1868). The general is dressed informally; there is no crowd to greet the Queen; the troops are few in number and for the most part only discernible in the distance by "the occasional glitter of helmets." The Queen arrives more than an hour late, her approach heralded by the "distant . . . piff-paff of guns"; her small procession (only two carriages) arrives at the back of the field, behind the spectators. Finally the ceremony begins, and the marching is "fine," but it is all over quickly and the Queen returns the way she came. Like the memorial unveilings to be discussed in the next chapter, this kind of public appearance, although a concession to the demand that she appear, emphasizes her continued obscurity more than it celebrates her return.

Her appearance in February 1872 at the service of Thanksgiving for the recovered health of the Prince of Wales had a different effect altogether.[69] This massively popular event, at which the Queen and her son performed generously and tirelessly, is generally thought to have brought to an end the worst consequences of her retirement, particularly the republican movement, by providing an occasion for public celebration of the monarchy. The Queen herself had been seriously ill in the summer and autumn of 1871 (with an infected throat and then an abcess on her arm) when the Prince of Wales fell ill with typhoid in November. In the same month, although she had made more public appearances in 1871 than in the previous ten years, Sir Charles Dilke in a speech at Newcastle condemned the Queen for her dereliction of duty and for the costliness of maintaining the royal family. Other signs of republicanism had emerged that fall: Charles Bradlaugh's speeches on the "Impeachment of the House of Brunswick" and a pamphlet entitled "What Does She Do with It?"[70] But popular sentiment sided with the Queen, who rushed to Sandringham to the bedside of her ailing child. The Queen writes in her diary: "The feeling shown by the whole nation is quite marvellous and most touching and striking, showing how really sound and truly loyal the people really are. Letters and telegrams pour in and no end of recommendations of remedies of the most mad kind."[71] By January 1872 it was clear that the Prince would recover, and plans were made for a Thanksgiving service to be held in St. Paul's.

Not only the Queen but the royal convalescent himself, riding in an open carriage with his mother, participated in the long procession to the cathedral and back to Buckingham Palace, although the *Times* pointed out the dubious wisdom of having him risk his health on that cold, wet day. Although the Queen had initially resisted having her participation in a religious observance put on display, these two crucial aspects of the event—the open carriages and her riding with the Prince—were her inspired ideas.[72] The newspapers regularly reported on the state of Bertie's health during his illness, and the procession celebrated the presence of his body, even to his balding head, on view when he doffed his hat to recognize the crowd's cheers. ("Bertie was continually with his hat off," writes the Queen in her diary [*Letters and Journals*, 216, 27 February 1872].) In an echo of the Queen's appearance at Aldershot in 1868, the report pauses over initial uncertainty as to whether the royal bodies will be visible. The first seven carriages in the procession are closed, but when the eighth and ninth, containing the royal family, turn out to be open, the crowd's pleasure is all the greater ("universal delight," according to the *Times*, 28 February 1872) for the drama of concealment that went before.

The news reports of the day's events are lengthy and celebratory, but according to the *Times* the rejoicing is as much for the reappearance of the Queen as it is for the recovery of the Prince of Wales. "By the inscriptions on most of the decorations, and by their inexhaustible cheering, the people of London endeavored to show that their Queen is as well beloved by them as ever, and that their delight at seeing her once more among them, performing a function of Royalty in the Metropolis of her Empire, was not less than that which they felt at the recovery of her heir." One banner reads, "With thee we mourned and with thee rejoice"; another reads, "Our sorrow is turned to joy." Thus the paper, eliding one "sorrow" with another, treats Bertie's illness as a stand-in for Victoria's years of mourning, and through the termination of Bertie's illness declares an end to that mourning. Moreover, in symbolic performance she is no longer alone, the position she had always adopted to express her widowhood:

> Every one seemed touched by a peculiar satisfaction at seeing Her Majesty in the same carriage with the Prince and Princess of Wales and their eldest son. [If they] had been in separate carriages ... the hearts of the people would not have been so deeply touched. ... The people cheered not so much a Queen and a Prince as the Mother and her Son. The recollection of all she had suffered in those cruel days and of her present joy blinded not a few eyes in the crowd, while others of sterner mould found relief in passionate outbursts of delight. (*Times*, 28 February 1872)

Again eliding one set of "cruel days" with another, the paper blurs one family tie with another and confers upon the Queen a recovered "joy" to make up for all losses (never mind the Queen's private skepticism about Bertie's morals and his fitness to reign after her). Albert's death is remembered only to be erased, as one middle-aged "Prince" silently replaces another. And indeed by all accounts she looked happy: she "had a smile and a bow for every one."

In addition to its erasure of the Queen's widowhood, the *Times* also reverses the relation of spectator and spectacle. Its report begins by asserting that "no monarch ever saw such a spectacle as Queen Victoria did yesterday." "The real spectacle of the National Thanksgiving," the report continues, is "the people, the never exhausted masses which covered all the pavements, filled all the windows and balconies and stands from street to housetop and spread themselves even over the roofs, and who, with a joy which is simply indescribable, exerted voices and arms and hands to greet the Prince and congratulate Her Majesty."[73] Even more so than in the report of the Queen's procession to open the Royal Exchange in 1844 (discussed in Chapter 1), the focus of this report is on the spectators. In 1844, the fine clothing of the spectators was stressed, as befitted a celebration of commerce, and there was much richer description of the Queen and her attendants as well: the perspective was that of the reporter on the ground. Here, the perspective is often that of the Queen looking out of her carriage ("Her Majesty received the expression of their loyalty ... with a feeling akin to delight"), and it is the turnout itself, rather than the people's economic strength, that is "the greatest marvel of all the marvels": the fact that they still care about their neglectful Queen, and the fact of their "mighty mass."

The lead editorial echoes these emphases on the Queen's prior absence and on the Queen as spectator of the "multitudes" in a way that confirms what I have been suggesting about the relation between her absence and popular representation.

> The sight which the Queen and the Prince saw in going and returning was more magnificent, more gratifying to the Heads of a reigning House, than the most brilliant assembly which rank and wealth . . . could furnish. . . . The younger people hardly remember the times when the Queen and the Prince Consort in the prime of life came freely among the public. They were popular then . . . but the numbers at yesterday's gathering, the occasion of their coming together, and, perhaps, the long period which has elapsed since they have had the opportunity of witnessing a similar spectacle, caused the cheers to be almost deafening.

The *Times*'s implication is clear: the Queen's absence means that when she returns, she returns as spectator to the spectacle of her loyal people more than as spectacle herself. Anticipating her future nonexistence by celebrating the survival of her heir and his heir, through her prolonged absence no longer entitled to a position as sole center of attention, the Queen now finds her popularity in her deference to her people. Although she has returned to performing her monarchy in person, the relation between her self-representations and theirs has been permanently changed: her appearing now serves only to show them how multitudinous, and how powerful, they themselves really are.

4

QUEEN VICTORIA'S
MEMORIAL ARTS

Albert Memorials

In the morning of the day in May 1867 when John Stuart Mill, MP for Westminster, moved that the word "person" be substituted for "man" in the language of the Reform Bill, so as to enfranchise single women, Queen Victoria made one of her rare public appearances of the 1860s to lay the foundation stone for the Royal Albert Hall. Although I have been emphasizing the scarcity of her appearances during this period and her effort to substitute for them written self-representations, Victoria did make exceptions for one kind of public ceremonial: unveiling or dedicating statues and other memorials of Albert.[1] Her books were also intended as memorials, a purpose that, as we have seen, reviewers tended to downplay, finding greater interest in the books' representations of the Queen herself. "While she tried to raise a monument to the Prince Consort, [she] added a stalwart buttress to her own throne," writes Charles Kingsley in his review of *Leaves* (*Fraser's* 77 [February 1868]: 154). Just so, public appearances intended to memorialize Albert were of interest to the public instead as opportunities to see her. Her speech at the building site of the Royal Albert Hall—where 7,000 elite ticket holders had packed into the tent to see her—captures this tension:

> It has been with a struggle that I nerved myself to a compliance with the wish that I should take part in this day's ceremony; but I have been sustained by the thought that I should assist by my presence in promoting the accomplishment of his great designs to whose memory the gratitude and affection of the country is now rearing a noble monument. (*Times*, 21 May 1867)

The speech (made "in so low a tone of voice as to be scarcely audible"), as much about herself as about Albert, ends with a performative: "It is my wish that this hall should bear his name to whom it will have owed its existence, and be called 'The Royal Albert Hall of Arts and Sciences.'" Acting out her love for Albert, she also and perhaps more saliently displays her unique powers and status as Queen, whose "presence" and whispered words can cause a building to rise and acquire a name. In addition to laying the foundation stone for the Royal Albert Hall, the Queen was "present at" the unveiling of a statue in Aberdeen in October 1863, "inaugurat[ed]" a statue in Wolverhampton in November 1866, "inspect[ed]" on 9 June 1863 a statue inaugurated the day before by the Prince of Wales, was "present at" the unveiling of a statue at Perth in August 1864 (a "trying and overpowering" event according to her journal), and traveled to Coburg in August 1865 to unveil a statue (a copy of which was sent to Sydney).[2] In the virtually empty calendar of her public appearances during these years, these loom large.

On 20 May 1867, while others were seeking the parliamentary representation of women (which she consistently opposed as "mad and utterly demoralising"),[3] she represented herself by representing Albert. Later on this day, back at Windsor, she also unveiled Theed's memorial statue of herself and Albert in Anglo-Saxon dress (now in the Frogmore mausoleum), a statue that portrays the Queen's devotion and reverence toward the departed Prince. With this triple coincidence, one could argue about these monuments (following Gallagher) that they, together with her books, constitute Arnoldian symbolic alternatives to parliamentary representation, particularly at this moment to the representation of women. They set an example of wifely deference, as well as of symbolic government, that would help silence the call for women's electoral representation. The report of the ceremony in the *Times* the next day calls attention to the "striking contrast" between the "robes of scarlet, fur, and ermine" worn by the dignitaries (all men) and the "bright, cool, light attire of the ladies around" ("the prevailing tints were white and green"). Although Victoria herself wore her customary black, as a visual spectacle the ceremony in which she participated thus illustrated the sex difference that formed the basis of the most vigorous objections to female suffrage—that (in the words of Mr. Laing, as reported in the *Times* two pages earlier) "between the two sexes it was abundantly evident that Nature had drawn clear lines of distinction." Victoria herself would have concurred: citing Tennyson's "beautiful lines" in *The Princess,* she writes, "God created men and women different—then let them remain each in their own position" (Martin, *Queen Victoria as I Knew Her,* 70). Despite the claim of one of Mill's few supporters in Parliament that Victoria's excellent governing makes the case for female suffrage, Victoria's actions earlier that day spoke for the precedence of symbolism over suffrage.

One could, however, also speculate (as in Chapter 3) that such monuments as Victoria inaugurated that day also constitute an indirect encouragement to democracy, even to female suffrage. For example, at the four corners of the Scottish national memorial (whose design the Queen selected in 1865) stand realistically depicted figures of people in modern dress paying tribute to an equestrian figure of Albert. Although these four groups represent the upper and laboring classes, the armed services, and the arts and sciences, they do so nonallegorically, setting an example for the viewers (including women) that they mimetically resemble (*Cult,* 70). The Queen, who supervised the construction of this memorial closely, particularly liked this feature of the plan; on unveiling day in 1876 she writes, "The effect of the monument as a whole, with the groups at the angles of the pedestal, is very good" (*More Leaves,* 142). These statues could be understood in the same way as the footnotes in *Leaves:* replacing popular self-representation yet also encouraging it by example. During the period of the Reform Bill debate, the Queen periodically tried to get Parliament to appropriate and increase funds for a national memorial to the Prince Consort. (In July 1866, for example, in the midst of a ministerial crisis and the Prussian war, Victoria induced the new Disraeli ministry to supplement the £50,000 already allocated in 1863). Of course, this preoccupation with her personal sorrows seemed self-centered, yet memorializing the Prince—even in monuments that do not include figures of ordinary citizens—also constitutes a symbolic equivalent (rather than alternative) to reform, in that both displace Victoria's iconic centrality.

As we shall see by the end of this chapter, the Queen is herself ultimately effaced by the process of memorializing Albert. Turning what might have been private grieving into a public national project, the Queen, on the one hand, draws attention—in what seems to be a monumentally self-centered way—to herself; on the other hand, this very self-centeredness comes to constitute the offering up to her subjects (women as well as men) of control over royal representations.

Elisabeth Darby and Nicola Smith provide a catalogue of memorials that present Albert's image in various media, and it is important to grasp the scale on which Albert was memorialized by the Queen in concert with her subjects. In addition to the national memorial on the site of the Crystal Palace there were Welsh, Scots, and Irish national memorials. Despite national fund-raising for the Hyde Park memorial, over twenty-five towns and cities in Britain and abroad erected their own sculptural monuments (see *Cult,* 67); still other localities allocated funds for less costly windows or paintings to be installed in public buildings. Royal memorials, some of which were made public or photographed for public consumption, included busts and full-size sculptures for the various royal residences, the Frogmore mausoleum on the grounds of Windsor Castle (consecrated 17 December 1862 and the Prince's body deposited in it the next day, in the presence of the Queen) and the Albert Memorial Chapel in Windsor (begun 1863 and opened to the public in 1875), an indoor statue for Balmoral unveiled 17 October 1863 and copied colossally in bronze for the grounds (unveiled 15 October 1867), and, of course, a cairn. Later in this chapter, we will consider two other kinds of cultural Albert memorials. Dickens wrote to a friend in 1864, "If you should meet with an inaccessible cave anywhere, to which a hermit could retire from the memory of Prince Albert and testimonials to the same, pray let me know of it. We have nothing solitary and deep enough in this part of England."[4] Because Victoria's mourning has become a nationwide project, the public sphere may be defined as that place where Albert is mourned; in the private sphere, Dickens's suppositional cave, Albert is not mourned, which is to say that it does not exist. Turning over to the public what should more properly be termed her melancholia (because her mourning is interminable), Victoria ultimately—as with her indirect encouragement of reform—reaffirms the monarch's disappearance and the assumption of the monarch's work by others.

Nonetheless, the monuments to Albert that "soon covered the land" (in Gladstone's phrase) did serve, in the absence of other representations, to represent the absent Victoria. Memorials raised to Albert by towns and cities were motivated as much by loyalty to the Queen as by enthusiasm for the Prince's memory (*Cult,* 58), and this chapter will begin by considering the Queen's acts of self-representation in creating and displaying monuments to Albert. Representing herself by implication as self-effacing and devoted, she nonetheless calls attention to herself, much as her appearance in widow's black makes her a visibly present absence in such representations as Frith's painting of the Prince of Wales's marriage (figure 28).

This situation is graphically illustrated by a substitution that occurred in the production of a monument to the Great Exhibition, planned in 1853, which was to have included a statue of Albert. During his lifetime, Albert had humorously resisted having his image used:

> [I]t would both disturb my quiet rides in Rotten Row to see my own face staring at me, and if (as is very likely) it became an artistic monstrosity, like most of our monuments, it would upset my equanimity to be permanently ridiculed and laughed at in effigy.[5]

Eventually an image of Victoria was chosen instead, the Queen presumably being more inured to her own monumentalization. After Albert's death, however, the Queen made it known that she wanted Albert's image substituted for hers, despite the Prince's stated wish. The monument was unveiled in June 1863. This episode set a precedent not only for making Albert memorials (*Cult*, 2) but also for using Albert's image to represent the Queen.

Her first major public appearance after Albert's death was her trip to Aberdeen to unveil, on 13 October 1863, Marochetti's seated figure of Albert in military dress, which she praised as "fine and like" (*More Leaves*, 19; see discussion in *Cult*, 84, 101–2). This occasion (discussed Chapter 2) dramatized the Queen's continued absence even when she was present, for citizens had been asked not to cheer or wave banners as she passed through the city. At the ceremony she silently handed a copy of her speech to the provost, who had silently handed a copy of his speech to her. The provost's address emphasized both the inadequacy of the memorial statue (which had been criticized for incongruously alluding to a speech the Prince gave to the British Association for the Advancement of Science in Aberdeen while also presenting him in military gear) and the remarkableness of the Queen's visit:

> No memorial is necessary to preserve the name of one who adorned the highest station of the land by the brightest display of intellectual and moral greatness. How inadequate for such a purpose the memorial we have erected must be, we ourselves must deeply feel. But that Your Majesty should have on this occasion graciously come forth again to receive the public homage of your loyal and devoted people, we regard as a ground of heartfelt thankfulness. (*More Leaves*, 21)

Thus attention was on the histrionically mourning Queen as much as or more than on the unmoving and inadequate image of Albert.

On 30 November 1866 she traveled to Wolverhampton to unveil the first statue of Albert erected by a municipality at its own expense, an equestrian statue of Albert in military dress chosen by the Queen despite—in the words of a local newspaper account—her husband's "gentle, science-loving" nature (quoted in *Cult*, 74). In the oft-told anecdote, the Queen was so pleased by the occasion that she borrowed a sword to knight the mayor; terrified, he thought she was about to behead him. As in Bagehot's *occupatio* construction of monarchy in *The English Constitution* (and recalling too Victoria's resemblance to the excessively violent Queen of Hearts, in Munich's reading), in this story the Queen demonstrates how vast and violent are her powers, even when held in check. Because of this anecdote, which rarely fails to accompany mentions of this statue, the visit to Wolverhampton comes to be about the Queen's powers, not about Albert or his memory. In the Queen's own epistolary account of the event she does not mention the mayor, but she does describe the "immense loyalty displayed" to her and the "unanimity" of the spectators, even including the "lowest, poorest people," and she notes her power to draw a crowd of 100,000 in a city of 75,000 (*Your Dear Letter,* 109–10). In the summer of 1866, in the midst of the Prussian war, she had just chosen a new ministry and set up a new foreign office. But given the invisible nature of these procedings, an event such as the nonbeheading of the mayor of Wolverhampton is the only way in which her powers can be made visible.[6]

As the jarring choice of a military pose for Wolverhampton suggests, monuments to Albert with which Victoria was associated are often generically inconsistent: they uneasily conjoin, or alternate between, what the Queen repeatedly refers to as "likeness" and what she calls allegory. The inclusion of the horse alludes to the traditional genre for celebrating military heroes. Benedict Read suggests that the widespread nineteenth-century creation of public memorials was sparked and given "major momentum" by the Napoleonic Wars; the Duke of Wellington was commemorated with more than one equestrian statue.[7] In this context, to portray Albert on a horse is to equate his deeds symbolically with military successes. Yet in the Wolverhampton statue his own figure is incongruously realistic, clothed in his customary modern civilian street wear of frock coat and trousers. This kind of generic inconsistency bears importantly on the way these monuments serve Victoria, for, as I will argue, it allows them at once to memorialize and to efface the Prince. Among the profusion of memorial statues and paintings there are portraits of Albert in contemporary dress, or in the symbolic costumes required to do things he actually did, as well as equestrian statues and other allegorical representations that would seem to submit Albert to another range of meanings altogether (see *Cult,* 82–83). Some images represent the man himself, others represent his offices (for example, chancellor of Cambridge, field marshall) or his accomplishments (the Great Exhibition, his speech at Aberdeen); still others make him explicitly allegorical (representing virtue or religion). The Queen's approval was always sought, and her preference was for good likenesses on the one hand (invariably the form her praise takes) and for equestrian statues on the other: for realism and for allegory. Although in death Albert becomes coextensive with his monuments (as the living Queen cannot quite do), the strain in those monuments between achieving his likeness and transforming him into allegory—a strain visible in the Queen's writings about them as well as in the memorials themselves—is a conflict between remembering him and remembering his death, between building monuments to him and building them to the fact that he is dead.

Many of Victoria's mourning practices have been interpreted by Adrienne Munich as expressing her "intention to treat the dead Albert as if he were alive" (*Secrets*, 87). Victoria was known to dislike "the word 'late' applied to the Prince" and to believe strongly "in the *Life presence* of the Dead."[8] Munich argues convincingly that the daily maintenance of the room where he died at Windsor (as what Victoria termed a "beautiful living monument" [quoted in *Cult*, 7, and *Secrets*, 87]), the habit of speaking of him as if he were alive and about to enter the room, and the preservation of every object ever to have passed the scrutiny of his taste answer to the Queen's need to defuse rumors, loud in the period 1866–71, about her intimacy with John Brown.[9] I would place alongside this argument another view. She hung at the head of every bed in which she slept a photograph not of Albert living but of him on his death bed.[10] Even as the Queen bitterly and with indisputable sincerity laments his death, the works of art to which she gave her approval memorialize his death more than they remember his life. They mark her continued existence and his disappearance into the generic conventions of the various arts in which he was memorialized and into the lofty meanings his person was now required to bear. Aided by and exaggerating a property intrinsic to any representational form (the tendency to displace what is represented), her melancholic refusal or inability to complete her mourning for him takes the form in public art of endless reminders that he is dead and that she is still alive to lament his loss.

Moreover, that she sponsored the making of monuments at all amounts to the ascendency of her will over his wishes. Although ten days after Albert's death Victoria wrote to her uncle King Leopold of her "*irrevocable decision, . . . that his wishes—his plans . . . are to be my law!*" soon she was merely paying "lip-service to her husband's wishes, provided they coincided with her own."[11] Her desire for "numberless" effigies directly contravened Albert's views.[12] "If I should die before you, do not raise even a single marble image in my name," he had written; if any monument were to be built, he had more than once stated a preference for a useful institution promoting arts or sciences.[13] But on the evidence of the choices she made, Victoria is representing not Albert himself—his wishes or even his likeness—but his death and her grief.

Furthermore, the shading of these monuments from likeness into allegory means the overshadowing of the Prince with meanings imposed on him. Walter Benjamin claims that melancholy makes objects allegorical and melancholics allegorists (as when Heathcliff exclaims, "The entire world is a dreadful collection of memoranda that she did exist, and that I have lost her!"), but Victoria's melancholy goes further.[14] Given the unusual scale on which she was able to manifest her melancholy, and given her power to extend her agency over the artwork of others by commissioning, selecting, and supervising it, she not only found but created allegory, and effaced not only "the entire world" but Albert himself in the process of turning everything into signifiers of his loss. As representations of Albert display the disjunctiveness of their parts and Albert's subordination to allegorical meanings, they represent the power of the Queen's melancholy and efface on her behalf the very memory to which she clings.

Although the Queen chose not to look again at the Prince's dead body after the first day, preferring to "keep the impression given of life and health than have this one sad though lovely image imprinted too strongly in my mind" (*Dearest Mama*, 24), that she saw him on that first day "beautiful as marble" (ibid.) and on the second apparently approved of his being photographed suggests that she had already begun the process of monumentalizing him. In the letter to her eldest daughter in which she reports this impression, dated 18 December 1861, she also reports that she has already—after lengthy exclamations about her debilitating, "weary" grief—chosen "a spot in Frogmore Gardens for a mausoleum for us." And again on 27 December, a mere two weeks after Albert's death, she is busy with plans for memorializing and allegorizing Albert in yet another location:

> Can't you think of allegorical pictures and decorations? The sacred room is to be dedicated to him—and I wish it to be very beautiful and put some Raphaels on china perhaps into it and busts etc. Mr. Gruner will be here in three or four days and then we shall talk all over! (*Dearest Mama*, 31).

The same rhythm structures all these letters: debilitating grief is followed by recuperation in the form of frenetic memorializing activity. Planning for the Frogmore mausoleum occupied much of the Queen's attention immediately after Albert's death, but it was to be her resting place as well as his. Writing to her daughter on 27 January 1862, the Queen allows herself to express delight about how "very fine!" will be the monument, for which she expects to lay the first stone (she did, on March 15), and "There is to be but one sarcophagus and we shall lie together!" (*Dearest Mama*, 45). Memorializing transforms grief for Albert into yet another self-representation, into aesthetic pleasure, even into a displaced eroticism.[15]

The statues Victoria was present to dedicate or unveil—including those she herself commissioned—cover the generic range from likeness to symbolism to allegory. The statues for Balmoral, for example, depict Albert in a kilt, which he did sometimes wear, but only for ceremonial occasions such as the Highlanders' Ball. A kilt, moreover, is invariably symbolic garb, signifying England's imperial union with Scotland (see Trevor-Roper, "The Invention of Tradition"). The significance of the sculptured kilt oscillates therefore between symbolizing Albert's "imperialist nostalgia" for Scotland and constituting a realistic representation of his appearance there.[16] As we have seen, the equestrian statue for Wolverhampton similarly mixes genres. The Coburg statue, by Theed, thought by Victoria to be an excellent likeness, portrays Albert surrounded by a salad of incompatible signifying objects "in Garter robes holding a Field Marshall's baton and a plan of the Great Exhibition" (*Cult,* 77–78); similarly, as we have seen, the Aberdeen statue awkwardly combines the field marshall's uniform with an academic scroll, and the whole strikes the city's provost as "inadequate" to memorializing the Prince's primarily intellectual and moral achievements.

Much Victorian figuralism shares in this generic inconsistency. In the 1840s and 1850s a controversy had raged over the suitableness of modern dress for sculptures of men. Gibson, who put Peel in a toga in 1852, had remarked that the "human figure [in] frock coat and trousers is not a fit subject for sculpture" (quoted in *Victorian Sculpture,* 166). Official garb, such as Garter robes, was thought to be a good solution. Benedict Read writes that "the image presented would be intentionally formal, with little room for 'the man within' except insofar as this persona is externalised in just such a formal icon" (*Victorian Sculpture,* 169). To put Albert in Garter robes, as in the Coburg statue and another at Birmingham, is thus to fulfill a version of Albert's own claim that his invariable principle was "to sink his *own individual* existence in that of his wife—to aim at no power by himself, or for himself."[17] To place even the best likeness of Albert in Garter robes, or even on a horse, is to subordinate the individual or "man within" to the public icon. Generic inconsistency enables these monuments at once to memorialize the Prince's likeness and to efface him, substituting for the "man within" various sets of abstract virtues projected by the Queen and her image makers, virtues most of which no one had ever associated with Albert.

Victoria's private comments on the ongoing work on various Albert memorials emphasize her concern to make allegory coincide with likeness and the difficulty of doing so. By allegory she seems to mean both a treatment of mimetic images or likenesses so as to endow them with spiritual meaning (blurring the boundaries between allegory, symbolism, typology, and emblem), and representations of spiritual ideals in which any apparently mimetic element is unimportant (as in her phrase "allegorical . . . decorations"). In January 1862 Victoria, on the one hand, admires the likeness of Theed's bust and records her impression that the eyes of a tinted photograph "quite look at me . . . as if to tell me what to do"; on the other hand, she also praises a representation of Albert in "a suit of allegorical armor."[18] In February 1864, at the same time that she is busy at Osborne assembling papers for "the precious Life" and conferring with General Grey and Arthur Helps about its progress (February 2 and 3), she also reports on supervising a monument being constructed at the local Whippingham church (February 11 and 12) and consulting with the painter Edward Henry Corbould about another memorial effort (figure 32). "Saw Mr. Corbould about his beautiful allegorical painting of my beloved one. The likeness was not quite good and needed some alterations, which I watched him carry out, after luncheon" (RA Queen Victoria's Journal, 12 February 1864). Allegory and likeness must meet in the Queen's memorials, and she has no more important royal work than to make sure they do.

Corbould has been copying into his design Robert Thorburn's 1844 miniature of Albert in armor, a birthday gift to her from Albert and known to be her favorite portrait. Although portraying a contemporary in medieval garb was quite an innovation (see *Cult*, 37), to have her husband painted in armor had been "an old wish of the Queen's."[19] Later she wrote that it was the best likeness she knew, adding that "on the last morning of his life, he was wonderfully like this picture."[20] That his features in dying should come to resemble a particular portrait, as if that were equivalent to praising a portrait for its likeness to his face, suggests how rapidly (as in Victoria's comment that Albert was already "beautiful as marble") Albert died into art, his living memory replaced by representations that took precedence over him. Dying, Albert becomes allegorical, for as Girouard points out the armor in Thorburn's painting (like the military poses of many of the public statues) could have no referential relation to Albert's experience: instead, it "symbolised his chivalrous qualities in civilian life" (*Return to Camelot*, 115). But Corbould's job is to render the likeness allegorical and to elevate the symbolism of the armor to the level of allegory, so, with a shift in the pose of the hands and the addition of biblical scenes and some lines of German, Albert becomes "a Christian Knight in the act of sheathing his sword, his good fight fought" (*Cult*, 17). "Ich habe einen guten Kampf gekampfet": to put words into the dead man's mouth, to say what cannot be said ("I have died"), is ostentatiously to subject Albert's death to the representational powers of the still living.

When Victoria comments on her own sittings with Graeffle (which have been going on since early January 1862), it is his likenesses she admires (15 February 1864), as we should expect given her preference for photographs and her habit of giving photos to portrait painters (see Chapter 1). Late the previous year, she objected to Frith's "picture, in which the likenesses are not very good" (RA Queen Victoria's Journal, 17 December 1863); and again on April 18 the marble statue of her mother just installed in her mausoleum earns praise as "*so* like." But to hire Corbould to produce works of art is to ask for

FIGURE 32   Edward Henry Corbould, *Memorial Portrait of Prince Albert in Armor.* Oil painting, 1864.

something in addition to likeness: as Girouard puts it, he was already "the official depicter of chivalry to royalty" (*Return to Camelot,* 124). Corbould continues his work, designing a statuette to be given as a christening present to the Prince of Wales's firstborn, Prince Albert Victor. "At my own particular request and desire only dearest Albert's statuette is to be brought in, taken from the beautiful allegorical picture in armour, sheathing his sword with the words 'I have fought the good fight'" (RA Queen Victoria's Journal, 16 February 1864). The figure of Albert was a composite: the pose and costume from Corbould's allegorical rendering of Thorburn's miniature, the head copied by the sculptor Theed—who had taken the Prince's deathmask—from his own bust of Albert. But despite Victoria's admiration for this "most beautiful" object (quoted in *Cult*, 17), the seams show. The head appears slightly too large for the body, and the head and hands are silver while the armored body is gold. The figure displays how much labor is required to render likeness allegorical and, even then, that the labor is merely that of attaching the one to the other. But the internal contradictions of this figure only exaggerate those of Thorburn's 1844 image, with its wholly symbolical armor grafted onto a likeness of the "man within" so effective that Theodore Martin had it detached and engraved for the frontispiece of his *Life of the Prince Consort.*

Henri de Triqueti's recumbent marble effigy for the Albert Memorial Chapel at Windsor (figure 33), completed in 1873 and opened to the public in 1875, imitates on the horizontal the statuette's allegorical pose and, in turn, Corbould's painting.[21] Clothed in armor, Albert sheathes his sword over the words "I have fought the good fight, I have finished my course." This effigy duplicates also the statuette's display of the misfit between likeness and allegory. Albert's comb-over is meticulously rendered, and his beard is shaved into fashionable long sideburns. This undisguisedly modern head jars awkwardly against the medievalesque pose and props of angels at his head and a dog at his feet (although it is a real dog's portrait—Albert's dog Eos). Grafting Albert to allegory may be intended to elevate his memory, but translated into the materials of visual art, this endeavor can only reveal its cumbersome and incomplete process. As is also true of the other works posing Albert over the same inscription, tying the image to words moreover implies that the image alone might not supply the desired meaning. Stephen Bayley, summing up the character of Victorian sculpture at this period, points to its combination of allegory and literalism, a literalism that took the form both of exacting detail and of dependency on labels to render the allegorical program legible (*Albert Memorial,* 56). In this case, without the inscription Albert might be unsheathing his sword, with rather unexpected implications for a funerary image. Head and body seem readily detachable, and so do the image and its spiritual meanings.

Theed's first bust of Albert was a relatively simple work representing the head alone, with the top part of the chest abstractly indicated and resting on an unadorned pedestal, said by Victoria to be "life itself." Rapidly executed, by 27 January 1862 it was ready to be placed between the two beds in the Blue Room.[22] Theed's second bust, also completed in 1862, was not installed at Osborne until 10 February 1864 because of the "minuteness of execution" required for the pedestal (*Cult*, 7), which Princess Alice had designed with an ornamental encrustation of cherubs and flowers. In this second bust, Albert's otherwise naked shoulder is adorned with drapery "held by a buckle carrying a portrait of the young Queen Victoria" (*Cult*, 7). The ornamentation of the base together with the drapery and signifying brooch allegorize Albert. In contrast to the first relatively literal, literally unadorned image, the second bust presents Albert as a celestial being (supported by cherubs) who wears his meaning on his shoulder as a fashion accessory. This meaning, moreover, is his subordinate relation to Victoria. Although the draping of a naked torso is a respectably masculine classical motif, the portrait brooch is a distinctly feminizing touch; Victoria and her daughters wore such pins on their chests and shoulders to commemorate Albert. Here, the dead Albert, commemorated not for himself but for his marriage, serves to memorialize a proleptically mourned Victoria. The sequential order of these two busts—a relatively literal and unadorned likeness of the Prince followed by a work so encrusted with ornament that its availability as an object for use was delayed by well over a year—suggests that to allegorize the Prince is both to feminize him and to begin to forget him.

The latter is exactly the concern that was expressed about the National Albert Memorial for Hyde Park (figure 34). Guided by a selection committee

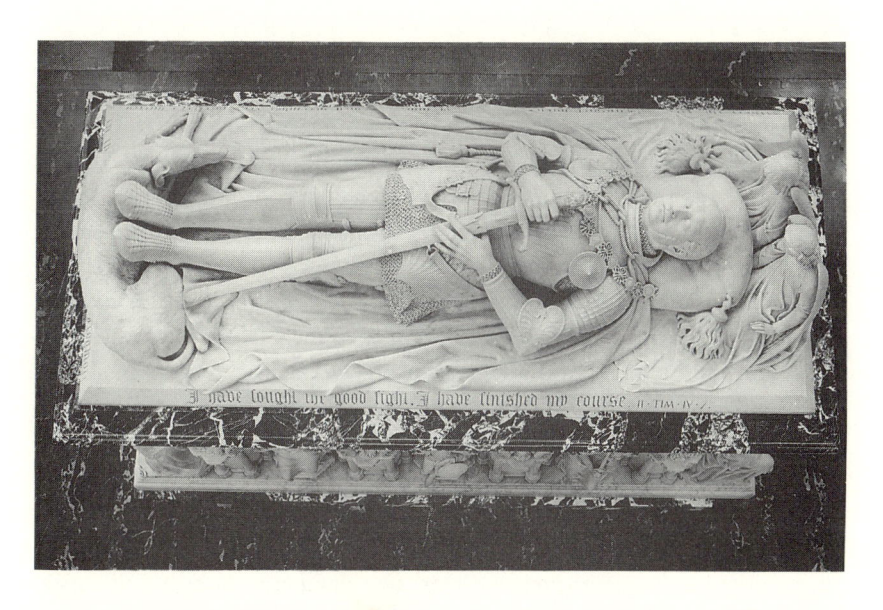

FIGURE 33   Henri de Triqueti, cenotaph of Prince Albert, Albert Memorial Chapel, Windsor, completed 1873. Detail.

and by her eldest daughter, the Queen in early 1863 chose George Gilbert Scott's elaborate and costly gothic design over various classical and abstract proposals.[23] A seated portrait statue of Albert was, by the Queen's wish, to be at the center of the memorial. Because the design competition was among the architects, however, the lion's share of public controversy and of public funds went to the architectural surround, the purpose of which, according to Scott's proposal, "is to protect and overshadow the statue of the Prince." His aim was to give "this overshadowing structure the character of a vast *shrine,* enriching it with all the arts by which it can be made to express the value attached to the object which it protects."[24] But reviewers criticized its extravagantly detailed ornamentation for failing to convey "true monumental character" and for conveying instead only a sense of lavishness and costliness; moreover, both the *Times* and the *Atheneum* complained that, with its elaborate sculptural programs, it memorialized not the Prince's character but the Great Exhibition and the arts and sciences he encouraged. The canopy over the statue's head also includes angels and allegorical figures of the virtues. Stephen Bayley suggests that for Scott it was a monument to the Gothic Revival as much as to Albert. Moreover, the shrine, completed in 1868, stood empty until 1872. The statue of Albert, put in place so long after the shrine was completed that it was never inaugurated and drew no public praise, lurks darkly, barely visible inside the colorful and allegorizing canopy, while the bas relief program around the base and the allegorical marble statues at the extended corners, made by sculptors selected by Victoria, draw the eye away from the interior.[25] Although Scott proposed the gothic style in part to conform with Albert's taste, the memorial representation, especially insofar as it endows the Prince with impersonal meanings (and, as we have seen, violates the Prince's wishes), literally overshadows what it purports to commemorate. The shrine conceals rather than enhances the precious object, and once again Albert's head and body are divided, created in this case by two different artists.

The two Theed busts, the plain and the fancy, appear in the many photographs taken of the Queen and her family in the days and years after Albert's death, the choice of bust depending on whether the photo was taken at Windsor or at Osborne. Despite their differences, they are often difficult to distinguish, because both tend to appear as whited-out patches of blankness in the mourning photographs, juxtaposed as they are to the voluminous black clothing of the posing mourners. Despite the acknowledged excellence of the actual busts' likenesses, Albert's barely legible marble whiteness in these photographs constitutes an opposite yet parallel spectrality to the spectral blackness of Victoria's mourning.[26] The one indeed technically contributes to producing the other: the material conditions of photography were

FIGURE 34 George Gilbert Scott, National Albert Memorial, Kensington Gardens, London, 1862–72. Detail.

such that mourner and mourned could not both be illuminated properly. Because the large expanse of Victoria's black dress (and those of the daughters generally portrayed with her) must be well lit to come into view, the bust is bathed in an excess of light that renders it nearly featureless; otherwise, the lower light that would bring out the bust's features would reduce Victoria to an undifferentiated pool of blackness. Photos of a bust by itself invariably come out better. Whited out, Albert becomes a faceless spirit. The same effect is produced by the distractingly elaborate allegorizing ornamentation of the Hyde Park memorial, on the one hand, and, on the other, the whited-out blankness with which the two busts make their appearance in the mourning photographs. In both cases, whether through depth of shadow or through excess of light, likenesses of Albert virtually disappear, to be replaced by allegorical meanings. Photo and monument alike evidence the obliterating power of Victoria's grief.

An 1862 photograph taken by Prince Alfred (figure 35) shows Victoria and Alice with the Osborne bust of Albert, which rises above and between them, Victoria in heavy mourning in a pose of extravagant, upward-turning devotion. Alice looking at the camera rather than the bust suggests an alternative to grieving, an alternative that another image from the same sitting, in which Alice wears an inappropriately lively expression, makes all the more vivid. Similar photographs pose this or the other bust with different groupings of family members; usually it appears above them all, if sometimes at one side of the composition. It would seem that the tendency of the late photographs of Victoria and Albert (see Chapter 1) to emphasize his height and her subordination simply continues after his death in exaggerated form. For example, the arrangement of this photograph is anticipated by another (figure 36), taken of Albert, Victoria, and Vicky on her wedding day (25 January 1858), in which again a static Albert towers above and between the two women, who seem undifferentiated—both downcast and nervous (to the extent that Victoria, long experienced in the art of holding still, spoiled the image by moving), both crowned, both busty, in similar white dresses. Photography here means adherence to middle-class norms that place Victoria on a level not with her husband but with her daughters, who actually became the consorts that some early cartoons wished Victoria herself had been. Victoria's abjection in the mourning photograph, not ironized by the public display of her person that mitigated her unregality in the marital photographs, may have seemed disturbingly genuine to her neglected subjects.[27]

Yet placing Albert's marble simulacrum on a pedestal also reduces him, in the ways that chivalry reduces the women who are so placed. His face a mere white blur in most reproductions of this and the other mourning photographs, he is gone and lamented, but from now on he is only what she makes of him, subjected to an idealization from which photography's de-idealizing approach to living subjects saves the living Queen. The same could be said of another frequently reproduced mourning photograph (figure 37), which poses Victoria and three of her children with the Windsor bust. While the living figures are posed against a variegated background that highlights the complexity of their features, the bust is photographed against a solid light-colored wall, its face turned toward the light coming in from an invisible window. The difference in backgrounds seems to divide the picture into two different realms, an effect exaggerated by the mourners appearing to ignore the bust (they are studying an unreadable photograph of Albert held by Victoria). Idealizing Albert beyond visibility, the mourning photographs, like the busts included in them, yield to a tension between documentary realism and allegorical extravagance, a tension made visible in the technical

FIGURE 35 Queen Victoria and her
second daughter, Princess Alice,
with a bust of Prince Albert, 1862.
Photograph by Prince Alfred.

FIGURE 36 Queen Victoria, Prince
Albert, and Victoria, Princess Royal,
on her wedding day, 25 January 1858.
Photograph by Williams.

difficulty of photographing masses of black and white together. Initially good likenesses of Albert, the two busts successively turn into allegories that obscure him as a spirit whose wishes can safely be ignored. Covering the land with statues testifying to her love and great loss, posing abjectly beneath a spiritualized image of her beloved, Victoria both deferentially effaces herself in black and calls attention to her vividly absent self and her undiminished if concealed sovereignty.

Roland Barthes's account of photography's relation to the dead may be of help here for understanding not only the memorial photographs but the array of memorial images Victoria sponsored. For Barthes, photography cannot be memorial in the sense of serving as an aid to memory. "Not only is the photograph never, in essence, a memory . . . , but it actually blocks memory, quickly becomes a counter-memory."[28] Instead, because "the referent adheres," because there can be no photograph without there having once been a tangible object stopped for however brief a moment before the camera, its effect "is not to restore what has been abolished (by time, by distance) but to attest that what I see has indeed existed" (*Camera Lucida,* 6, 82). This for Barthes is "the melancholy of Photography itself" (79). Because the photograph is "an emanation of past reality" (88), it attests to the fact that what existed for the photographer exists no more. "In front of the photograph of my mother as a child, I tell myself: she is going to die. . . . Whether or not the subject is already dead, every photograph is this catastrophe" (96).

More historically oriented critics have similarly connected photography with the nineteenth-century fascination with the dead. Terry Castle, speculating that "the very pattern of human invention was determined by preexisting emotional needs," suggests that photography was invented to meet the nineteenth century's "spectralizing habit," its tendency to prefer mental simulacra to the thing itself.[29] Marina Warner, meditating on the connection between early photography, shadows, and the shades of the dead, writes in a similar vein that "the era of melancholic romanticism set the stage for a new pictorial medium that intrinsically possessed the power to make permanent the crepuscular phantoms of imagination and of personal loss and historic elegy."[30] Barthes, Warner, and Castle stress that the photograph makes permanent not the living memory of the dead but the loss itself: the photograph does not so much "call up the past" (*Camera Lucida,* 82) as confirm the spectrality of the dead.[31] And this confirmation is melancholic: for both Barthes and Warner, photography cannot aid the work of mourning, because it makes loss permanent.

Perhaps this confirmation of loss would have been (and is) the effect of looking at a photograph of the living Albert after he died; Victoria sur-

FIGURE 37 Queen Victoria, Victoria, Crown Princess of Prussia, Princess Alice, and Prince Alfred with a bust of Prince Albert, March 1862. Photograph by Bambridge.

rounded herself with an ample selection of these (St. Aubyn, *Queen Victoria*, 349). But because Barthes excludes from consideration any photograph whose principle force is not documentary and evidentiary, as typified by the snapshot of his mother, his claims would not seem to be readily applicable to all photographs. Barthes uses a photograph of Victoria—in black, seated on a horse whose head is held by John Brown—to illustrate his definition of *punctum* in the first half of *Camera Lucida*.[32] Oddly, Barthes does not discuss this picture in relation to the photograph of his dead mother, even though this picture would serve well to demonstrate the "melancholy" of photography; nor does Barthes register that it is a mourning photograph, as are all images of Victoria after 1861: a photograph of absent people that refers to a still more absent figure. (Indeed, by focusing on the possibility of action implied by the photograph, he refuses both its thematic and its constitutive references to the dead.) Had he registered this aspect of the image, he might have had to acknowledge other genres of photography beyond the documentary. Nevertheless, Victoria's mourning photographs, together with the photograph of Albert dead, do literalize the function Barthes claims for documentary photographs: they reveal the death of the person represented. In this regard they mesh with widespread Victorian practices linking photography and the dead, such as the compilation of memorial photo albums, the practice of photographing dead children, and the fashion of incorporating a photograph into grave markers (see Linkman, *Victorians,* 119–22).

Moreover, Victoria's memorials in other media invite us to extend to them the reading Barthes, Castle, and Warner make specific to photography. Barthes stresses that no writing, painting, or other representation can offer this "certificate of presence" (87), and Warner and Castle differentiate photography from other nineteenth-century arts. I would argue, to the contrary, that for the grieving Victoria all media potentially function in the same way. Her interest in ensuring the "likeness" of every statue and painting, made effectual by her power to keep her artists working till they got it right, suggests that for her all arts function as photographs do for Barthes, as memoranda that Albert did exist and that she has lost him. But in this case it is not the likeness itself that makes permanently present his death so much as the array of allegorical practices applied to the likeness that, through overshadowing, overencrustation, or whiting out, idealize him out of all memory. When Victoria commissions or approves a work of art in which likeness is subordinated to allegory, she is at once acting out her melancholic refusal to part with the dead and obscuring the dead, making him a permanently present absence.

Early in her reign, Victoria and Albert's marriage involved gender reversals as well as conformity to the doctrine of separate spheres. Victoria described Albert as an "angel" with a "cheek like a rose," and the press mocked the feminity of his subordinate position (see Chapter 1). At the same time Victoria offered plentiful evidence of her wifely deference.[33] After his death, the gendering of their relation—if such it can be termed—is similarly contradictory. He is feminized by being turned into a blank icon of purity, much as he is by being made a prop for allegorical decorations. Although this process could also be described as his subjection to the same process to which

Shelley subjects the dead Keats in *Adonais,* whose transformation into a star at once idealizes him and renders him safely remote and static, Susan Wolfson's observation that Shelley in doing so feminizes Keats can be extended to the memorial idealization of Albert as well.[34] By 1861 generally regarded as an important statesman as well as patron of the arts and sciences, mourned as author of the Trent memorandum that kept Britain out of the U.S. Civil War, Albert was not by the time of his death so readily seen as girlishly dependent and subordinate as he had been in 1840. Yet the handling of his image by Victoria and her iconographers suggests the continuance or revival of the ambiguous gender positioning of earlier years.

The divide in his memorial images between realist portraiture and allegory can be understood in these gendered terms. To the extent that he was important in himself, he receives realistic depiction, in the manner of portraits and memorials of other great men. But his subordination to allegorical meanings indicates that his position has rendered him feminine, even when his portrayed body consists of armor. We will observe this inconsistency in another form in Julia Margaret Cameron's photographs, in which the men are photographed in realist portrait style for their character and accomplishments, while the women are photographed for their beauty and are generally used as allegorical figures. (The most readily available collection of Cameron's photographs is titled *Victorian Photographs of Famous Men and Fair Women.*) Scott based his design for the most prominent of all Albert memorials in part on the "Eleanor Cross," monuments erected by Edward I to commemorate the funeral journey of his Consort's body (see *Albert Memorial,* 21, 40, 45, 46, and *Cult,* 46–48); the Eleanor Cross again provided the model for a memorial to the Duchess of Sutherland, for which Victoria laid the foundation stone in 1872 (*More Leaves,* 89). But it is not only his role as Consort that feminizes Albert in death. The genres available for representing premature death contribute to this effect as well. Victoria's memorials commemorate Albert as a great man, but they also assimilate him to the Victorian topos of the languishing or dead female beauty whose death, though grieved, inspires the male artist to new heights of accomplishment.

Critiques of women dying so that men can create, a subset of the larger topos of the objectification of the female body, have been a staple of feminist literary criticism since its second wave inception. Judith Fetterley's 1978 discussion of Hawthorne's "The Birthmark," in which a male scientist kills his wife in endeavoring to perfect her body's beauty, is a classic of this genre.[35] In 1978, writing on Wordsworth's "Lucy" poems, I discussed the benefit to the male poet of representing Lucy's death as noncatastrophic, as in the lines, "She died, and left to me / This heath, this calm, and quiet scene."[36]

"Though Lucy leaves the speaker bereft, her legacy to him is synonymous with the natural world of which she herself has become a part," I wrote, the natural world that is the material of Wordsworth's most familiar pastoral verse.[37] A feminist perspective on Barthes would call attention to the fact that it is his dead mother whose image he so productively contemplates in the second part of *Camera Lucida*, her momentary motionlessness before the camera and then her death moving him to brilliance. Associations of woman with death—as with darkness, the oceanic, and the irrational—are so prevalent in representation in the West as hardly to need documentation. ("They give birth astride of a grave," says Pozzo in *Waiting for Godot*.)[38] It is not that mens' deaths go unrepresented; rather, in the world of high cultural production that has been dominated by men, women are linked with death for reasons that Elizabeth Bronfen gives as follows:

> [B]ecause the feminine body is culturally constructed as the superlative site of alterity, culture uses art to dream the deaths of beautiful women. Over representations of the dead feminine body, culture can repress and articulate its unconscious knowledge of death which it fails to foreclose even as it cannot express it directly.[39]

Woman as culture's other must bear the burden of embodying death so that men, repressing their knowledge of death, can go on creating.

Tennyson and the Pre-Raphaelite painters were among the chief producers of icons of such desirable deaths, from "The Lady of Shalott" to Rossetti's portraits of an intensely spiritualized Elizabeth Siddall. Millais's "Ophelia," for which Siddall served as model, lying—in the famous anecdote—gorgeously clothed in a tub of cold water until she caught pneumonia, is probably the most celebrated of such images, for its merging of real and fictive female deaths and for its conversion of Ophelia's manic suicide into Siddall's gradual and unprotesting "deanimation" (*Over Her Dead Body*, 170). Like Aylmer's wife in Hawthorne's story or Wordsworth's dead Lucy, such figures can be understood as muses for male artists, as both Bronfen and Carol Christ have argued (Christ in relation to Tennyson).[40] But in Britain in this period they can also represent the male artist himself, as is arguably the case with the Lady of Shalott (Tennyson's trial run at Elaine of Astolat in *Idylls of the King*, discussed at greater length below), who both suffers the fate of women who act on their desires and, as a weaver and singer, presents the dilemma of the artist of any sex whose separation from the world allows him or her to create but prevents that creation from being more than "shadows."

Tennyson, Rossetti, and other male Victorian poets suffered from a "feminization of the poet" that coincided with the nineteenth-century relegation of poetry to the private, middle- and upper-class female sphere of leisure and conspicuous consumption.[41] As a luxury commodity, poetry was seldom any longer the stuff of heroic or civic action. Tennyson's position as laureate on the one hand, and, on the other, his identification with the lady (and with his other languishing female artist figures such as Mariana) suggests multiple gender identifications, the complexity of which offer a model for understanding the gendering of Victoria's Albert memorials. Albert appears in Victoria's memorials divided in two (realist head, allegorical body) or self-canceling (his distinctive features represented but overshadowed or whited out), because he was both a maker of signification in the masculine world of commerce and politics and culturally feminine both by his position and by his early death, the passive recipient of meanings imposed by others. In dying young and suffering Victoria's aggressive memorializing, Albert in part merges—incongruous as it may sound—with such icons as Tennyson's lady, Millais's Ophelia, and Elizabeth Siddall: dead and lamented but leaving his memorializer to live and create. Although constructed as thoroughly feminine (private, unthreatening) by the reception of her memorial books, Victoria as monument builder occupies a potentially more masculine position. While the books' popularity underscores public contentment with their feminine posture, Victoria's apparent aggressiveness as a monumentalist exacted a price.

Albert, Tennyson, and Victoria all assume multiple gender identifications. Although Victoria followed (some would say took advantage of) conventions for the behavior of widows in grieving, she also allowed her grief to take up public space in a way that disgusted, for example, Mrs. Oliphant, whose code of female behavior required less self-indulgence and more self-sacrifice. As we will see, in scenes of grieving that mirror Victoria's memorial arts in grafting likeness to allegory, the figures of Elaine and Arthur in Tennyson's *Idylls of the King* and in Julia Margaret Cameron's photographic illustrations allow mourner and mourned multiple gender identifications as well. Victoria explicitly identified herself with Tennyson as a grieving maker of memorials, and, as will be seen in the next part of this chapter, Tennyson's *Idylls* constitutes a memorial for Albert that both advances Victoria's mixed project to recall and to obscure his features through allegorical elaboration and continues those memorials' ambiguous gendering of the dead.

Tennyson's *Idylls of the King* as an Albert Memorial

For her laureate, Victoria presciently chose a professional mourner, for Tennyson shared with his Queen and Isle of Wight neighbor a near lifelong and highly public preoccupation with the death of the beloved. Just as the death of Albert shaped Victoria's monarchy and royal representations after 1861, the death of Arthur Hallam in 1833—when Tennyson and his friend were just out of Cambridge—dominated the subject matter and shaped the formal concerns of virtually all of Tennyson's verse. England's most articulate mourner even in 1850, when he published *In Memoriam* and was named laureate to succeed Wordsworth, Tennyson was, unbeknownst to him, preparing throughout his early career to be the poet of the widowhood Victoria never anticipated when she (on Albert's advice) appointed him. Even poems written before Albert's death became, after 1861, poems in Albert's memory. The Queen found *In Memoriam* to be her greatest source of consolation after religious writings (*Dear and Honoured Lady*, 71). Peter Sacks's reading suggests how attuned it was to the Queen's melancholia: in it Tennyson "accumulates rather than lets go."[42] Victoria identified with Guinevere and with Mariana. Even more, it could be said that, as Victoria's laureate, everything Tennyson wrote became her expression, even though she claimed she "never could make two lines meet in my life" (*Dear and Honoured Lady*, 84, quoting a letter by Emily Tennyson). Just so, her having only once had the temerity to attempt Albert's likeness (despite her training and talent as an artist and her copious sketches of her children and others) does not stop the monuments whose design she approved and the other artworks she commissioned from being hers. The laureate's poems, like those memorials, speak for her in much the same way as her ministers and her government express her will: symbolically, even fictionally, but nonetheless powerfully.

Their collaboration, in 1864, on lines to be inscribed on the Frogmore memorial statue of the Queen's mother (whose death had preceded Albert's by nine months), may be taken as an exemplary limit case defining Tennyson's poetic practice as laureate. Having asked for some lines, the Queen politely rejected Tennyson's first attempt, which began "O blessing of thy child as she was thine," as being on the one hand "too presuming" ("as she was thine") and on the other more appropriate for the tomb itself, located elsewhere (*Dear and Honoured Lady*, 79–80). She requested that he take as his motto instead "Her children arise and call her blessed." The verse then produced was satisfactory and was sent to the sculptor. Attempting to flatter his patron as well as the dead, Tennyson had not understood the first time that, for Victoria, direct flattery is not needed, since all royal monumentality refers to her in any case. In the successful attempt, flattery of the dead serves quite adequately to memorialize Victoria herself:

> Long as the heart beats life within her breast,
> Thy child will bless thee, guardian-mother mild,
> And far away thy memory will be bless'd
> By children of the children of thy child.

The verse celebrates Victoria's fertility and durability as well as the value of her blessing, even while it ostensibly celebrates the Duchess, and thus Victoria gets her laureate to praise her in just the manner she likes best, in a kneeling pose that nonetheless amply displays her virtues. Her use of Tennyson here recalls her use of General Grey to write her memoir of Albert or her excuses to the *Times:* the verse is a self-representing royal utterance even if it happens to be spoken by someone else.

The Queen's reading of *In Memoriam* suggests a similarly collaborative effort. She found herself "much soothed and pleased" (RA Queen Victoria's Journal, 5 January 1862) by reading it, and was reported to find particular solace in the early poems, "the sadder ones especially" (*Dear and Honoured Lady*, 67, 71). She quoted to Tennyson a verse (from poem LI) that articulated her belief in the "*Life presence* of the Dead"; this poem gave her the language to say that Albert "watch[es] . . . with larger other eyes than ours," a phrase she liked to use. In February she showed the Duke of Argyll her copy of *In Memoriam,* so that he could see and report to Tennyson how much it meant to her. She had marked "many passages" and even added revisions and commentary to render some of the poems collaborative works, as if she were showing her laureate how to rewrite them for her. "She had substituted 'widow' for 'widower' and 'her' for 'his'" in poem XIII, to make the male speaker's tears and empty arms her own. Victoria had also annotated XXV, XXIX, and LXVI to indicate how they applied to her and Albert. For example, next to the line "How dare we keep our Christmas-eve" (poem XXIX) she wrote: "We did not keep it in 1861," making herself the poem's referent (*Dear and Honoured Lady,* 67). *In Memoriam* influenced her idea of how to mourn, but she also read *In Memoriam* selectively, carving out her own canon from its verses to suit her melancholic cast of mind. The early verses, including those she marked, contain no hint of completed mourning. The poem lends its language to her beliefs, and she in turn appropriates the poem to suit her needs.

The collaboration could also go the other way, Tennyson's poems sometimes saying more for her than she might have wished. When Tennyson visited her in April 1862 she remarked, "I am like your Mariana now." While no doubt she had in mind Mariana's endless "dreary" grieving for him who "cometh not," the poem's aestheticizing pleasures and Mariana's erotic self-sufficiency (dramatized, for example, in Millais's famous 1851 painting) hint at the self-indulgence of interminable mourning and prefigure the Queen's pleasure at the prospect of lying with Albert in a beautiful tomb. Similarly her admiration for *Guinevere (G)*—the idyll in which Arthur's pristine virtue is most on display—suggests also that the Queen enjoyed identifying masochistically with Guinevere's abjection, as she "grovelled with her face against the floor" (*G,* 412) at Arthur's feet.[43] Victoria uses Tennyson to speak for her and makes his words refer to her, but these poems sometimes speak against the grain of her apparent intentions, revealing the secret pleasures of her melancholy. Later, she traded books with Tennyson, liking to consider herself a fellow-artist. She had Lady Augusta Bruce give him a copy of the Prince's speeches at the same time that she asked him to write welcoming verse for the future Princess of Wales. She sent him a copy of *Leaves* in January 1868 with an inscription: "Trusting he will not criticize too severely"; and when he published "To the Queen" as epilogue to the *Idylls* in 1873, she reciprocated with the offer of a tour of her magnum opus, the mausoleum (*Dear and Honoured Lady*, 85, 91). Perhaps this insistence on being his peer (if not his equal) as an artist was a way of keeping his artistic production under her control.

While not conceived as laureate work, Tennyson's *Idylls of the King*—whose origins can be traced back to 1833–34 with the writing of "Morte d'Arthur," or to 1832 with "The Lady of Shalott," or even to 1830 with some of the writing of "Sir Launcelot and Queen Guinevere"—retroactively becomes laureate work after 1850, and especially in 1862 when Tennyson dedicated the idylls published in 1859 (the two *Geraint* idylls, *Merlin and Vivien [MV]*, *Lancelot and Elaine [LE]*, and *Guinevere*) to the memory of the Prince. Alice had asked Tennyson, on her mother's behalf, for something that would "idealise" the Prince. Tennyson, finding it difficult to comply, at first (it seems, on the evidence of an unsent letter) planned to recommend the Queen read *In Memoriam;* but he then decided to add a verse dedication "To the Prince Consort" to a new edition of the *Idylls* already at the printers (see *Dear and Honored Lady*, 60–63). With this dedication, as Swinburne jocularly put it, the poem became "the Morte d'Albert."[44] Idylls added subsequently—*The Coming of Arthur (CA)*, *The Holy Grail (HG)*, *Pelleas and Ettarre*, and *The Passing of Arthur (PA)*, published together in 1869; *The Last Tournament*, published in 1871; and *Gareth and Lynette (GL)*, 1872—were thus by definition already dedicated to the Prince. Like *In Memoriam* originally a memorial for Hallam, in which Hallam was equated with Arthur (and like that poem, an "accretive" work that accumulates rather than letting go), under the Queen's patronage *Idylls* memorializes Albert, and thus (like all Albert memorials) celebrates Victoria herself.[45] That this was so is confirmed by the belated framing of the dedication as an address to the Queen: "Break not, O woman's-heart," begins the last ten lines, which end with the hope that God's love will "set Thee at His side again." The poem directly addresses and celebrates Victoria again in the epilogue, "To the Queen," written at Emily Tennyson's suggestion in 1873 about the 1872 thanksgiving service for the Queen's and the Prince of Wales's recovery from illness.[46] Although from

Tennyson's point of view these dedicatory verses may simply have been an economical way of doing his job, getting him laureate credit for the vast work he would have continued to work on anyway, Tennyson's decision also invites a reading of *The Idylls of the King* as a poem for and about the Prince and the Queen, a poem constituting one more item in the "collection of memoranda that [he] did exist, and that I have lost him."

The dedication to the Prince opens:

> These to His Memory—since he held them dear,
> Perchance as finding there unconsciously
> Some image of himself—I dedicate,
> I dedicate, I consecrate with tears—
> These Idylls.

Like the Queen's remark that Albert on his deathbed became "wonderfully like" a picture painted fifteen years before, the retrospective syntax that produces the antecedent for "these" so belatedly ("These . . . These Idylls") models the curiously convoluted temporal sequence by which poems already long published could now be discovered to be not only dedicated to Albert but about him. (Swinburne captures this chronological oddity, or lucky coincidence, when he calls the poem "the Morte d'Albert . . . after the princely type to which . . . the poet has been fortunate enough to make his central figure so successfully conform.") Albert might find in the *Idylls* "an image of himself," as if Albert had been the model for Arthur; but Albert can be that model only insofar as he is or has become like the already written Arthur. If Albert with his dislike of monuments to himself "held [the *Idylls*] dear," it is unlikely to be because he found in Arthur an image of himself, but it is under this condition of enforced retrospective reference that Tennyson can memorialize the Prince. In any event, the very act of claiming resemblance between the Prince and the King renders them similar, for in making this claim Tennyson transfers to Albert Arthur's representational status: both are at once individuals and allegories, and the Prince is rendered half-allegorical in the act of even notionally assimilating him to the half-allegorical Arthur. As we have seen, to render Albert allegorical is to commemorate and celebrate him, but it is also to dissolve him into an undifferentiated field of white.

Much of Tennyson's verse is characterized by an uncertainty about its representational status. Coventry Patmore writes in his copy of *The Princess*, "Is this allegory? If not, Ida is most unjustifiably disagreeable."[47] Tennyson himself expressed uncertainty about Arthur's allegorical status, on the one hand claiming that he was "allegorical" and on the other wishing him to be appreciated for his human qualities. According to his son Hallam, Tennyson said of the *Idylls,* "My meaning was spiritual. I only took the legendary stories of the Round Table as illustrations. Arthur was allegorical to me. I intended him to represent the Ideal in the Soul of Man coming into contact with the warring elements of the flesh."[48] Or again, quotes his son, "'the whole,' he said, 'is the dream of man coming into practical life and ruined by one sin.'"[49] If Arthur is allegorical, then the Prince who might have found in him an "image of himself" is also allegorical, his meaning residing not in himself but in Arthur and in turn in those qualities Arthur allegorizes. By contrast, Tennyson also claimed to reject the kind of allegory in which "'*This* means *that*,' because the thought within the image is much more than any one interpretation" (Hallam Tennyson, *Memoir,* 2:127). Moreover, "my father thought that perhaps he had not made the real humanity of the King sufficiently clear" (2:129), so in 1891 he added the words "Ideal manhood closed in real man" to "To the Queen," just as the dedication to Albert also alludes to real events in the Prince's life ("dear to Science, dear to Art") as well as idealizing him as "Albert the Good."

Recent critics have emphasized the equivocal nature of Tennyson's allegory, whether symptomatically (by asserting one possibility or the other) or by adducing this equivocation as a characteristic of the *Idylls.* Robert Martin finds that the ideas and the narrative and descriptive elements fail to cohere: "[T]he allegorical values of the poem remain unexceptionable theories that are unsupported by adequate intensity in the characters and events meant to embody them," and he concludes "that the literal is less believable than the allegorical" (*Tennyson,* 495, 496). Similarly, John Rosenberg finds *Guinevere* confusing when Arthur both speaks (as usual) as an allegorical figure of godlike moral rectitude and, for the first time, expresses human desire, lamenting the loss of his Queen's "golden hair, with which I used to play": "[I]f . . . Arthur feels sexual passion for Guinevere . . . then he had no business losing [her] in the first place."[50] But in contrast to Martin, Rosenberg praises in the poem the parts where characters and story exceed the allegory.[51] He asserts that "the *Idylls* is not an allegory and . . . those who so read it are forced into simplistic conclusions" (*Fall of Camelot,* 22). (He may have in mind a book such as that of John Reed, who baldly states that the *Idylls* is "an allegorical poem with a moral point.")[52] After all, Rosenberg points out, Tennyson mocks schematic allegory when, in *Gareth and Lynette,* he renders as "burlesque" Gareth's "mock-heroic encounters" with four "costumed, allegorical brethren" who represent Morning, Noon, Evening, and Death (*Fall of Camelot,* 105). Rosenberg prefers to read the *Idylls* as a symbolist poem, and Gerhard Joseph too emphasizes that Tennyson would have shared Coleridge's preference for symbol over the "mechanical" "picture-language" of allegory. Joseph settles on "allegory in the distance" as the best term for "the properly flickering genre" of the *Idylls*.[53] John Dixon Hunt asserts that the poem is "iconic" and an instance of Victorian typology, through which Tennyson can identify actual contemporaries (Hallam, Albert) with historical or mythic figures (Arthur, and behind him Jesus), but Hunt soon merges the term "typology" with "ideal" or "type" in the sense of "typical" ("The Poetry of Distance," 116), and he acknowledges that Tennyson sustains only intermittently Arthur's identification with Christ (117).

Tennyson's contemporaries, reviewing the *Idylls* as they came out, likewise equivocated as to its status as allegory. According to Valerie Pitt, the first four idylls were neither presented nor taken as allegories,[54] but the *Holy Grail* volume of 1869 was. Reviews of the 1859 *Idylls* volume emphasize Tennyson's talent for characterization. Tennyson's reputation as a writer of dramatic monologues—together with recent debates over whether, in *Maud*, the central character's wild speech is characterization or the poet's views—had accustomed reviewers to thinking of him as a poet of character. Walter Bagehot, writing in 1859, extols "the character of Arthur" as "the very type of the highest abstract or ascetic character," as if the point of the poem were its delineation of human qualities.[55] William Gladstone, reviewing the same volume, contrasts the success of these *Idylls* to *The Princess,* where "the persons are little better than mere personae . . . . weak *media* for the conveyance of ideas" (in *Critical Heritage*, 243). Gladstone's praise is hyperbolic: *Guinevere* (which was according to Martin "wildly popular with most of Tennyson's readers," *Tennyson,* 423) marks "the highest point which the poetry of our age has reached," and Gladstone ascribes his overall admiration for the volume to its exhibition of "the first among the poet's gifts—the gift of conceiving and representing character" (*Critical Heritage,* 256, 263). Likewise both Gladstone and Bagehot praise Tennyson's eye for descriptive detail.[56]

By contrast, J. T. Knowles writing on the 1869 *Idylls* confidently asserts their status as allegory (although not "that most tedious of riddles a formal allegory," *Critical Heritage,* 313), in which all the characters "stand for" the soul and its various trials. Yet in summarizing his view, he acknowledges the slipperiness of what the allegory might mean ("Such or suchlike seems to be the high significance and under-meaning of this noble poem," 315), and he notes too the likelihood that the poem's touches of realism will prevent many readers from noticing the allegory at all (the supernatural version of Arthur's birth could be explained as a shipwreck, for example).[57] Tennyson praised Knowles's analysis as "the best, and indeed . . . the only true critique of the *Idylls*" (quoted in *Critical Heritage,* 11), but it would be difficult to say whether Tennyson praises Knowles's grasp of the poet's intentions or his analysis of how those intentions might miscarry. The anonymous 1870 reviewer for the *British Quarterly Review,* in describing Tennyson's "idealized and modernized King Arthur," both praises the poet for granting the characters "significance beyond themselves" and criticizes the allegorical program of *The Holy Grail* where "the cross play of allegorical meanings has really, to some extent, put under water the genuine human interest of the story."[58] Moreover, even the 1859 *Idylls,* after 1869, become retroactively allegorical. The same reviewer complains also that "the whirl of the poet's fancy by which the Elaines and Viviens are translated into abstractions is too sudden" (*Victorian Scrutinies,* 318). A century later John Reed, pursuing an allegorical reading, does not differentiate among the different sets of *Idylls,* finding them all grist for his mill.

These readings, contemporaneous and more recent, may be taken as symptomatic of something about the experience of reading the *Idylls* that has remained constant in its inconsistency since the poems' publication. If Arthur and Albert are equivocally allegorical, intermittently plausible human characters and figures for the Ideal, then they also could be understood, in the terms of our discussion of pathetic fallacy in Chapter 2, as failed allegories or personifications in whom the gap between character and intended allegorical meaning—or the effort required to graft the latter onto the former—is more conspicuous than that meaning itself, as when Albert's balding, realistically depicted modern head is seen emerging from and iconographically conflicting with his "allegorical armor." I use the term "failed allegory" not to pass moral judgment but rather to preserve (as *occupatio* can preserve) the allegorical possibility while also indicating its incomplete achievement. The difficulty of getting the allegory to work is suggested by the balanced antitheses that characterize Tennyson's remarks about Arthur, both within and outside the poem: "Ideal manhood closed in real man" ("To the Queen"); "the highest and most human too" (*G,* 644). The content or apparent intention of these phrasings is belied by their persistently binary rhetoric. Ruskin's aspiration to fit middle-class British women into a royal allegory (as we saw in Chapter 2) reveals itself to be instead an instance of pathetic fallacy or failed allegory, when the essay closes with Tennyson's talking flowers, Ruskin's own chief example of pathetic fallacy; Carroll mocks Ruskin's attempt to make pathetic fallacy look like genuine allegory when he has the Red Queen "thump, thump" heavily through the Looking-Glass garden. Think of Tennyson's program to make Soul or an icon of purity (as Arthur is alternatively rendered in allegorical readings) into a plausible husband as the counterpart to Ruskin's attempt to make ordinary British housewives into idealized queens.

For Swinburne Tennyson's apparent attempt at allegory has a similarly absurd effect. In his attempt to render Arthur a figure for moral purity by eliminating from the story Arthur's incest (which in Malory makes Arthur fallible and thus human), Swinburne argues, Tennyson has inadvertently made Arthur all the more "pitiful and ridiculous" ("Under the Microscope," 406). Removing Guinevere's motive has the effect of

> reducing Arthur to the level of a wittol, Guinevere to the level of a woman of intrigue.... All the studious care and exquisite eloquence of the poet can throw no genuine halo round the sprouting brows of a royal husband who remains to the very last the one man in his kingdom insensible of his disgrace. ("Under the Microscope," 405–6)

Arthur's failure as a poetic subject comes not simply from the conspicuousness of his "debased" humanity but from the attempt to graft onto it elevated allegorical meanings. To see Arthur as "wittol" is to describe a collapse of allegorical aspirations just as complete as that indicated by Carroll's absurdly literalist Red Queen. The effigy of Albert with modern head attached to Gothic, armored body could also be termed failed allegory, in that the balding yet fashion-conscious head can be seen to undermine the high seriousness of the allegorical armor. In the first section of this chapter, I emphasized rather that the difficulty lay the other way: that in most of the Albert memorials the allegory "overshadows" the realist elements. The term "failed allegory" still applies, however, as allegory cannot survive the gravitational pull of realist depiction that we perceive as such; what we then see, in the Albert memorials as in Swinburne's view of Arthur, is the awkward graft itself.

This "duality in Arthur's character" (*Fall of Camelot*, 127) that we will term "failed allegory" is given thematic life in the poem's alternative accounts of his origins. Either he is human, the child of Ygerne's rape by Uther; or he is supernatural, delivered to the shore by a dragon-shaped boat and a wave "gathering half the deep / And full of voices" (*CA*, 379–80). Similarly, in Leodogran's alternative dreams Arthur is either "a phantom king" in a warscape of smoke and haze (*CA*, 435) or the heavenly king of an unreal earth. Merlin repeats these alternatives when he decribes to Gareth the enchanted building of Camelot by fairies:

> For there is nothing in it as it seems
> Saving the King; though some there be that hold
> The King a shadow, and the city real.
> (*GL*, 260–62)

If when human Arthur is "debased," when allegorical he suffers, as does the memorialized Albert, from a tendency to become shadowy, attenuated, or ghostly, not because allegory is necessarily disembodied but because of the imperfect grafting in him of human and ideal. Having chosen Arthur because he believes him to be supernatural, Leodogran asks, "think ye this king / . . . Hath body enow to hold his foemen down?" (*CA*, 249–52). (Joseph describes this tendency elsewhere in Tennyson as a fearful yet attractive "drift toward insubstantiality," *Tennyson and the Text*, 58.) That being a failed allegory disables Arthur from serving as an effective monarch again recalls the memorial representations of Albert that divide him between honored statesman and overshadowed icon.

When Guinevere sees him last, after his paradoxical performance as God and impassioned cuckold, he has become especially insubstantial, as if exhausted by the failed effort to embody "Ideal manhood closed in real man":

> The moony vapour rolling round the King,
> Who seemed the phantom of a Giant in it,
> Enwound him fold by fold, and made him gray
> And grayer, till himself became as mist
> Before her, moving ghostlike to his doom.
> (*G*, 597–601)

The "doom" to which Arthur moves could be either his death at the hands of his traitor knights or his apotheosis and return to immortal Avalon; readers of the *Idylls* tend to praise it (and *In Memoriam*) for its tactful handling of doubt in the context of belief. These lines suggest, however, that these alternatives differ little. Either way, just as the mourning photographs turn a good likeness of Albert into an abstract patch of whiteness, and just as Scott's decorated architectural surround overshadows the image of the man within it, the image of an idealized Arthur "moving ghostlike to his doom" renders him simultaneously grand and vaporous. Whether this Arthur is modeled retroactively on Albert, or the dead Albert is reconstructed to match Arthur, the image matches perfectly the effect of the Queen's memorial representations that efface Albert even while monumentalizing him. With the dedication of the poem to the Prince, the Queen has her laureate idealize Albert—in lushly decorative verse—into "gray" nonexistence.

Tennyson himself, in "To the Queen," defines failed allegory by the degree to which a name exceeds what it refers to. To his poem's presumptively successful allegory—"Sense at war with Soul, / Ideal manhood closed in real man" (lines 37–38)—Tennyson contrasts the unembodied Arthur of faded legend:

> Rather than that gray king, whose name, a ghost,
> Streams like a cloud, man-shaped, from mountain peak,
> And cleaves to cairn and cromlech still.
> ("To the Queen," lines 39–41)

But, as we have seen, this regrettable ghostliness characterizes Arthur within the poem as well, whenever the effort to make him allegorical becomes strained. Thus "To the Queen" glosses the *Idylls'* preoccupation with Arthur's attenuation as a worry over the relation between names and persons. For his allegorical burden to exceed his plausibility as a character is like having his name exceed his identity, as when Tennyson's Ulysses says, in his discontent, "I am become a name." The entire *Idylls* is haunted by the worry that not just Arthur but all the characters will shrink to their own ghostly but famous names, "mere personae . . . weak *media* for the conveyance of ideas."

The most optimistic of the Round Table idylls, *Gareth and Lynette* (published in 1872 but in the story's sequence the second after *The Coming of Arthur*), is plotted around Gareth's project to establish his name by deeds, to ensure that his name does not become "a ghost [that] / Streams like a cloud." At his mother Bellicent's request, he starts out incognito ("nor seek my name," *GL, 438*), serving in Arthur's kitchen. Once he gets his arms, he wants to remain nameless until after his first quest: "Let be my name until I make my name" (562). According to Gareth's Adamic notion of naming, his name will emerge as the exact expression of his deed. The foolish Lynette, insisting on his name of "kitchen knave," is displeased at his appointment to undertake her quest in place of Lancelot, the brand-name knight she had requested. Her faulty attitude toward names is mocked by the send-up of allegory encountered in the form of Gareth's opponents, the knights who have named and costumed themselves by copying pictures of knights representing times of day ("yon four fools have sucked their allegory / From these damp walls, and taken but the form," 1169–70). When Gareth succeeds in vanquishing the enemy, Lynette apologizes for having "missaid thee" (1136) and acknowledges his identity: "I marvel what thou art" (1141). To this Gareth replies, "You said your say; / Mine answer was my deed" (1145–46). Allegory is thus castigated as the predominance of an empty name over real actions, in contrast to names or words that match their referents.

When Gareth fights his final opponent, the knight dressed as "Nox" or "Mors," the poem describes a figure of such horrific appearance that "a maiden swooned," only to reveal the comical disparity between the "night-black arms" and death's-head mask and their contents:

> Then with a stronger buffet he clove the helm
> As throughly as the skull; and out from this
> Issued the bright face of a blooming boy
> Fresh as a flower new-born, and crying, "Knight,
> Slay me not: my three brethren bad me do it."
> (*GL*, 1371–75)

The bright face of an untrained boy poking out of a terrifying suit of black armor recalls, and is no less internally contradictory than, the armored effigies of the civilian Albert, in which the head and the armor seem to come from different historical and material worlds. Like Swinburne's derisive vision of the self-contradictory Arthur as "wittol," this humorous image hints at the unintended comedy of some of the Albert memorials.

Oddly, given this idyll's stated preference for putting deeds ahead of words, when facing his most feared opponent Gareth accepts Lancelot's offer to trade shields, so as to scare "Nox" into submission: "'Peradventure he, you name, / May know my shield'" (1266–67), suggests Lancelot. Gareth complains of Nox's "ghastly imageries," but he himself relies on imagery to fight this battle, which in any case turns out to be no battle at all. Fighting under Lancelot's falsely assumed colors, Gareth can fight only a sham battle that nearly reduces his entire quest to comedy and almost undermines the value of his hard-earned "name."

Borrowing Lancelot's shield seems innocuous enough in context, but *Lancelot and Elaine* (one of the 1859 *Idylls* later dedicated to the Prince) makes it clear later in the sequence what is wrong with the gesture. Lancelot suffers from believing that his name is greater than the deeds that should match it (an excess of name over deeds), a problem he seeks to correct in *Lancelot and Elaine*, where what had been a clever strategy—relying on name or "imagery" alone—becomes a pathology. At Guinevere's suggestion, Lancelot sets out to fight in a tournament anonymously. As she puts the problem,

> we hear it said
> That men go down before your spear at a touch,
> But knowing you are Lancelot; your great name,
> This conquers: hide it therefore; go unknown:
> Win!
> (*LE*, 147–51)

Neatly inverting the plot of *Gareth and Lynette*, *Lancelot and Elaine* shows Lancelot questing to reverse the ascendency of his name over his deeds, to escape the power of his shield or name to fight his battles for him. The situation resembles that of Albert emblematically memorialized over the words "I have fought the good fight," a situation in which a kind of naming supersedes and determines what is being named. The image itself is considerably more ambiguous without the words than with them. Only this imposed allegorical construction causes us to read what he is doing as sheathing his sword. Albert is unable to speak for himself (or choose to keep silent), and without the words, he might be unsheathing his sword, preparing to prove by deeds that he is greater than his label. As we shall see in the last section of this chapter, this is an ambiguity that Julia Margaret Cameron's photographic illustrations make explicit; here it will serve as a reminder that the memorialized Albert is implicated in all of Tennyson's figures who themselves struggle between allegory and characterization.

Guinevere offers her suggestion not because she believes it worthwhile but because she disdains the "wit" of both her men. In order to stay at the castle with Guinevere, Lancelot has made the mistake of telling Arthur he will miss the tournament. Because this will arouse Arthur's suspicions, she scornfully invents an excuse for Lancelot ("If I must find you wit") to fool that "moral child without the craft to rule" (*LE*, 147, 145). Although Lancelot conceals his name in order to conceal their adultery, the ruse quickly exceeds the intentions of its inventor, just as Lancelot's name has exceeded the deeds it should refer to. Generating a plot of its own, the ruse of Lancelot's anonymity results in another representational problem, when Elaine mistakes her part in Lancelot's disguise for a sign of his true love. At her suggestion he goes into battle not only with a borrowed, blank shield but also with her sleeve attached to his helmet, for, Elaine tells him, since he "never yet [has] worn / Favour of any lady in the lists," "in wearing mine / Needs must be lesser likelihood, noble lord, / That those who know you should know you" (*LE*, 361–65; Lancelot is slow to get the idea here, too). Knowing he has accepted her favor only in order to complete his disguise, Elaine nonetheless convinces herself that it signifies his love, "And loved him, with that love which was her doom" (259).

This error is one of many instances in this idyll of a name or sign that ceases to refer to what it is intended to refer to and instead acquires its own self-referential elaboration (Lancelot's shield that fights his battles for him is the first such instance). Elaine makes a silken case for the heavily scarred shield Lancelot leaves behind at Astolat, and this case becomes the idyll's central figure, as it is also its chief example of the practice of failed allegory. The opening *in medias res* passage traces the process by which Elaine elaborates a representation that exceeds what it represents. Having at first simply "Guarded the sacred shield of Lancelot" in her bedroom,

> Then fearing rust or soilure fashioned for it
> A case of silk, and braided thereupon
> All the devices blazoned on the shield
> In their own tinct, and added, of her wit,
> A border fantasy of branch and flower,
> And yellow-throated nestling in the nest.
> (*LE*, 4, 7–12)

This added "border fantasy" exceeds the frame to which it would seem initially to be confined, just as Scott's shrine overshadows the figure of Albert within it, and just as the words "I have fought the good fight" impose a meaning possibly belied by the image to which they are juxtaposed. The excessive shield case has also the same relation to Lancelot that the disembodying gray vapor has to Arthur. Hunt, emphasizing that Elaine herself is "iconic," calls her embroidery a "ludicrous multiplication of image upon image" ("The Poetry of Distance," 96). Her reading of the shield itself works in just the same way. She daily locks herself into her room and

> Stript off the case, and read the naked shield,
> Now guessed a hidden meaning in his arms,
> Now made a pretty history to herself
> Of every dint a sword had beaten in it,
> And every scratch a lance had made upon it,
> Conjecturing when and where: this cut is fresh;
> That ten years back; this dealt him at Caerlyle;
> That at Caerleon; this at Camelot:
> And ah God's mercy, what a stroke was there!
> And here a thrust that might have killed, but God
> Broke the strong lance, and rolled his enemy down,
> And saved him: so she lived in fantasy.
> (*LE*, 16–27)

The narrator summarizes brutally as "fantasy" the almost imperceptible change from "guessed" to "made," from historical "conjecture" to melodramatic reconstruction (and from description to symbolic representation), even though this is exactly the poet's procedure in embellishing Malory. Similarly Elaine dwells on Lancelot's remembered face, which becomes "the face" that "lived, / Dark-splendid, speaking in the silence, full / Of noble things, and held her from her sleep" (*LE*, 335–37).

John Dixon Hunt refers to her fantasies about the naked shield and the "meaning in his arms" as "a curious and erotic scene of vicarious experience behind a barred door" ("The Poetry of Distance," 96). Her artistic self-sufficiency is also erotic self-sufficiency, echoing that of Mariana "within the dreamy house" who, especially in Millais's illustration, broods voluptuously on pleasures not to be. Victoria's identification with Mariana helps us see how closely Elaine's response to Lancelot's departure resembles Victoria's response to Albert's death: both immediately start making works of art that have increasingly little to do with the departed man. Victoria, appropriating Albert for her own designs, indulges in her grief and looks forward to "ly[ing] together" in so "fine" a tomb. These 1859 lines about Elaine cannot strictly be said to be a portrait of Victoria in 1862 (or only in the same sense in which the already written Arthur becomes in 1862 a portrait of Albert), but from Elaine (as from Mariana) Victoria may have learned some of the consolations of mourning: you can stay in your room forever, you can spell out your fantasies in art, and (with regard to the end of Elaine's story) you can make yourself into a cynosure that people long to see.

Lancelot wins the tournament in disguise, but only after his own kin hurt him in attempting to defend his reputation, a bit of plotting that literalizes the division of Lancelot's name from his deeds. A long stretch of narrative recounts Elaine's faithful nursing of his wound, during which Lancelot comes to value but not to love her. Here and again after Lancelot has recovered and gone home, Elaine's state of mind is compared to sounds that lose their meanings from repetition:

> "He will not love me: how then? must I die?"
> Then as a little helpless innocent bird,
> That has but one plain passage of few notes,
> Will sing the simple passage o'er and o'er
> For all an April morning, till the ear
> Wearies to hear it, so the simple maid
> Went half the night repeating, "Must I die?"
> . . . .
> And "Him or death," she muttered, "death or him,"
> Again and like a burthen, "Him or death."
> (*LE*, 888–98)

When the recovered Lancelot takes his shield away, leaving "only the case, / Her own poor work, her empty labour," she continues to fetishize his image—"still his picture formed / And grew between her and the pictured wall" (983–86)—and repeats a song that itself repeats the words "sweet," "love" and "death" (997–1011). The narrator now contributes this comparison:

> As when we dwell upon a word we know,
> Repeating, till the word we know so well
> Becomes a wonder, and we know not why,
> So dwelt the father on her face, and thought
> "Is this Elaine?"
> (*LE*, 1020–24)

A repetitive user of words when love obsessed, Elaine now resembles a word that, through repetition, has become "a wonder" (to her father and, by extension, to the reader)—an object in itself, no longer signifying anything else. This condition is continuous with her practice of making failed allegories, as when her shield case with its abstract decorations and nestling bird, her invented battle narratives, and her fantasmatic image of Lancelot lay claim to meanings quite separate from the man they purport to represent; now, however, it is Elaine the artist who is rendered blank, rather than Lancelot the referent of her art.

The narrator of this idyll repeats Elaine's name three times in the first two lines in an incantatory sequence of phrases beginning "Elaine, the . . ."; in 1859, when the printed title was *Elaine*, the word appeared four times in a small space. This repetition anticipates as an aspect of the narration the stuttering effects described above as characteristics of Elaine. Tennyson reported deriving his earliest sense of immortality from repeating a name:

> A kind of waking trance I have frequently had, quite up from boyhood, when I have been all alone. This has generally come upon me thro' repeating my own name two or three times to myself silently, till all at once, as it were out of the intensity of the consciousness of individuality, the individuality itself seemed to dissolve and fade away into boundless being. (Hallam Tennyson, *Memoir*, 1:320)

What gives Tennyson intimations of poetic immortality—the detachment, through repetition, of word or name from meaning—only renders Elaine immobile: static as an icon and, in terms of plot, unable to move or change. Detaching representation from what it represents, this kind of repetition structurally resembles failed allegory. Tennyson's anecdote is about his successful mobilization of this kind of nonsignification into incipient poethood; but for Elaine making failed allegory means death, just as for Lancelot (uncertain whether he or his name conquers) it means loss of identity. Tennyson himself repeats words—as above, "his picture formed / . . . the pictured wall"—with sufficient frequency for Gladstone to remark on it as a defect. (Gladstone's example is the repetition of "face" and "darkness" within four lines describing the groveling Queen in *Guinevere* [*Critical Heritage*,

257]; Gladstone's objection would apply equally to the dedication to the Prince, discussed above, with its circular temporal structure and repetitive language.) But for Tennyson repetition is the hallmark of poethood, a reminder that words have incantatory powers beyond those of reference.

Electing to die and elaborately staging her death and commemoration in advance, Elaine has her brother write a letter to be placed in her hand when she is dead and has her body and deathbed decked "like the Queen's / For richness" (*LE*, 1111–12), placed on a barge, and made into a message to be delivered downriver to the court. She is "cheerful" (1124) after convincing her family to comply with her wishes, because her death will complete what Elisabeth Bronfen calls the "closed circuit of her love" (*Over Her Dead Body*, 153): it will allow her, in fantasy, to playact Guinevere (whose role as Lancelot's lover Elaine steadfastly disbelieves), riding to meet Lancelot on her bed. Becoming her own monument, Elaine fulfills the iconic promise of the idyll's opening and becomes "an image of purified stasis" (Shaw, *Tennyson*, 134), the paradigm of all Victorian females killed into art. Her self-objectification contrasts with (and graphically justifies) Albert's wish not to be monumentalized either during his lifetime or after death, knowing as he did that monuments erase rather than preserve memory.

In monumentalizing herself she also chooses to make herself allegorical, a figure for chaste and faithful love. It would seem that in death "her inner idea . . . coincide[s] perfectly with her appearance, because her body as a 'dead letter' suggests a perfect congruence between signifier or material form of expression and signified" (*Over Her Dead Body*, 155). But allegory here as elsewhere depends upon misrepresentation, a problem signaled when Elaine's family adds to the decoration of her funeral barge "the silken case with braided blazonings" (*LE*, 1142), chief emblem of her representational problem. The letter she composes constitutes a fantastic falsification of the situation at court. Despite her father's effort to disillusion her, her letter constructs Lancelot as "a knight peerless" and Guinevere and her ladies as worthy of her prayers, in a courtly fantasy that only Elaine could credit. Elaine's allegorical fantasy is nearly broken up by modern emotional realism when Guinevere, jealous because Lancelot wore Elaine's favor, throws Lancelot's painfully won diamonds into the river a moment before Elaine's barge floats by. And although Elaine has complete confidence that she radiates her intended meaning, no one in the court can figure out what that meaning is. When her barge floats in, the court becomes "mouths that gaped, and eyes that asked / 'What is it?'" (*LE*, 1241–42), and the next several lines detail their wild and inapt speculations (has she "come to take the King to Fairyland?" 1249). Although she unites in her body representation and represented, she fails to convey her allegorical message because it depends upon the superimposition of an idealized courtly meaning on a sordid actuality of weak morals and weaker reading.[59]

Elaine's burial (after Arthur has read her letter aloud and the court has marveled at and pitied her) does not so much resolve this idyll's representational problem as reify it. She is buried "with gorgeous obsequies . . . like a queen" (*LE*, 1324–25) in the royal shrine, and Arthur orders her tomb:

> "Let her tomb
> Be costly, and her image thereupon,
> And let the shield of Lancelot at her feet
> Be carven, and her lily in her hand.
> And let the story of her dolorous voyage
> For all true hearts be blazoned on her tomb
> In letters gold and azure!"
> (*LE*, 1328–34)

Radiating significance, doubling its chances of being read by combining descriptive representation with symbolism (her image and her story as well as the lily and the shield), the tomb is intended to make permanent Elaine's self-transformation into a message "for all true hearts," an allegory of innocent and faithful love. Yet the allegory once again fails. As Bronfen points out, the tomb replaces Elaine's chosen medium (her body) with stone (in Bronfen's words, the court "replac[es] Elaine's iconic recoding with complete retextualisation") and substitutes inscription for "the central notion expressed by her body-text . . . the more global statement 'I am dead'" (*Over Her Dead Body*, 156). As with the inscription under Albert's figure in the memorial chapel, words speaking for the dead can never get it right.

Moreover, the only described consequence of Elaine's allegorical burial is to ironize Lancelot's continued suffering. After the burial, Arthur harasses Lancelot about his failure to reciprocate Elaine's love and his consequent failure to perpetuate his "name and fame" by producing sons (1361). Sitting alone, Lancelot reproaches himself and broods on Arthur's imperative:

> Why did the King dwell on my name to me?
> Mine own name shames me, seeming a reproach,
> Lancelot, whom the Lady of the Lake
> Caught from his mother's arms . . .
> . . . .
> For what am I? what profits me my name
> Of greatest knight? I fought for it, and have it:
> Pleasure to have it, none; to lose it, pain.
> (*LE*, 1391–1404)

Although his name has "[n]ow grown a part of me" (*LE*, 1405), because he won the tournament and reaffirmed his right to the epithet "greatest knight," he fears that having done so will only make "sin seem less, the sinner seeming great" (1407). The ironic relation of Elaine's allegorical purity to the corrupt court is repeated in Lancelot's empty recovery of his name.

In eliminating Arthur's original sin and making Guinevere's adultery solely responsible for dismantling the Round Table, Tennyson makes the representational problem exemplified by Elaine the foundational moral problem of Camelot. Told no fewer than three times, the story of Guinevere's love for the wrong man is a story of representational error. (One of Tennyson's earliest Arthurian efforts from the early 1830s, "Sir Launcelot and Queen Guinevere," tells the story more cheerfully but suggests the centrality of the episode to Tennyson's thinking about Arthurian matters.) Arthur, having glimpsed Guinevere once from a procession, and having successfully petitioned her father Leodogran, sends Lancelot to collect her for the wedding. Arthur supposes there is no difference between his intentions and the actions of his representative ("his warrior whom he loved / And honored most," *CA*, 446–47), but Guinevere falls in love with Lancelot the representative rather than Arthur the represented. From Arthur's point of view, the only indication of a problem is that Guinevere speaks her vows "with drooping eyes" (468). In Merlin's account, when Lancelot arrived as "ambassador . . . to fetch her," "she took him for the King, / So fixt her fancy on him" (*MV*, 772–75). As Guinevere recalls it, her error was less accidental and more thoughtful. Her having met Lancelot first, and having passed the "maytime" of their journey "Rapt in sweet talk or lively, all on love / And sport and tilts and pleasure" (*G*, 383–85)—not to mention their having passed together through half a dozen lines of luscious Tennysonian landscape description loaded with "sheets of hyacinth" and "silk pavilions"—was enough to make the "cold, / High, self-contained, and passionless" Arthur seem lackluster by contrast (*G*, 402–3). The representational excesses of Tennyson's verse (those sheets of hyacinth and silk pavilions) lend weight to the possibility that one might well have difficulty choosing the message over the messenger. As when Elaine takes her image of Lancelot for Lancelot himself, Guinevere in each version of the story takes the figure literally, taking Lancelot for her lover, not as a representative for her lover.

Such representational excesses are rendered threatening not only to the moral health of the Round Table but even to Arthur's continued bodily existence. Statues representing Arthur are associated with the haze that generally signals his "drift toward insubstantiality" (*Tennyson and the Text*, 58). Hunt points out that Arthur is three times "presented as if he himself were a statue or stained glass window" ("The Poetry of Distance," 102), the third time to be disparaged by the skeptical Tristram.[60] Elaine, her body made a statue-like representation of love, her image carved into a signifying memorial statue, demonstrates the incompatibility between life and allegorizing monuments. Just before Guinevere sees Arthur vanish into the mist, allegorized into nonexistence, she sees not his face but his armor, his body already turning into sculpture, encased as it is in "The Dragon of the great Pendragonship" (*G,* 594), the emblem of his office. The question of whether Arthur is human or supernatural, real or allegorical crops up repeatedly in descriptions of Camelot and its sculptural decorations. *Gareth and Lynette,* the most optimistic idyll after *The Coming of Arthur,* brings Gareth into Camelot by way of Merlin's story of fairies building Camelot; Merlin offers as alternatives the realness of Arthur (in a fairy-built castle) and the realness of the city (and "the King a shadow"). Approaching the city, Gareth and his companions see "the silver-misty morn / Rolling her smoke about the Royal mount" (*GL,* 186–87), and they see its "spires and turrets" alternately flashing and disappearing. When they reach the gate, they see a sculptural program that represents the Lady of the Lake, the Three Queens, and Arthur's wars (his fairy origins and the fairy builders of the city) but not Arthur himself. That the fairies are depicted but Arthur is not justifies Merlin's claim that Arthur is real. This is the idyll in which, as we saw, representations do not yet exceed what they represent; it is not yet time for Arthur to be transformed into a statue of himself.

In *The Holy Grail,* by contrast, a different sculptural program testifies to the growing disjunction in Camelot between representations and what they represent. Arthur, away from home when the Grail makes its alluring appearance (having untypically chosen to serve as his own representative on a quest), returns to see his "great hall . . . rolled in thunder-smoke" (*HG,* 220). As Percival describes it to the monk Ambrosius, this is what Arthur sees endangered by the Grail and the passions it arouses. The towers and spires of the city all climb

> to the mighty hall that Merlin built.
> And four great zones of sculpture, set betwixt
> With many a mystic symbol, gird the hall:
> And in the lowest beasts are slaying men,
> And in the second men are slaying beasts,
> And on the third are warriors, perfect men,
> And on the fourth are men with growing wings,
> And over all one statue in the mould
> Of Arthur, made by Merlin, with a crown,

And peaked wings pointed to the Northern Star,
And eastward fronts the statue, and the crown
And both the wings are made of gold, and flame
At sunrise till the people in far fields,
Wasted so often by the heathen hordes,
Behold it, crying, "We have still a King."
(*HG*, 231–45)

Arthur rides up, "In horror lest the work by Merlin wrought, / Dreamlike, should on the sudden vanish" (*HG*, 259–60). This sculptural program, unlike the one on the gate in *Gareth and Lynette*, not only includes Arthur but is devoted to him, placing him at the top of a hierarchy of being that he both supervises and supersedes. It allegorizes him, and, recalling the full array of Albert memorials, it does so both through representational excess and through blankness. That the statue's wings "flame" connects them all too closely to the "folds of rolling fire" Arthur fears will obliterate them and him. Moreover, to have a fancy allegorical statue is precisely *not* to "have . . . a King," just as in "To the Queen" Arthur is "gray" when his "name, a ghost, / Streams like a cloud," exceeding him. Because the description of this sculpture appears where it does, it signifies not Arthur's ascendency but his approaching failure to keep the Round Table together and defeat the forces of evil. Recalling and indeed prefigured by Elaine's sculptural tomb, Arthur's statue signifies his absence and forecasts his coming nonentity. Just as for Albert as well as for Elaine, allegorizing sculptural depiction of Arthur is incompatible with continued existence. In *Gareth and Lynette*, Arthur's realness obviated sculptural representations of him; nearing the end of his reign, his unrealness—his existence only as shadowy allegorical meaning—is signified by his extravagant memorialization, his body as a character replaced by his body in abstract art.

In their writings from the days immediately after Albert's death, the Queen and her eldest daughter associate Tennyson and his *Idylls* with Albert and specifically with their project to memorialize, monumentalize, and allegorize him. On 21 December 1861, after a paragraph on "our new life of sorrow and desolation" and its allegorical consolations ("Papa's love shines like a bright star"), Vicky writes of her last visit with her father: "Papa read to me from the 'Idylls of the King' at Osborne and wished me to draw something for him, and it has been my occupation for weeks—thinking of him, whether the drawings would please him." As in her mother's mourning letters, grief is followed by aesthetic activity. The next paragraph congratulates the Queen on her choice of Frogmore for a mausoleum and expresses her happiness at being consulted about its planning because "I knew Papa's taste so well." Finally, in the next sentence, Papa is again made allegorical: "As he was the most perfect model of all that was pure, good, virtuous, and great—so was his judgement in all things concerning art—unerring" (*Dearest Mama*, 25). Encouraged by the *Idylls*, Vicky like her mother uses Albert's allegorical status as an excuse for her own pleasurable artistic activities. A model of purity, Albert becomes the muse of art. The service the *Idylls* performs for Albert's relicts is not only to provide an idealized image of him but also to vindicate, by mirroring it, their own practice of setting up feminized allegorical abstractions that could never have coexisted with the living man.

When Vicky writes to Tennyson in February 1862 to thank him for dedicating the *Idylls* to her father, she explains that he had read aloud to her the last two or three pages of *Guinevere* (her first experience of any of the *Idylls*, which she now knows "by heart"). She continues, "I cannot separate the idea of King Arthur from the image of him whom I most revered on earth!" (Hallam Tennyson, *Memoir*, 1:481). The last "two or three pages" of the 1859 edition include no speech of Arthur's but only Guinevere's repentant hagiography of Arthur after he has gone: Guinevere compares him to "the conscience of a saint / Among his warring senses" (*G*, 634–35) and calls him God's "highest creature" (651). Vicky's identification of her father with Arthur thus arises from his reading a memorial allegorization of Arthur that is now, thanks to the dedication, a memorial allegorization of the deceased reader himself. In Vicky's letter, thanks to Tennyson, Albert justifies his own transformation into mist-filled allegory.[61] Later, Vicky and her mother would find *The Holy Grail*, the idyll that launched the trend toward allegorical readings, admirable yet incomprehensible.[62] Yet in their early responses to Albert's death they associate the *Idylls* and Tennyson with their desire to turn Albert into an allegorical monument. Tennyson's disjointed allegorical method corresponds to their own memorializing gestures, in which Albert's known wishes and his likeness are erased or concealed by the never-ending effort to construct and celebrate his higher meaning. Written (according to Emily Tennyson) to gratify "the Queen's wish, and that of the Crown Princess" (quoted in Martin, *Tennyson*, 478), appearing in 1869 as many of the more ambitious sculptural Albert memorials were nearing completion, Tennyson's statue of Arthur in *The Holy Grail* fulfills both his own and his Queen's memorial programs: to "think of allegories," even, or especially, those which in their beauty mystify any possible mimetic elements or realist meanings.

Tennyson's second dedicatory poem, "To the Queen" (1873), printed at the end of every subsequent edition of the *Idylls*, not only airs many of these issues about naming, allegory, and the uneasy fit between "ideal [and] real" but also links this subject—and the memory of Albert—to justifications for the maintenance of the British Empire. Up to now we have focused on the fact of Albert's subordination to allegorical meanings, and on the implications of that subordination for his memory and for Victoria as memorialist; by attending briefly to some of the content of those meanings, I would like to suggest what else was at stake in grafting larger meanings onto Albert's image. Dead and idealized, Albert can be made to mean anything any iconographer—in the name of praise—pleases to have him mean.

The occasion for "To the Queen" was the thanksgiving celebration for the Queen's and the Prince of Wales's recovery from illness in February 1872, which as we saw in Chapter 3 inspired the *Times* to shift its attention from the Queen as spectacle to the subjects to which she will hereafter be the spectator. This topical subject leads into Tennyson's rebuttal to the proposal "that Canada should sever her connection with Great Britain, as she was 'too costly.'"[63] Presenting the empire as a benign institution that only the shortsighted penuriousness of Britons would bring to an end, Tennyson yokes love of the Queen and her heir to continuation of empire.

> The loyal to their crown
> Are loyal to their own far sons, who love
> Our ocean-empire with her boundless homes
> For ever-broadening England . . .
> ("To the Queen," lines 27–30)

The rhetoric of these lines distantly echoes the *Times* account of Victoria's 1844 appearance to open the new Royal Exchange: domestic love and love of empire ("the reign of kindness") reinforce one another. Soon after these lines, a period and a dash link this part of the poem to the next section, with its references to the *Idylls* and to Albert. Like the imperfect grafting of Albert's modern head onto medieval armor, the dash calls attention to the awkward break and jump from current events to the "old imperfect tale" (36) and the topics it raises. The *Idylls* are generally understood by critics to convey enthusiasm for Britain's imperial projects, celebrating as they do Arthur's conquest of the "heathen" and his strong-armed if temporary maintenance of peace in his and neighboring kingdoms. No one has seriously disputed Tennyson's support for Britain's empire at this period of his career, and "To the Queen" ends predictably by comparing the loss of Canada to the loss of Arthur's last battle.[64] But the awkward linking of current events to the matter of Arthur and Albert—like the many instances we have surveyed of imperfect grafts of allegory and likeness—reminds us of yet another vast and overshadowing project that the memory of Albert could be made to allegorize and thus to justify. Just so, allegorical marble groups representing "the Continents" guard the four corners of the National Albert Memorial. These groups, striking for their predictably Victorian primitivizing and feminizing of the Other, allude to the Great Exhibition and Albert's work to bring the nations together there; in their positioning, in their bright blankness and their elaborating detail, they also serve as a first line of defense to distract the viewer from seeing the dark and diminished Prince inside his spectacular shrine. In both works—"To the Queen" and the national memorial—Albert is linked disjunctively to, and diminished by, allegorical representations endorsing the vast machinery of Britain's empire, a machinery far larger than any likeness of Albert or even of his Queen.

Julia Margaret Cameron's photographs, by contrast, as we shall see, both "think of allegories" and take them apart, and in so doing make visible the human cost—to women and to men—of the monumentalizing project.

Cameron's Photographic *Idylls:* Allegorical Realism and Memorial Art

Tennyson's other illustrious neighbor on the Isle of Wight during the 1860s and 1870s was Julia Margaret Cameron. Expansive, hardworking, and imperious, Cameron was, like Victoria, a woman at the top of her line of work who both obeyed and flouted Victorian norms of femininity. Cameron lived next door to the Tennyson family and was notorious for commandeering her own and adjacent families, visitors, and innocent bystanders to sit for her as models. Children who posed for her later recalled her as "terrifying . . . with a plump eager face and piercing eyes, and a voice husky and even harsh, yet in some way compelling and even charming"; "we trembled (or we should have trembled had we dared to do so) when the round black eye of the camera was turned upon us."[65] Like Victoria—or perhaps even more like Lucilla Marjoribanks or Dorothea Brooke—"Cameron often managed to safely bypass the confines of her gender by enlarging the bourgeois woman's part in both her art and life."[66] Like Victoria, she did her work at home. Unlike Victoria's, however, her work disrupted her domesticity: she kept her servants so busy modeling for her that she sometimes served bacon and eggs three meals a day. She never met or photographed the Queen, despite the close connection through Tennyson and despite Cameron's membership in a ruling class family (Cameron's critics often begin by reciting her pedigree—sister to the famously beautiful Pattle sisters, great-aunt of Virginia Woolf). Victoria would have been more likely to visit a home among the "lower orders" than to enter Cameron's studio.[67] A sort of alternative Queen through the looking-glass, Cameron presided over a glassed-walled studio that stood in some ways as a parodic miniature of some of the Queen's own spaces, her vast greenhouses and above all the Crystal Palace. Robert Douglas-Fairhurst points out that "the crowds at the Great Exhibition could marvel at the sights of the world being fitted under a giant version of the glass roofs which already covered wealthy photographers' studios. In a sense, they were inside the world's largest photograph, a photograph of the world."[68] But Cameron's unprofessional backyard studio was a renovated henhouse, said to be "very untidy and very uncomfortable" (quoted in Gernsheim, *Cameron*, 53), and the photographs she produced within its no doubt far from crystal-clear walls were famous not for their transparent reflection of the world but for their soft focus, their spots and streaks, and their self-dramatizing pictorial extravagance. Her artistic values would seem to invert those for which Victoria stood.

Nonetheless, when in 1874 and 1875 Julia Margaret Cameron made, at Tennyson's request, a series of fifteen photographic illustrations for the *Idylls of the King,* her work joined Tennyson's 1862 "To the Prince Consort" in retroactively making poems of the 1850s perform the work of later Victorian mourning.[69] Most simply, her pictures memorialize Albert by illustrating the poem that was dedicated to his memory and thus by picturing the ideal Arthur in whom the Prince was to have found his "image." But they also memorialize the Prince generically and, in so doing, comment critically on other memorial works of art. As we have seen, the case can be made that all photographs are melancholic if not memorial with regard to their referents.[70] In making this claim, Barthes and those writing after him assume that the primary force of photography is evidentiary, as when he writes, "from a real body, which was there, proceed radiations which ultimately touch me, who am here" (*Camera Lucida,* 80). He takes for granted that what can never be completely mourned is the being that stood still for an instant before the camera. But few readers of Cameron's work have considered it primarily evidentiary.[71] Allegorical and illustrative photographs such as those Cameron made for the *Idylls* have a different and more complicated relation to referentiality, for, as will be seen in more detail below, not only do they offer likenesses of the models who stood before the camera, they also refer to the story that the models' poses illustrate and, moreover, to the allegorical meanings that the story is supposed to convey. Consequently, like the mourning photographs of Victoria's family with the marble Albert, they serve as memorial art not because the people posing in them were to be dead one day (Barthes's argument) but because their representational form duplicates Victoria's and Tennyson's memorial representations of Albert and Arthur, the form that serves so well both to monumentalize Albert and to allegorize him into blankness. They also comment critically on the memorial arts they practice.

Several commentators on Cameron have noted the generic ambiguity of her photographs that can make the same image appear, by turns, as realist portrait and as allegory. To borrow Joseph's phrase for the *Idylls,* Cameron's is a "flickering genre," or "allegory at a distance." For example, in September 1872 Cameron made a photograph of Alice Liddell, by then twenty years of age. The portrait is full length; the subject, elegantly coiffed and dressed in an unmistakably adult style, leans her face pensively on her hand and looks directly at the photographer and the viewer. Over the title "Alice Liddell, Freshwater, September 1872" this photograph would seem to be a firm rejoinder to Charles Dodgson's wish not to see his little Alices—the real Alice he photographed and the imaginary Alice of his stories—grow up.[72] Although we have seen how Lewis Carroll mocks the attempt, by the likes of the Red Queen and Ruskin, to make girls signify, Dodgson's use of Alice Liddell to hold onto a certain idea of womankind and to signify Alice in a timeless Wonderland are notorious. By contrast, Cameron's Alice Liddell is a modern adult, signifying only herself. Cameron did with this image, however, what she often did with portraits, especially those of women: she retitled it to make it allegorical. "Another print from this same negative was titled 'Pomona' by Mrs. Cameron," writes Anita Mozley. "It is one of those portraits of women in which Mrs. Cameron saw both the real person and recalled the legendary character that the real person seemed to her to personify. Alice, so richly alive in this photograph, reminded her of the Roman goddess of fruitfulness."[73] Cameron reallegorizes the woman whom the image itself would seem to have just defended from allegorization. Finally, however, the outcome is equivocal: that she gives Alice Liddell this particular meaning, on the one hand, suggests a complicity with Dodgson's vision—Mozley speculates that "Pomona" alludes to the "riper years" projected for Alice after the end of *Wonderland*—and, on the other hand, confirms the rejoinder to Dodgson, since Alice becoming "ripe" was what he most lamented. Another image of the adult Liddell uses her strictly allegorically (her profile head and loose hair posed against a wall of vines), as "Alethea"; still, Dodgson is known to have disliked Cameron and her photographs and to have avoided her when he visited the Tennysons.[74]

One way to understand Cameron's intermittently allegorizing approach is to follow Mike Weaver's claim that Cameron shared the Pre-Raphaelites' attraction to typology and that, as a deeply religious person, Cameron believed in the seamless correspondences that constitute typology.[75] Weaver (in a discussion that has become a touchstone in Cameron criticism) argues that, rather than "vaguely allegorical," her photographs are "typological or typical—illustrative in a profound, biblical sense," and that she "found personifications of [biblical types] among her famous friends and domestic relations" (Weaver, *Cameron*, 15). The meaning of her photographs lies "in the space between idealist fiction and realist fact. She was turning actual models into ideal subjects" (26). Sir John Herschel in a velvet cap is at once "a German Nazarene painter [and] a Paterfamilias" (20). Very similar poses by the same people (Mary Hillier with a scarf on her head hovering over a sleeping baby) can be titled "My GrandChild" and "The Shadow of the Cross"; a portrait of Florence Fisher is interchangeable with an image of the same child as "A Study of the John the Baptist" (23). Not only do her friends and relations embody ideal types, but they can also embody several types at once, through typological connections: "Young Freddy Gould could impersonate Astyanax, a classical type of Christ, as well as Cupid" (23). At one point Cameron thought she had found her Lancelot—whose face, according to Tennyson, had to be "well worn with passion"—in Cardinal Vaughan (Gernsheim, *Cameron*, 30). By only a slight stretch of the same logic, the same model—or even the same photograph—can represent Iago and Christ, Mary Magdalene and the Angel at the Tomb. The Pre-Raphaelites themselves (especially Rossetti) incurred the wrath of critic Robert Buchanan in 1871 for making the spiritual "fleshly," for making (in Adrienne Munich's words) "a revisionary use of typological symbolism" that "erases distinctions between body and soul" and between the chaste and the unchaste.[76] Cameron's use of typology too suggests an undoing of the very distinctions a religious typology would seem to depend upon.

Cameron conveyed the belief that individuals bore intrinsically the meaning of the characters they illustrated. The woman who modeled Vivien in the *Idylls* illustrations was unhappy about representing so "objectionable" a character, as if the photograph were to reveal the sitter's innate likeness to the evil Vivien. Cameron searched high and low before she found the right models for certain characters, locating Arthur in the porter at Yarmouth pier and trying out countless combinations for Lancelot and Guinevere.[77] And yet if by a switch of captions the same image can represent Alice and Pomona, or even saint and sinner, then Cameron's art also may be said to call attention to the arbitrariness with which typological or allegorical meanings are assigned to (or even "found in") real models. The meaning cannot be intrinsic to the image, much less to the model, if different captions can produce such contrary meanings. As we saw earlier, only the caption "I have fought the good fight" determines whether Albert is sheathing or unsheathing his sword. As in those works I have characterized as failed allegory, Cameron's art exposes the constructedness of what is passing for typology, the human work of projection that can be necessary to making typological connections appear intrinsic.

This is not to say that, having exposed its mechanisms, Cameron objects to the arbitrary grafting of meaning onto natural forms. The image that concludes the second volume of her Tennyson illustrations affirms this very process (figure 38). A young woman poses with her face and upper body in profile against Cameron's brick garden wall. On it grows a passion-flower vine in such blooming profusion that one tendril reaches out from the wall to encircle the woman's shoulder. The text, which identifies the woman as Maud, is the verse that we know so well from Ruskin's double quotation and Carroll's mockery of that act of quotation. It is as though Victorians knew only one verse of Tennyson's poem and repeated it over and over, its incantatory power defining their favored representational practice:

> There has fallen a splendid tear
> From the passion-flower at the gate,
> She is coming, my dove, my dear;
> She is coming, my life, my fate;
> The red rose cries, "she is near, she is near";
> And the white rose weeps, "She is late";
> The larkspur listens, "I hear, I hear";
> And the lily whispers, "I wait."

As the final image in the volume that was to be her last major photographic work before she left England for India, this photograph constitutes Cameron's signature, and she signs off with the hallmark of Ruskinian pathetic fallacy. The image diverges little from a familiar Cameron formula, a young woman with loosened hair posed meditatively with signifying flowers (more typically lilies or roses). As is often the case, real objects (a woman, a vine) are asked to signify not themselves but symbols in a poem. But by grafting her image onto lines that are themselves about the awkward grafting of meaning onto natural objects, Cameron adds another layer to the pathetic fallacy already at work in the kind of image this one typifies. With this signature photograph, she affirmatively identifies the art of the Tennyson volumes not with seamless religious typology but with the passionate awkwardness of personification or failed allegory.

Cameron's photographs have provoked strong and at times gendered responses. Writing in 1948, Helmut Gernsheim rapidly dismisses her tableaux pictures, asserting that in attempting narrative illustrations she "diverted the camera from its true function" and "lost her sense of proportion" (*Cameron*, 52); her portraits, by contrast, "her magnificent large heads," earn his un-

FIGURE 38
Julia Margaret Cameron, Maud. Photograph in *Illustrations to Tennyson's Idylls of the King and Other Poems,* 1875. "There has fallen a splendid tear / From the passion-flower at the gate . . ."

bounded praise, and he carefully lists all the great men she took (63). Gernsheim's judgmental tone might appear to be a phenomenon of the 1940s, but so recent and fine a critic as Gerhard Joseph—writing for an audience more wary of evaluation—delivers much the same judgment when he dismisses "the portraits of her grandchildren in swans' wings, the allegorical subjects, or her illustrations of the *Idylls of the King*" as "all those conventional genre-tradition *tableaux vivants* that parade forth the limitations of her Victorian sentimentality all too clearly." Her reputation, Joseph continues, derives instead from her "portraits, some of women, but mostly of the 'representative men,' the Carlylean (or Emersonian) heroes of Victorian society." He praises her "Herschel Album" where many of these portraits are to be found as "perhaps the finest album of Victorian photographs in existence" and ends the paragraph—in a gesture like Gernsheim's—with a list of some of the famous men she "captured" (*Tennyson and the Text,* 78–79).

By contrast, Victoria Olsen and Linda Shires take Cameron's Tennyson illustrations seriously, and what both find worth noting is their representation of women's powers.[78] Carol Mavor, disagreeing explicitly with Gernsheim, extolls Cameron's quasi-narrative photographs of Madonnas and children: "I love Cameron's fallen Madonnas . . . *altered* images of Mother, scratched with sexuality and printed with flesh" (*Pleasures Taken,* 44). Mavor also praises the messiness of Cameron's plates, the evidence they bear (strands of hair, fingerprints, blots) of having been touched by the photographer's body. Cameron's contemporaries, needless to say, join Gernsheim in finding this aspect of her work, like her use of soft focus, merely a sign of ineptitude. Lindsay Smith also finds, but differently values, gendered meanings in Cameron's deliberate choice of soft focus for portraits of children: when contrasted with Dodgson's sharp focus on little girls who are placed (back to the wall) in geometrically defined spaces, Cameron's soft focus "constitutes a critique of the ideology of perceptual mastery" ("The Politics of Focus," 250).[79] The straightforward portraits of great men are generically clear: they are realistic and refer unequivocally to the sitter. By contrast, what has made male viewers squeamish—her attempts to portray narrative, her messiness, her sentimentality, her generic uncertainties—has appealed to Cameron's women fans.

Cameron's project in illustrating the *Idylls* was to use photography against its commercial grain, in which naturalism and sharp focus were valued most highly, to create an "ideal representation" of the *Idylls,* which were themselves "allegory in the distance."[80] In Victoria Olsen's view, Cameron claims "the equal status of the poet and photographer" ("Photography," 126) when she writes out the Tennyson passages in her own hand opposite each photograph. But because she was using real models, Olsen writes, "Cameron was forced to make difficult compromises between the referentiality of photography and the imaginary scenes of Tennyson's Arthurian poem" (127). For Gernsheim, these compromises were unequivocally defects: continuing his disparagement of the *Idylls* illustrations, he remarks that despite her intention to offer ideal representations of Tennyson's idealizing poem, "her compositions persist in producing a realistic effect which can only be termed incongruous" (Gernsheim, *Cameron,* 61). In thus criticizing her, he is repeating Coventry Patmore's complaint about "the effect of the 'realistic' air which most of her groups persist in maintaining for themselves, after all has been done to bring them into the pure region of ideality."[81] Among even the most sympathetic recent critics, Hopkinson finds the illustrations "over-literal transcriptions of his poetic images" (Hopkinson, *Cameron,* 131) and cites G. B. Shaw remarking that the "truthfulness" of the *Idylls* illustrations makes them "ridiculous." Those who praise the *Idylls* photos at all tend to emphasize the ones that benefit from Cameron's skill as portraitist; the photos of Enid and of Elaine with the shield (figure 41) were even marketed individually. The complicated group composition of Arthur in his barge from *The*

Passing of Arthur (figure 45) has generally been the limit case in evaluations of Cameron: singled out for detailed criticism both by Gernsheim and by Hopkinson, its jarring mismatch between material circumstances and apparent sublime allegorical aims recalls the memorable image from the rained-out Eglinton Tournament, a knight in armor carrying an umbrella (*Return to Camelot*, 103).

Guidance toward a different view of the *Idylls* illustrations can be found in Carol Mavor's enthusiasm for the tactile qualities of Cameron's Madonna pictures, which she sees as pictures of mothers touching children, and for the prints' visual evidence of the photographer's touch. If Cameron accepts her pictures' so-called technical flaws to the extent that she thematizes them, making touch the very subject of her pictures, then accusations about her technique can have little purchase. By the same token, having chosen to illustrate an allegorical work with a documentary medium, Cameron displays rather than trying to hide the bodily particularity of her models; the "realistic effect" may indeed contrast with the "ideality" of the scene illustrated, but it cannot be condemned as an error. Cameron values generic ambiguity and often, as we have seen, takes it as her subject. Her compositions and her technique guide the viewer to see simultaneously the discrepancy between the actual model and the ideal character and their coexistence. For me the "punctum" in these pictures is often the women models' greasy long hair, separating into stiff strands as it is loosed from its accustomed bindings; looking at the pictures, I think of how itchy the models' heads must have been as they sat or stood motionless (without even the headrests commercial photographers provided) for the three to ten minutes of Cameron's exposures. The pictures, in other words, unravel allegorical meaning even as they constitute it, by enabling the viewer to see—in a "flickering" way—now the model, now the idealized allegory, and at all times the difference between them. (Weaver's undeveloped claim that the meaning lies "in the space between idealist fiction and realist fact" hints at much the same point.) Cameron's typological art, if such it is, is also an art of flamboyantly failed allegory—allegory that continuously displays the effort of its construction and the ease with which it could fall back into naturalism. Just so, the doubling of the portrait of Alice Liddell as a typological representation of "Pomona" recalls Carroll's pleasure in exposing the Ruskinian attempt at allegory. Even as Alice rises to the status of Pomona, Pomona sinks to the level of a well-dressed young Briton.

Similarly, several of the *Idylls* images show, as if by mistake, the inside of Cameron's studio; but what embarrasses Gernsheim can again be read as part of these photographs' exposure of the mechanics of allegory making. He faults the *Idylls* illustrations as having "overshot the mark of what is acceptable—at least to our generation—in artificiality" and finishes his amused description of Arthur in his barge with the three queens (figure 45) in this way: "Our description is not complete without reference to the background of the studio—needless to say, for such an ambitious composition the background cloth does not stretch far enough, and reveals odd corners and part of the roof of the studio" (Gernsheim, *Cameron,* 61). The studio walls and peaked roof are conspicuous as well in the image of Elaine on her barge (figure 43), where one can also easily discern the strings holding the shield case above Elaine's head. Cameron was known to take and retake photographs until she got it right, exhausting her sitters. By her estimate, she took over two hundred pictures to get the fifteen she finally published, forty alone of the scene of Lancelot and Guinevere. The picturing of her studio equipment, like the "incongruous" effect of using real models for ideal scenes, cannot in any simple sense be taken for a mistake; rather, it allows the photographs to identify themselves as photographs. The pictures display the effort that went into transforming friends and henhouse into mythic beings and spaces.

Although by 1874 Cameron could have chosen to illustrate any of the *Idylls* except *Balin and Balan* (1885), her photographs concentrate on the 1859 set: of the fifteen *Idylls* photographs, eleven illustrate figures and scenes from those four. Linda Shires points out that the illustrations also concentrate on women characters, as do photographs of other Tennyson poems included in the two volumes, such as "Mariana," *The Princess,* and *Maud.*[82] Whether an interest in photographing women caused her to focus on the first four idylls—named, in 1859, for their central women characters: Enid, Vivien, Elaine, and Guinevere—or whether focusing on those idylls led logically to focusing on women, in selecting figures and scenes to illustrate, it is as if Cameron had returned to the 1859 edition. Enid is pictured alone in the two images from that idyll. The four images of Elaine (figures 41, 42, 43, and 44) give her story and point of view, with Lancelot's tournament and moral struggles nowhere to be seen. Victoria Olsen points out that the two images of *Merlin and Vivien* attend to the turning points of Vivien's ascendency ("Photography," 127–28), in images that suggest an analogy between woman villain and woman artist. And when Cameron includes an image of Arthur from *Guinevere,* she chooses to illustrate the moment when the King is turning into vapor (figure 39); she underlines "who seemed the phantom of a giant." (Men do appear: Cameron's white-bearded husband Charles served both as Merlin and as the dumb oarsman who brings Elaine to Camelot, appearing in four pictures altogether; Arthur appears in three; and Lancelot, Galahad, and Gareth appear as well; but women clearly predominate.) She took, but did not publish, a picture of Guinevere groveling at Arthur's feet and another of Guinevere alone with text about her jealousy of Elaine; she thus edited out Guinevere's less savory appearances.[83] Both Linda Shires and Joanne Lukitsch point out that the photographs illustrate moments of power for these women characters and that Elaine is idealized as a dreamer of Arthur's stature when both are represented traveling to immortality in their boats (figures 43 and 45; Lukitsch, *Cameron,* 29, 35; Shires, "Glass House Visionary," 120).

Cameron's emphasis can be explained thematically, through something analogous to the "theological feminism" she shared with Anna Jameson, which led her also to emphasize, among her biblical images, Mary and other female figures (Weaver, *Cameron,* 23). Her emphasis on female figures in the *Idylls* illustrations may simply reflect her gynocentric point of view, as Shires, Lukitsch, and Olsen's readings imply. But the emphasis on women can also be explained generically, in the context of the photographs' apparently chosen artificiality, as images of the models as well as of allegorical figures. When she photographed men, the image was usually referential; although Herschel becomes in one image "The Astronomer," Tennyson, the famous man who sat for her most often, refused to be allegorized, refusing even to let her place lines of verse underneath his portrait that served as frontispiece to the *Idylls* volume. (The epithet "dirty monk" was Tennyson's nickname for the image after he saw it, not a formal title of Cameron's.) Although she took named portraits of women, images of women are more likely than those of men to serve double duty as types or allegorical figures. In thus gendering her genres, Cameron was hardly diverging from standard Victorian practice. For example, in the sculptural program of the National Albert Memorial female figures—neatly labeled to make it clear they are allegories and not the scantily clad women they appear to be—represent the continents (Asia, for example, is a half-naked woman unveiling herself astride an elephant) and the skills (agriculture, commerce, etc.), while the bas relief offers 169 realistic portraits of men, likenesses of actual artists, musicians, poets, and architects.[84] Hopkinson argues that Cameron "approached the photography of women and men differently" because she saw women as male photographers and purchasers would have done, through the lens of separate spheres (Hopkinson, *Cameron,* 15, 110). But the focus on women in the *Idylls* is also consistent with Cameron's career-long pattern of finding women more illustrative, more susceptible to being discovered as types or turned into allegories. Women, for her, more easily enable the double referentiality required in illustration (or the triple referentiality of illustrating an allegorical work): where a famous man arrests the chain of referents at himself, a woman allows referentiality to slide from her face to the story to the story's "ideal."

The two pictures in the dining-room of Pointz Hall in *Between the Acts,* the last novel by Cameron's great-niece Virginia Woolf, illustrate the same gender difference and suggest additionally how it reflects—for good or ill—the conditions of patriarchy. "[T]he man was an ancestor. He had a name. He held the rein in his hand" (*Between the Acts,* 36). A "talk producer," the talk he produces is Mr. Oliver's referential account of his history. Having wished to be painted and to be buried with his "famous" dog, he is linked to his elderly descendant, who dozes dreaming of himself with gun and helmet in the India of his youth, with "the dog at his feet . . . look[ing] a stone dog, a crusader's dog, guarding even in the realms of death the sleep of his master" (17). "The lady," by contrast, "was a picture, bought by Oliver because he liked the picture" (36). She is linked not to referential history and conquest but to the picture's material surface and to artistic creation itself: "[S]he led the eye up, down, from the curve to the straight, through glades of greenery and shades of silver, dun and rose into silence" (36), a silence that the narrative then elaborates as one of its valued terms. Her yellow robe connects her also to the flower, which "blazed a soft yellow, a lambent light under a film of velvet; it filled the caverns behind the eye with light" (11), the flower that represents the child George's incipient artistic vision and its terrifying interruption by his grandfather. A painting of painting itself because she has no known historical significance, the lady recalls Woolf's great-aunt's photographs of photography, photographs enabled by the choice of female models. The man who produces talk only about himself recalls Cameron's portraits of famous men. The lady, by contrast, like Cameron's allegorical pictures of women, is a silent producer of silence who lends herself to being used to tell other stories than her own. From the vantage point of 1939, Woolf can write both affectionately and critically about the gendered aesthetic conventions in which her Victorian ancestress was embedded; she can show at once how they reflect patriarchal values and how they might serve a woman artist. Photographing the artifice of photography itself while photographing women, Cameron calls attention to the gender as well as to the awkward artistry of her allegorical practice.

The focus on women, then, defines the images as a group generically. Although the illustrations include three images of Arthur, to which I will turn shortly, as pictures primarily of women the *Idylls* illustrations memorialize Albert more by playing on the same generic ambiguity that characterizes both Victoria's and Tennyson's Albert memorials than by simply picturing Albert as Arthur. As we have seen, during her mourning Victoria sought to have images of Albert made that offered both good likenesses and allegorical meanings, images that often foreground the difficulty of grafting one onto the other and that efface Albert's particularity in the process. In much the same way, Tennyson understood the *Idylls* to represent "[i]deal manhood closed in real man," one of many formulations that captures the strain between realistic and allegorical elements, a strain that often results in Arthur's effacement. Cameron's focus on women and particularly on Elaine, together with the images' self-consciousness about their own awkward artifice, do not so much draw attention away from Arthur/Albert as memorialize the Prince by calling attention to the difficulty with which allegory may be gotten to serve as memorial art, given the tendency of allegory to overshadow or detach from the dead to whom they may purportedly refer. Even when Cameron photographs Arthur, in images that allude to existing Albert memorials, it is as much through their reflections on generic questions as through direct allusion that they comment on the practice of memorializing Albert. We will look first at two images of Arthur that function in this way, then turn to the four images of Elaine that comment on the process of memorialization through a figure who is both agent and object of memorialization, and look finally at the series' concluding image of Arthur in his barge, which—by consensus the most outrageous image of the group—brings together in a particularly heightened way generic questions about the genders of realistic allegory with the image of Arthur as Albert.

Volume One closes with two images of Arthur alone, one illustrating Arthur vanishing into the mist in *Guinevere* (figure 39), the other illustrating Arthur about to kill Modred and receive his mortal wound in *The Passing of Arthur* (figure 40). Surprisingly, these images are virtually identical. In both images Arthur is presented as a half-length portrait of the porter at Yarmouth pier, dressed in the same suit of mail and cape, holding his sword as if either sheathing or unsheathing it. Although he has changed helmets between pictures, not only the camera angle and his pose but his expression are virtually unchanged: he looks dreamily off to his left, his face composed in a solemn and elevated expression. If there is any difference detectable, it is that Arthur looks more martial in the domestic scene, as he wears a gauntlet and the fancier of his two helmets. The pose and expression closely resemble that of Corbould's 1864 allegorical painting of Albert over the legend "Ich habe eine guten Kampf gekampfet" (figure 32), although Albert wears plated armor and no helmet. These images of Arthur appear, by the least interpretive stretch, to refer to Albert by alluding to an existing image, and the pictures of Arthur are allegorical portraits, as Corbould's is. But especially in light of how much of the *Idylls* she omitted, there is something peculiar about Cameron's having included two such similar images, and something preposterous about having virtually the same image portray a scene of domestic melodrama and a battle scene. Exaggerating the effect of the armored and captioned Albert, these interchangeable images depend exclusively on words to identify their meaning; like Alice Liddell/Pomona, they call attention to the arbitrariness with which a text can assign allegorical meaning to an image. As in the armored Albert memorials, only the words determine whether he is sheathing or unsheathing his sword.

It is also preposterous—given Cameron's skill with and liking for blurred images and soft focus—that two of the clearest images in the series should illustrate moments in which a figure is becoming ghostly, since Arthur is being enfolded in vapor in the first image and fighting his last battle in the second. (Amanda Hopkinson in fact criticizes the first of these images for its failure to portray the mistiness of the scene.) The clarity of the images and their resemblance to portraiture suggest that Cameron is assimilating Arthur to her "famous men" series, and Gernsheim predictably exempts the Arthur portraits from his general condemnation of the *Idylls* illustrations. Nonetheless, the images can never be anything but failed allegories, as the "portraits"—unlike, say, the volume's frontispiece—are of a fictional character. But if we take seriously the volume's claim that the image illustrates the text, rather than reading the juxtaposition as one more of Cameron's silly mistakes, we have to conclude that for Cameron Arthur becomes ghostly through the very act of taking a sharp photograph of him. The sharper the image, she implies, the more completely the subject vanishes, because that is what allegorization does, just as the realistically rendered modern head of Albert only accentuates, by resisting it, the subordination of the figure to Victoria's medievalizing aesthetic. They are pictures of the patient Yarmouth porter disappearing into the role he was assigned; pictures of Arthur disappearing into the allegory he is assigned; and pictures, too, of Albert disappearing into Victoria's grand allegorical projects, with their noisy articulateness and their silent blankness. Finally, what we see is not the porter impersonating Albert (by way of Arthur) but Cameron commenting on the difficulties of the memorial arts.

Elaine's story in Tennyson's poem, as we have seen, is a story of representations that exceed and become independent of what they represent—the shield case, her hallucinatory mental picture of Lancelot, words that lose their meanings through repetition, her dead body as an allegorical work of art out of step with the sordid realities of Arthur's court. Cameron included more illustrations of *Lancelot and Elaine* than of any other idyll, and she makes Elaine's shield case the striking focal point of three of those four photographs. The first two images (figures 41 and 42), presented in the first volume as a pair, depict as virtually identical the opening retrospect of the

FIGURE 39
Julia Margaret Cameron, King Arthur in *Guinevere*. Photograph in *Illustrations to Tennyson's Idylls of the King and Other Poems*, 1875. "The moony vapour rolling round the King, / Who seemed the phantom of a Giant in it, / Enwound him fold by fold, and made him gray / And grayer, till himself became as mist . . ."

FIGURE 40
Julia Margaret Cameron, King Arthur in *The Passing of Arthur*. Photograph in *Illustrations to Tennyson's Idylls of the King and Other Poems*, 1875. "King am I, whatsoever be their cry; / And one last act of kinghood shalt thou see/ Yet, ere I pass."

idyll—Elaine alone in her tower, making the shield case with its encrustation of ornament—and the moment after Lancelot has taken his shield away, when Elaine has "only the case, / Her own poor work, her empty labour, left" (*LE*, 983–84). May Prinsep is seated in profile sideways on what appears to be the same carved chair. In the first (figure 41), she looks up at an ornamented disk representing Lancelot's shield, while part of her arm rests against the embroidered case, the nestling bird—apparently a paper cutout attached to an existing prop—clearly visible just under her hand.[85] In the second (figure 42), the shield is gone (the upper right corner of the photograph a dark blank where it was), and over her lap is draped the case, on which she rests her hands and at which she looks down; her right forefinger appears slightly to be lifting the bird, which seems not well stuck down to the cloth. Particularly noticeable about this pair of images is the lack of resemblance between the shield and the case. In the text reproduced opposite the photograph, the case is said at least initially to duplicate the appearance of the shield (she "braided thereupon / All the devices blazon'd on the shield / In their own tinct"). But in the photograph, the case is square and the shield is round, their differing shapes emphasized by their juxtaposition and their angle parallel to the picture plane. The embroidery on the case resembles not in the least the designs on the shield.

There is one obvious explanation: Cameron was working with props from her own household, among them treasures brought back by the trunkload from India (see Hopkinson, *Cameron,* 47) and objects left over from the amateur theatricals that preceded photography as the household art form.[86] What appear to be an ornamental disc and an embroidered table mat (or perhaps emptied pillow cover) no doubt came to hand.[87] But she went to great lengths to locate the right models and turned to costume rental agencies for armor and helmets. As in the case of her allegedly inadvertent inclusion of the studio walls, her searching no further for a better matched pair of props suggests her acceptance of photography's material conditions. Moreover, the diminutive and rather delicate-looking "shield" bears no traces of the "dints" and "scratches" said to have been made by Lancelot's opponents.[88] Cameron thus calls attention to the disparity between the shield and its representation even prior to Elaine's having "added, of her wit, / A border fantasy of branch and flower, / And yellow-throated nestling in the nest." On the shield case in the photograph the "border fantasy" and "nestling bird" are particularly conspicuous; indeed, they are all that can be seen on the heavily fringed velvet surface. Because Elaine's words later on are birdlike (line 889), the nestling bird may be her autobiographical touch. As an ostentatiously added-on image (added both by Elaine and by Cameron) that exceeds what

FIGURE 41
Julia Margaret Cameron, Elaine in *Lancelot and Elaine*. Photograph in *Illustrations to Tennyson's Idylls of the King and Other Poems*, 1875. "Elaine the fair, Elaine the loveable, / Elaine, the lily maid of Astolat . . ."

FIGURE 42
Julia Margaret Cameron, Elaine in *Lancelot and Elaine*. Photograph in *Illustrations to Tennyson's Idylls of the King and Other Poems*, 1875. "So in her tower alone the maiden sat: / His very shield was gone; only the case, / Her own poor work, her empty labour, left."

it refers to, the bird is equivalent to Elaine's solipsistic fantasy image of Lancelot.

In short, the only part of the text's description of the shield and case that Cameron illustrates is the part about Elaine's personal additions; otherwise, the props flaunt their infidelity to the original. What the case does slightly resemble is the carving on the chair behind Elaine, a similarity all the more conspicuous in the second image (figure 42), in which the carving is in sharper focus and directly above and almost parallel to the embroidered border of the case. In the first photograph (figure 41), Elaine seems to be holding her embroidery up to the shield to see how they match; perhaps her dazed look comes from her recognition that her work of fantasy has already displaced the object it was to portray. The second image, which calls attention to the resemblance between the case and the furnishings in Elaine's room, implies an explanation for this disparity: Elaine never even attempted to make her embroidery represent Lancelot's shield; she was representing herself all along, by representing her fantasy and her furniture. Here, she contemplates the shield case whole, as she also contemplates her hands, which rest on the embroidery in much the same way as the nestling bird appliqué does. The implied autoeroticism is accentuated by the recurrence of the same intricately carved chair in the image of "Mariana" in the second volume, in which a female figure radiating the kind of sexual heat not explicit in the Elaine pictures rests her "weary" but fully embodied arm on the familiar chair back. Here also is the Mariana-like Victoria alone in her castle, designing a beautiful tomb in which to lie with Albert, with other memorials that reflect her wishes and resemble him not in the least.

These two images of Elaine, in their similarity and difference, suggest a narrative, as if they were nearly adjacent stills from a movie: first she makes the case, then she loses the shield. But even as the pictures imply one narrative (that of Elaine's fetishistic love and loss), they also erase another one. Nearly a thousand lines go by—including a tournament and Lancelot's lengthy recovery from his wound—between the two episodes, yet the sameness of Elaine's pose implies that the time passed has been only the blink of an eye. (Similarly, with the two identical portraits of Arthur Cameron might be suggesting that there is no narrative duration between Arthur leaving Guinevere and receiving his mortal wound.) The solipsism of Elaine's art and of her pleasure is thus reinforced by the camera's selectivity, which eliminates Lancelot fully as much as Elaine does herself.

The mismatch between shield and case is the effect of Cameron's naturalistic medium, in which props must be found or materially constructed rather than spun at will out of words or paint. It also constitutes Cameron's way of interpreting the poem, in exaggerating the already extreme detachment of representation from ostensible referent that characterizes Elaine's art, language, and history. These features of the photographs need to be understood in relation to each other. On the one hand, Cameron is portraying real people and things: her household goods and May Prinsep with her uncomfortable-looking hair as well as the interior walls of her studio and her own fingerprints. "The referent adheres," as Barthes remarks (*Camera Lucida*, 6). On the other, she is portraying an idea about an idea, a different kind of referent than the one Barthes indicates. It is the stubborn realness of the props that forces—or, in my reading, enables—her to emphasize the overelaboration of Elaine's artwork and its self-referring detachment from what it fails to represent. The deidealizing force of the naturalist medium in this case works together with, not against, the particular kind of idealizing the poem undertakes, which is to make Elaine into a figure for failed allegory. Although in the allegorical reading of Tennyson's poem Elaine is supposed to be a figure for innocent love (a reading whose limitations, as we have seen, the poem itself exposes), in Cameron's pictures she becomes a figure for the breakdown of idealizing forms of representation, exposing—with the help of her awkward props—the machinery by which allegorical meanings can intermittently and effortlessly be grafted onto characters.

In this reading Elaine emerges not so much like Arthur as like Victoria, mourning fetishistically over relics of the beloved departed and, by authorizing allegorical memorials, obscuring his image rather than preserving it. But because Elaine mourns and then is mourned, she makes possible multiple identifications. The images of Elaine dead in her barge in the second volume of illustrations (figures 43 and 44) link her iconographically to Arthur and Albert. Allegorized, like Albert, she is an object rendered inert, blank, and at once to-be-read and unreadable. Both Albert and Arthur have been discussed in terms of the ambiguity of their gender. For Elliot Gilbert, the "restrained, almost maidenly" Arthur is the "Female King" ("The Female King," 863); deprived of the "phallic incident of the sword in the stone" that is prominent in Malory, he stands for sexual innocence ("The Female King," 868, 872) and stays at home while his knights go on quests in his name. As we have seen, both Victoria and the public press feminized Albert early in her reign, and the work of Bronfen, Christ and others on the iconic centrality to Victorian culture of the beautiful dead woman suggests that supine images of Albert ("beautiful as marble") may have been assimilated to this feminine image. The poems' and illustrations' equation between Elaine and Arthur suggests that the dead Elaine represents Albert as much as the living Elaine resembles Victoria.

FIGURE 43
Julia Margaret Cameron, Elaine in *Lancelot and Elaine*. Photograph in *Illustrations to Tennyson's Idylls of the King and Other Poems*, 1875.
"Then rose the dumb old servitor, and the dead, / Oared by the dumb, went upward with the flood— / In her right hand the lily, in her left / The letter..."

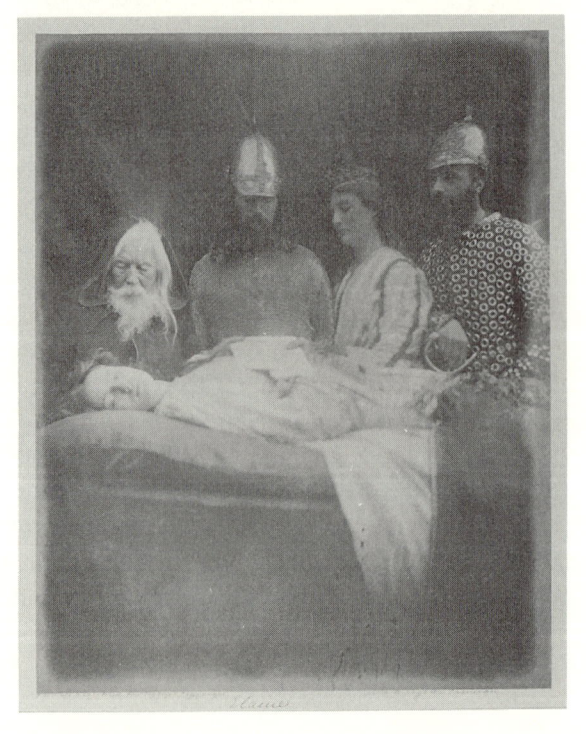

FIGURE 44
Julia Margaret Cameron, Elaine in *Lancelot and Elaine*. Photograph in *Illustrations to Tennyson's Idylls of the King and Other Poems*, 1875.
"But Arthur spied the letter in her hand, / Stoopt, took, brake seal, and read it..."

In the first image of her lying in the barge (figure 43), attention is again drawn to the artificiality of the shield case—the most prominent object in the photograph, hung in midair over Elaine's head—this time through exposure of the strings suspending it from the equally visible studio ceiling. By locating the case so conspicuously, and by permitting the nestling bird again to appear so obviously glued on, Cameron has further accentuated what was already excessive in the text: Elaine asked only to have the letter placed in her hand, and it is her family that decides to send the case along with her (*LE*, 1142). By exposing the mechanics of its suspension, Cameron makes the case the single most striking feature of Elaine's funereal pose. Doré does not include it in his illustration of the same scene, with which Cameron was vying for commercial success.

The second image of the dead Elaine (figure 44), the next to last in the *Idylls* series, portrays Elaine's barge in Camelot, her body transformed into a mysterious object for interpretation and her letter apparently being studied by Arthur, Lancelot, and Guinevere. Actually, Arthur holds the letter at such an angle as to prevent him from reading it; the letter is instead proffered to the viewer to read, as the viewer also reads the pale body on which the letter reposes and with which it merges. But no one could read this letter: it appears as a blank in the image, a mute reminder that allegorization strips away referential specificity. The letter whitely merging with Elaine's pale dress recalls the posing of Albert's marble bust against a white wall (figure 37). In both cases, what is presented for admiring reading is simultaneously rendered blank. If at the center of the first three Elaine images is the overly elaborate shield case that invites the eye to do all too much reading, at the center of the last image is a blank that calls attention to its own unreadability.[89] These alternatives recall the Albert memorials (encrusted and blank) and Tennyson's representations of Arthur (excessive and misty); all of these sets of equivalent alternatives point up the awkwardness of assigning meaning to human forms. The blank page may also allude to the art of photography itself, whose early practitioners were "sun artists": at the center of another Cameron allegorical image, titled "Cupid's Pencil of Light," is a radiantly blank white paper on which a winged child is writing or drawing, while rays of light stream down from above. The paper is propped on a box camera, and Cupid is therefore drawing with light: a sun artist whose work of art is a blank but glowing page.

This final image of Elaine in her barge also links her iconographically to Arthur, because the very next image in the volume (figure 45), the last in the *Idylls* series, is of Arthur similarly posed horizontally in a boat surrounded by standing figures, in this case the three queens and, behind them, three or four

FIGURE 45
Julia Margaret Cameron, King Arthur in *The Passing of Arthur*. Photograph in *Illustrations to Tennyson's Idylls of the King and Other Poems*, 1875. "So to the barge they came. There those three Queens / Put forth their hands, and took the King, and wept. / But she, that rose the tallest of them all / And fairest, laid his head upon her lap . . ."

"stately forms, / Black-stoled, black-hooded, like a dream" (*PA*, 364–65). The boat is portrayed in the two images by the same prop, a painted, curved board placed across the studio, and one of the three queens wears Guinevere's costume from the last Elaine illustration. The presentation of Elaine's dead body as a text to be read (figure 44) encourages the reader to see Arthur, on the next page, in the same way, even though no letter is present in figure 45 to guide the viewer.

In the context of these similarities, the most striking difference between the two images is in the degree of comfort the two bodies convey. While Elaine appears unprotestingly supine, comfortable to be merged with the letter resting on her body, Arthur appears to be struggling to get out of the boat, while two of the three queens appear gently but firmly to be holding him down. Or if he is not struggling, he is at least manifestly uncomfortable in his pose. Nor does he seem to be acceding with any grace to his coming death: his eyes appear to be open and looking up and out beseechingly at the viewer. The poem itself obscures and attenuates the moment of Arthur's death; it is not clear whether he is literally dying and becoming a spirit as he goes off with the queens, or whether his going off with them to Avilion is a substitute for death. Cameron's illustration accentuates this uncertainty and represents it through the model's protest against what he is required to do. It is a protest more readily imaged with a male model than with a female one, given Cameron's Victorian predilection for allegorizing young women. Once again the material features of the photographic situation work not against but with the poem's allegorical project, if we understand that project as the exposure of the labor of making allegories.

The model's pose and apparent struggle, which so graphically render Arthur's struggle between life and death and between realism and allegory, also act out the tension we observed within the armored memorial figures of Albert, where the modern and realistically depicted head contrasts so glaringly with the armored, nonrepresentational body. Indeed, the Yarmouth porter's pose quite closely duplicates one of Triqueti's sketches for his recumbent figure of Albert (figure 46), in which Albert lies not on his back (as in the version finally executed in marble) but propped on his side, his lower leg extended forward and his upper arm held diagonally across his body. In Triqueti's sketch, Albert is holding the sword that demonstrates his having "fought the good fight"; in the photograph, Arthur's arm extends near what appears to be a broom or rake handle representing his barge's oar, which angles downward in a sword-like direction. In the sketch, Albert is borne aloft by four angels; in the photograph, Arthur is held down by the three queens. Although the Albert Memorial Chapel was open for public viewing by the time Cameron made her photographs, it is not likely that she would have seen Triqueti's sketch, yet her unintentional literalization and parody helps us see her photograph's closeness to the finished effigy in the chapel at Windsor and to the other medievalizing images that exhibit Albert inhabiting his allegorical role so inconsistently.

Moreover, that Arthur looks so much more uncomfortable than Elaine in his recumbent pose—not dead yet, not ready to be read, his modern head at odds with his allegorical costume—recalls Tennyson's refusal to let Cameron allegorize him and her preference for allegorizing women. Although the blank letter of Elaine's message makes her, too, finally inscrutable, Elaine at least appears to acquiesce gracefully to being laid out for interpretation, in contrast to the effort manifestly required to render a man an allegorizable object, an effort that fails even more spectacularly than in the case of Elaine. Although Shires and Lukitsch argue that Cameron elevates Elaine to Arthur's status by juxtaposing their barge scenes, the juxtaposition equally emphasizes Arthur's unwilling feminization, his assimilation, under protest, to Elaine "the lily maid" who allows herself to be whited out into allegory. Even as it attempts with a straight face to incarnate Tennyson's sublime transformation of Arthur into a god, the photo also flaunts its own preposterous awkwardness, in order to anatomize and critique the process by which anyone—woman or man—can be turned into allegory. As an Albert memorial, it both allegorizes the Christian Knight and attempts to rescue him from allegorization. It gives Albert a voice, however mute, with which to protest his subjection to the representational regime of the monument. That her king seems trying to get someone to notice that he is still alive may be Cameron's witty literalization of the Queen's stated but unfulfilled aim to keep alive the Prince's living memory. He could be alive, the picture says back to Victoria, if only it weren't for your fatal allegories.

Assimilating Arthur to the topos of the Victorian woman killed into art and subordinated to vague, higher meanings not of her own devising, a topos represented by the beautifully dead Elaine and then carried over to the near-supine Arthur in his barge, Cameron's drag image defamiliarizes that topos and permits a critique unavailable through her comparable images of women. Her picture criticizes Victoria for doing to Albert what she and other Victorian artists do to images of women routinely; indeed, although she allows Arthur to protest against his allegorization, she ends the last volume with an image (figure 38) that, as we have seen, returns to and reaffirms the use of a female figure in the explicit manufacture of pathetic fallacy or failed allegory. But to return to the point I have been making about the public claim on and transformation of Victoria's memorial fantasies: participating in Victoria's memorial project by treating it with skepticism, Cameron's Tennyson illustrations make visible the vacuity as well as the obliterating force of Victoria's high-serious allegories. By appropriating the authorship of Victoria's project, they enact the critical claim also conveyed thematically within the images: allegorizing Albert makes Victoria herself a vanished presence.[90] Victoria resembles the still living Elaine, heatedly making allegorical memorials for Lancelot, and this chapter as a whole has considered Victoria as a maker or authorizer of art that objectifies her feminized husband. But the power of allegory to efface likeness exerts its force even on the living Victoria.

The evacuation of Victoria as author is rendered as a sort of signature to the Triqueti effigy in the Albert Memorial Chapel, if I can so describe a curious image of Victoria carved for its base (figure 47), an image variously known as "Mourning Royalty" or "Mourning Queen." Originally the Queen wished to see images of Albert's family surround the effigy's base, in bronze, gilt, and enamel, but the decision later to portray Albert in medieval armor coincided with the decision to ornament the base instead with allegorical images and to make the whole of marble. Angels lift the effigy at the corners; along the sides "are statuettes representing Truth, Justice, Charity,

FIGURE 46   Henri de Triqueti, sketch for the cenotaph of Prince Albert, Albert Memorial Chapel, Windsor.

Hope, Mourning Science, and Mourning Royalty—a crowned figure, presumably intended to represent Queen Victoria, kneeling on a prie-dieu emblazoned with the Royal Coat of Arms, in a niche beneath Prince Albert's feet" (*Cult,* 37). "Presumably" begs the question: granted that the figure does not much resemble Victoria, the only crowned royalty who would so mourn was Victoria, as if this allegorical figure were a residue from the earlier scheme to represent the family in this position.[91] The representation oscillates between individuated (if not realistic) reference on the one hand and allegory on the other. Whereas carved letters clearly label the figure representing "Truth" (a robed woman baring one breast), the mourning figure is unlabeled, perhaps because it cannot so simply be reduced to its allegorical import. Weeping under Albert's feet, Queen Victoria seems, at least at a distance, both herself and the type of Mourning Royalty. The figure thus would seem to bring together portraiture and allegory, much as the many images of Albert we have discussed attempt and fail to do, and much as Oliphant's parting image of Lucilla as her own statue wishfully does. But marble allegory, as we have seen, has a way of overshadowing individuated portraiture; allegory can only work when mimetic referentiality is effaced.

FIGURE 47 Henri de Triqueti, cenotaph of Prince Albert, Albert Memorial Chapel, Windsor, completed 1873. Detail.

And unlike Albert, Victoria was still around to pay the price of the attempt to merge personal likeness and public meaning; this image registers that price as accurately as it captures anything else. When I visited the chapel, I knelt down to confirm my suspicion: behind its veil, the figure has no face.

As the sponsor of the effigy's design, Victoria authorized the overshadowing of her husband's likeness with allegorizing trappings; as one among those trappings, however, pictured beneath his body, a small and relatively insignificant part of the whole, Victoria herself suffers, not just the overshadowing of her own monumental artistry but the complete obliteration of her person. That process continues to this day: we use the word "Victorian" without thinking about Queen Victoria; her name designates a diffuse global culture before it designates a person who once lived, wrote, and made aesthetic judgments. I have tried to trace here one of the processes by which her authorship came to be diffused into the culture that bears her name, in an age when the hierarchical organization of society began gradually to be dismantled. The faceless image at Albert's feet expresses both a pervading anxiety of Victoria's reign and the price she paid for making that anxiety into her own wish: for, having eagerly embraced her role as symbolic monarch, she indeed found herself, as her subjects both wished and feared, as much effaced by that choice as if she were herself in the grave. That is a wish her subjects unwittingly helped her to fulfill, and we continue to make it come true.

EPILOGUE: EMPIRE OF GRIEF

> Grandcourt had an intense satisfaction in leading his wife captive after this fashion: it gave their life on a small scale a royal representation.
>
> **George Eliot,** *Daniel Deronda,* 1876

This book has explored selected representations from the first four decades of Victoria's reign, up through the mid-1870s. We have seen her image—created, chosen, accepted, or merely suffered by her—change from that of the private, domestic wife who holds monarchic power by giving it away, to that of the self-aggrandizing, self-effacing allegorist of the Albert memorials, passing by way of the widow whose absence requires, from her and from her subjects, a plethora of substitute representational forms, including the emphatic representation of her absence. We have also observed some of the political work performed by these changing representations as they helped to smooth the transition to a symbolic monarchy. Early domestic images, for example, answered the paradoxical demand for a monarch who was not too strong but strong enough; later, the Queen's popular writings and representations emphasizing her absence served to support those reforms that she sometimes, in private, opposed. The mid-1870s mark a turning point in her reign, both because the public, the press, and politicians ceased to complain so much of her lack of visibility and because Victoria became Empress of India in 1876.[1] After 1876, empire and imperialism must become the focus of attention for any study of the Queen's representations. Moreover, once the Queen's absence became less pronounced, the disjunction between "the image and the political reality" (to return to Simon Schama's formulation) took a wholly new form from those we have observed thus far. This Epilogue will glance at some of the new representational forms imperial monarchy took in the decade beginning in 1876: Victoria's attempts at political intervention in imperial policy, George Eliot's 1876 definition of the term *empress,* and finally the Queen's last published book. Although promotion to Empress might seem to have granted Victoria new scope for her active political might, these representations instead suggest how the Queen's active embrace of her diminution, her passive acceptance of her empire, served the aims of empire building in an era eager to see the growth of empire as natural or inevitable, as natural as tears.

It is a commonplace that the idea of Queen Victoria served to justify the extension and maintenance of Britain's—or rather "Her"—empire, and indeed her image traveled the globe in the service of this project.[2] The Queen's correspondence presents a record of enthusiastic support for the most aggressive imperial policies. Although some kind of imperialism was favored by most Britons, there were partisan differences over the form it should take, and Victoria's opinions in this regard were decidedly Tory.[3] She urged her ministers to maintain a strong military as well as official presence wherever possible, as when—before Parliament had committed the funds—she "at once supported and encouraged" Disraeli's impromptu and risky purchase of the Suez canal, "which gives us complete security for India, and altogether places us in a very safe position" (*Letters and Journals,* 241, 24 November 1875). She repeatedly reproaches the "mad, unpatriotic" Gladstone, whose lack of imperial resolve during the 1880s led, in her view, to the sacrifice of British lives.[4]

Early in 1881, when shown the draft of "her" speech opening Parliament, she objected so strongly to its announcement that all British troops would be withdrawn from Afghanistan (where the British had been fighting since 1878 to prevent its being taken by Russia) that, on the morning of the Privy Council meeting at which she was expected to approve the speech, she "telegraphed to Mr. Gladstone to have the Speech altered, or the part about Candahar left out" (*Letters and Journals,* 266, 3 January 1881). Just a few months earlier General Frederick Roberts had led a "wonderful march" to the strategically critical Kandahar and achieved "brilliant victory" there; it was typical of Gladstone's foreign policy not to build on such a victory. Controversy erupted between the Queen and her Cabinet: Sir William Harcourt insisted that "this was really the Cabinet's speech," while the Queen, refusing to "tolerate . . . the disrespect and contempt of her position shown her," objected to "being kept in ignorance and then forced at the last moment to assent."[5] The Queen won her point, for the Queen's Speech as delivered on 6 January 1881 reads in part as follows:

The war in Afghanistan has been brought to a close, and, with the exception of the Candahar force, my troops have been recalled within the Indian frontier. It is not my intention that the occupation of Candahar shall be permanently maintained, but the still unsettled condition of the country, and the consequent difficulty of establishing a Native Government, have delayed for a time the withdrawal of the army from that position. (*Queen's Speeches*, 336–37)

The tone of measured benignity that suffuses this announcement is consistent with the Queen's official tone in conducting much public imperial business; when in 1858 the government of India was transferred to Britain, she had Lord Derby rewrite the proclamation "bearing in mind that it is a female Sovereign who speaks.... Such a document should breathe feelings of generosity, benevolence, and religious toleration" (quoted in St. Aubyn, *Queen Victoria*, 307).

Nonetheless, it was not the Queen who delivered the Queen's 1881 speech—in this case, truly hers—to Parliament, which was opened once again by commission; but even had she delivered it in person, no listener would have credited to her its policies. The imperial aggression of Queen Victoria could not be displayed as such. The publicly nonpartisan Queen could preside over imperial policy only as an image or as a name. "Make what use of the Queen's name Lord Beaconsfield wishes," she writes, urging Disraeli (now Lord Beaconsfield) to accelerate Britain's controversial and unpopular involvement in Turkey's war against Russia (*Letters and Journals*, 248, 13 November 1877). Although she telegraphed him almost hourly during the crisis, her passionate views were not for public consumption: "[I]f the Queen were a man, she would like to go and give those Russians, whose word one cannot believe, such a beating!"[6] One of her most conspicuous changes in outer appearance—her acquisition of the title Empress—did not perhaps create the substantive change it might have seemed to promise; when she became Empress of India, only her picture traveled there. And in this period of Victoria's active but largely secret involvement in foreign policy, the gap between her benign, aging-maternal appearance and her private wishes and actions widened while becoming more predictably configured than in earlier years of her reign. Her political agency consistently took the traditional monarchic form of explicit attempts to influence the direction of foreign policy, while the appropriateness of hiding those actions derived from the obvious need to preserve the monarchy's image of neutrality.

In 1876 Victoria successfully lobbied Parliament (through Disraeli) to pass the Royal Titles Act, making her Empress of India. She was proclaimed

Empress, in her conspicuous absence, in a vast and visually extravagant ceremony in Delhi on 1 January 1877. Having achieved this aim, however, she seems to have understood that the title could potentially and ironically diminish her status. Apparently, her chief reason for wanting the new title was that "Queen" no longer ensured her precedence over the Emperor of Germany or the Tsar, or indeed over her own daughter, who would one day be an Empress; nor did it sufficiently impress her Indian subjects, whom she ruled, according to Disraeli, "through their imagination" (St. Aubyn, *Queen Victoria,* 434). But as so often happened during her reign, what would seem to aggrandize her powers did not unequivocally do so. In seeking passage of the Royal Titles Act she exposed herself to "disgraceful agitation" from the opposition and to insinuations about her aggressiveness; Gladstone (then out of power) felt impelled to publish a letter in the *Observer* refuting the rumor that the Queen had tried to get the title during earlier ministries.[7] She might become an Empress, but she must through her evident passivity make the title seem the natural expression of her state of being rather than the object of her desire; "Empress" is a worthy title only if it does not indicate a power aggressively sought.

The Queen also registers concern that the addition of the supplementary "Empress" will diminish her original title by appearing to render it inadequate on its own. Thus she writes to Theodore Martin that she wants him to insert in the papers

> a small paragraph to this *effect,* only worded by himself: "There seems a very strange misapprehension on the part of some people, which is producing a mischievous affect; viz. that there is to be an *alteration* in the *Queen's and Royal* family's *ordinary* appellation. Now this is utterly false. The Queen will always be called 'the Queen' . . . and *no* difference whatever is to be made except *officially adding* after *Queen* of Great Britain, '*Empress of India,*' the name which is best understood in the East, but which Great Britain (which *is an empire*) never has acknowledged to be *higher* than Queen or King." (*Letters,* 2d series, 2:450, 14 March 1876)

Accepting the new title introduces the possibility that neither title is supreme, if "Empress" is only for show while the status of "Queen" must be so vehemently defended. Whereas to be Queen of England could once be imagined to be the highest position in the world, now, despite or because her reach extends so far, such a title must be supplemented, yet even thus augmented it conveys less precedence, not to mention less power, than it once did. She is to be Empress of India—merely an exotic, decorative title—while, over Great Britain, "which is an empire," she is only to be Queen, a title that loses its chivalric luster in an era and a world so much larger than that of Ruskin's gardens. In the event, unsurprisingly, she used "Victoria R & I" with increasing frequency (Thompson, *Queen Victoria*, 130).

And indeed contemporary uses of "queen" and "empress" reveal a new kind of diminution. As we have seen, the Queen's image was reduced by the uses to which it was put and especially by its multiplication. Examining, as in earlier chapters, the ways in which representational uses of her idea and image actively construct the Queen (instead of looking only at how those representations draw on an idea of the Queen presumed to be fixed and knowable) reveals that empire not only expands the Queen's reach; it also diminishes her. In Chapter 2 we glanced at some of George Eliot's novels of the 1860s as examples of the multiplication of queens during Victoria's absence and as instances of the use of a queenly image to suggest an ironic gap between splendid appearance and curtailed personal power. *Daniel Deronda*, Eliot's last novel, published in the year Victoria became an Empress, supplies a biting summation of this negative image of queenliness in the expansive context of imperialism.[8] Here, a queen who is also a sometime empress enjoys a power that is at best illusory and at worst self-destroying. The novel brings the image of disempowered queen in Eliot's 1860s novels forward into the context of imperial expansion, a context whose breadth diminishes even further the regal heroine. In 1876, a queen who becomes an empress may find her agency constricted even further than it was before.

As in other Eliot novels, nomination as queen celebrates the heroine's beauty but also signals the limitation of her freedom. Gwendolen Harleth is regal when unmarried, and even more so—to the public eye—as Mrs. Grandcourt, because of the social promotion her marriage brings (Hans Meyrick's name for her is the Vandyke Duchess). She nonetheless suffers the deepest of private humiliations, in her marriage but also before and after. Having been discouraged from a career as an artist and facing a hated future as governess, Gwendolen is "a queen dethroned" whose "lovely lips and eyes and majestic figure" contrast pitifully against her "helplessness" (*Daniel Deronda*, 334–35). Just a few pages before, however, Grandcourt has been described (as he is throughout the novel) as exercising an "imperious spell" (331), and although Gwendolen will soon—with the arrival of Grandcourt's letter asking to see her alone—feel "her power" and "a sort of empire over her own life" (337), it is Grandcourt whose "empire of fear" (479) will eventually prove the stronger. Like Harold Transome in *Felix Holt*, who subdues his "queenly" mother by exploiting an Eastern-tinged language of chivalry, Grandcourt fosters Gwendolen's illusion of "command" and "empire" over him during courtship, but exerts his greater force—he is associated with tiger hunting and compared to a colonial governor—once they are married.[9] It is in this context that the phrase "royal representation" (736) is used to denote Gwendolen's "captiv[ity]" and Grandcourt's "despotism" on board his yacht. Eliot is drawing on a vocabulary of ambiguous female sovereignty supplied by the example of Queen Victoria, critiquing the consequences for women of the illusions fostered by the chivalric revival; at the same time, "royal representation" now connotes an inversion of expectation and fulfillment far more severe for the expansiveness of its imperial reference. For Victoria to have become Empress means that purportedly foreign, Eastern styles of power—despotism over captives—now become part of the British vocabulary of familial power. Victoria's possession of an Eastern empire supplies the metaphor for Gwendolen's captivity, but Gwendolen's captivity may in turn shed an ironic light back upon Victoria Regina et Imperatrix, dwarfed by her own grandiose ambitions.

It is not only the cruel colonial governor Grandcourt who makes the queenly Gwendolen suffer. The interplay of personal subjection and public regality is evident also in Gwendolen's relation with Deronda, as in the following passage from Book 6, at a party where Gwendolen has been frustrated in her desire to talk to Deronda. (At this point in the novel, Deronda is the focus of Gwendolen's emotional life; she does not yet know how fully absorbed he is in his growing attachment to Mirah and Mordecai.)

> Deronda was there at last, and she would compel him to do what she pleased. Already and without effort rather queenly in her air as she stood in her white lace and green leaves, she threw a royal permissiveness into her way of saying, "I wish you would come and see me tomorrow between five and six, Mr. Deronda."
>
> There could be but one answer at that moment: "Certainly," with a tone of obedience. (*Daniel Deronda*, 670)

Violating conventions of gender relations by issuing the invitation, but doing so with the excuse of her rank (as Victoria proposed to Albert), Gwendolen publicly performs a regality that only thinly masks her subjection, not only to her husband but also to Deronda. That chivalry's language of masculine deference conceals masculine predominance is revealed by the next sentence, which underscores Deronda's emotional freedom contrasted to Gwendolen's dependence: "Afterwards it occurred to Deronda that he would write a note to excuse himself." Gwendolen's "royal permissiveness" here means something more like abjection. The abject Gwendolen, a representation of the Queen who at the same time provides the resource for Eliot's regal metaphor, constitutes Eliot's hard vision of the losses that queens may sustain when illusions fostered by chivalric discourse encounter such social and erotic exigencies as the male privilege chivalry disguises. A queen who loses in the hard world of realist fiction (and *Deronda* is Eliot's only novel set in the present time of the novel's writing), Gwendolen dramatizes the possibilities suggested in some of Victoria's late marital photographs (see Chapter 1), images that seem uncannily to anticipate Albert's death: a queen who looks frantically off camera or upward from her low seat to search out the meeting eye of the man she loves, only to find that he has moved off into worlds beyond her.

After Grandcourt's death Gwendolen, lonely and dressed in black, comes most to resemble these yearning images of Victoria as well as the Queen as a widow, even if it is not her husband she mourns. Twice described as her own statue, Gwendolen starts to look like the marble "Royal Mourning" at Albert's effigied feet: "She had never smiled since her husband's death. When she stood still and in silence, she looked like a melancholy statue of the Gwendolen whose laughter had once been so ready when others were grave" (*Daniel Deronda*, 841). The only future "to which she turned her face with a willing step" is one reliant on Deronda (867). But that face is soon to be effaced, like Victoria's beneath the effigy. Deronda's plan to found a Jewish homeland in the East sets Gwendolen's queenly diminishment in the context of imperial expansionism.[10] Whereas Deronda contemplates his future with "visionary joy" (867),

> [t]he world seemed getting larger round poor Gwendolen, and she more solitary and helpless in the midst. The thought that he might come back after going to the East, sank before the bewildering vision of these wide-stretching purposes in which she felt herself reduced to a mere speck. (875)

"Dislodged from her supremacy" (876), Gwendolen can only feel "self-humiliation" and show to Deronda "[h]er withered look of grief" (878). The further he is to go, the smaller she becomes ("a mere speck"), because she credits his perspective over her own (after all, she might have perceived that Deronda was to become the "speck"). The global scope of Deronda's ambitions, and the narrative's overvaluation of them, render the expansion of empire just another source of this queen's abjection.

Staying at home, without even the consolation of having her image transported abroad, Gwendolen enacts a grim parody of the domestic white queen whose "sitting" (as mocked in Churchill's *Cloud 9*) was to inspire the expansionist deeds of her imperial warriors. Gwendolen is neither burdened nor rewarded with responsibility for such deeds, nor will she gain anything from Deronda's outward journey. She loses even the dubious privilege of being allegorized. In the Introduction to this book I argued that we should look for Victoria's agency in places where historians have not looked: not just in her formation of foreign policy but in her permitting pictures to be made, not just in words she wrote but in words others spoke on her behalf, in her being and seeming as forms of doing. Eliot, however, empties the potential for queenly (or indeed imperial) agency even from such gestures as "sitting" when she gives us Gwendolen Grandcourt at the end of the novel, reduced to repeating Deronda's hollowly inspirational words as her spoken and, finally, written refrain, "it shall be better with me because I have known you"; "I said . . . I said . . . it should be better . . . better with me . . . for having known you" (510 and 882; 878; more fragments 879, 882).[11] Like Elaine's stuttering repetitions in the *Idylls,* these words after a few repetitions lose their power to signify anything but the fact that they are being repeated. By her repetitions we know Elaine as a failed allegorist who will soon die, and no other future seems imaginable for Gwendolen, Eliot's last queen-empress, who is here cut off altogether from world historical "movement" (876) and represented in the end by a virtually posthumous letter. Like Tennyson's "To the Queen" only in this regard, *Daniel Deronda* displays the detachment of royal causes from world historical effects. Empire and history move onward, leaving behind a sorrowing queen, a queen whose speech—like that of the Queen whose rewriting of imperial policy must remain invisible—is radically cut off from her being.

Victoria's frustration over not being able to speak out publicly and have her way in foreign and imperial policy became especially acute during Gladstone's ministry of 1880–85, as if Gwendolen's immobilization and frustrated yearning not only looked back to the proleptically widowed Victoria but also anticipated the Victoria of this later period. As we have seen, she disputed Gladstone's policy in Afghanistan, and won a small victory over the Queen's Speech of 1881; a larger imperial problem, and source of greater differences between the Queen and her minister, was Britain's involvement in Egypt.[12] Through the early 1880s, Victoria was urging the reluctant Gladstone and the deeply divided Liberal party not to withdraw from Egypt, to assume actively the responsibility for governing Egypt that Britain had incurred in destroying Egypt's army (in 1882, in the battle of Tel-El-Kebir) and making it dependent on Britain for defense against the Mahdist revolt in the Sudan; her letters call for the army to remain while Gladstone pursues a policy of "rescue and retreat." When General Gordon, who had been sent to Khartoum to help the British troops there withdraw, was killed in January 1885— reinforcements having been sent too late to be of use—the nation reacted strongly against Gladstone's policies that had "betrayed" this hero and his troops. Yet even so the Liberal majority in Commons later that spring voted against continued aggression in the Sudan.

The Queen blamed Gladstone and disagreed with the nation's Liberal majority, but the only acceptable protest she could make publicly was to send an open letter of condolence to General Gordon's bereaved sister, praising her "dear, noble, heroic brother" and castigating Gordon's "betrayers" for the "*stain*" left upon England" (quoted in St. Aubyn, *Queen Victoria*, 456). (She also had sent Gladstone an unciphered telegram blaming him for Gordon's death, but the post office kept her indiscreet gesture from reaching the public.) Any Briton could agree with these sentiments, but the policy implications of her views—that "[w]e must not retire without making our power felt" and that "[s]ome means must be found to try and place some *sort of Government* at Khartoum, or try to *treat* with the rebels"—could only be expressed privately, here to Ponsonby (*Letters*, 2d series, 3:598, 5 February 1885). She writes, futilely, to Gladstone:

> Think it would be fatal to our reputation if we were to *abandon* active operations in and still more to withdraw from the Soudan. It would be such an exhibition of weakness, and of the *triumph* of savages over British arms, that it would seriously affect our position in India and elsewhere. (*Letters*, 2d series, 3:635, 14 April 1885)

Thinking as an aggressive global imperialist, but able to speak out only through the acceptable vocabulary of a widow's sympathy, Victoria is—for good or ill—Empress only in name.

Victoria did, as we know, have other avenues of publicity, and in 1884 she published her last book, *More Leaves from the Journal of a Life in the Highlands from 1862–1882*, a collection of diary excerpts from the years after Albert's death. Once again a book from the Queen was highly successful (she mentions "some thirty or forty different articles—really beautifully written") because, once again, she gave the public the verbal performance it wanted: "I have always been fully aware of what I was doing—and know perfectly well what my people like and appreciate and that is 'home life' and simplicity."[13] This book, I will suggest, uses Victoria's persona as grieving widow to say something about empire that could not be said directly to the public. Published with an eyebrow-raising dedication to John Brown, who had died suddenly in 1883, this book maps the Queen's grief—explicitly for Albert, but implicitly for Brown—onto the Scots landscape through which she makes a series of extensive proprietary tours, in this gloomy sequel to the less conspicuously imperial *Leaves* of 1868. Whereas the focus of the earlier *Leaves* and its reception was on themes and forms of concealment, public appearances abound in *More Leaves*;[14] instead, the focus is on Scotland itself, as a location that conjoins Victoria's interest in her empire with her preoccupation with death. Through the lens of her grief everything she sees on her travels in Scotland becomes "a dreadful collection of memoranda that [he] did exist, and that I have lost [him]."[15] Imperial possession is celebrated, but finally the value of empire appears in its capacity to reflect back its Queen-Empress's grief; empire itself, not just its lady, becomes a "speck," in this last of the Queen's published self-representations. While this volume performs the old trick of *Leaves* of pretending the Queen is living a wholly private life even while (outside the text) she is actively involved in politics, this volume conceals not the Queen's absence, as was necessary in 1868, but rather her imperial aggression.

Death and its memory fill this volume, from its opening description of Albert's memorial cairn at Balmoral to its ending with the death of Brown. Travel itself is a life-threatening business: the road cannot be found, the carriage suffers an accident, Brown's legs are injured, their luggage is left behind, her private train won't fit in a tunnel and has to be changed, the tea things cannot be found. Death fills the landscape, and the pages. Friends and other relatives die or become incurably ill—her friend the Duke of Blair, our old friend Widow Grant of *Leaves,* a local child who drowns, the Duchess of Sutherland (for whose monument Victoria lays the foundation stone), Dr. Norman MacLeod—recalled for ten pages, her own daughter Alice (for whom she erects a memorial cross in 1879), Brown's parents, and on and on. She attends funerals, visits graves, sets up monuments, writes memorials. But most of all, she finds and visits memorials to Albert, and she visits places where the history of Scotland's losses are remembered. Time and space are filled up with these two linked kinds of remembrance, to the point that in bringing the entries to a close on an ostensibly high note of imperial victory, memory appropriates the present even as Victoria's grief has appropriated everything around her.

The cairn being built to Albert's memory at Balmoral is to be forty feet wide and thirty-five feet high, with all the "orphans'" names to be carved in it; after viewing its foundation Victoria visits the old cairn built and celebrated in *Leaves;* and the next May the newly completed cairn can be seen, "a fine sharp pyramid," thus an imperial hybrid of Egyptian form and Scots function (*More Leaves,* 13). Compared "to former times," these visits are "dreadfully sad," and whenever she revisits a place once visited with Albert, she never fails to note the sadness of the difference. But there are memorials to Albert not built by Victoria's command, nor even projected by her memory. They crop up in unexpected places, as if spontaneously exuded by the memory-saturated landscape. In September 1865 she sees a well built to commemorate her and Albert's having drunk some water on the spot years ago; in stones appear the words, "pray for Scotland's Queen." In September 1869 she revisits a place where Albert found some white pebbles he had made into a bracelet for her; the same pebbles can still be seen on the ground. In Ballachulish, in September 1873, she stops to drink from an old Highlander's silver quaich, from which both Prince Charles (Bonnie Prince Charlie) and Albert had drunk; he "begged I would do the same" (117). Albert's memory is everywhere, and everywhere merged with the terrain and history of Scotland.

As the volume proceeds, Albert's memory is increasingly linked with the memory of Scotland's tragic past. The day after finding Albert's white pebbles she visits a graveyard and then the "burial-place of the MacGregors (whose country this is or, alas! rather was), which is a chapel standing in a wood" (64). Victoria enjoys her sensations of melancholy, recording funerary inscriptions and calling it an "interesting and beautiful drive." The next day at Loch Lomond the travelers board "the fine steamer 'Prince Consort' (a pleasant idea that that dear name should have carried his poor little wife, alas! a widow, and children, on their first sail on this beautiful lake which he went to see in 1847)" (65). Her reiterated "alas!" links grief for Albert to pity for Scotland's losses and renders all Scots war memorials effectively Albert memorials too. Her widowhood authorizes her pity, while her pity appropriates the landscape. She passes or tours battlefields of "the forty-five": in September 1872 on a train trip "[w]e passed Culloden, and the moor where that bloody battle, the recollection of which I cannot bear, was fought" (83), and the next night she "felt strange—such a dinner in a strange place for the first time without my dear one!" (87). What "recollection" of the "bloody battle" more than a century ago can she have? The presentness of her personal grief compresses time. Just as eleven years seem as nothing to the widow who still finds it strange to dine without Albert, so the battle of Culloden moor might as well have been yesterday. Albert and Bonnie Prince Charlie have, after all, drunk from the same silver quaich, although they must have meant rather different things when they did so.[16]

In September 1873 she visits a series of places in the neighborhood of Inverlochy associated with the forty-five and Prince Charles's hopes and failure. Here, Victoria sympathetically emphasizes Scotland's suffering and the present peace literally embodied in her reign, but there is no doubting who was the victor, for she begins with Scotland's capitulation in the end: "Here Glencoe came to take his oath to William III" (112). She tours the vicinity of Lochiel and records an exchange with Ponsonby:

It was, as General Ponsonby observed afterwards, a striking scene. "There was Lochiel," as he said, "whose great-grand-uncle had been the real moving cause of the rising of 1745—for without him Prince Charles would not have made the attempt—showing your Majesty (whose great-great-grandfather he had striven to dethrone) the scenes made historical by Prince Charles's wanderings. It was a scene one could not look on unmoved."

Yes; and I feel a sort of reverence in going over these scenes in this most beautiful country, which I am proud to call my own, where there was such devoted loyalty to the family of my ancestors—for Stuart blood is in my veins, and I am now their representative, and the people are as devoted and loyal to me as they were to that unhappy race. (*More Leaves*, 113)

Having earlier and throughout the text emphasized her descent from "my poor ancestress Queen Mary" (124), and here incorporating Scotland's doomed nationalism into her bloodstream, she makes their sorrows her own and converts their bitter separatist nationalism into a united British nationalism. By a quick turn of the genealogical tables, loyalty to those who would have overthrown her ancestors is also loyalty to those very ancestors. United in her sorrowing body, there can be no differences between Scots and English sorrows, or Scots and English interests, even if the entire effort of Scots nationalism was to resist exactly this incorporation. Thus her empire of grief is put into effect.

At the bottom of the pass of Glencoe she meets "Mrs. MacDonald, a descendent of one of the unfortunate massacred MacDonalds." Appropriating this perspective of the mourning female relict, Victoria goes on to describe the mountains rising up on either side,

> without any sign of habitation, except where, halfway up the pass, there are some trees, and near them heaps of stones either side of the road, remains of what once were homes, which tell the bloody, fearful tale of woe. The place itself is one which adds to the horror of the thought that such a thing could have been conceived and committed on innocent sleeping people. How and whither could they fly? Let me hope that William III knew nothing of it. (*More Leaves*, 115–16)

British imperialism was often justified through pity for the sufferings of natives under local tyrants. Victoria claimed, for example, that annexing New Guinea "will enable us to protect the poor natives and to advance civilization";[17] this is the sort of claim that is echoed by the representation of Gwendolen as the pitiable captive of a despot, or as likely to "burn herself in perpetual suttee" for Daniel (*Daniel Deronda*, 871). Just so, Victoria's pity for the sufferings of the Scots—her "imperialist nostalgia"—justifies her intruding her own all-appropriating sorrow everywhere she goes. Encountering "heaps of stones" halfway up the pass, remains that more closely resemble authentic Scots cairns (in that their remaining there is what "tell[s] the bloody, fearful tale") than do the fancy commissioned artworks the Queen calls cairns, the Queen nonetheless turns these, too, into Albert memorials. Her tour of Bonnie Prince Charlie memorabilia concludes with a viewing of "a very ugly monument to Prince Charles Edward," a repetition of her claim to be descended from both sides, and finally an exhibit of relics: the Prince's snuff mill, his watch, a ring made with his hair. This memorabilia recalls and merges with the official grief of *More Leaves*, for what else has this text been full of but ugly monuments to and strange relics of Albert? Scotland's loss of its cultural and political independence is granted no significance apart from Victoria's personal loss.

The volume's last entries include two records from Britain's far-extending imperial history, records that would seem to move the interest outward from the claustrophobic world of a grief-saturated Scotland. In June 1879 the Queen is haunted by nightmares about the death, at the hands of Zulu warriors, of the Prince Imperial, the only son of her friend the exiled French Empress. Victoria's own son Arthur is in the military, serving in Egypt, and so grief over the Prince Imperial is compositionally balanced by Prince Arthur's success, and the success of the British army, in defeating "the enemy" at Tel-El-Kebir in September 1882. But the entry, and the volume, ends with the reversion of Empire to home; for the interest for the diarist is in repeating a domestic scene from the past. After toasting the victory in Egypt, the Queen has a bonfire lit on Craig Gowan, "just where there had been one in 1856 after the fall of Sevastopol, when dearest Albert went up to it at night with Bertie and Affie . . . very nearly the same time twenty-six years ago!" (*More Leaves*, 170). All imperial victories are the same, for as we saw in Chapter 3, the 1856 bonfire was itself in turn a symbolic celebration of the defeat and annexation of Scotland: the site of the bonfire is the cairn built to celebrate the royal family's taking possession of Balmoral, and by extension England's possession of Scotland itself. This "most beautiful country" is, after all, "my own" (113). All cairns commemorate Albert; imperial losses and victories alike serve as reminders that he did exist and is no more. In Victoria's empire of grief, as the text of *More Leaves* constructs it, time and space shrink to one grieving woman and her memories. This is, of course, a very different image of empire than the one to be found in the records of Britain's political leaders, armed forces, and colonial governors, or indeed in Victoria's private correspondence and journal entries omitted from *More Leaves*. But it is the form that imperial aggression can take when expressed through the vocabulary of an officially nonpartisan Queen, whose public persona is the grieving widow. Feigning a lack of involvement in imperial policy, Victoria enacts an acceptable form of textual imperialism in appropriating global sorrows to represent her own.

More Leaves ends not with these final entries but with a "Conclusion," added during the editing in 1883 and expanding upon the volume's opening dedication to John Brown. The "Conclusion" begins: "The faithful attendant who is so often mentioned throughout these Leaves, is no longer with her whom he served so truly, devotedly, untiringly." The Queen records his illness and sudden death, "respected and beloved," tautologically, "by all who recognized his rare worth and kindness of heart, and truly regretted by all who knew him." She concludes:

> His loss to me (ill and helpless as I was at the time from an accident) is irreparable, for he deservedly possessed my entire confidence; and to say that he is daily, nay hourly missed by me, whose lifelong gratitude he won by his constant care, attention, and devotion, is but a feeble expression of the truth. (*More Leaves*, 170)

Whereas the opening dedication to Brown includes also "My Loyal Highlanders," and is visually balanced by the formal inscription on Albert's Egyptian cairn on the first page of journal entries, these concluding words about Brown make it impossible to ignore the Queen's indiscretion, recalling as they do the scandalous rumors, cartoons, and pamphlets of the late 1860s. Brown was still not popular with the Queen's staff, friends, and family, who had continued to discourage what they considered an embarrassing and degrading familiarity.[18] Yet just as in the late 1860s this notorious connection may have served the not unhelpful political purpose (however inadvertently on the Queen's part) of lowering her to the level of her subjects, the dedication here too does some cultural work. At a time when the Queen's imperial aggression far outstripped that of her popular Prime Minister Gladstone, the dedication of her book to Brown renders the hawk a newly mourning dove. The scandal of her emotional vulnerability covers the scandal of her imperial political agency, even while the vehemence of that agency reappears in a negative form, in the shrinking of Empire down to the size of a commoner's grave.

For Brown is indeed everywhere in *More Leaves*, at first in the role of dedicated servant, and then increasingly as friend.[19] Like the nation he personifies, he serves the Queen precisely by offering her a gratifying and reassuring image of his autonomy and thus by providing her with a worthy object of her sympathy. That Brown is always to be seen wearing a kilt serves as a reminder that Scotland's autonomy is as illusory as his, the kilt signifying the pretense or "invention" of autonomous Scots traditions by the conquering English. Thus Brown's most valued services take the form of the apparently unservile acts of a friend, freely given, not required. Brown hurts his legs walking in the rain to guide her carriage on a rough road; Brown and Grant arrange for a "merry" housewarming party for Glassalt Shiel, her new small house at Balmoral; on a journey in 1869 "(Brown as always, unless I mention to the contrary, on the box)" (57), or again, "(Brown going each day of course with us on the box)" (119), or again, "(Brown remaining in his place on the carriage)" (125); Brown joins the search for the drowned child; the Queen and Brown exchange gifts; Brown picks a sprig of white heather for luck; Brown breaks the news, more than once, of the death of a friend; Brown defends the Queen from intrusive reporters.[20]

When Brown's parents die, his father in 1875 and his mother in 1876, the Queen attends the funeral, comforts the widow as only another widow can ("I . . . tried to soothe and comfort dear old Mrs. Brown, and gave her a mourning brooch with a little bit of her husband's hair" and "told her the parting was but for a time," 139), and then sympathizes with Brown when he has to appear at a public festivity a fortnight after losing "his much loved mother" (143). Later in the 1870s it is not Brown who brings the news of a friend's death but rather Brown to whom she sends the news, for his sympathetic reaction; Brown is "shocked" (156), "distressed" (163). On Albert's birthday in 1878 she gives presents to her daughter Beatrice and to "my faithful Brown"; "the tears came to his eyes" and he says, "'It is too much.' God knows, it is not, for one so devoted and faithful" (159). Even more than when the Queen's footnotes in the 1868 *Leaves* granted to her servants a life and value apart from her own, Brown's tears in 1878, anticipating and substituting for Victoria's on his death in 1883, endow him with full human subjectivity, if only from the perspective of his loss. Like her attitude to Scotland itself, pity for the conquered subject's suffering becomes a pleasurable and a blameless form of imperialism.

In the end, the "Conclusion" subordinates all the mourning in the book—for Scotland, for Albert—to the loss of Brown, by reframing public losses as representations of one private loss. Powerfully and willfully Victoria shrinks the world to a pocket-sized memorial for her most private griefs. But the effect is not merely to trivialize the Queen, to make her appear a "speck" unconcerned with world-historical matters. To represent her Scots servent (thus doubly a subservient being) as a human being endowed with subjectivity and emotions, and thus to be able fully and publicly to mourn him, legitimates and naturalizes imperial deeds—in Scotland and, implicitly, around the globe—as acts of human sympathy. Privately anxious to secure Britain's predominance by keeping its troops at the ready around the globe, furious at her "incorrigible" government for failing to do so, the Queen nonetheless in this last "Queen's Book" found a way to present herself in the softened and familiar image of the grief-stricken relict too distracted to care about foreign policy. Thus, even while appearing to separate herself from official actions, she presents a model of imperialism justified by her own subjects' admiration for "'home life' and simplicity." Although in mourning her Highland servant she has imperially appropriated him and his nation to her regal needs, she creates for the imperial monarchy a harmless image ostentatiously isolated from the nastier realities of policy; she renders imperialism palatable to those who prefer not to attribute the growth of empire to any human agency, least of all to the singular aggression of their female monarch. While the display of feeling for Brown brought down on her the familiar complaints about her lack of reticence, mourning the death of a free Scotsman who was also preeminently "my own" offers Victoria in the frustrating Gladstone years an occasion to express imperial aggression in a relatively acceptable—or at least by now expected—form. Seeming a bit indiscreet, seeming to have forgotten how a Queen-Empress ought to appear, Victoria appears in *More Leaves* exactly as it served her monarchy best to have her appear. Like the other representations we have surveyed in this book, *More Leaves* constitutes a form of royal representation that displays the Queen as both the captive and the despot of her own regime.

Notes

Introduction

1. Told by his advisor Thurlow that "Your Majesty seems more yourself," George III replies, "I have always been myself even when I was ill. Only now I seem myself. That's the important thing. I have remembered how to seem"; Alan Bennett, *The Madness of King George* (screenplay; New York: Random House, 1995), 71. In Bennett's diagnosis, the King may owe his temporary recovery to his own or his doctor's efforts or to the accidents of his disease. Moreover, the scene of his recovery is his performance of King Lear, a performance that further emphasizes the ironic gap between "myself" (the man as bare, forked animal) and "myself" (the royal figure Thurlow is relieved to find once again).

2. For this formulation, I am indebted to Sharon Aronofsky Weltman's insight that woman's function in Ruskin's "Of Queens' Gardens" is like that of a constitutional monarch, who guides but does not determine; "'Be no more housewives, but Queens': Queen Victoria and Ruskin's Domestic Mythology," in *Remaking Queen Victoria,* ed. Margaret Homans and Adrienne Munich (Cambridge: Cambridge University Press, 1997), 105–22.

3. Aristotle, *Poetics.* See also Elaine Hadley's argument that Victoria is the heroine of a melodrama, a role that would appropriately transpose the ancient grandeur of Oedipus Rex into the more pedestrian terms of nineteenth-century British monarchy, but that nonetheless similarly indicates Victoria's function of embodying her audiences'/subjects' fantasies about power and abjection: *Melodramatic Tactics: Theatricalized Dissent in the English Marketplace, 1800–1885* (Stanford: Stanford University Press, 1995), 138–39.

4. A recent example is William Kuhn, who studies Victorian royal ceremonials from the point of view of the "public men" who managed them. In his (not untypical) view, Albert "laid plans for the monarchy," and his death left a "vacuum" to be filled by "influential men." Even when Kuhn's research provides evidence of Victoria's active contributions to making these events succeed, he presents her as at best resistant to the political work undertaken by these "men" for her own good (see, e.g., his discussion of the Thanksgiving ceremony of 1872, reviewed below in Chap. 3). William Kuhn, "Ceremony and Politics: The Management of British Royal Ceremonial, 1861–1911" (Ph.D. diss., Johns Hopkins University, 1989), 13, 3.

5. Simon Schama, "The Domestication of Majesty: Royal Family Portraiture, 1500–1850," *Journal of Interdisciplinary History* 17, no. 1 (Summer 1986): 155–83, quotation p. 157.

6. Sarah Stickney Ellis, *The Women of England: Their Social Duties, and Domestic Habits* (London, 1838; Philadelphia: Carey and Hart, 1839), 68.

7. The word "Victorian" is used almost always without reference to the Queen: witness the titles of books, such as Richard Stein's *Victoria's Year: English Literature and Culture, 1837–1838* (New York: Oxford University Press, 1987); Peter Gay's *The Bourgeois Experience: From Victoria to Freud*, vol. 1: *The Education of the Senses* (New York: Oxford University Press, 1984); or Esther Schor's *Bearing the Dead: The British Culture of Mourning from the Enlightenment to Victoria* (Princeton: Princeton University Press, 1994); books that have nothing (or next to nothing—Schor includes one paragraph) to say about the Queen herself. I wish to put Victoria back into Victorian.

8. Dierdre David, *Rule Britannia: Women, Empire, and Victorian Writing* (Ithaca: Cornell University Press, 1995), 7.

9. Caryl Churchill, *Cloud 9* (London, 1979; rev. American ed., New York: Methuen, 1984).

10. Virginia Woolf, *Between the Acts* (New York: Harcourt Brace Jovanovich, 1941), 161–62.

11. See Adrienne Munich, *Queen Victoria's Secrets* (New York: Columbia University Press, 1996), 153–54, for a reading of this picture as conveying Victoria's domestication.

12. Locke, from whom we get the theory of constitutional monarchy, rooted all liberty (or agency) in "the power to *suspend* the prosecution of this or that desire," in our ability not to act. John Locke, *An Essay concerning Human Understanding* (1690; 4th ed., 1700; Oxford: Clarendon Press, 1975), 263. In this regard the Queen is like any subject of a constitutional state, yet her not-doing takes on special meanings in light of her extraordinary prerogatives.

13. Elizabeth Longford, *Queen Victoria: Born to Succeed* (New York: Harper and Row, 1964), 15.

14. All that was needed to render the government's request acceptable was to remove the words "for purposes aforesaid," so as to make clear that she approves only the debate, not its outcome. The editorial concludes by urging that the language be thus changed, so that this phase of Irish reform can go forward. The Irish Church was disestablished starting in 1871.

15. Jean Ingelow, *Mopsa the Fairy* (London: Longmans, Green, 1869; repr., New York: Garland, 1977), 205.

16. F. Sidney Ensor, ed., *The Queen's Speeches in Parliament from Her Accession to the Present Time: A Compendium of the History of Her Majesty's Reign Told from the Throne* (London: W. H. Allen, 1882), 7.

17. See the Epilogue for one such episode in 1881.

18. See the history of this idea in Ernst H. Kantorowicz, *The King's Two Bodies: A Study in Medieval Political Theology* (Princeton: Princeton University Press, 1957), quotation p. 3. Kantorowicz's study focuses more on the identity of the ruler than on his powers and discusses power only in the context of cultures that identified the king's divine and natural bodies.

19. See the first chapter of Gail Turley Houston's forthcoming book on Victoria in the context of legal constructions of the monarch's gender, "Professional Royalties and Representations: Queen Victoria, the Laurel Crown, and the Gendering of Authority."

20. The royal "we" in ambiguous conjunction with the wife's married "we" further complicates the assignment of agency to a speaker. Although "she" says "I" to Parliament, in the title of her 1868 book *Leaves from the Journal of Our Life in the Highlands* it is precisely unclear whether "our" refers to her own singular historical subjectivity speaking in the royal plural, or whether she is referring to the joint marital life in which she submerged her personal identity in yet another way. The institution of marriage intersects with the institutions of monarchy in obscuring the identity of the royal speaking subject.

21. Quoted in *Life at the Court of Queen Victoria 1861–1901*, ed. Barry St-John Nevill (Exeter: Webb and Bower, 1984), 55. In this account and in the Queen's diary entry, she does audi-

bly express her "admiration" for the Hall, but what happened next isn't quite clear: in the Queen's diary, she does not whisper, and "Bertie declared the Hall open" (*Queen Victoria in Her Letters and Journals,* ed. Christopher Hibbert [New York: Viking, 1985], 224).

22. Frank Hardie, *The Political Influence of Queen Victoria 1861–1901* (London: Oxford University Press, 1935), 7, 21. See Kuhn, "Ceremony and Politics," for a less respectful view of Victoria's political contributions. Both define the sphere of her activity more narrowly than I do.

23. Giles St. Aubyn, *Queen Victoria: A Portrait* (New York: Atheneum, 1992), 600–601.

24. Susan Frye, *Elizabeth I: The Competition for Representation* (New York: Oxford University Press, 1993). Frye and other feminist New Historicists are indebted to Stephen Greenblatt, whose *Renaissance Self-Fashioning: From More to Shakespeare* (Chicago: University of Chicago Press, 1980) and other works taught a generation of scholars how to think about power and constraints on individual agency in a Foucauldian context.

25. Louis Adrian Montrose, "The Elizabethan Subject and the Spenserian Text," in *Literary Theory/Renaissance Texts,* ed. Patricia Parker and David Quint (Baltimore: Johns Hopkins University Press, 1986), 303–40, quotation p. 310, as quoted in Frye, *Elizabeth I,* 10.

26. The passage from Montrose that Frye quotes is: "Elizabeth was more the creature of the Elizabethan image than she was its creator" ("Elizabethan Subject," 310, quoted in *Elizabeth I,* 152). Frye's awkward misquotation (she writes "createe" instead of "creature") indicates uneasiness about the need to decide the matter one way or another.

27. Dorothy Thompson, *Queen Victoria: The Woman, the Monarchy, and the People* (New York: Pantheon, 1990), 87–88.

28. Munich, *Secrets,* 5, 222; or again, "Victorian culture accommodated ideas of Victoria to represent its self-interested moment"; "Her uniqueness enabled those of differing interests and needs to create the Victoria of their particular dreams. . . . Further, to the extent that Victoria shaped her own image, she could not control many of its cultural meanings" (*Secrets,* 2, 13). For Frye, Elizabeth I is an almost infinitely interpretable allegory (*Elizabeth I,* 16–18), and this is the case with Munich's Victoria as well.

29. Nancy Armstrong, *Desire and Domestic Fiction: A Political History of the Novel* (New York: Oxford University Press, 1987). Armstrong does not discuss Victoria; I am speculating about what her approach would lead one to say about the Queen.

30. Elizabeth Langland, *Nobody's Angels: Middle-Class Women and Domestic Ideology in Victorian Culture* (Ithaca: Cornell University Press, 1995), 20, quoting Judith Butler, *Gender Trouble: Feminism and the Subversion of Identity* (New York: Routledge, 1990), 147. Later, discussing the queenly Lucilla Marjoribanks's performance of both the powers and the limitations of her gender, Langland cites Butler's account of performativity, in which the stylized repetition of social conventions may nonetheless lead to their being "'rework[ed],' enacting a destabilization that facilitates resignification" (*Nobody's Angels,* 166, quoting Judith Butler, *Bodies That Matter: On the Discursive Limits of "Sex"* [New York: Routledge, 1993], 117).

31. This survey could continue. On the opposite end of the spectrum from Langland is, for example, Elaine Hadley, who, writing incidentally of Victoria in her discussion of Victorian melodrama and its equivocal effects of containment and subversion (its celebration and critique of patriarchal domesticity), sees Victoria as a "largely supernumerary figure" (*Melodramatic Tactics,* 166), her role as melodramatic heroine who aids in "the regulation of social energies" (139) entirely scripted for her by her governments.

32. Susan Frye, by contrast, implies that Elizabeth's approval of an image would mean it "represents her voice," the only question being then whether or not she approved (*Elizabeth I,* 10). In the case of Victoria, there is much documentation as to her approval or disapproval, but that documentation does not answer the question of what approval means.

33. Nancy K. Miller, "The Text's Heroine: A Feminist Critic and Her Fictions," *Diacritics* (Summer 1982): 48–53, quotation p. 53; more generally see Miller, *Subject to Change: Reading Feminist Writing* (New York: Columbia University Press, 1988).

34. Cynthia Huff, almost alone in reading Victoria's diaries as texts (not just for the historical information they impart), writes that the diaries both resemble and differ from those of ordinary Victorian women; see Huff, "Private Domains: Queen Victoria and Women's Diaries," *Auto/Biography Studies* 4 (1988): 46–52.

35. Jay Clayton and Eric Rothstein, "Figures in the Corpus: Theories of Influence and Intertextuality," in *Influence and Intertextuality in Literary History*, ed. Jay Clayton and Eric Rothstein (Madison: University of Wisconsin Press, 1991), 3–36, quotation p. 11.

36. Analogously, Terry Eagleton points out, about both feminism and nationalism, that revolutionary politics tend to require temporary reliance on the very concept being overturned. "Women are not so much fighting for the freedom to be women . . . as for the freedom to be fully human; but that inevitably abstract humanity can be articulated in the here and now only through their womanhood, since this is the place where their humanity is wounded and refused." For this effect Eagleton uses the term "irony." See Terry Eagleton, "Nationalism: Irony and Commitment," in *Nationalism, Colonialism, and Literature*, ed. Terry Eagleton, Frederic Jameson, and Edward W. Said (Minneapolis: University of Minnesota Press, 1990), 23–39, quotation p. 24.

Chapter One

1. Thompson, *Queen Victoria*, 98. The ballad excerpted for the second epigraph to this chapter appears in Thompson, *Queen Victoria*, 38. Among the images discussed in this chapter are some of the popular representations of Victoria that Thompson's book reproduces but does not closely read.

2. Adrienne Auslander Munich, "Queen Victoria, Empire, and Excess," *Tulsa Studies in Women's Literature* 6 (1987): 265–81, quotation p. 265. I follow Munich in finding that Victoria's uncompromisingly female monarchy could only be represented through paradoxes, but unlike me, Munich focuses on the moments when those paradoxes lead to representational excess—"contradiction, nonsense, massiveness" ("Victoria, Empire, and Excess," 278; see also *Secrets*, 207).

3. Thompson argues (*Queen Victoria*, 98) that whatever popular dislike there was for Victoria arose chiefly from the expensiveness of her growing family to the taxpayers (along with Albert's foreign birth); this point suggested to me the analogy between queen and wife. Thomas Richards argues, with reference to the Great Exhibition and the Queen's two Jubilees, that the monarch was constituted as consumer and as promoter of consumption: the culture of advertising and the success of the monarchy depended on each other. See *The Commodity Culture of Victorian England: Advertising and Spectacle, 1851–1914* (Stanford: Stanford University Press, 1990), 17–118. While Richards does not focus on the monarch's gender, Nancy Armstrong argues specifically that Victorian women (but not the Queen in particular) were seen as consumers, especially of goods coming in from the empire, whose desires were both dangerous and essential to commerce (see "The Occidental Alice," *Differences* 2, no. 2 [Summer 1990]: 3–40). These arguments together suggest the way in which Victoria's identification with the middle classes came about through representations of her as consumer, and indeed Munich discusses Victoria's role as consumer in *Secrets*, 28–30. Although I will briefly discuss one such representation (the ceremony to open the new Royal Exchange), this chapter will chiefly explore how she came to be constructed as middle class through another kind of representation, that of marital hierarchy.

4. Leonore Davidoff and Catherine Hall, *Family Fortunes: Men and Women of the English Middle Class, 1780–1850* (Chicago: University of Chicago Press, 1987), 149.

5. Sarah Stickney Ellis, *The Wives of England: Their Relative Duties, Domestic Influence, and Social Obligations* (London, 1843; New York: Appleton, 1843), 24–25.

6. John Ruskin, "Of Queens' Gardens," in *Sesame and Lilies* (1865; London: J. M. Dent, 1907), 58; Charles Darwin, *The Descent of Man and Selection in Relation to Sex* (London, 1871); excerpted in *Women, the Family, and Freedom: The Debate in Documents*, vol. 1: *1750–1880*, ed. Susan Groag Bell and Karen M. Offen (Stanford: Stanford University Press, 1983), 411.

7. Linda Colley, *Britons: Forging the Nation 1707–1837* (New Haven: Yale University Press, 1992), 206–7, 212–15, 231–32.

8. David Cannadine argues that royal ritual became elaborated in inverse proportion to the power of the monarchy; see "The Context, Performance, and Meaning of Ritual: The British Monarchy and the 'Invention of Tradition,' c. 1820–1977," in *The Invention of Tradition*, ed. Eric Hobsbawm and Terence Ranger (Cambridge: Cambridge University Press, 1983), 121 and passim. See also Judith Williamson on the media's construction of the spectacular ordinariness of the present royal family, "Royalty and Representation," in her *Consuming Passions: The Dynamics of Popular Culture* (London: Marion Boyars, 1986), 75–89.

9. Louis Adrian Montrose, "*A Midsummer Night's Dream* and the Shaping Fantasies of Elizabethan Culture: Gender, Power, Form," in *Rewriting the Renaissance: The Discourse of Sexual Difference in Early Modern Europe*, ed. Margaret W. Ferguson, Maureen Quilligan, and Nancy J. Vickers (Chicago: University of Chicago Press, 1987), 65–87, quotation p. 67.

10. *Debrett's Queen Victoria's Jubilees 1887 and 1897*, ed. Caroline Chapman and Paul Raben (London: Debrett's, 1977).

11. Munich, citing Victoria's preference for bonnets, makes a similar point about the popular idea that Victoria refused to wear her jewels, and that she could do so precisely because her empire was so great that she had no need to show off (*Secrets*, 73–74).

12. *The Letters of Queen Victoria: A Selection from Her Majesty's Correspondence between the Years 1837 and 1861*, 3 vols., ed. Arthur C. Benson and Viscount Esher (London: John Murray, 1908), 2:27. The letter is dated 29 October 1844.

13. Reprinted in Louis James, *English Popular Literature 1819–1851* (New York: Columbia University Press, 1976), 340, 341. Broadsheets and street ballads provide important evidence of popular views of the Queen, especially before 1855 when the repeal of the tax on newspapers made them so cheap that even members of the working classes could obtain them. See Richard Altick, *The English Common Reader: A Social History of the Mass Reading Public 1800–1900* (Chicago: University of Chicago Press, 1957), 354.

14. For the afterlife of "petticoat rule" as a pornographic trope of Victoria's reign, see *Secrets*, 156–86.

15. Reprinted in Richard Balzer, *Optical Amusements: Magic Lanterns and Other Transforming Images* (catalogue of an exhibit at the Museum of Our National Heritage, Lexington, MA, 1987).

16. Writing about Victoria's later years as a widow, Munich discusses her massiveness ("Victoria, Empire, and Excess"), her subjects' fears of her irrational tyrannizing, and her dangerous appetites ("'Capture the Heart of a Queen': Gilbert and Sullivan's Rites of Conquest," *Centennial Review* 28, no. 1 [Winter 1984]: 23–44).

17. See Nicola J. Watson, "Gloriana Victoriana: Victoria and the Cultural Memory of Elizabeth I," in *Remaking Queen Victoria*, 79–104.

18. *The Girlhood of Queen Victoria: A Selection from Her Majesty's Diaries between the Years 1832 and 1840*, 2 vols., ed. Viscount Esher (London: John Murray, 1912), 1:268, 1 February 1838.

19. *Queen Victoria in Her Letters and Journals*, ed. Christopher Hibbert (New York:

Viking, 1985), 30, ed. note. Although most quotations from Victoria's letters and journals come from their first published sources (and in later chapters from manuscripts), I am indebted to Hibbert's selection for shaping my own. I quote from Hibbert's edition, however, only where he prints hitherto unpublished material. Cited hereafter as *Letters and Journals*.

20. By contrast, Elizabeth I is invoked repeatedly and favorably in the *Times*'s account of the 1844 opening of the new Royal Exchange, Elizabeth having opened the first one with an even more splendid ceremony than Victoria's. Rendered benign as an early sponsor of commerce, she also is rendered part of the safely distant past, as the paper calls attention to the transformation and vast expansion of commerce in the intervening years.

21. Frances Wynn quoted in John Ashton, *Gossip in the First Decade of Victoria's Reign* (London: Hurst and Blackett, 1903), 2.

22. On Victoria's white satin appearance in Parliament, Ashton quotes "one evening paper" in terms that make her an object of chivalrous admiration but with emphasis on her femininity rather than on her position as monarch: "Her emotion was plainly discernible in the rapid heaving of her bosom, and the brilliancy of her diamond stomacher, which sparkled out occasionally from the dark recess in which the throne was placed, like the sun on the swell of the smooth ocean, as the billows rise and fall" (*Gossip*, 4). An oceanic force of nature, her body is at once vulnerable and potentially threatening, seeming more to invite institutional control by chivalrous men than to provide it for them. See also Munich's account of Victoria's much publicized tears, visible when she made her first public appearance as Queen: to her contemporaries, her tears could only mean her anxious vulnerability (*Secrets*, 19). On pictures of Victoria as girlish Queen, see Susan Casteras, "The Wise Child and Her 'Offspring': Some Changing Faces of Victoria," in *Remaking Queen Victoria*, 182–99.

23. The quarrel between Victoria and Peel was heated by her deliberate misunderstanding: that he intended to replace them all rather than just those married to Whig ministers. She insisted that it was the same: to change one was as much a violation of her rights as to change them all. For full accounts of the crisis see Longford, *Queen Victoria*, 109–14; St. Aubyn, *Queen Victoria*, 110–15; and Karen Chase and Michael Levenson, "'I Never Saw a Man So Frightened': The Young Queen and the Parliamentary Bedchamber," in *Remaking Queen Victoria*, 200–218.

24. Nonetheless, Victoria did win her point, and she may even have contributed to Peel's failure to form a successful government, although he also lacked a majority in Commons. The public "applauded her pluck in standing up for her rights, and admired the 'vein of iron' which ran through her character" (St. Aubyn, *Queen Victoria*, 114). Still, although Melbourne returned for two more years, that was to be his last term of office. It would be difficult to say whether Victoria narrowed her power in the attempt to assert it, or whether she actually gained power by narrowing her claims for it.

25. Cecil Woodham-Smith reports that Melbourne told Victoria that Lady Flora was the Duchess of Kent's rival (Cecil Woodham-Smith, *Queen Victoria: Her Life and Times 1819–1861* [London: Hamish Hamilton, 1972], 167).

26. Margaret Oliphant, *Miss Marjoribanks* (1866; London: Virago, 1988), 342.

27. *The Early Years of His Royal Highness the Prince Consort*, compiled, under the direction of Her Majesty the Queen, by Lieut.-General the Hon. C. Grey (London: Smith, Elder, 1867), 318.

28. Munich (*Secrets*, 8–10) provides an elegant account of Prince Albert's project to reconcile Victoria to her wifely dependence on him, the dependence that the public had been eager for her to display. Munich argues persuasively that Albert's letter about sinking his existence in hers "did *not* mean that he would accept Victoria as he found her" (9).

29. The London *Times* reported the entire service the next day (11 February 1840), includ-

ing her vows (among them, "to love, cherish, and to obey"), and this report is reprinted in an appendix to *Early Years,* quotation p. 454.

30. Ira Nadel, "Portraits of the Queen," *Victorian Poetry* 25 (1987): 169–91, quotation p. 173.

31. Schama suggests that domestic royal family portraiture in England and on the Continent preceded the reality it would seem to reflect, and that such domestic portraits were motivated not so much by an imitative response to "the onward and upward march of the nuclear family" as by a wish to co-opt French Revolutionary imagery of "republican sovereignty" ("Domestication of Majesty," 158). Because I am considering images of Victoria specifically, I will take more seriously than does Schama the relation of the royal domestic portrait to the bourgeois family.

32. On the Anglo-Saxon memorial statue, see *Secrets,* 49–53; for fuller discussion of Thorburn's painting and other images of Albert in armor, see Chapter 4.

33. Laurence Lerner, "Private Feelings: Public Forms (Are Elizabeth Browning's Letters Literature?)" (paper given at Vanderbilt University, October 1989).

34. George Eliot, *The Mill on the Floss* (1860; Harmondsworth: Penguin, 1979), 524.

35. George Eliot, *Daniel Deronda* (1876; Harmondsworth: Penguin, 1967), 670, 348, 350, 361, 659.

36. For an account of this ball and of the political meanings of costumes in the contexts of ethnic nationalism and of Chartism, see Munich, *Secrets,* 27–34.

37. The Jennings Albums at the Paul Mellon Center for British Art contain pages of such images, clipped from newspapers and magazines.

38. Longford, *Queen Victoria,* reproduces the version from the British Museum that has the full surround (and an additional child); copies of the version with the paper doors can be seen at the Royal Archives and at the Paul Mellon Center for British Art.

39. The railway car and carriage images are in the Royal Archives, reprinted in Helmut and Alison Gernsheim, *Victoria R.: A Biography with Four Hundred Illustrations Based on Her Personal Photograph Albums* (New York: G. Putnam's Sons, 1959), 80–81. The stately boat is part of a series of ten images published in 1845 by Dean and Co., a set of which is in the Paul Mellon Center for British Art, as is the 1844 lithograph discussed in the next paragraph.

40. Schama finds the painting's endorsement of "domestic virtues" to consist in the wife's appearance of attending on her husband ("Domestication of Majesty," 157). About this painting Munich writes, "Two dogs . . . act out Victoria's adoration" (*Secrets,* 135). Like me, Munich finds that the painting represents Victoria as both monarch and subordinate (see 134–36), whereas Schama sees little regality in it at all.

41. Anne Hollander, *Seeing through Clothes* (New York: Viking, 1975), 425.

42. William Gaunt, *Court Painting from Tudor to Victorian Times* (London: Constable, 1980), 211–14.

43. Quoted in Marina Warner, *Queen Victoria's Sketchbook* (London: Macmillan, 1979), 112.

44. Quoted in David Piper, *The English Face* (London: Thames and Hudson, 1957), 265.

45. Caroline Norton, *A Letter to the Queen on Lord Cransworth's Marriage and Divorce Bill* (London: Longman, 1855); repr. in *Selected Writings of Caroline Norton: Facsimile Reproductions,* ed. James O. Hoge and Jane Marcus (Delmar, NY: Scholars's Facsimiles and Reprints, 1978), 4.

46. I will refer to Elizabeth Barrett Browning by her unmarried name, as the writing discussed here dates from before her marriage.

47. Barrett's poems are quoted from "Cambridge Edition," *The Poetical Works of Elizabeth Barrett Browning,* ed. Harriet Waters Preston (1900; Boston: Houghton Mifflin, 1974).

48. Helen Cooper reads "The Young Queen" to reveal Barrett's identification with the Queen: "token women who attain public prominence feel ambivalent about their status" (*Elizabeth Barrett Browning, Woman and Artist* [Chapel Hill: University of North Carolina Press, 1988], 44). Munich argues that Barrett's 1838 Queen poems render as grief- and anxiety-filled an experience that Victoria faced with equanimity (*Secrets*, 15).

49. *The Letters of Robert Browning and Elizabeth Barrett Browning 1845–1846*, 2 vols., ed. Elvan Kintner (Cambridge: Harvard University Press, 1969), 1:3. The letter is dated 10 January 1845.

50. For example, Laura Haigwood, drawing on the "Essay on Shelley," finds that Browning identifies his poetry as objective in contrast to Shelley's and Barrett's subjective styles, which Browning disparages: "Browning comes close to suggesting that many of his peers, including his wife, who continue to write in a 'more or less' subjective style are producing merely 'sentiments' according to a 'convention' (Laura E. Haigwood, "Gender-to-Gender Anxiety and Influence in Robert Browning's *Men and Women*," *Browning Institute Studies* 14 [1986]: 97–118, quotations pp. 99–100). Dorothy Mermin, however, takes Browning's remark to Barrett, and further epistolary comments in the same vein, as a sincere compliment and as an expression of his poetic aim to put more of himself into his poems (Dorothy Mermin, *Elizabeth Barrett Browning: The Origins of a New Poetry* [Chicago: University of Chicago Press, 1989], 122). Daniel Karlin points out that Barrett grew tired of hearing from Browning about this identification between herself and her poems, which might suggest that she did not take it wholly as a compliment (Daniel Karlin, *The Courtship of Robert Browning and Elizabeth Barrett* [Oxford: Clarendon Press, 1985], 52). Recent readers of the letters have not seen the extent to which Barrett and Browning belittle each other directly (if subtly), in addition to condemning each other to idealization with their excessive compliments.

51. Readers of the dialogue between the married poets' poems have discovered a comparable range of competitiveness mixed with compliments. Munich calls the relation of *The Ring and the Book* to *Aurora Leigh* "appropriative and admiring, diminishing while it possesses"; "Robert Browning's Poetics of Appropriation," *Browning Institute Studies* 15 (1987): 69–77, quotation p. 75. Others who have written on the Brownings' poems to and about each other include Nina Auerbach, "Robert Browning's Last Word," *Victorian Poetry* 22 (1984): 161–73; and U. C. Knoepflmacher, "Projection and the Female Other: Romanticism, Browning, and the Victorian Dramatic Monologue," *Victorian Poetry* 22 (1984): 139–59. My discussion, however, will not reach far enough forward in time to engage with that discussion.

52. Betty Miller, *Robert Browning* (New York: Charles Scribner's Sons, 1953), 101. Miller emphasizes, however, that Barrett eventually, with regret, "consent[s] . . . to be worshipped" (101); Miller argues that in their married life Browning's desire to "obey" his wife had unfortunate consequences for him personally and poetically.

53. Angela Leighton, *Elizabeth Barrett Browning* (Bloomington: Indiana University Press, 1986), 93–94. Leighton links artistic to amatory competition, as does Laurence Lerner, who writes that some letters "seem like a contest to claim that each is beneath the other. They argue endlessly . . . about which has gained more from the other. . . . Sometimes they grovel" ("Private Feelings").

54. Yopie Prins, "Elizabeth Barrett, Robert Browning, and the *Différance* of Translation," *Victorian Poetry* 29 (1991): 435–51, quotations (including "secondary") pp. 436, 445.

55. I am drawing here on my memory of Leslie Brisman's reading of "Pauline" in a graduate seminar at Yale years ago; for a related argument about this poem see Leslie Brisman, "Back to the First of All: 'By the Fireside' and Browning's Romantic Origins," in *Robert Browning: A Collection of Critical Essays*, ed. Harold Bloom and Adrienne Munich (Englewood Cliffs, NJ:

Prentice-Hall, 1979), 39–58. Robert Browning's poetry is quoted from *Browning: Poetical Works 1833–1864,* ed. Ian Jack (London: Oxford University Press, 1970).

56. Miller, in *Browning,* 116, quotes from "Pauline" to describe Browning's desire to be led by Barrett, although she does not link Barrett to Shelley.

57. Browning's invocation of Shelley reinforces poetic patrilineage, as his star figure alludes to Shelley's sonnet on Wordsworth which in turn alludes to Wordsworth's sonnet on Milton.

58. It was a key project of feminist criticism of the late 1970s to explain why Harold Bloom's "anxiety of influence"—the critical theory that underwrites this kind of attention to Browning's struggle with Shelley—could not be generalized to include women poets (see esp. Joanne Feit Diehl, "'Come Slowly—Eden': An Exploration of Women Poets and Their Muse," *Signs* 3 [1978]: 572–87). But even Barrett's best feminist critics—such as Mermin, Leighton, Prins, and Lerner—are overlooking such differences (of which they are quite aware when it comes to reading the poetry) when they see Barrett and Browning performing in the correspondence symmetrical acts of humility, each worshipping from beneath and desiring to use that position for subtle advantage.

59. Leighton reads the same poem, it seems to me less plausibly, as an optimistic account of a girl's success in combining the very roles Mermin sees she cannot combine.

60. Of recent readers of the correspondence, Lerner notes this gender asymmetry the most explicitly. When Browning speaks "from beneath," Lerner writes, in a passage quoted above, his chivalric pose "looks too like a tactical inversion of the real relations of power" between men and women, who "are called goddesses by the men because they are going to have to treat the men as gods" ("Private Feelings").

61. Mermin, contrasting the poem to the gloomy romances that precede it in the 1844 volume, sees the poem as wish-fulfillment, Barrett's successful fusion of the roles of beloved (object) and of poet (subject) in a woman character (Mermin, *Barrett Browning,* 110–12). Likewise Glennis Stephenson stresses the equality between Bertram and Geraldine, because each one speaks and each worships the other: "[T]he roles of lover and beloved are as interchangeable as the positions of narrative subject and object" (Glennis Stephenson, "The Vision Speaks: Love in Elizabeth Barrett Browning's 'Lady Geraldine's Courtship,'" *Victorian Poetry* 27 [1989]: 17–31, quotation p. 22). Only Cooper stresses the poem's ultimate "inability to imagine a woman poet" (Cooper, *Barrett Browning,* 93): Geraldine, she accurately notes, is placed on a pedestal and made the poet's muse.

62. In fact, Barrett Browning herself, and not Browning, was nominated to be laureate by the Atheneum in 1850, when Wordsworth died; the Queen, on Albert's advice, appointed Tennyson.

63. See Eagleton's use of "irony" (in "Nationalism").

64. As we shall see in Chapter 2, Lucilla Marjoribanks's independence also depends upon her ability to maintain irony: keeping others from deciding whether she is joking or not puts her in control of the conversation.

65. Cooper points out that it was, specifically, Barrett's complimentary mention of his "Bells and Pomegranates" that "won [his] heart" (Cooper, *Barrett Browning,* 90); more generally, Mermin sees Browning imitating Bertram in the style of his first letter (Mermin, *Barrett Browning,* 116).

66. William S. Peterson detects realism behind Barrett's poetic self-abasement: any forty-year-old unmarried woman would be merely reflecting Victorian convention if she viewed herself as unworthy of a suitor ("Introduction," *Sonnets from the Portuguese: A Facsimile Edition of the British Library Manuscript* by Elizabeth Barrett Browning, ed. William S. Peterson

[Barre, MA: Barre Publishing, 1977], xv). Peterson quotes Browning's comments on the sonnets from a letter to Julia Wedgwood (xvii).

67. Patrick J. Noon, "Miniatures on the Market," in John Murdoch, Jim Murrell, Patrick J. Noon, and Roy Strong, *The English Miniature* (New Haven: Yale University Press, 1981), 207; see also Peter Galassi, *Before Photography: Painting and the Invention of Photography* (New York: Museum of Modern Art, 1981), 12.

68. Jennifer Green-Lewis, *Framing the Victorians: Photography and the Culture of Realism* (Ithaca: Cornell University Press, 1996), 30.

69. The royal family's patronage had much to do with the rapid early development of photography, and by the end of her life the Queen had amassed 110 albums containing 100,000 "photos" (Victoria's coinage), largely of herself and her family. See Gernsheim and Gernsheim, *Victoria R.,* 256–66; see also Frances Dimond and Roger Taylor, *Crown and Camera: The Royal Family and Photography 1842–1910* (Harmondsworth: Penguin, 1987). On the relation of oils to portrait photography at mid-century, see Lauren Chattman, "Pictures of Privacy: Femininity on Display in the Nineteenth-Century British Novel" (Ph.D. diss., Yale University, 1993).

70. There is one exception from this period, a photograph of the Queen in evening dress wearing her crown, a pose requested by and produced for the Queen of Spain.

71. George Eliot, *Adam Bede* (1859; Harmondsworth: Penguin, 1980), 221–23. See also George Levine's articulations of this idea in *The Realistic Imagination* (Chicago: University of Chicago Press, 1981); and in "Looking for the Real: Epistemology in Science and Culture," in *Realism and Representation: Essays on the Problem of Realism in Relation to Science, Literature, and Culture,* ed. George Levine (Madison: University of Wisconsin Press, 1993), 3–23.

72. Green-Lewis, *Framing the Victorians,* 35. Nancy Armstrong argues that fiction made the visual its chief criterion of the real at just the moment when photography became popular ("Fiction in the Age of Photography," lecture at CUNY, 2 May 1997). Photography became a paradigm for the idea of the real through, among other things, its association with the glass lenses and plates used in the evolving technology of photography and with the glass walls of photographers' studios, which resembled plate glass shop windows. See also Andrew Miller, *Novels behind Glass* (Cambridge: Cambridge University Press, 1995).

73. Green-Lewis, *Framing the Victorians,* 26, with reference to the idea of realism as the product of social "consensus," in Elizabeth Deeds Ermarth, *Realism and Consensus in the English Novel* (Princeton: Princeton University Press, 1983).

74. Mrs. Henry Wood, *East Lynne* (1861; New Brunswick: Rutgers University Press, 1984), 505.

75. Richard Ormond writes, "Where the painters offer us a highly flattering impression of the Queen's appearance, the camera records her glum expression and dumpy figure without subterfuge of any kind... [R]eality... communicates a force of character far more effectively than the facile gloss of the artist" (*The Face of Monarchy: British Royalty Portrayed* [Oxford: Phaidon, 1977], 36). Although I would question Ormond's view that photography is "without subterfuge," the contrast he draws does hold true.

76. The album where these images may be found in the Royal Archives was made in 1891 and consists of carbon prints made from older negatives by various photographers to preserve them, the original prints (made with such materials as albumen) being quite vulnerable. I have not seen the original prints, and my conclusion that there are ten is based on inspection of the carbon print album. Although they are scattered through the album, intermixed with the work of other photographers, it is clear that they are from the same session because the same clothes as well as the same settings appear in each image.

77. The first of these is no. 3502 in the album; the second was printed as a *carte* but apparently only for family use.

78. The second of Miss Day's images of Victoria seated and Albert standing, while it reads in roughly the same way as figure 16, could not have been engraved because it was blurred; she looks awkwardly at his legs, in any case.

79. See, for example, Audrey Linkman, *The Victorians: Photographic Portraits* (London: Tauris Parke Books, 1993), 62.

80. This is no. 3201 in the album; in a similar pose (no. 3210) she appears relatively composed.

81. Neither of these seated poses appears to have been publicly circulated: if she is to appear alone, there is perhaps something unseemly about her apparent needfulness. That all four images of Victoria alone—the regal and the needful—were posed and taken suggests that Victoria, or Albert, or Mayall, or all three expected the public might like seeing the Queen both regally independent and abject; or perhaps none of the participants anticipated what these images would reveal.

82. This image was apparently made into a *carte* only for private circulation.

83. Two of these, nos. 1010 and 3501 in the album, versions of figure 24, are virtually indistinguishable and might be prints of the same image.

84. In the fourth image of her standing and him seated (no. 210), the drama of relationship that informs all the other images seems to be missing: he looks down at his book, ignoring her, while she stands, equally oblivious of him, looking neither abject nor in command.

85. The carbon print album also contains prints of Victoria alone made by cropping negatives of the couple; it is unclear whether these cropped images were made only at the time the album was assembled or were part of Mayall's original project. Of the seven or eight different images of the couple together, there are four basic poses, with two or three exposures of each, in which the sitters' eyes may be looking in slightly different places.

86. Unnamed Victorian photographers quoted in Linkman, *Victorians*, 46.

87. A variant (no. 3337) poses her in three-quarters profile and him in profile, their arms linked in the same stiff way.

88. Another image (no. 208) is virtually identical but has her looking more directly into his eyes; yet another (no. 3340) has her head slightly tipped sideways.

Chapter Two

1. Lytton Strachey, *Queen Victoria* (1921; Harmondsworth: Penguin, 1971), 176; quoted in Hardie, *Political Influence*, 17.

2. Walter Bagehot, *The English Constitution* (1867; Ithaca: Cornell University Press, 1965), 64, 85; see Chapter 3 for a fuller discussion of these issues and of Bagehot.

3. See St. Aubyn, *Queen Victoria*, 343; Stanley Weintraub, *Victoria: Biography of a Queen* (London: Unwin Hyman, 1987), 308, 324.

4. Lucy Brown, *Victorian News and Newspapers* (Oxford: Clarendon Press, 1985), 147; her source is *The History of the Times*, vol. 2: *The Tradition Established: 1841–1884* (London: Printing House Square, 1939), 358.

5. The Vautier painting is reproduced in Dorothy Marshall, *The Life and Times of Victoria* (London: Weidenfield and Nicolson, 1972), 128; and in Gernsheim and Gernsheim, *Victoria R.*, 109.

6. See Stephen Orgel, *The Illusion of Power: Political Theater in the English Renaissance* (Berkeley: University of California Press, 1975), 10–16.

7. Elisabeth Darby and Nicola Smith, *The Cult of the Prince Consort* (New Haven: Yale University Press, 1983), 101–2, paraphrasing *Illustrated London News*, 24 October 1863, 414.

8. *Scotsman*, 14 October 1863; quoted in Queen Victoria, *More Leaves from the Journal of a Life in the Highlands from 1862–1882* (New York: Harper Brothers, 1884), 20.

9. *Aberdeen Journal*, 14 October 1863, 8; quoted in *Cult*, 102.

10. In a letter to her daughter Alice, 9 April 1864, the Queen writes that this letter was "put in by Mr. Delane's wish and written by the General:—that *is I* insisted on there being something put forth to stop demands which were quite *impossible* for *me—ever* to comply with" (RA Add Mss U. 143 Reel 2). This equivocation over the agency behind the letter—it is put in by the wish of Mr. Delaine, publisher of the *Times*, yet at the Queen's insistence; it is written in the Queen's voice, but by General Grey—anticipates the equivocation over the authorship of *The Early Years of His Royal Highness the Prince Consort*, discussed in Chapter 3.

11. Longford describes the episode in *Queen Victoria*, 329–30.

12. Barbara Leigh-Smith [Bodichon], *A Brief Summary in Plain Language of the Most Important Laws concerning Women, Together with a Few Observations Thereon* (London, 1854), 3; quoted from *Women, the Family, and Freedom*, vol. 1: *1750–1880*, ed. Bell and Offen, 301.

13. Adrienne Munich discusses Alice's queening, "the hyperbole of three Queens," and what she finds to be allusions to Victoria's excesses ("Queen Victoria, Empire, and Excess," 269–70; and *Secrets*, 194–96).

14. Cathy Shuman, however, calls "queen" in Ruskin's usage an "obsolete" class category because, she astutely notes, Ruskin appears to refer not to Victoria but to a medievalesque but essentially ahistorical fantasy of queenship ("Different for Girls: Gender and Professional Authority in Mill, Ruskin, and Dickens" [Ph.D. diss., Yale University, 1994], 106–7). Perhaps in surrounding "queen" with a feudal aura Ruskin is commenting wishfully upon his own Queen as well as on the middle-class women of his day.

15. Langland, *Nobody's Angels*, 62–79, quotation p. 67; Weltman, "'Be no more housewives.'" For similar but less fully developed readings of Ruskin, see Elizabeth Helsinger, Robin Lauterbach Sheets, and William Veeder, *The Woman Question: Society and Literature in Britain and America 1837–1883*, 3 vols. (Chicago: University of Chicago Press, 1983), 1:77–102; and Nina Auerbach, who also sees Ruskin registering women's power in his symptomatic desire to restrict them, although without reference to Queen Victoria, in *Woman and the Demon: The Life of a Victorian Myth* (Cambridge: Harvard University Press, 1982), 59–60.

16. Millett's reading appears in *Sexual Politics* (New York: Doubleday, 1969), 126–51.

17. For example, Poovey writes that "these deployments of the domestic ideal helped depoliticize class relations at midcentury, partly by translating class difference into psychological or moral difference." See *Uneven Developments: The Ideological Work of Gender in Mid-Victorian England* (Chicago: University of Chicago Press, 1988), 1–23, quotation p. 9; see also Armstrong's *Desire and Domestic Fiction*, "Introduction," 3–28.

18. Weltman's "'Be no more housewives,'" in reading "Of Queens' Gardens" against Patmore's *Angel*, emphasizes the difference between the terms "angel" and "queen," to give Ruskin credit for not making his women ineffectual angels but effective queens.

19. The writers who connect Queen Victoria to Ruskin's queens understand that Victoria's powers as domestic and maternal Queen were compromised and paradoxical: Weltman notes that Victoria's role as constitutional monarch made her power resemble the "guiding but not determining" power Ruskin attributes to middle-class women ("'Be no more housewives,'" 114); and Langland acknowledges the complexity of Victoria's imposture as a domesticated Queen (*Nobody's Angels*, 62–66). But when these critics condense this complex Victoria into the referent for Ruskin's word "queen," the conclusion they reach is that being compared to a queen lends a person more power.

20. RA M58.163, December 1864.

21. This point was suggested by Melissa Levine in a seminar discussion, February 1995.

22. In contrast to my reading here, Nina Auerbach and U. C. Knoepflmacher see Mopsa as a figure of power and "imaginative superiority," in *Forbidden Journeys: Fairy Tales and Fantasies by Victorian Writers,* ed. Nina Auerbach and U. C. Knoepflmacher (Chicago: University of Chicago Press, 1992), 207–13; more recently, in a reading closer to my own, Knoepflmacher characterizes Mopsa as Ingelow's "magically potent yet powerless queen," in "Male Patronage and Female Authorship: The Case of John Ruskin and Jean Ingelow," *Princeton University Library Chronicle* 57, no. 1 (August 1995): 13–46, quotation p. 46.

23. Christina Rossetti, *Speaking Likenesses* (London: Macmillan, 1874), 5, 18, 26, 33.

24. Thus it is an irony that reverses the irony upon which pictures of the married Victoria depend, in which real royal identity is highlighted by its absence from (or muteness in) Victoria's appearance.

25. On 28 November 1860 Eliot reports in her journal that, according to Arthur Helps, the Queen has "been speaking to him in great admiration of my books, especially the Mill on the Floss. It is interesting to know that Royalty can be touched by that sort of writing." *The George Eliot Letters,* 9 vols., ed. Gordon S. Haight (New Haven: Yale University Press, 1954–74), 3:360. It would be interesting to know what the Queen thought of the image of queen projected in Eliot's novels.

26. George Eliot, *Felix Holt* (1866; Harmondsworth: Penguin, 1972), 149, 160. Munich quotes the latter passage also, to make a point about the moral value of avoiding finery, which Esther learns from Felix, just as Victoria submitted to Albert's taste (*Secrets,* 70).

27. George Eliot, *Romola* (1863; Harmondsworth: Penguin, 1980), 95, 249 (where Eliot quotes Renaissance writer Agnolo Firenzuolo).

28. George Eliot, *Middlemarch* (1872; Harmondsworth: Penguin, 1965), 250, 879.

29. Margaret Oliphant, *Miss Marjoribanks* (Edinburgh: Blackwood, 1866; repr., London: Virago, 1988). Page numbers will not be given for words and phrases used—as are "a comfort to papa" or "society"—so frequently as to be catch-phrases.

30. Joseph O'Mealy, "Mrs. Oliphant, *Miss Marjoribanks,* and the Victorian Canon," *Victorian Newsletter* 82 (Fall 1992): 44–49, quotation p. 47. O'Mealy is quoting Patricia Stubbs, *Women and Fiction* (Sussex: Harvester, 1979), 7.

31. Langland sees Lucilla's rescue of Mr. Cavendish as an example of the "influence" that both Ruskin and Victoria urge women to exercise (*Nobody's Angels,* 195; see also her fuller discussion of this episode, 161–64). But Lucilla's aims are not precisely moral: she saves Mr. Cavendish because to admit that he had imposed on Grange Lane would be to admit her own fallibility as social arbiter.

32. Margaret Oliphant, "The Great Unrepresented," *Blackwood's* 100 (September 1866): 367–79; a response to Barbara Bodichon's 1866 petition (eventually presented by J. S. Mill to Parliament in 1867), this essay appeared just after the serialization of *Miss Marjoribanks* in *Blackwood's.* Those who debated both sides of Mill's motion to enfranchise single women (on 20 May 1867) agreed that "women possessed great power"; the question was whether it was to become "responsible power" (Mill's phrase, as quoted in the London *Times,* 21 May 1867; see Chap. 4 for a brief discussion of this debate).

33. Langland notes that the novel's "rhetoric of sovereignty" recalls both the young and the widowed queen, but she does not distinguish one part of the reign from another in identifying Lucilla's connection to the Queen (*Nobody's Angels,* 158).

34. Lewis Carroll, *Alice's Adventures in Wonderland* (1865); and *Through the Looking-Glass* (1871), in *Alice in Wonderland,* ed. Donald Gray (New York: Norton, 1971).

35. J. Hillis Miller, "Catachresis, Prosopopoeia, and the Pathetic Fallacy: The Rhetoric of

Ruskin," in *Poetry and Epistemology: Turning Points in the History of Poetic Knowledge,* ed. Roland Hagenbüchle and Laura Skandera (Regensburg: F. Pustet, 1986), 398–407.

36. Harold Bloom, "Introduction," *John Ruskin: Modern Critical Views,* ed. Harold Bloom (New York: Chelsea House, 1986), 1–14, quotations pp. 11, 13. Andrew Miller uses the term "failed allegor[y]" in a way related to my own when he points out that in Thackeray's commodity-stuffed novels "objects are simply objects, not harbingers of enduring contentment... Thackeray is an allegorist manqué" (*Novels behind Glass,* 50, 36–37).

37. Dinah Birch, "Ruskin's 'Womanly Mind,'" *Essays in Criticism* 38 (1988): 308–24; David Sonstroem, "Millett versus Ruskin: A Defense of Ruskin's 'Of Queens' Gardens,'" *Victorian Studies* 20 (1977): 283–97. Birch sees them as projections of Ruskin's own feminine position as judge but not creator of art and of his need to make his feminine position a more active one; for Sonstroem, Ruskin seeks to enlist yet another constituency in furthering the social ideal he was pushing in the 1860s.

38. Sheila Emerson, *Ruskin: The Genesis of Invention* (Cambridge: Cambridge University Press, 1993), especially 207–28.

39. Sharon Aronofsky Weltman, "Gender and the Archtectonics of Metaphor: Ruskin's Pathetic Fallacy in *The Ethics of the Dust,*" *Prose Studies* 16, no. 2 (August 1993): 41–61, quotation p. 59.

40. Paul Sawyer, "Ruskin and the Matriarchal Logos," in *Victorian Sages and Cultural Discourse: Renegotiating Gender and Power,* ed. Thais Morgan (New Brunswick: Rutgers University Press, 1990), 129–41, quotation p. 140.

41. Nina Auerbach argues, by contrast, that Ruskin's queens constitute his celebration of woman's powers and makes her garden "a large visionary world" (*Woman and the Demon,* 59–60).

42. John Stuart Mill, *On the Subjection of Women* (1869; Buffalo, NY: Prometheus Books, 1986), especially pp. 32–34 (close of chap. 1).

43. The delicate ironies of *Miss Marjoribanks* likewise ask the question, "but then,—is she a queen?"

44. Tennyson, *Maud,* pt. I, 22:10; quoted in Ruskin, *Modern Painters,* 5 vols. (London: Smith, Elder, 1873), 3:172 (pt. 4, end of chap. 12).

45. According to Sheila Emerson, Ruskin in his earliest experience of learning to read and write responded to words more as "visible objects, pictures" than as "representations of sound, or signifiers of ideas" (*Ruskin,* 211); and in *Fors Clavigera* he celebrates the "picture writing" of a six- or seven-year-old girl cousin for its "Adamic bond between name and thing" (217).

46. Weltman ("Gender and the Archtectonics," 51) discusses this practice in *The Ethics of the Dust,* where Ruskin gives a bogus etymology for "wife" to connect it to "weave."

47. Emerson's main thesis on Ruskin and gender is to link his identification with girls to his persistent focus on words as things, words as intrinsically meaningful, even though she resists definitively characterizing the literal as feminine or associated with the mother (*Ruskin,* 213). My reading of "Of Queens' Gardens" is thus indebted to (but different from) Emerson's reading of, chiefly, other Ruskin texts on women and words.

48. Carroll wrote *Alice's Adventures under Ground* in 1862–63 and presented the illustrated bound manuscript to Alice Liddell in November 1864 as a "Christmas Gift," just before Ruskin delivered his lecture; he completed his expansion of it (about double the length of the original) into *Alice's Adventures in Wonderland* in July 1865. *Wonderland* may conceivably respond to Ruskin's lecture, which appeared in print in *Sesame and Lilies* in July 1865; *Through the Looking-Glass,* about which I would make more definite claims, was written mainly in 1867–69. There is a facsimile of the manuscript *Alice's Adventures under Ground* (London: Pavilion Books and the British Library, 1985).

49. But Auerbach and Knoepflmacher emphasize Mopsa's mature powers, which they see as opposite to Carroll's wish to keep girl-queens small (*Forbidden Journeys*, 212–13).

50. Jerome Buckley called attention to this three-way connection only to dismiss "the English common sense of Alice," in his *Tennyson: The Growth of a Poet* (Cambridge: Harvard University Press, 1960), 145. Tennyson's biographer, Robert Martin, calls this part of *Through the Looking-Glass* "an obvious parody of parts of *Maud*" (see *Tennyson: The Unquiet Heart* [Oxford: Clarendon Press, 1980], 487).

51. Miller, "Catachresis, Prosopopoeia," 406; John Hollander, "Carroll's Quest Romance," in *Lewis Carroll: Modern Critical Views*, ed. Harold Bloon (New York: Chelsea House, 1987), 141–51. Chess too, Hollander points out, is a traditional marker of allegory (146).

52. Alwin L. Baum, "Carroll's Alices: The Semiotics of Paradox," *American Imago* 34 (1977); repr. in *Lewis Carroll*, ed. Bloom, 65–81, this point p. 68. Baum points out that "the heterogeneity of approaches to Carroll's *Alices* is sanctioned by the overdetermination of semantic possibilities" (66).

53. *Miss Marjoribanks*, seen in this light, might be said to end by cheerfully realizing the Red Queen's fantasy of identifying the monumental and the real.

54. She does not count herself as a queen here, yet in the next chapter she is certain she is entitled to her own bell on the door marked "Queen Alice," a bell marked something other than "Servants" and "Visitors." Munich, as noted above, precedes me in noting that this tripling of queens points to the excessive Victoria.

55. Here my emphasis differs from that of Munich, who finds the Alice books to represent "ruling women as excessive: large, nonsensical, but potentially violent and ultimately destructive figures" ("Victoria, Empire, and Excess," 270).

56. *Alice's Adventures under Ground* underscores this point about multiple queens in another way. When Alice meets the white rabbit for the second time he is anxiously muttering, "The Marchioness! The Marchioness! . . . She'll have me executed, as sure as ferrets are ferrets!" In *Wonderland*, the rabbit is anxious about "The Duchess! The Duchess!" who will "get me executed" and who turns up as a character in her own right. In *under Ground*, however, there is no Duchess, and when Alice meets the rabbit again and asks after the Marchioness, she learns that "The Queen's the Marchioness," the "Marchioness of Mock Turtles." This doubling of the Queen's titles diminishes her queenliness; and Carroll's later addition of the Duchess suggests that female authority figures could be exfoliated endlessly in Wonderland.

57. The latter is Munich's idea ("Victoria, Empire, and Excess," 269; and *Secrets*, 195); Florence Becker Lennon finds the queens refer to Victoria because of their shared "immaturity" (*Victoria through the Looking-Glass: The Life of Lewis Caroll* [New York: Simon and Schuster, 1945], 11).

58. The Continental Historical Society (author and publisher), *Queen Victoria's Alice in Wonderland* (San Francisco: Continental Historical Society, 1984).

Chapter Three

1. Catherine Gallagher, *The Industrial Reformation of English Fiction: Social Discourse and Narrative Form 1832–1867* (Chicago: University of Chicago Press, 1985), especially chapters 8 and 9, 187–267. Here she discusses "a number of nineteenth-century writers concerned with the relationship between political and literary representation" (188), including Coleridge, Carlyle, Disraeli, Arnold, and Eliot.

2. Summarizing Eliot's views, Gallagher writes that "the working class . . . should be represented, not in Parliament, but in novels" (*Industrial Reformation*, 224); ultimately, in *Felix*

Holt, "pure politics and literature . . . strive to represent merely one another" (225). Her discussion of the issues summarized in this paragraph appears chiefly on pp. 218–28.

3. Walter Bagehot, *The English Constitution* (London, 1867; Ithaca: Cornell University Press, 1963), 59 (the first page of Bagehot's text). This edition includes Bagehot's 1872 introduction to the second edition.

4. R. H. S. Crossman, "Introduction," in Bagehot, *The English Constitution,* 8–9.

5. The phrase is Mill's, cited by Crossman, p. 7; Crossman and Gallagher agree in thus refuting Mill's self-description as a democrat. Kuhn reports ("Ceremony and Politics," 20, 43–47) on the reviews (contemporaneous and recent) that complain of Bagehot's opposition to extending the franchise, despite being lukewarm in his reverence for the monarchy.

6. F. B. Smith, *The Making of the Second Reform Bill* (Cambridge: Cambridge University Press, 1966), 6–7.

7. Mill's amendment was rejected, 73–196; that there were even so many "for" votes suggests that MPs knew the motion would fail anyway and wanted to appear gallant; Lord Galway, "believing that the Committee were anxious to proceed to more important business," appealed to Mill "to withdraw his motion, which, if pressed to a division, would place many gentlemen, who were great admirers of the fair sex, in an embarrassing point" (London *Times,* 21 May 1867). Galway insisted that Mill himself served as an adequate "Representative" for women, who therefore did not need the franchise.

8. "The Commons and the Lords' Amendments," *Saturday Review* 24, 10 August 1867, 165; "The Amendments of the Lords," *Saturday Review* 24, 3 August 1867, 131.

9. Disraeli's love of symbolic representation lingers on in his insistence, on which he was eventually defeated, that voters be only those who pay their taxes personally, making a direct equivalence between the symbolism of money and the symbolic act of voting.

10. "The Session," *Saturday Review* 24, 17 August 1867, 209; also "The Commons and the Lords' Amendments," 165.

11. For example, Maurice Cowling takes to task earlier histories of the Reform Act (including F. B. Smith's) for overestimating its radicalism, its responsiveness to popular agitation, and its contribution to the reforms of the 1870s (Cowling, *1867: Disraeli, Gladstone, and Revolution: The Passing of the Second Reform Bill* [Cambridge: Cambridge University Press, 1967], 1–3). Eric J. Evans, in *The Forging of the Modern State: Early Industrial Britain 1783–1870* (London: Longman, 1983), attempts to bridge both positions. Balanced antitheses such as the following are typical: "It is indisputable that the number of people enfranchised by 1867 was very large. The electorate almost doubled within three years. . . . Yet in 1870 less than two Englishmen in five had the vote" (351–52). The chapter is titled "'The Principle of Numbers': Towards Democracy, 1867–1870," but the section summarizing results begins, "The 1867 Reform Act, then, did not turn the political world upside-down overnight" (355).

12. Quoted in Orgel, *The Illusion of Power,* together with James I's similar "A King is as one set on a stage, whose smallest actions and gestures, all the people gazingly doe behold" (from his *Basilikon Doron,* quoted p. 42). Others who quote and discuss both or either of these remarks include Stephen Greenblatt, "Invisible Bullets: Renaissance Authority and Its Subversion," *Glyph* 8 (1981): 40–61, quotation p. 57; Christopher Pye, "The Sovereign, the Theatre, and the Kingdome of Darknesse: Hobbes and the Spectacle of Power," *Representations* 8 (Fall 1984): 85–106, discussion p. 85; Frye, *Elizabeth I,* 9.

13. To be sure, this did not start with Victoria's monarchy; Linda Colley discusses the increasing importance of "sentimental feminine attachment to the British monarchy" beginning in the reign of George III (219). Elaine Hadley discusses some of the same passages from Bagehot that I discuss—including the one about theatricality and this one about the spectacle

of a royal wedding—in the process of discussing the Queen's function as melodramatic heroine whose "royal melodrama" helps to contain the anarchic forces of the free market. But whereas Hadley states that the Queen's invisibility together with the invisibility of the Cabinet "threatened to evacuate the public sphere," I will argue that the Queen's invisibility is itself spectacular (see Hadley 171–74 for her discussion of Bagehot).

14. Bagehot's ambivalence toward the monarchy and its ceremonials—a mix of reverence and cynicism—is central to Kuhn's discussion, "Ceremony and Politics," 33–39.

15. The Queen apparently disliked Bagehot's book, but later sovereigns took it seriously. The future George V studied it in the 1880s and wrote a summary of its guidance for English sovereigns that is preserved in the Royal Archives. This summary notes that "the Queen nonetheless retains an immense unexhausted *influence* which goes some way to compensate for the formal *powers* which have been lost" (Harold Nicolson, *King George the Fifth: His Life and His Reign* [London: Constable, 1952], 61–63). Elizabeth II was given tutorials in Bagehot's book.

16. In making this argument about the correspondence between Victoria's and Bagehot's texts and their shared distrust of "representation," I am contravening a more commonsense historical view. William Kuhn argues that Bagehot's remarks about the monarchy as a good show were intended to urge Victoria to resume a showy daily display and performance of monarchy ("Ceremony and Politics," 47–52). But Kuhn's view that, for Bagehot, the Queen's scanty visibility "was undoing the work of the prince consort" and arousing the "constant concerns of the men who had some responsibility for the monarchy's public affairs . . . after the prince consort's death" (61–62) does not adequately recognize Victoria's agency in representing the monarchy in this period, however strangely; nor does it appreciate Bagehot's textual—if unintended—recognition that representation always requires and creates absence.

17. *Your Dear Letter: Private Correspondence of Queen Victoria and the Crown Princess of Prussia, 1865–1871,* ed. Roger Fulford (London: Evans Brothers, 1971), 120. The letter is dated 5 February 1867.

18. *The Letters of Queen Victoria,* 9 vols., ed. Arthur Benson and Viscount Esher (1st ser.), and George Earle Buckle (2d and 3d ser.) (London: John Murray, 1907–31), 6:166, 25 December 1880; quoted in Hardie, *Political Influence,* 121.

19. This wish for the spectacle to remain showy is what Kuhn's reading brings out; here, in what I hope is a more nuanced reading, I see that wish balanced by its opposite.

20. Anthony Trollope, *Can You Forgive Her?* (1864–65; London: Dent, 1994), 394.

21. Leonard Tennenhouse, *Power on Display: The Politics of Shakespeare's Genres* (New York: Methuen, 1986), especially chapter 4, pp. 147–86; see also an earlier version of parts of that chapter, "Representing Power: *Measure for Measure* in Its Time," *Genre* 15 (1982): 139–56.

22. This is literally true: only with the publication of her letters after her death did it become clear how much influence she and Albert had actually exerted especially on foreign affairs; even through the 1860s as well as later she insisted to a sequence of ministers that they show her drafts of foreign dispatches in time for her to approve or disapprove of them (see *Letters and Journals,* 161, 164, 178, 180, 181, 201; Bagehot discusses this matter, *English Constitution,* 110–11).

23. These books are, according to their title pages: *The Early Years of His Royal Highness The Prince Consort,* compiled, under the direction of Her Majesty the Queen, by Lieut.-General the Hon. C. Grey (London: Smith, Elder, 1867) (a more conventional bibliographic entry is not possible, given the complexity and uncertainty of the relation of director to compiler, and in the absence of a clearly identifiable author, as will be discussed below); and Queen Victoria, *Leaves from the Journal of Our Life in the Highlands, from 1848 to 1861,* ed. Arthur Helps (Lon-

don: Smith, Elder, 1868). It would be possible to discuss both books in terms of the issues raised in Chapter 1 of this book: the Queen's strategy of asserting her powers by appearing slavishly devoted to Albert. For a sketch of such a reading of *Early Years,* see Gail Turley Houston, "Reading and Writing Victoria: The Conduct Book and the Legal Constitution of Female Sovereignty," in *Remaking Queen Victoria,* 159–81, especially pp. 173–75. As is true also of memorial images of Albert sponsored by the Queen, the story of their relative powers continues after his death.

24. Queen Victoria, *More Leaves from the Journal of a Life in the Highlands from 1862–1882* (London, 1884; New York: Harper Brothers, 1884); see the Epilogue for a brief discussion. To complete the roster of her memorial writings, she also drafted, but never published, a memoir of John Brown's life after his death in 1883. The project was sternly discouraged (in 1884, after the publication of *More Leaves*) by those close to her; for the story, see, for example, St. Aubyn, *Queen Victoria,* 425–26. Munich incorrectly reports that it was "more leaves from her Highland journals" that she was persuaded not to publish (*Secrets,* 160).

25. St. Aubyn, *Queen Victoria,* 350; Giles St. Aubyn, "Queen Victoria as an Author," in *Essays by Divers Hands* 38 (1975): 127–142, quotation p. 128.

26. Weintraub (*Victoria,* 337) gives no source for attributing this feeling to Grey; perhaps there is a source in Grey's papers in Durham.

27. Weintraub, *Victoria,* 340; Weintraub does not, however, connect these episodes.

28. *Dearest Mama: Letters between Queen Victoria and the Crown Princess of Prussia, 1861–64,* ed. Roger Fulford (London: Evans Brothers, 1968), 169.

29. [Charles Anthony Froude,] "The Late Prince Consort" [review of *Early Years*], *Fraser's Magazine* 76 (September 1867): 269–83, quotations pp. 270, 271.

30. "Article VIII—*The Early Years*" [review], *London Quarterly Review* 29 (October 1867): 199–222, quotations p. 199.

31. [Margaret Oliphant,] "A Royal Idyll" [review of *Early Years*], *Blackwood's* 102 (September 1867): 375–84, quotations pp. 375, 376.

32. "The Early Years of H.R.H. the Prince Consort" [review], *Saturday Review* 24, 3 August 1867, 151–53, quotation p. 151.

33. [Charles Kingsley,] "Leaves from the Journal of Our Life in the Highlands" [review], *Fraser's Magazine* 77 (February 1868): 154–67, quotation p. 154. Another review of *Leaves* similarly opens with equivocation about the authorship of *Early Years:* [H. Reeve,] "Article IX—*Leaves*" [review], *Edinburgh Review* 127 (January 1868): 281–300.

34. "The Queen's Book," *London Quarterly Review* 123 (October 1867): 147–61, quotations p. 147.

35. The "revelation" to which the vulgar might object appears to be the Queen's passion for the Prince. The volume contains "ever-recurring proof of the greatness of the wedded love . . . which for once invested with its sacred brightness the throne of England" (158). The reviewer celebrates love because "it elevates every character which it does truly possess," and because "the sight of the majesty of deep affection is always ennobling," but clearly love is a potentially risky thing on which to lift the veil, and it is at every point possible converted into domestic virtue. Summarizing his defense of the revelation of the Queen's love, the reviewer concludes on the benefits to the nation of letting "the throne be seen to have been the central point of that true, pure, loving family life which has ever been so dear to the heart of England" (158).

Moreover, if the Queen's revelations were potentially vulgar, they appeared at a time when even more vulgar accusations about her relations with John Brown were appearing freely in the press; the rumor had been circulating since 1866 that she had had a child by him, and in August 1867 (virtually simultaneous with the publication of *Early Years*) *Tomahawk* published its notorious cartoon, "A Brown Study," which pictures John Brown more or less in possession of the throne (see Thompson's review of the salacious gossip in and out of the press, in her *Queen Victoria*, 61–86). The timing of the publication of *Early Years* with the rise of this kind of talk lends support to Munich's view, in *Secrets*, that Victoria published the books in part to distract the public from her connection to Brown. This argument is persuasive, although I would take it as one of many aims and effects of the books.

36. The note continues: "Poor prince! What a bore his life must have been to him." Letters to Blackwood are quoted in Vineta Colby and Robert A. Colby, *Equivocal Virtue: Mrs. Oliphant and the Victorian Literary Marketplace* (New Haven: Archon, 1966), 116–17. Hard on the Queen for her self-indulgence in mourning, Oliphant was willing to "tackle the holy Albert" only on condition that she not be asked to review further volumes of his life: "I am sick of the name of him and so I suppose is everyone else." Colby and Colby treat *Early Years* as if it were written by Grey, but note Oliphant's assumption that it is the Queen's work: "It is a dreadful thing to begin writing, she may be going in for novels yet if she is to get a review in *Blackwood's* every time she takes pen in hand" (*Equivocal Virtue*, 117).

37. As recently as 1975 St. Aubyn revives the belief that the monarch's words are uniquely empowered to make their writer present: "The Queen is dead, but in the pages of her letters and journals, Long lives the Queen. Every word she wrote provides a self-portrait" ("Queen Victoria as an Author," 140). He ends his essay giving Victoria the last word to emphasize her truthfulness.

38. D. A. Miller's *The Novel and the Police* suggests to the contrary that the realist novel, as the literary equivalent of the modern regime of surveillance, ought to be Victoria's literary model; but her books, like her other performances of absence, follow a more antique representational model. See Greenblatt, "Invisible Bullets," 57, for a brief discussion of this difference.

39. The romantic teleology is of course not merely plot convention, as their marriage was discussed when they were babies, and Albert was raised to think his vocation might well be to marry the Queen of England. Although one reviewer complains that the book doesn't follow the model of a courtship novel because it traces the couple's first year of marriage, the book ends with an appendix detailing the marriage ceremony and thus does technically adhere to the courtship novel convention.

40. Margaret Oliphant, "Autobiographies. No. VI—In the Time of the Commonwealth: Lucy Hutchinson—Alice Thornton," *Blackwood's* 132 (July 1882): 79–101, quotation p. 92.

41. The *Daily Telegraph*, which as I have noted distinguishes in the body of its main review between Grey as author and the Queen as source of quoted notes and diary passages, nonetheless in a "second notice" printed two days later obscures that distinction in the following passage: "'The letters she then received from the Prince are,' she writes, 'the greatest treasures now in her possession.'" The book makes it clear that these words are quoted from the Queen's memorandum, but the newspaper makes them seem continuous with the narrative (29 July 1867).

42. In a letter to Theodore Martin written after reviews of *Leaves* came out, Victoria called on him to "rectif[y] and explain" publicly their suggestion "[t]hat the Queen wrote *The Early Years*. Pray, have that contradicted" (Sir Theodore Martin, *Queen Victoria as I Knew Her* [Edinburgh: Blackwood, 1908], 29). This insistence (to which Martin diplomatically declined to yield) suggests the importance to her of controlling the public appearance of her (non)authorship.

43. "The Commons and the Lords' Amendments," 165.

44. "The Bill as It Is," *Blackwood's* 102 (August 1867): 245–56, quotation p. 255.

45. "The Residuum," *Saturday Review* 24, 3 August 1867, 135.

46. "Article II—*Leaves from the Journal...*"[review], *London Quarterly Review* 124 (January 1868): 29–43, quotation p. 29.

47. "Article IV—*Leaves from the Journal...*"[review], *London Quarterly Review* 30 (April 1868): 84–98, quotation p. 84.

48. [Margaret Oliphant,] "The Queen of the Highlands" [review], *Blackwood's* 103 (February 1868): 242–50, quotation p. 242.

49. [H. Reeve,] "Article IX—*Leaves from the Journal...*" [review], *Edinburgh Review* 127 (January 1868): 281–300, quotations pp. 281 and 283.

50. The volume did have an editor, Arthur Helps who also wrote the introduction, but inferences about changes he or Victoria introduced are difficult to make, since the original was selectively copied and then burned by Victoria's youngest child, Beatrice; Beatrice (tendentiously, I believe) omits many of the passages I consider of greatest interest below. Judging by her correspondence, Victoria took a very active interest in seeing *Leaves* through publication—more so than in the case of *Early Years*.

51. RA Y167/103, 27 October 1869. This letter is excerpted in Martin's *Queen Victoria as I Knew Her*, 43–44, but there it is dated 20 October 1868.

52. In Beatrice's edited transcription of her mother's original journals, the phrases "council of war" and "lucky foot" are omitted (although "luck" is mentioned). Beatrice thus further silences the already muted political undertone of the passage. One would be tempted to speculate that, to the contrary, Beatrice has transcribed faithfully, and it is the Queen or Mr. Helps who has added these phrases for publication. There is ample evidence, however, that Beatrice did a great deal of cutting as she transcribed, and there is no evidence that this is not yet another instance of that practice.

53. Munich calls Victoria and Albert's love of the Highlands "another colonizing masquerade" and Balmoral a "colonial outpost" (*Secrets*, 39, 41). Even the act of dressing in kilts and plaids—as the royal family liked to do when in Scotland—is an act of domestic imperialism, as the kilt was not a native tradition but the invention of an Englishman after the Union, a garment requiring factory-made cloth; see Hugh Trevor-Roper, "The Invention of Tradition: The Highland Tradition of Scotland," in *The Invention of Tradition*, 15–41. Trevor-Roper's work suggests that most of what Victoria and her family romanticized as authentic Highland tradition was of recent, and foreign, invention.

54. Beatrice omits the second cairn—perhaps she too finds it perplexingly excessive—and Victoria's detail of "put[ting her sketch] on a stone. Beatrice also renders the story of Albert's day more gratifying than it is in the published version, which is likely in this case to be closer to the original: at the end of the day, Albert takes another shot; in the published text Albert only wounds it and is "unaware of having killed the stag," whereas Beatrice's version makes Albert "very glad at his success." Did Beatrice think her mother made Albert look undignified?

55. For their full accounts of the Queen's role in the war, see St. Aubyn, *Queen Victoria*, 294–98; and Longford, *Queen Victoria*, 242–56.

56. Kingsley's review in *Fraser's*, which quotes less than other reviews, selects only "Visits to the Old Women" for extensive quotation, 157; see also, for example, *Edinburgh Review* 127 (January 1868): 291.

57. Beatrice's transcription omits this detail. For a fuller discussion of Victoria's assumption of clothes indistinguishable from those of her subjects, see *Secrets*, chapter 3: "Dressing the Body Politic," especially 59–60 (on Victoria in Scotland).

58. Quoted in *Dear and Honoured Lady: The Correspondence between Queen Victoria and Alfred Tennyson*, ed. Hope Dyson and Charles Tennyson (Rutherford, NJ: Fairleigh Dickinson University Press, 1969), 87.

59. Victoria's emphatic "delight" over these incognito tours may have resonated for readers with the "revelation" of her passion for Albert in *Early Years,* the revelation that one reviewer suggested might be "vulgar" (see above), and, too, more risky, with rumors prevalent in the 1860s that Victoria had traveled incognito to the Continent to bear in secret a child by Brown. (The Prince of Wales was also known to use incognito travel to conduct illicit affairs on the Continent.) Secrecy may always have an erotic charge, even without these specific contexts.

60. In the privately printed edition of *Leaves,* Tomantoul is not only poor and wretched but has "a look of disreputability about it, which reminded Lady Churchill of an Irish village." This comparison—as insulting to Tomantoul as it is to Ireland—is omitted from the published edition and also from Beatrice's transcription, but its presence in the private edition means that the Queen wrote it originally. For publication, impolitic remarks are obscured along with Lady Churchill's identity, confirming that editing is yet another form of royal disguise. There are other examples of Helps's editing for politeness: in the entry on Albert killing the royal stag, the original has Macdonald remarking on the Queen's luck "in his peculiar English." For further discussion of the toning down of the passage about Tomantoul, see John R. De Bruyn, "Sir Arthur Helps and the Royal Connection," in two parts, *Bulletin of the John Rylands University Library of Manchester* 66, no. 1 (Autumn 1983): 54–87; and 66, no. 2 (Spring 1984): 141–76.

61. Beatrice's transcription of the original journal omits the first of these passages and most of the second. She also omits mention on the same page that General Grey "bought himself a watch in a shop for 2£!" These and other editorial changes in Beatrice's version suggest she finds her mother's sometimes colloquial hilarity improper. Together with her omissions in the "Visits to the Old Women" episode, they suggest a concerted effort to minimize the journal's preoccupation with concealment and revelation, an effort that calls all the more attention to it; they also suggest she is wishing the published edition out of existence.

62. The quotation appears in *London Quarterly Review* 30 (April 1868): 88, and in *London Quarterly Review* 124 (January 1868): 34. The *Edinburgh Review* (127 [January 1868]: 287–88) mentions deerstalking but does not quote this passage.

63. Beatrice's transcription of the original journal omits this improperly amusing passage about the roe turning into an old woman.

64. St. Aubyn's point is that Victoria had the "gift" of "knowledge of what her subjects were thinking," but Salisbury's remark implies, to the contrary, that the Queen shared their views rather than knowing them.

65. RA Add A32/5, 1 October 1867, to Arthur Helps (partially quoted in De Bruyn, "Sir Arthur Helps," 85; De Bruyn's transcription of Victoria's underlinings differs from mine).

66. Oliphant argued against parliamentary suffrage for women on the grounds that their representation would diminish their status; the vote would be the supplement that implies that something was lacking before they got it, whereas Oliphant maintains that their powers of influence without the vote are great, and adequate. See [Margaret Oliphant,] "The Great Unrepresented," *Blackwood's* 100 (September 1866): 367–79. For further discussion of Victoria and women's suffrage, see Chapter 4.

67. If Victoria had something to hide about Brown, she certainly flaunts the connection here, as she does later in dedicating *More Leaves* not to Albert's memory but to Brown's. As mentioned above, in 1867 public criticism of Victoria's attentions to Brown had been intense in the press. See Thompson, *Queen Victoria,* 61–86, and Munich, *Secrets,* 158–64, for some of the rumors and cartoons about "Mrs. Brown" as well as Munich's argument that the publication of books dedicated to Albert was motivated in part to deflect public attention away from

the Queen's notorious connection to Brown. The footnote to Brown, however, could hardly have been expected to deflect attention away from him.

68. RA Add U143 reel 3, 31 May 1865.

69. For a fuller exposition of the events and especially Gladstone's motives for planning this service and its attendant royal procession, see Kuhn, "Ceremony and Politics," 58–95; his evidence confirms that the Queen played an important role in scripting the event even though she initially resisted Gladstone's wish to put her on display.

70. For full discussion of republicanism in the period see Thompson, *Queen Victoria*, 105–18; Thompson cites the "usual" view of the significance of the Thanksgiving service in ending republicanism, p. 114; Kuhn also discusses the danger of republicanism as the chief motivation for the ceremony, in "Ceremony and Politics," 65–70.

71. 10 December 1871; in *Life at the Court of Queen Victoria 1861–1901*, ed. Nevill, 74.

72. Kuhn, who emphasizes the Queen's resistance to Gladstone's shrewd management of the ceremony, nonetheless supplies this information about the Queen's contributions (from the correspondence of the Queen and Gladstone), in "Ceremony and Politics," 88, 90.

73. Unsurprisingly, the Queen's diary also emphasizes the size and enthusiasm of the crowd. She writes: "The deafening cheers never ceased the whole way, and the most wonderful order was preserved. We seemed to be passing through a sea of people." Afterward, "Could think and talk of little else, but today's wonderful demonstration of loyalty and affection, from the very highest to the lowest" (*Letters and Journals*, 216, 27 February 1872). What is notable is that the *Times* too should adopt the perspective of the Queen as spectator. Gladstone also emphasized the size and orderliness of the crowd in his diary (see Kuhn, "Ceremony and Politics," 61–64).

Chapter Four

1. Elisabeth Darby and Nicola Smith write that "during the 1860s she was rarely seen in public except to unveil statues of the Prince Consort. . . . The melancholy spectacle of yet another inauguration ceremony was no substitute for the great public celebrations which were expected" on such an occasion as the Prince of Wales's wedding. Elisabeth Darby and Nicola Smith, *The Cult of the Prince Consort* (New Haven: Yale University Press, 1983), 102.

2. The terms quoted in this sentence are from the Lord Chamberlain's Annual Report, listed under "Incidents" for the year, in the Royal Archives.

3. Quoted in St. Aubyn, *Queen Victoria*, 368. In a letter of 1870 she inveighed against "this mad, wicked folly of 'Women's Rights.' . . . It is a subject which makes the Queen so furious that she cannot contain herself"; in Martin, *Queen Victoria as I Knew Her*, 69–70.

4. *Charles Dickens to Charles Leech*, privately printed by Walter Dexter, 1938, 42. Quoted in *Cult*, 102.

5. In Sir Theodore Martin, *The Life of His Royal Highness the Prince Consort*, 5 vols. (London: Smith, Elder, 1874–80), 2:537.

6. She had decided also to give Helena away in marriage on July 5, with "great crowds and enthusiasm"; *Your Dear Letter*, 78.

7. Benedict Read, *Victorian Sculpture* (New Haven: Yale University Press, 1982), 87.

8. *Dear and Honoured Lady: The Correspondence between Queen Victoria and Alfred Tennyson*, ed. Dyson and Tennyson, 69; the quotations are from a letter from the Duke of Argyll to Tennyson.

9. Munich argues that Victoria maintained her monarchy by preserving the illusion that she was still married and still under proper patriarchal control; see *Secrets*, 96–100.

10. The photograph was probably taken two days after his death by William Bambridge. See Linkman, *The Victorians: Photographic Portraits*, 122. A death mask was taken also, and Corbould made a watercolor painting of Albert after his death.

11. *Letters and Journals*, 157, 24 December 1861; St. Aubyn, *Queen Victoria*, 348.

12. Quoted from an unidentified source in H.R.H the Duchess of York with Benita Stoney, *Victoria and Albert: Life at Osborne House* (London: Weidenfeld and Nicolson, 1991), 166.

13. "If I should die . . . " is quoted without source in St. Aubyn, *Queen Victoria*, 349. Albert's 1853 letter about the Great Exhibition monument concludes: "If I were officially consulted, I should say, 'Mark the corners of the building by permanent stones, with inscriptions containing ample records of the event, and give the surplus money to the erection of the museums of art and science'"; Martin, *Life of the Prince Consort*, 2:537. In a letter of 23 April 1862 General Charles Grey describes Albert's wish for an institutional memorial "promoting Science and Arts as applied to productive industry"; quoted in Stephen Bayley, *The Albert Memorial: The Monument in Its Social and Architectural Context* (London: Scolar Press, 1981), 147. Albert did, of course, eventually get such a memorial, but the Queen gave it a lower priority than monuments including his image.

14. Walter Benjamin, *Illuminationen* (Frankfurt: Suhrkamp, 1982), 242; Emily Brontë, *Wuthering Heights* (1847; Harmondsworth: Penguin, 1965), 353.

15. Reading such passages more boldly than I, Munich finds that "Victoria's extravagant mourning included an additional sensation: if not quite pleasure, it was a quickening" (*Secrets*, 80). She emphasizes the erotic component of Victoria's mourning when she argues that its purpose was to deflect criticism of her relationship with Brown. Referring to the photo at the head of Victoria's bed, she writes, "Queen Victoria took Albert to bed with her wherever she went" (*Secrets*, 98).

16. See Renato Rosaldo, *Culture and Truth: The Remaking of Social Analysis* (Boston: Beacon Press, 1989), 68–87.

17. Best known from its having been quoted (without the italics) in *Early Years*, 318, and then in reviews of that book, this statement was first published in *The Principal Speeches and Addresses of His Royal Highness the Prince Consort* (London: John Murray, 1862), 77. The context is an 1850 letter by Albert explaining to the Duke of Wellington why he cannot accept the offer of the position of commander-in-chief of the army, a position offered to him because the monarch was a woman and thus could not so serve herself.

18. The first quotation is from RA Queen Victoria's Journal, 20 January 1862, quoted in the Duchess of York, *Victoria and Albert*, 166; "allegorical armor" is the Duchess's phrase, 166.

19. According to her Lady of the Bedchamber Lady Lyttelton, who echoes Victoria's journal for her birthday: "[M]y beloved Albert is painted in armour, which I so much wished"; RA Queen Victoria's Journal, 24 May 1844; cited in Mark Girouard, *The Return to Camelot: Chivalry and the English Gentleman* (New Haven: Yale University Press, 1981), 115.

20. Martin, *Life of the Prince Consort*, 1:212; the Queen said this on 20 December 1873; cited in *Cult*, 17.

21. This connection is suggested both in *Return to Camelot*, 126, and in *Cult*, 17. That Triqueti's Arthur wears armor was a controversial innovation in funerary monuments, even though there was ample precedent for the cenotaph's other gothic features; see *Cult*, 37; and *Victorian Sculpture*, 194. The newspapers took only small notice of the opening of the Albert Memorial Chapel for public viewing; the *Times* does not mention it at all, and the *Daily Telegraph* printed a brief notice, remarking generally on the "magnificent" decoration and architecture, the "exquisite" proportions, and the "feeling" of "solemnity," but paying more

attention to the limited size of the quiet but appreciative crowd; *Daily Telegraph*, 2 December 1875.

22. The quotation is from a letter to the Crown Princess, 27 January 1862, quoted in *Cult*, 7. Although this bust does not actively display the kind of internal contradiction discussed above with regard to the use of armor, it is worth noting that in 1890 E. Roscoe Mullins, making general remarks on unclothed busts, writes that "this treatment would look strange if applied to a head with long side whiskers," which Albert indeed sports; quoted in *Victorian Sculpture*, 172.

23. On the design competition and the Queen's choice, see *Albert Memorial*, 26–41; *Cult*, 45–46; and *Victorian Sculpture*, 97.

24. Quoted in *Cult*, 48, and *Albert Memorial*, 40. These two works are the sources of the information in this paragraph: see *Cult*, 48–57, and *Albert Memorial*, 14, 40, 45, 66, and passim. Scott's proposal was later reprinted in the journal *Builder* (21 [1863]: 176–77). Strangely, as Darby and Smith point out, the decoration of the exterior of the shrine was made of far more vulnerable materials (glass mosaic and semi-precious stones) than the seated figure itself, and Henry Cole—director of the South Kensington Museum—recommended that it be enclosed in a glasshouse for protection, as if the Crystal Palace were to return to memorialize itself and its maker. Cole was right: the Albert Memorial has been closed to the public for years because of falling debris and is now undergoing a major restoration.

25. To be fair, the statue was originally gilded; the gold was stripped off during WWI.

26. The equivalency of black and white is suggested again when Tennyson visited the mausoleum and the Queen was pleased by his "wish . . . that funerals could be in white" (*Dear and Honoured Lady*, 92).

27. Although there has been much recent debate about how Victorians read photographs, at least some assumed photos represented the real. Beaumont Newhall discusses the shocked public reaction to Henry Peach Robinson's 1858 art photograph "Fading Away," in which the death of a young girl is represented by models. "The very fact that it was a photograph implied that it was a truthful representation"; Beaumont Newhall, *The History of Photography from 1839 to the Present Day*, 4th ed. (New York: Museum of Modern Art, 1964), 61.

28. Roland Barthes, *Camera Lucida: Reflections on Photography*, trans. Richard Howard (New York: Farrar, Straus and Giroux, 1981), 91.

29. Terry Castle, "The Spectralization of the Other in *The Mysteries of Udolpho*," in *The New Eighteenth Century*, ed. Laura Brown and Felicity Nussbaum (New York: Methuen, 1987), 251, 310.

30. Marina Warner, "Stolen Shadows, Lost Souls: Body and Soul in Photography," *Raritan* 15, no. 2 (Fall 1995): 35–58; quotation p. 50.

31. On the photo album as souvenir—"the nostalgic is enamored of distance, not of the referent itself"—see also Susan Stewart, *On Longing: Narratives of the Miniature, the Gigantic, the Souvenir, the Collection* (Durham, NC: Duke University Press, 1993), 145.

32. Although Barthes seems not to know or care who Brown is, for Barthes the punctum is Brown holding the bridle, which makes Barthes wonder, "[W]hat if the horse suddenly began to rear? What would happen to the queen's skirt, *i.e.* to *her majesty?*" (57). Given Barthes's apparent ignorance about Brown, his discernment of the picture's hinted-at sexuality is astute.

33. See also Elliot Gilbert's astute if schematic claim that Victoria and Albert "revers[e] the usual male-female roles" even while a contemporary representation such as Tennyson's "Dedication" of the *Idylls of the King* to Albert's memory portrays them in conventional gender roles; Elliot Gilbert, "The Female King: Tennyson's Arthurian Apocalypse," *PMLA* 98 (1983): 863–78, quotation p. 864.

34. Susan Wolfson, "Feminizing Keats," in *Critical Essays on John Keats*, ed. Hermione de Almeida (Boston: G. K. Hall, 1990), 322.

35. Judith Fetterley, *The Resisting Reader: A Feminist Approach to American Fiction* (Bloomington: Indiana University Press, 1978), 22–33.

36. William Wordsworth, "Three Years She Grew in Sun and Shower," in *Wordsworth: Poetical Works*, ed. Thomas Hutchinson, rev. Ernest de Selincourt (Oxford: Oxford University Press, 1969), 148.

37. Margaret Homans, *Women Writers and Poetic Identity* (Princeton: Princeton University Press, 1980), 22.

38. Samuel Beckett, *Waiting for Godot* (New York: Grove Press, 1954), 57.

39. Elisabeth Bronfen, *Over Her Dead Body: Death, Femininity, and the Aesthetic* (Manchester: Manchester University Press, 1992), xi.

40. Carol Christ, "Victorian Masculinity and the Angel in the House," in *A Widening Sphere: Changing Roles of Victorian Women*, ed. Martha Vicinus (Bloomington: Indiana University Press, 1977), 146–62.

41. See Kathy Psomiades, "Subtly of Herself Contemplative: Women, Poets, and British Aestheticism" (Ph.D. diss., Yale University, 1990).

42. Peter M. Sacks, *The English Elegy* (Baltimore: Johns Hopkins University Press, 1985), 168.

43. Quotations from the *Idylls* are from *The Poems of Tennyson*, ed. Christopher Ricks (London: Longman, 1969). "To the Prince Consort" (1862) and "To the Queen" (1873) frame the poem at beginning and end.

44. "Under the Microscope," in *The Complete Works of Algernon Charles Swinburne*, ed. Sir Edmund Gosse and Thomas James Wise (London: William Heinemann, 1926), 16:403.

45. John Dixon Hunt points out that "Morte d'Arthur" (written 1833–34, published 1842) "was first written in a manuscript book among early versions of five sections of *In Memoriam*"; see "The Poetry of Distance: Tennyson's *Idylls of the King*," in *Victorian Poetry*, ed. Malcolm Bradbury and David Palmer (London: Edward Arnold, 1972), 89. Without referring to the laureateship, Elliot Gilbert suggests that the *Idylls* are about Victoria and Albert when he briefly discusses the feminization of Arthur as a version of the "sexual role reversal" ("The Female King," 865) embodied by Victoria and Albert.

46. Robert Bernard Martin, *Tennyson: The Unquiet Heart* (Oxford: Clarendon Press, 1980), 442, 500.

47. Quoted as an epigraph in Marion Shaw, *Alfred Lord Tennyson* (Atlantic Highlands, NJ: Humanities Press International, 1988), 110.

48. *Tennyson and His Friends*, ed. Hallam Tennyson (London, 1911), 498; quoted in Mike Weaver, *Julia Margaret Cameron 1815–1879* (Boston: Little, Brown, 1984), 66.

49. Hallam Tennyson, *Alfred Lord Tennyson: A Memoir by His Son*, 2 vols. (London: Macmillan, 1897), 2:127.

50. John D. Rosenberg, *The Fall of Camelot: A Study of Tennyson's "Idylls of the King"* (Cambridge, MA: Harvard University Press, 1973), 130.

51. J. Philip Eggers echoes the point that the characters escape the constrictions of allegory when he argues that although the "moral scheme has a clear polarity of abstract good and evil," Tennyson "refuses . . . to exempt the virtuous from error or defects." See his *King Arthur's Laureate: A Study of Tennyson's Idylls of the King* (New York: New York University Press, 1971), 81.

52. John R. Reed, *Perception and Design in Tennyson's Idylls of the King* (Athens: Ohio University Press, 1969), 48.

53. According to Joseph, the first of these phrases is Tennyson's; Hunt attributes the phrase

to Benjamin Jowett, in "The Poetry of Distance," 116. See Gerhard Joseph, *Tennyson and the Text: The Weaver's Shuttle* (Cambridge: Cambridge University Press, 1992), 161.

54. Valerie Pitt, *Tennyson Laureate* (London: Barrie and Rockliff, 1962), 183–84.

55. Walter Bagehot, unsigned review from *National Review* (October 1859) of *Idylls of the King*, in *Tennyson: The Critical Heritage*, ed. John D. Jump (London: Routledge and Kegan Paul, 1967), 215–40, quotation p. 229.

56. Joseph works out some of what he means by the poem's "flickering" genre by discussing the poem's alternation between sharp-focus naturalism and the Tennysonian proclivity for things "far, far away."

57. Dwight Culler points out that none of the poem's supernatural occurrences are given the authority of being spoken in the poet's voice; all appear in characters' speeches; see Dwight Culler, *The Poetry of Tennyson* (New Haven: Yale University Press, 1977), 225; see also Kerry McSweeney, *Tennyson and Swinburne as Romantic Naturalists* (Toronto: University of Toronto Press, 1981), 119.

58. *Victorian Scrutinies: Reviews of Poetry 1830–1870*, ed. Isobel Armstrong (London: Athlone Press of the University of London, 1972), 321, 316, 318.

59. Bronfen too finds Elaine's self-objectification to fail in its aims, but for reasons having to do with the properties of all representation: "Any signification is always such that the body functions as a signifier whose signified and whose referent is inevitably gliding and whose materialization is never complete"; *Over Her Dead Body*, 155. I agree, but would add that the poem undermines her allegorical intentions through the particulars of its events as well. For a woman to be her own statue has, in context, other negative associations: Guinevere's ability to cover up her emotions about Lancelot when Gawain brings news of his return is "such and so unmoved a majesty / She might have seemed her statue" (*LE*, 1163–65).

60. Hunt's instances of Arthur being compared to statuary differ from the passages I will consider here, in which Arthur is assimilated to statuary in the narrative.

61. In another seemingly random association of Tennyson with allegorizing Albert, when the Queen writes back to Vicky about the plan to elaborate allegories around Albert in the Blue Room, the paragraph begins "I send you the copy of a beautiful letter from Tennyson," as if Tennyson's condolences, or simply the beauty of his writing, led naturally to the thought of allegorizing Albert; *Dearest Mama*, 31.

62. The Queen writes: "[B]eautiful as are passages in it—it . . . leaves me quite bewildered"; Vicky answers: "I own they are beyond me. I cannot quite understand them"; *Your Dear Letter*, 255, 257, 12 and 14 January 1870.

63. Tennyson's note, quoted in *The Poems of Tennyson*, 1755.

64. See, for example, Deirdre David's view that "To the Queen" "domesticate[s] empire, mak[ing] it an extension of British loyalty to the Queen"; *Rule Britannia*, 170–71.

65. Quoted in Helmut Gernsheim, *Julia Margaret Cameron: Her Life and Photographic Work* (London: Fountain Press, 1948), 22.

66. Carol Mavor, *Pleasures Taken: Performances of Sexuality and Loss in Victorian Photographs* (Chapel Hill, NC: Duke University Press, 1995), 45. Mavor remarks, about the recollections of a woman who modeled for Cameron as a child, "Cameron feels large and ominous, like Queen Victoria" (45); but I have not located any explicit comparison made by a contemporary.

67. Amanda Hopkinson reports that Cameron "shared Emily Tennyson's adulation of Queen Victoria" and found it a "bitter pill" that none of her *cartes de visite* were in the royal albums; Hopkinson speculates that H. P. Robinson—for whose prints Prince Albert had placed a standing order, and who disapproved of Cameron's technique—had turned the royal family

against Cameron; rumors of Cameron's bizarre housekeeping perhaps kept the Queen away as well; Amanda Hopkinson, *Julia Margaret Cameron* (London: Virago, 1986), 161.

68. Robert Douglas-Fairhurst, "Mirror with a Memory," *TLS*, 1 March 1996.

69. Cameron's illustrations for the *Idylls* and other Tennyson poems were published in two volumes, of which few copies were made, as the images are full-sized photographic prints; the books resemble albums more than printed books. Each copy is different, owing to variations in printing and in Cameron's handling of the prints; the one I examined belongs to Harvard's Houghton Library; Julia Margaret Cameron, *Illustrations to Tennyson's Idylls of the King, and Other Poems*, 2 vols. (London: Henry King, 1875).

70. Discussing this issue in relation to Cameron, Gerhard Joseph cites Abigail Solomon-Godeau's Barthesian observation that the photographic portrait is "a commemorative trace of an absent object, the still picture of a frozen look"; Solomon-Godeau, "The Legs of the Countess," *October* 39 (1986): 65–108, quotation pp. 67–68; cited in *Tennyson and the Text*, 79, together with Carol Christ's account (in a lecture) of the Pre-Raphaelite painters' tendency to fetishize the woman's body as dead.

71. Lindsay Smith argues that Cameron's categorization as "fine art" photographer in an age dominated, in John Tagg's view, by the use of photography for surveillance has marginalized her work and obscured the originality and importance of her technical innovations; Lindsay Smith, "The Politics of Focus: Feminism and Photography Theory," in *New Feminist Discourses: Critical Essays on Theories and Texts*, ed. Isobel Armstrong (London: Routledge, 1992), 241. She alludes to John Tagg's influential book, *The Burden of Representation* (London: Macmillan, 1986); on realism and surveillance, see also D. A. Miller, *The Novel and the Police*.

72. As Amanda Hopkinson suggestively puts it (*Cameron*, 120), Cameron began photographing Liddell after Dodgson had ceased to do so.

73. Anita Mozley, catalog entry no. 42, *Mrs. Cameron's Photographs from the Life* (catalog of exhibit, January–March 1974), Stanford University Museum of Art (1974).

74. See Hopkinson, *Cameron*, 117; see also *The Golden Age of Photography 1839–1900*, ed. Mark Hayworth-Booth (New York: Aperture, 1984), 120. Two critics, Gernsheim and Lindsay Smith, describe as a polar opposition the difference between their photographic styles: Gernsheim to Dodgson's advantage, Smith to Cameron's. See Gernsheim, *Cameron;* and Smith, "The Politics of Focus."

75. Mike Weaver, *Julia Margaret Cameron 1815–1879* (Boston: Little, Brown, 1984). Despite the "disappearance of god," which made full-fledged allegory untenable in the nineteenth century, typology thrived in the context of Victorian religious revival because it values the present avatar more than allegory does; for a full discussion of these issues, see George P. Landow, *Victorian Types/Victorian Shadows: Biblical Typology in Victorian Literature, Art, and Thought* (London: Routledge, 1980). See also, for example, McSweeney on why allegory and even typology are likely to fail as nineteenth-century genres: "God disappeared in the nineteenth century, taking with him the religious certainties of centuries and the supernatural sanctions of morality. The Renaissance conception of a hierarchically ordered universe, rich in correspondences and analogies among its levels, which provided the organizing principles and the typological potency of the *Faerie Queen* and *Comus*, also disappeared"; McSweeney, *Tennyson and Swinburne*, 102.

76. Adrienne Munich, *Andromeda's Chains: Gender and Interpretation in Victorian Literature and Art* (New York: Columbia University Press, 1989), 88–89. Munich argues that Rossetti blurred these boundaries as a way of calling attention to the problem of sexual difference; see p. 93.

77. Gernsheim, *Cameron*, 29–30, 51; for fuller discussion of the issues raised by Cameron's

practice with models, see Victoria Olsen, "Photography in the Victorian Art World: Julia Margaret Cameron's Photographs for Alfred Tennyson's *Idylls of the King*," *Dickens World* 8 (Summer 1992): 122–36.

78. Olsen, "Photography," 128–30; Linda Shires, "Glass House Visionary: Julia Margaret Cameron among the Writers," *Princeton University Library Chronicle* 57, no. 1 (Autumn 1995): 107–25, especially 120.

79. Hopkinson too contrasts Cameron's photos of children to Dodgson's, focusing not so much on technique as on "prurience [and] voyeurism," which she finds wholly absent in Cameron; Hopkinson, *Cameron*, 117. Gernsheim states (Gernsheim, *Cameron*, 46) that Cameron's soft focus was the result of poor technique, even though he quotes a letter in which Cameron says she chooses it for its superior beauty. No doubt critical appreciation of all Cameron's work by both sexes will increase in future.

80. Cameron uses the phrase "ideal representation" to indicate (possibly to paraphrase or to quote) Tennyson's praise for the illustrations. Weaver (*Cameron*, 66) quotes a letter from Cameron to Francis Fox, 15 December 1874, found in the Metropolitan Museum's copy of her *Idylls*. Weaver says that "her illustrations were ideal representations of other works which were themselves ideal representations of legendary subjects" (Weaver, *Cameron*, 67). But Robert Martin casts doubt on Tennyson's admiration for the illustrations, claiming that Tennyson's request "suggests an act of deliberate kindness since he hated illustrations of his poems"; Martin, *Tennyson*, 508.

81. Coventry Patmore, "Mrs. Cameron's Photographs," *Macmillan's* 13 (1866): 231; quoted in Weaver, *Cameron*, 20.

82. Shires, "Glass House Visionary," 118–20; Hopkinson points out that of approximately 3,000 pictures she took in England, Cameron made approximately the same number of men and children, but twice as many of women; Hopkinson, *Cameron*, 16.

83. See Joanne Lukitsch, *Cameron: Her Work and Career* (Rochester, NY: International Museum of Photography at George Eastman House, 1986), 33–34.

84. Benedict Read points out that bas relief was generally used for realistic depictions, for example, of scenes from the memorialized person's life, while allegorical figures were more likely to be freestanding, but he does not make this point about gender; *Victorian Sculpture*, 148–50.

85. This reading is confirmed by Anita Mozley, catalogue entry no. 46, *Mrs. Cameron's Photographs*.

86. While a number of critics note the resemblance between amateur theatricals and some of Cameron's more elaborately staged photographs, Robert Martin points out that the *Idylls* themselves recall "unconvincing . . . playacting," "the props more believable than the actors"; Martin, *Tennyson*, 499.

87. Hopkinson identifies the "shield" as the same that appears in a 1868 photograph of "Little Alamayou," the Prince of Abyssinia; but unless the round "Abyssinian" shield (and it is not clear whether this is Cameron's prop or the Prince's property) is the reverse side of Lancelot's shield, it is hard to see how they could be the same; see Hopkinson, *Cameron*, 64 and 128, for her comments on the two images. In any case it is clear, as Hopkinson points out later about the final image of the series, that "the props she accumulated bear very little resemblance either to the medieval version of the Arthurian legend or to the wild outside" (139).

88. In the Harvard copy, someone (presumably Cameron) has scratched on the surface of the "shield," but only to whiten the highlights on its decorations, not to suggest battle damage. The gesture only emphasizes the purely ornamental nature of the shield.

89. In the Harvard copy of figure 43, in which the eye is drawn to the suspended shield case, it is clear that something like the blank letter of figure 44 was also posed on Elaine's body, only

to have been ineffectively covered up later by what appear to be squiggles made with a pen on the negative. That Cameron had originally intended to show Elaine's letter here as well as in the next image is also suggested by the accompanying text, which mentions the letter. In the print reproduced here, the white patch is more effectively covered by flowers strewn across Elaine's body, but the glow from the white patch is still perceptible. Perhaps Cameron wanted to clarify that the shield case and the letter are equivalents.

90. Cameron's participatory approach to Victoria's project produces other ironies as well. On the day John Stuart Mill tried in vain to extend the suffrage to women, Victoria was setting up memorials to her late husband and so representing herself. She did not need the vote in order to take a responsible interest in politics (one of Mill's arguments in favor of female suffrage): she alone of all British women had an interesting government job. Cameron, a woman whose suppositional vote in parliamentary elections the Queen so adamantly opposed, succeeded a decade later in participating in the national representational project of memorializing the Prince. Like all citizens, male and female, implicitly invited to take part, Cameron took up that work in the sphere of art rather than of politics. Like "woman's influence," a woman's cultural productions may accomplish both more and less than would the fulfillment of her frustrated electoral responsibilities; perhaps, lacking the vote, Cameron still managed to do for herself what Victoria herself ultimately chose not to do: make a name that still signifies concrete accomplishments in the world.

91. Similarly, Read calls the figure "Mourning Queen . . . who can only be Queen Victoria" (*Victorian Sculpture*, 194).

Epilogue

1. Britain's history is imperial throughout the period of Victoria's reign; I treat 1876 as a boundary because I am considering here primarily Victoria's representations. Frank Hardie states that "the growth of royal popularity" from 1875 to the Queen's death in 1901 "was part of the general growth of imperialism which was one of the principal movements in the history of these years," and that the Queen benefited from the growth of empire because of Disraeli's project, which marked a departure from earlier styles of monarchy, "'to identify the symbolism of monarchy with the symbolism of Empire'"; Hardie, *Political Influence*, 176–77, quoting, in the second instance, from Kingsley Martin in *Edinburgh Review* (April 1926): 384. Writing more recently, St. Aubyn concurs that Disraeli's ministry of 1874–80 transformed Victoria from reclusive into "vigorous and imperious"; *Queen Victoria*, 445.

2. See, for example, Munich, "Victoria, Empire, and Excess"; and Janet Winston, "Queen Victoria in the *Funnyhouse:* Adrienne Kennedy and the Rituals of Colonial Possession," in *Remaking Queen Victoria*, 235–57.

3. Describing this consensus and the differences within it Dorothy Thompson writes, "Tories and Conservatives favoured military conquest, Liberals relied on free trade imperialism without formal conquest, while Fabians and many other socialists favoured cooperative efforts to share enlightenment"; *Queen Victoria*, 128.

4. *Letters and Journals*, 260, 5 April 1880. The Queen also objected strongly to Gladstone's democratic tendencies, to which she links his foolhardy views on empire: if she must ask Gladstone to form a ministry, she writes to Ponsonby that "there must be no democratic leaning, no attempt to change the Foreign policy (and the Continent are terribly alarmed), no change in India, no hasty retreat from Afghanistan, and no cutting down of estimates"; *Letters and Journals*, 260, 8 April 1880. Disraeli's ministry of 1874–80 had launched numerous imperial campaigns, just to her taste.

5. Frederick Ponsonby, *Sidelights on Queen Victoria* (London: Macmillan, 1930), 142, 145. Quotations are from an account of the incident written by Henry Ponsonby and from a letter by the Queen to Ponsonby, 5 January 1881. The Queen eventually sought Disraeli's opinion, and he of course supported her: "The principle of Sir W. Harcourt, that the speech of the Sovereign is only the speech of the Ministers, is a principle not known to the British Constitution. It is only a piece of Parliamentary gossip"; *Sidelights*, 155–56.

6. Quoted in Strachey, *Queen Victoria*, 212, from W. F. Monypenny and G. E. Buckle, *The Life of Benjamin Disraeli, Earl of Beaconsfield*, 6 vols. (1910–20), 6:217. Although Disraeli and the Queen shared the desire not "to see the Mediterranean becoming a Russian lake" (St. Aubyn, *Queen Victoria*, 436), most of Disraeli's Cabinet and the country were strongly anti-Turkey because of Turkey's notorious "Bulgarian atrocities."

7. For the text of his letter see *The Queen and Mr. Gladstone*, vol. 1: *1845–1879*, ed. Philip Guedalla (London: Hodder and Stoughton, 1933), 455–56.

8. Eliot was finishing *Deronda* during the spring of 1876 when Victoria's promotion was being debated; but my point here about Eliot's construction of a diminished empress would not depend on Eliot's following the debate and its result; Eliot and Victoria are simultaneously making such an image, in different ways.

9. For a fuller exposition of the novel's account of Gwendolen and Grandcourt's figurative relations to empire, see Susan Meyer, *Imperialism at Home: Race and Victorian Women's Fiction* (Ithaca: Cornell University Press, 1996), 162–67. See also Deirdre David, *Fictions of Resolution in Three Victorian Novels* (New York: Columbia University Press, 1981); and Ann Cvetkovich, *Mixed Feelings: Feminism, Mass Culture, and Victorian Sensationalism* (New Brunswick: Rugters University Press, 1992).

10. I am relying here on Meyer's highly persuasive argument that the novel's "proto-Zionism" is a form of British imperialism that doubles as antisemitism, in that it seeks at once to remove the Jews from England and expand Britain's reach in the Middle East; see *Imperialism at Home*, 183–91.

11. For calling my attention to Gwendolen as one "in" whom "things repeat" (*Deronda*, 840), I am indebted to Margery Sokoloff, "The Nothing That Was: Trauma at Home in the Works of George Eliot, Rebecca West, and Virginia Woolf" (Ph.D. diss., Yale University, 1997).

12. For a vivid but detailed account of Britain's muddled involvement in the Suez, Egypt, and the Sudan during the 1870s and 1880s, see Ronald Robinson and John Gallagher with Alice Denny, *Africa and the Victorians: The Official Mind of Imperialism*, 2d ed. (1961; London: Macmillan, 1981), 76–159. See also St. Aubyn, *Queen Victoria*, 453–57, on the Queen's position.

13. *Beloved Mama: Private Correspondence of Queen Victoria and the German Crown Princess 1878–1885*, ed. Roger Fulford (London: Evans Brothers, 1981), 159, 160.

14. *More Leaves* includes entries on some of the Albert memorial statue unveilings considered in earlier chapters, such as the visits to Aberdeen in October 1863 and to Edinburgh in August 1876. Even when she is traveling to visit friends she makes public stops in towns along the way. In Kelso on 21 August 1867 fifty ladies strew her way with flowers, and she receives an address; another time she opens a waterworks in Aberdeen.

15. Brontë, *Wuthering Heights*, 353.

16. There seems to be an allusion here to the topos in Sir Walter Scott novels of Scots nationalists punningly toasting their own King while appearing to toast the English King, by holding their glasses over their water goblets and thus drinking to the King over the water.

17. Hardie, *Political Influence*, 174, quoting a letter to Lord Derby, *Letters*, 6:525, 8 August 1884.

18. As Thompson summarizes, "[T]he queen's children, particularly her eldest son, bitterly resented Brown" (*Queen Victoria*, 77). Victoria had to be sternly discouraged from going on with her own memoir of Brown's life in 1884 (see Chap. 3, n. 24). She arranged to have placed secretly in her coffin tokens suggesting greater intimacy with Brown than with Albert. For this story, which comes from Victoria's physician Sir James Reid, see Thompson, *Queen Victoria*, 76–77.

19. Strachey, with some exaggeration, calls Brown "in effect the hero of the book"; *Queen Victoria*, 218.

20. This last episode is, with all necessary cinematic exaggeration (one reporter's telescope turns into a flock of them), nicely rendered in John Madden's 1997 film *Mrs. Brown*.

INDEX

Afghanistan, 230–31, 236
Africa, xxii, 139, 236–37, 241
Albert, Prince Consort (1819–61):
life and career: as husband and consort, 4–7, 15, 17–32, 84, 118, 121–25, 135, 139–41, 143–46, 169, 239, 267n.17; as father, 23–32, 239; as ruler, actual or imagined, xxxi, 10–19, 22, 27, 32–33, 114, 118, 127, 141, 177; identification with the middle class, 5–8, 21–24, 26, 44–56; *Speeches and Addresses* by, 117, 165, 267n.17; death of, xxx, 3, 48–49, 58–60, 117, 155, 179–80. *See also* Victoria, widow
representations of: in ballads, broadsheets, cartoons, and popular prints, 17–20, 22–28; as a blank, 170–76, 188, 199, 203–4, 221; as Cameron's Elaine, 219–22, 224; as Cameron's King Arthur, 212–15, 223–24; on his deathbed, 163, 267n.10; as feminine, 17–18, 24–26, 28–30, 176–79, 219–24; as hunter, 28–29, 139–40, 144–46, 265n.60; in memorial sculptures, 62, 67, 158–79, 224; in oil portraits, 21–23, 28–32, 166–68; in photographs, 44–57, 170–76, 221; in realist allegorical works, 162–74, 183–88, 190, 199–202, 212–15, 219–24; as Tennyson's King Arthur, 182–91, 199–202. *See also* memorials; Victoria, works

NOTE: Italic folios indicate works of art.

Albert Edward, Prince of Wales ("Bertie"), later King Edward VII: images of as child, 23–28, 30–32; Thanksgiving service for, 153–56, 201; as substitute for Victoria, xxx, 63, 247n.21; wedding of, 60–63, 107–8
Alfred, Prince, Duke of Edinburgh, 172–*173*
Alice, Princess, later Grand Duchess of Hesse, 182; as designer of memorial, 168–69; memorial to, 238; in royal family pictures, 23–28, 30–31, 172–73
Alice books. *See under* Lewis Carroll
allegory and "failed allegory": in Albert memorials, 162–72, 176–79, 201–2, 224–27; in Cameron, 203–24; in Carroll, 90–99, 186–87; in Ruskin, 86–95, 98–99, 186; in Tennyson, 183–88, 191–202. *See also* realism
Altick, Richard, 249n.13
Armstrong, Nancy, xxxiii–xxxiv, 2, 69, 82, 247n.29, 248n.3, 254n.72
Arnold, Matthew, 101–3, 116
Arthur, Prince, Duke of Connaught, 241
Auerbach, Nina, 252n.51, 256n.15, 257n.22, 258n.41

Bagehot, Walter, *The English Constitution*: on the monarchy relative to the government, 59, 64, 102–3, 106–8, 110–15, 120, 126, 136, 148; on parliamentary representation, 103–6, 110, 146, 260n.5; on Tennyson, 185; on Victoria, 113–15, 136, 148, 161

277

Balmoral Castle, 5, 62, 133–35, 138–42, 150, 164, 238, 241, 243
Barrett, Elizabeth: courtship correspondence, 33–43; "Lady Geraldine's Courtship," 34, 39–42; likeness to Victoria, xxxvi–xxxvii, 33–34, 39–42; "The Lost Bower," 38; poems about Victoria, 34; *Sonnets from the Portuguese*, 42–43. *See also* Elizabeth Barrett Browning
Barthes, Roland, 174–76, 203, 219, 268n.32
Baum, Alwin, 259n.52
Bayley, Stephen, 168, 170
Beatrice, Princess ("Baby"), then Princess of Battenberg: as editor of Victoria's journal, 152, 264nn.50, 52, 54, 57, 265nn.61, 63; in royal family photographs, 46, 48
Bennett, Alan, xx, 245n.1
"Bertie." *See* Albert Edward, Prince of Wales
Between the Acts (Virginia Woolf), xxiii–xxiv, 212
Birch, Dinah, 86–87, 258n.37
Blackstone, William, xxix
Blackwood's, 120, 122, 125, 128–30, 147
Bloom, Harold, 86–87
Bodichon, Barbara Leigh-Smith, 67, 69, 71–72
Bright, John, 101, 105, 113, 131, 146
Brisman, Leslie, 252n.55
Bronfen, Elisabeth, 195–96, 219, 270n.59
Brown, John, 143, 151, 163, 237–38, 242–44, 262nn.24, 35, 265nn.59, 67, 268n.32, 275n.18
Brown, Lucy, 62
Browning, Elizabeth Barrett, 251n.46. *See also* Elizabeth Barrett
Browning, Robert, courtship correspondence of, 33–43; *Pauline*, 37–38, 40
Butler, Judith, xxxiii–xxxiv, 247n.30

cairns, 139–40, 146, 160, 238, 241
Cameron, Julia Margaret: "Cupid's Pencil of Light," 221; gender difference in photos by, 177, 211–13, 219–224; *Illustrations to Tennyson's Idylls of the King, and Other Poems*, 203–25, 207, 215, 217, 220, 222; portraits by, 177, 204–7, 211–14. *See also* Albert; allegory; photography; realism; Victoria
Canada, 201
Cannadine, David, 249n.8
Caroline, Queen, 12–13
Carroll, Lewis: *Alice's Adventures under Ground*, 90, 258n.48, 259n.56; *Alice's Adventures in Wonderland*, 67, 73, 90–91, 94, 96, 98, 115, 258n.48; *Through the Looking-Glass*, 67, 73, 90–99, 115, 186–87, 258n.48, 259n.54. *See also* Charles Dodgson
cartes de visite, 46–48, 53–57
Casteras, Susan, 250n.22
Castle, Terry, 174, 176
Chase, Karen, and Michael Levenson (coauthors), 250n.23
chivalry, Victorian revival of: 13–14, 21–23, 28–29, 33–42, 55, 166–68, 172, 189–91, 195–97, 209, 233–34. *See also* gender hierarchy; Ruskin; Tennyson
Christ, Carol, 219, 271n.70
Churchill, Caryl, *Cloud 9*, xxii–xxiv, 235
Clayton, Jay, xxxvi
Colby, Vineta, and Robert Colby (coauthors), 263n.36
Colley, Linda, 4, 260n.13
Conroy, John, 15
Continental Historical Society, 96
Cooper, Helen, 37, 39, 42, 252n.48, 253nn.61, 65
Corbould, Edward Henry (painter), 166–68, 167, 213, 267n.10
Cowling, Maurice, 128, 260n.11
Culler, Dwight, 270n.57

Daily Telegraph, xxv, xxvii–xxviii, 62, 117, 119–20, 122, 127, 129–31, 137, 263n.41, 267n.21
Darby, Elisabeth, and Nicola Smith (coauthors), 159–62, 266n.1, 268n.24
Darwin, Charles, 3
David, Deirdre, xxii, 270n.64
Davidoff, Leonore, and Catherine Hall (coauthors), 2–3, 12–13, 39
Day, Miss (photographer), 46–49, 47, 49, 254n.78
de Bruyn, John R., 264n.60
Dickens, Charles, 160

Disraeli, Benjamin (later Lord Beaconsfield), 2, 61, 101–2, 105, 107, 230–32, 260n.9, 274nn.5, 6
Dodgson, Charles: 85, 204, 208. *See also* Lewis Carroll
Douglas-Fairhurst, Robert, 203

Eagleton, Terry, 248n.36
Edinburgh Review, 132–33, 138, 144, 147
Eggers, J. Philip, 269n.51
"Eleanor Cross," 177
Eliot, George, queenly heroines in, 68; *Adam Bede*, 45; *Daniel Deronda*, 22, 229, 233–36, 274n.8; *Felix Holt*, 74–75, 103, 233, 259n.2; *Middlemarch*, 75, 118; *The Mill on the Floss*, 21–22, 55, 74, 257n.25; *Romola*, 75; theory of political representation in, 101–3
Elizabeth I, xxxii–xxxiii, 4–5, 11–13, 81, 106–7, 138, 250n.20
Ellis, Sarah Stickney, 3, 39; *The Wives of England*, 1, 7–8, 79; *The Women of England*, xxi, 2, 5–6
Emerson, Sheila, 87, 258nn.45, 47
Evans, Eric J., 260n.11

female rule, fears of, 1–4, 7–11, 18–19, 32, 48, 51–57, 85–87, 92, 96, 114–15, 161, 177–79, 202, 210, 222, 227, 244. *See also* gender hierarchy
feminist scholarship, xxxiv, xxxvi, 177–78, 253n.58
Fetterley, Judith, 177
Fraser's Magazine, 119–20, 122–23, 125, 136, 146–49
Frith, William Powell (painter), 60–61
Frogmore (mausoleum), 160, 164
Froude, Henry, 119–20, 122–23
Frye, Susan, xxxii–xxxiii, 247n.32

Gallagher, Catherine, 100–103, 107, 117, 158, 259nn.1, 2
gender hierarchy, xxxv–xxxvii, 1–3, 21–24, 28–57, 87, 125, 151, 158, 172–73, 176–79, 226–27, 233–36, 244. *See also* Cameron; influence; woman's "sphere," women's rights; Victoria; Victorian ideology
George III, xix, 4, 260n.13

Gernsheim, Helmut, 206–10, 271n.74, 272n.79
Gernsheim, Helmut, and Alison Gernsheim (coauthors), 44, 46, 48
Gilbert, Elliot, 219, 268n.33, 269n.45
Girouard, Mark, 166–67, 209
Gladstone, William, xxvii–xxviii, 185, 194–95, 230, 232, 236–37, 242–44, 266n.69, 273n.4
Grant, John, 143, 150, 243
Grant, Mrs. (Victoria's neighbor), 142, 152
Great Exhibition, xxv, xxvi, 6, 61, 165, 202–3, 248n.3
Greenblatt, Stephen, 106, 247n.24, 263n.38
Green-Lewis, Jennifer, 45, 254nn.68, 72, 73
Grey, Charles: as character in *Leaves*, 143–45, 265n.61; as ghostwriter for Victoria, 117–20, 124–27, 145, 148, 256n.10

Hadley, Elaine, 33, 109, 245n.3, 247n.31, 260n.13
Haigwood, Laura, 252n.50
Hardie, Frank, xxxi–xxxii, 273n.1
Hastings, Lady Flora, 15–16
Helena, Princess, 32, 266n.6
Helps, Arthur, 119, 131, 137, 148–49, 151, 264n.50
Hibbert, Christopher, 12, 249–50n.19
Hill and Saunders (photographers), xxiv, xv
Hollander, Anne, 251n.41
Hopkinson, Amanda, 208–9, 211, 270n.67, 272nn.79, 87
Houston, Gail Turley, xxix, 246n.19, 262n.23
Huff, Cynthia, 248n.34
Hunt, John Dixon, 185, 192–93, 198, 269n.45

Idylls of the King. See Tennyson
imperialism and Britain's empire, xxii–xxv, xxxi, 138–43, 201–2, 229–244, 273n.1; as theme of *Leaves* and *More Leaves*, 138–43, 237–44; women as passive agents of, xxii–xxv, 230
India, 142, 216, 229–32

280 / INDEX

influence: of Queen Victoria, xxi–xxii, xxxi, 55, 261n.15; of women, xxi–xxii, 3, 68–69, 72–73, 75, 78–79
Ingelow, Jean, *Mopsa the Fairy*, xxvii, 68, 73–74, 92, 95, 257n.22
Ireland, 138–139, 265n.60; (Anglican) Church of, xxv, xxvii–xxviii, 246n.14

James, Louis, 249n.13
Jennings Albums, 251n.37
Joseph, Gerhard, 184–185, 206, 270n.56

Kantorowicz, Ernst H., xxix, 246n.18
Karlin, Daniel, 252n.50
Kent, Victoire, Duchess of (Victoria's mother), 15–16, 34, 166, 180–81
Kingsley, Charles, 120, 123, 137–38, 146–50, 152, 157, 263n.56
"king's two bodies," xxix, 4–5
Knoepflmacher, U. C., 252n.51, 257n.22
Kuhn, William, 245n.4, 247n.22, 260n.5, 261nn.14, 16, 19, 266nn.69, 70, 72, 73

Lami, Eugene Louis, *Opening of the Great Exhibition 1 May 1851*, xxv, *xxvi*
Landseer, Sir Edwin, 22, *23*, 28–*29*, 45, 55
Langland, Elizabeth, xxxiii–xxxiv, 44, 68–69, 72, 80, 247n.30, 256n.19, 257n.31, 33
Leighton, Angela, 36, 42, 252n.53, 253n.58
Lerner, Laurence, 21, 251n.33, 252n.53, 253nn.58, 60
Levine, George, 254n.71
Liddell, Alice, 85, 204, 258n.48
Linkman, Audrey, 50, 53
London Quarterly Review, 119–23, 125, 144–45
Longford, Elizabeth, xxv, xxxi–xxxii, 11, 61–62, 64, 81, 109, 116–17, 141, 151
Lukitsch, Joanne, 211, 223

McSweeney, Kerry, 271n.75
Martin, Robert, 259n.50, 272nn.80, 86
Martin, Theodore, 137, 263n.42
Mavor, Carol, 207–9, 270n.66
Mayall, John E. (photographer), 45–46, 48, 50–57, *50*, *52*, *54*, *56*, 255nn.81, 84
Melbourne, Lord, 12–17
memorials: to Prince Albert: 157–79; —, in Aberdeen, 158, 161, 274n.14; —, at Balmoral, 164, 238; —, in Coburg, 158, 165; —, at Edinburgh, 159, 274n.14; —, at Windsor, 158, 168–69, 224, 267n.21; —, in Wolverhampton, 158, 161–62, 165; to Alice, 238; to the Duchess of Kent, 166, 180–81; to the Duchess of Sutherland, 177, 238; to Scots nationalists, 239–41. *See also* National Albert Memorial; Royal Albert Hall; Albert, representations of
Mermin, Dorothy, 36–38, 42, 252n.50, 253nn.58, 61
Meyer, Susan, 274n.10
Mill, John Stuart, 69, 87, 102–3, 157–58, 257n.32, 260nn.5, 7, 273n.90
Millais, John Everett, "Ophelia," 178–79, "Mariana," 181
Miller, Andrew, 254n.72, 258n.36
Miller, Betty, 36, 252n.52, 253nn.56, 58
Miller, D. A., 263n.38
Miller, J. Hillis, 86
Miller, Nancy K., xxxvi
Millett, Kate, 69
Miss Marjoribanks. *See* Oliphant
Montrose, Louis Adrian, xxxii–xxxiii, 4–5, 247n.26
More, Hannah, 3
Morning Post, 70
Mozley, Anita, 204
Munich, Adrienne: on Victoria, xxxiii, 1–2, 5, 22, 137, 161–62, 246n.11, 247n.28, 248nn.2, 3, 249nn.11, 14, 16, 250n.28, 251nn.32, 36, 40, 252n.48, 256nn.13, 26, 259nn.54, 55, 57, 263n.35, 264n.53, 265n.67, 266n.9, 267n.15; on Victorian art and poetry, 205, 252n.51, 271n.76

Nadel, Ira, 21, 251n.30
National Albert Memorial, 159, 169–71, 202, 211, 268nn.24, 25
Noon, Patrick, 254n.67
Norton, Caroline, 33, 251n.45

Oliphant, Margaret: on autobiography, 124; *Miss Marjoribanks*, 16, 67–68, 75–85, 98–99, 257nn.29, 31, 259n.53; reviews of the Queen's books, 120, 122, 125, 144,

INDEX / 281

147; private comments on Victoria, 122, 263n.36; on women's suffrage, 78, 257n.32, 265n.66
Olsen, Victoria, 207–8, 210–11
O'Mealy, Joseph, 77
Orgel, Stephen, 61, 106, 113
Ormond, Richard, 254n.75
Osborne House, 5, 46–48

Patmore, Coventry, 69, 183, 256n.18
Peel, Sir Robert, 14–15
Peterson, William, 253n.66
photograph albums, royal, 44–57, 254nn.69, 76, 255nn.85, 87, 88, 270n.67
photography: as quasi-allegory, 203–224; as documentary, 44–46, 203; as memorial that obliterates, 170–76, 178, 203; as royal iconography, 46–57, *See also* names of photographers and subjects
Pitt, Valerie, 185
Ponsonby, Arthur, 137, 239–40, 274n.5
Poovey, Mary, 69, 256n.17
Prins, Yopie, 37, 252n.54, 253n.58
prosopopoeia. *See under* Ruskin, pathetic fallacy
Psomiades, Kathy, 178
Punch, cartoon of Victoria, 65–67, 84, 99
Pye, Christopher, 147–48

queens, multiple fictional, 67–99
"Queen's Book." *See under* Victoria
"Queen's Speech." *See under* Victoria

Read, Benedict, 162, 165, 272n.84
realism: in fiction and photography, 43–46; grafted to allegory, 162–74, 183–88, 201–26. *See also* allegory
reform bill of 1867, 64, 80, 100–101, 104–6, 108–9, 116–17, 127–31; Lords' amendments to, 127–28, 130; lodgers clause, 127–28, 130; minority clause, 105–6, 130
representation: anxieties about, 85, 89, 95, 102; descriptive vs. symbolic, 101–8, 128–30, 146–48, 158–59; disguise and misrepresentation as forms of, 63, 100–15, 119–21, 126, 136, 148; excessive, 169–70, 192–99, 209–10;

parliamentary, 80, 100–105, 116–17, 127–28, 157–58. *See also under* Albert; allegory, Bagehot; memorials; photography; realism; reform bill; Victoria; women's rights; *and see names of artists and authors*
republicanism, 59–60, 83–84, 113, 154
Richards, Thomas, 248n.3
Robinson, Henry Peach, 268n.27, 270n.67
Rossetti, Christina, xix, xxv, xxxiv, xxxvi, 68, 73–74
Rothstein, Eric, xxxvi
Royal Albert Hall, xxx–xxxi, 157–58
Royal Exchange, 6–7, 155
"royal representation," 229, 234
Ruskin, John: 85–96, 99; *The Ethics of the Dust*, 88; *Modern Painters*, 88, 93; "pathetic fallacy" in, 86–94, 98–99, 186, 206; "Of Queens' Gardens," 3, 44, 67–74

Sacks, Peter, 180
Saturday Review, 104–5, 120, 125, 128–29
Sawyer, Paul, 87
Schama, Simon, xxi, 4, 21–22, 229, 251nn.31, 40
Scotland, 116–17, 135, 137–46, 164, 238–44, 264n.53
Scott, George Gilbert (architect), 170, *171*, 177, 192
Shelley, Percy Bysshe, 37, 177, 253n.57
Shires, Linda, 207, 211, 223
Shuman, Cathy, 69, 92, 256n.14
Smith, F. B., 104–6, 128
Smith, Lindsay, 208, 271nn.71, 74
Sokoloff, Margery, 274n.11
Sonstroem, David, 86–87, 258n.37
St. Aubyn, Giles, xxxi–xxxii, 59–60, 109, 116–17, 141, 147, 232, 237, 250n.24, 263n.37
Stephenson, Glennis, 253n.61
Stewart, Susan, 268n.31
Strachey, Lytton, 58–59, 143, 275n.19
Swinburne, Algernon Charles, 183, 187
Symons, Widow (Victoria's neighbor), 142, 151

Tagg, John, 271n.71
Tennenhouse, Leonard, 112

Tenniel, John, 95–97
Tennyson, Alfred: *The Idylls of the King*, 181–202; —, addressed to Victoria and Albert, 182–83, 200–2202; —, debate over allegorical method of, 183–87; —, as commentary on and instance of realist or failed allegory, 187–200; "Mariana," 181, 193, 218; *Maud*, 88–89, 93, 206–7; *In Memoriam*, 180–82; *The Princess*, 69, 158; as Victoria's laureate and friend, 179–83, 268n.26. *See also under* Cameron; Albert; Victoria
Theed, William (sculptor), 158, 165, 168–75, *173, 175*, 179, 268n.22
Thompson, Dorothy, xxvii, 1, 3, 11, 15, 68, 233, 248nn.1, 3, 265n.67, 266n.70, 273n.3, 275n.18
Thorburn, Robert (painter), 21–22, 48–*49*, 51, 166–68
Times (London), xxiv, xxviii, 6–7, 15, 58, 60, 62–63, 70–71, 99, 119–20, 122, 127, 135–36, 154–58, 256n.10, 266n.73
Tomahawk, 28, 65, 67, 99, 262n.35
Trevor-Roper, Hugh, 263n.53
Triqueti, Henri de (sculptor), 168–*169*, 223–27, *225, 226*, 267n.21
Trollope, Anthony, *Can You Forgive Her?* 111–12
typology, 165, 185, 204–6, 271n.75. *See also* allegory

Vautier (painter), 60
Victoria, Queen (1819–1901)
  life and career: accession and coronation, 8–13, 34; unmarried queen, xxi, 14–16; courtship, 17–18, 20, 41, 123–24, 263n.39; wife, xxxv, 2–7, 17–34, 42–58, 132–33, 140, 149, 262n.35; mother, 5–7, 23–32, 44, 46, 48, 58, 122, 238; widow and mourner, xxviii, xxx–xxxi, xxxiv–xxxv, 57–67, 80–85, 110–36, 146, 153–83, 193, 199–201, 218–19, 224–47; memorialist, xxxv, 146, 157–79, 199–202, 218–19, 224–27; abdication, rumored, xxviii, 62, 65, 83; Empress, xxv, 2, 229–44; jubilees, 3, 5, 153; prerogatives and state powers, xxvii, xxxi–xxxii, 67–68, 113–15, 137–41, 161, 230–32; public appearances, xxix–xxv, 6–7, 58–64, 107–11, 122, 153–58, 161–62, 201, 238, 250n.22; speeches, xxviii–xxxi, 64–65, 98–99, 110, 114, 118, 126, 131, 230–31
  attributes as Queen: absence and invisibility, xxxv, 58–60, 62–67, 82–86, 91, 95–96, 98–101, 108–18, 122–23, 126, 130–33, 136, 146–48, 152–57, 160, 226–27; agency, xix–xxxvii, 111–13, 147–48, 157–58, 236; constitutionality, xx, xxiv, xxvii–xxxi, xxxv, 29, 100–101, 107–13, 129, 147–48; domesticity; identification with the middle class, 2–8, 16, 18, 21–24, 26, 33, 44–60, 69–72, 77, 84, 128–29, 133–37, 141–42, 147–56, 172, 248n.3; apparent privacy, xxx–xxxi, 4–5, 13, 23–33, 120–22, 125–26, 132–46, 237–44; symbolic monarchy, xx, 2–7, 16, 18, 29, 44, 55–59, 79, 85, 106–8, 148, 158, 227.
  representations of, xxi–xxvi, xxxi–xxxvii; by Bagehot, 113–15, 136, 148, 161; by Barrett, 33–34, 39–43; in broadsheets, cartoons, street ballads, and popular prints, 1, 8–13, 17–20, 22–28, 57, 59, 62, 65–67; as Cameron's Elaine, 218–19, 224; by Carroll, 67–68, 90–99, 115; in disguise, 135–36, 141–46, 265n.59; by Eliot, 22, 68, 74–75, 233–36; by Ellis, xxi; as Queen Hermione, 65–67, 84, 99; in newspapers and magazines—*see under individual titles;* in oil paintings, 13, 22–23, 28–32, 60–61, 65; as Oliphant's Lucilla, 76–85, 98–99; in photographs, 44–57; as "Queen of Trumps," 57, 85; as rose, 11–12, 32, 48; as Ruskin's "queens," 67–69, 71–74, 85–96, 99, 115; in stone, 225–27; by Tennyson, 180–82, 193, 200–202
  views: on empire, 230–31, 236–44, 273n.4; on democracy and

parliamentary reform, 108–10, 127–28, 131, 146, 273n.4; on women's rights, 14, 158

works, xxxv–xxxvi; *Leaves from the Journal of Our Life in the Highlands,* 116–17, 131–53, 237–38, 265n.60; *More Leaves from the Journal of a Life in the Highlands,* 117, 144, 161, 177, 237–44; *The Early Years of His Royal Highness the Prince Consort* (contributing author), 17, 115–33, 145; drawing, *31–32*

Victoria, Princess Royal ("Vicky"), later Empress of Prussia: images of as child, 23–31, 45; as substitute for Victoria, 63; on *Leaves,* 151; wedding of, 172–73; on Tennyson, 199–200, 270n.62

Victorian ideology, xx–xxiii, xxxi–xxxvii, 33–34, 41, 125. *See also* gender hierarchy; woman's "sphere"

Warner, Marina, 174, 176
Watson, Nicola J., 11
Weaver, Mike, 204–5, 209, 211, 272n.80
Weintraub, Stanley, 59, 109, 117–18, 137
Weltman, Sharon Aronofsky, 68–69, 72, 87–88, 256nn.18, 19, 258n.46

widowhood. *See under* Victoria
William IV, 34
Williamson, Judith, 249n.8
Windsor Castle, xxiv, 60–63, 158, 168, 223–27
Winterhalter, Franz Xaver, 11, 29–32, *31,* 44–45
Wolfson, Susan, 177
woman's "sphere," xx, 1–3, 23, 26–27, 32, 39, 77, 125, 202. *See also* gender hierarchy; Victorian ideology; *see also under* Victoria
women, middle-class, as "queens," xxi–xxii, xxxiii–xxxiv, 67–99. *See also under* Victoria
women's rights: divorce, 33; suffrage, xxv, 104, 149, 157–58, 257n.32, 260n.7, 265n.66, 273n.90
Wood, Mrs. Henry, *East Lynne,* 45
Woodham-Smith, Cecil, 250n.25
Woolf, Virginia, 201; *Between the Acts,* xxiii–xxiv, 212
Wordsworth, William, 40–41, 89, 177–78, 253nn.57, 62

York, Duchess of, and Benita Stoney (coauthors), 163, 267nn.12, 18